BALTHASAR AND PRAYER

T&T Clark Studies in Systematic Theology

Edited by

Ian A. McFarland
Ivor Davidson
Philip G. Ziegler
John Webster[†]

Volume 38

BALTHASAR AND PRAYER

Travis LaCouter

LONDON • NEW YORK • OXFORD • NEW DELHI • SYDNEY

T&T CLARK
Bloomsbury Publishing Plc
50 Bedford Square, London, WC1B 3DP, UK
1385 Broadway, New York, NY 10018, USA
29 Earlsfort Terrace, Dublin 2, Ireland

BLOOMSBURY, T&T CLARK and the T&T Clark logo are trademarks of Bloomsbury Publishing Plc

First published in Great Britain 2021
Paperback edition published 2023

Copyright © Travis LaCouter, 2021

Travis LaCouter has asserted his right under the Copyright, Designs and Patents Act, 1988, to be identified as Author of this work.

For legal purposes the Acknowledgments on p. ix constitute an extension of this copyright page.

All rights reserved. No part of this publication may be reproduced or transmitted in any form or by any means, electronic or mechanical, including photocopying, recording, or any information storage or retrieval system, without prior permission in writing from the publishers.

Bloomsbury Publishing Plc does not have any control over, or responsibility for, any third-party websites referred to or in this book. All internet addresses given in this book were correct at the time of going to press. The author and publisher regret any inconvenience caused if addresses have changed or sites have ceased to exist, but can accept no responsibility for any such changes.

A catalogue record for this book is available from the British Library.

Library of Congress Cataloging-in-Publication Data
Names: LaCouter, Travis, author.
Title: Balthasar and prayer / Travis LaCouter.
Description: London, UK ; New York, NY, USA : Bloomsbury Academic, 2021. | Series: T&T Clark studies in systematic theology ; volume 38 | Includes bibliographical references and index. |
Identifiers: LCCN 2021013477 (print) | LCCN 2021013478 (ebook) | ISBN 9780567701862 (hb) | ISBN 9780567701916 (paperback) | ISBN 9780567701879 (epdf) | ISBN 9780567701909 (ebook)
Subjects: LCSH: Balthasar, Hans Urs von, 1905-1988. | Prayer–Christianity. | Catholic Church–Doctrines.
Classification: LCC BX4705.B163 L33 2021 (print) | LCC BX4705.B163 (ebook) | DDC 248.3/2–dc23
LC record available at https://lccn.loc.gov/2021013477
LC ebook record available at https://lccn.loc.gov/2021013478

ISBN: HB: 978-0-5677-0186-2
PB: 978-0-5677-0191-6
ePDF: 978-0-5677-0187-9
eBook: 978-0-5677-0190-9

Series: T&T Clark Studies in Systematic Theology, volume 38

Typeset by Deanta Global Publishing Services, Chennai, India

To find out more about our authors and books visit www.bloomsbury.com and sign up for our newsletters.

CONTENTS

List of Figures	viii
Acknowledgments	ix
Abbreviations	x

INTRODUCTION   1

Chapter 1
MAPPING BALTHASAR STUDIES   7
- 1.1 Which Balthasar?   7
- 1.2 Whose Balthasar?   12
  - 1.2.1 The First Wave: Seeing the Form   12
  - 1.2.2 The Second Wave: Characters in Conflict   19
  - 1.2.3 The Third Wave: Integration   27
- 1.3 Reading Balthasar Today   32

Chapter 2
PRAYER'S ROLE   35
- 2.1 Theology and Prayer   35
  - 2.1.1 The "Contemplative Style" of Theology   35
  - 2.1.2 Balthasar's Personal and Polemical Resonances   42
- 2.2 Placing *Das Betrachtende Gebet*   45
- 2.3 Mysticism Considered   49

Chapter 3
PRAYER'S SOURCE: TRINITARIAN DIMENSIONS   57
- 3.1 Positing Trinitarian Prayer   57
- 3.2 The Spirit's Role   61
- 3.3 Characterizing Trinitarian Prayer   65
  - 3.3.1 *Aletheia*   66
  - 3.3.2 *Emeth*   69
- 3.4 Contemporary Perspectives on Distance   72
- 3.5 Consolidation   77

Chapter 4
PRAYER'S SHAPE: CHRISTOLOGICAL DIMENSIONS — 79
- 4.1 Christ as Prayer — 81
  - 4.1.1 "Christ As the Language of God" — 81
  - 4.1.2 God's Language in Historical Form — 84
- 4.2 Christ at Prayer — 86
  - 4.2.1 Mission-Consciousness and Prayer — 87
  - 4.2.2 The "Pistis Christou" and Prayer — 92
  - 4.2.3 Trinitarian Inversion — 95
- 4.3 The Ecclesial Dimensions — 98
  - 4.3.1 The Church's Prayer Constitution — 99
  - 4.3.2 Prayer and Sacrament — 102
- 4.4 Consolidation — 105

Chapter 5
PRAYER'S EFFECTS: ANTHROPOLOGICAL DIMENSIONS — 107
- 5.1 Against the Anthropological Approach — 107
- 5.2 Predisposition — 111
  - 5.2.1 Shame — 111
  - 5.2.2 Confession — 114
- 5.3 Response — 116
  - 5.3.1 *Parrhesia* — 117
  - 5.3.2 Silence — 119
  - 5.3.3 The Marian Word — 122
- 5.4 Life and Mission — 123
- 5.5 Consolidation — 127

Chapter 6
PRAYER'S END: ESCHATOLOGICAL DIMENSIONS — 129
- 6.1 Theocentric Eschatology — 129
- 6.2 Prayer and (Salvation) History — 133
  - 6.2.1 Sanctifying History — 133
  - 6.2.2 Intercession — 136
- 6.3 Action — 139
- 6.4 Consolidation — 145

Chapter 7
PRAYER'S POWER: CRITICAL DIMENSIONS — 147
- 7.1 Prayer and Power — 149
  - 7.1.1 The Example of the Prophets — 150
  - 7.1.2 "The Encounter" — 152

7.2	*Parrhesia* Revisited	155
	7.2.1 Foucault's Account	155
	7.2.2 Theological Transposition	157
7.3	Consolidation	163

CONCLUDING REMARKS   165

Appendix   179
Bibliography   181
Index   214

FIGURES

1 Balthasar, *Das Betrachtende Gebet* (Einsiedeln: Johannes, 1955), 162   4

ACKNOWLEDGMENTS

This book arose rather directly out of my doctoral work. I thus owe the largest and most obvious debt of gratitude to my supervisors at the University of Oxford. James Hanvey's dogged efforts to hold me to his characteristically high standards were nothing short of heroic, and I am grateful for his persistence, his guidance, and above all his passion for theology. Graham Ward added to the project greatly with his insights, his encouragement, and by his faith that I had something of value to say as a theologian. In their own inimitable ways, they have both shaped everything that is of any value in this work.

Campion Hall, Oxford, was my intellectual and spiritual home during the time this study was conceived of and written. It was a place to share joys, find refuge from burdens, and to learn to see the world anew. Would that every young scholar knew the gifts of community life. I am particularly grateful for the steadfast help and friendship of Philip Kennedy, Sarah Gray, and Nicholas Austin, SJ, who as Master of the Hall during the pivotal final stages of my writing ensured that I was given adequate space and resources to bring this work to a successful end. Wilma Minty was always responsive and conscientious in acquiring necessary materials for the Hall's library.

I am also grateful to the Society of Jesus for all the work it does supporting institutions of higher learning across the world.

I must also acknowledge the generosity of spirit that was shown to me by a number of more senior colleagues who took the time to discuss or offer comments on aspects of this work, including especially Lucy Gardner, Peter Tyler, Joel Rasmussen, Carol Harrison, Philip McCosker, Karen Kilby, Luigi Gioia, Werner Jeanrond, Dermot Power, Gavin Flood, Jennifer Cooper, Patrick Riordan, Junius Johnson, Sean Larsen, and Stephan van Erp. Whether they realize it or not, their suggestions, comments, and challenges all helped to impose some much-needed discipline upon my often haphazard drafts.

I am not a person who thinks best, or even particularly well, in isolation, and so the presence of a number of friends, critics, and interlocutors have been of the upmost importance for the development of this work. There are of course too many to name but I should like to single out Mark Aloysius, Russell Bogue, Pavlo Smytsnyuk, Tatiana Kalveks, James Lorenz, Naomi Richman, Nikolaas Deketelaere, Gerard Ryan, William Campbell, Dritëro Demjaha, Kate Bresee, Anne Ploin, Joseph Simmons, Matthew Dunch, and Alejandro Olayo-Méndez.

I am extremely grateful to my benefactors and especially to Bill Loschert for his generosity, his commitment to Catholic education, and his friendship.

And lastly to my family—my parents Jeanne and Steve and my brother Nick—for their unflagging love and support.

ABBREVIATIONS OF SELECT ENGLISH-LANGUAGE WORKS BY HANS URS VON BALTHASAR

(See Bibliography for full list of citations and German cross-references.)

2SS	*Two Sisters in the Spirit: Thérèse of Lisieux and Elizabeth of the Trinity*
3FG	*The Threefold Garland: The World's Salvation in Mary's Prayer*
CA	*The Christian and Anxiety*
CL	*Cosmic Liturgy: The Universe According to Maximus the Confessor*
CM	*Christian Meditation*
CSL	*The Christian State of Life*
DWH?	*Dare We Hope That All Men Be Saved?*
EG	*Engagement with God*
ET.1 (etc.)	*Explorations in Theology*, Vols. 1–5
FF	*In the Fullness of Faith: On the Centrality of the Distinctively Catholic*
FGAS	*First Glance at Adrienne von Speyr*
"FSO"	"The Fathers, the Scholastics, and Ourselves"
GL.1 (etc.)	*Glory of the Lord: A Theological Aesthetics*, Vols. 1–7
GW	*The Grain of Wheat: Aphorisms*
HW	*Heart of the World*
LAC	*Love Alone is Credible*
LLC	*The Laity in the Life of the Counsels: The Church's Mission in the World*
MCW	*The Moment of Christian Witness*
MiH	*Man in History: A Theological Study*
MP	*Mysterium Paschale: The Mystery of Easter*
MWiR	*My Work in Retrospect*
NE	*New Elucidations*
"Norm"	"The Gospel as Norm and Test of All Spirituality of the Church"
OPSC	*The Office of Peter and the Structure of the Church*
OSF	*Origen: Spirit and Fire*
OT	*Our Task: A Report and a Plan*
Prayer (H)	*Prayer* (translated by Graham Harrison)
Prayer (L)	*Prayer* (translated by A. V. Littledale)
RB	*Razing the Bastions: On the Church in this Age*
"Résumé"	"A Résumé of My Thought"
SPUL	*A Short Primer for Unsettled Laymen*

TA	*A Theological Anthropology*
"Task"	"On the Tasks of Catholic Philosophy in Our Time"
TD.1 (etc.)	*Theo-Drama: Theological Dramatic Theory*, Vols. 1–5
TE	*Test Everything and Hold Fast to What Is Good*
TH	*A Theology of History*
TL.1 (etc.)	*Theo-Logic: Theological Logical Theory*, Vols. 1–3
TS	*Truth is Symphonic*
TuG	*Tragedy Under Grace: Reinhold Schneider on the Experience of the West.*
Unless	*Unless You Become Like this Child*
VBR	*The Von Balthasar Reader* (eds. Kehl and Löser)
WiC?	*Who is a Christian?*
YCYYG	*You Crown the Year with Your Goodness: Sermons*

INTRODUCTION

What, for Balthasar, is prayer? How does it work, and what does it do? Furthermore, while seeking answers to these questions, how can we be sure to render a properly *theological* account of prayer, one which does not fall back on purely sociological or psychological answers? In this book, I will pursue answers to these questions, and, in doing so, I will not only uncover more fully the depths of Balthasar's theological vision but will thereby help contribute to the reintegration of theology and prayer, which was one of his primary concerns and which has been one of the major efforts of recent Anglophonic theology.[1] The topic of prayer is relevant today in a particular way in light of these ongoing debates and in light of the broader debates about theology's place in the modern university. However, there are even more fundamental reasons why Christian theology should never abandon the question of prayer nor confine it merely to the genre of "spirituality." These have to do with the essential questions that are necessarily implicated by any Christian account of prayer: How does the finite creature come to know the infinite God? How, in knowing God, does the creature engage with God? What effect does this interaction have on the one who prays, and through them, the world? In other words, through the dramatic interaction of freedom that prayer is, the Christian theologian has a view to the entire eschatological drama that unfolds between

---

1. For some recent arguments in favor of the reintegration of theology and spirituality, see: Sarah Coakley, *God, Sexuality, and the Self* (Cambridge: Cambridge University Press, 2013); Graham Ward, *How the Light Gets In*, Vol. 1: *Ethical Life* (Oxford: Oxford University Press, 2016); Romanus Cessario, *Theology and Sanctity*, ed., Cajetan Cuddy (Ave Maria, Florida: Sapientia Press, 2014); Rowan Williams, *Wrestling with Angels: Conversations in Modern Theology* (London: SCM, 2007), especially the first chapter on Lossky; Andrew Prevot, *Thinking Prayer: Theology and Spirituality amid the Crises of Modernity* (South Bend: University of Notre Dame Press, 2015); Bernard McGinn, "The Letter and the Spirit: Spirituality as an Academic Discipline," in *The Study of Christian Spirituality*, eds. Elizabeth Dreyer and Mark Burrows (Baltimore: Johns Hopkins University Press, 2005); and Philip Sheldrake, *The Spiritual Way: Catholic Traditions and Contemporary Practice* (Collegeville: Liturgical Press, 2019). By grouping these authors together, I do not mean to imply that their various theological projects necessarily cohere, merely that they all make some form of the argument that Christian theology must maintain an organic connection to spiritual practice lest it misrepresent the object of its inquiry. Balthasar's arguments for the integrity of theology and prayer are among the strongest in the twentieth century.

God and the world.[2] In this book, I aim to depict that drama—the drama of God's crossing over in love which is the drama of prayer—in its proper breadth and depth. It was Balthasar's contention and it is mine now that a thorough account of prayer draws on and has implications for a number of traditional *loci theologici* such as Trinitarian theology, Christology, theological anthropology, eschatology, and ecclesiology. Accordingly, I adopt a systematic approach in order to consider each essential aspect of prayer in turn—naturally, this means that something of the full picture of prayer will only emerge when the various chapters are taken together, although I will at all times write with an eye to the whole. (By adopting this "systematic" approach to the topic, I obviously make no claim to account for each and every subjective experience in prayer but rather seek to illuminate the essential structure of prayer so as to better address the theological questions I have already mentioned.)

This is not to say that Balthasar's account of prayer will merely be uncritically reproduced. Indeed, I aim to place his theological arguments in their proper historical, doctrinal, and metaphysical contexts. This is necessary to do for at least three reasons. First, while Balthasar's theology is often said to bear some kind of connection to prayer or spirituality, it is usually left unsaid just how this matters to the shape and substance of his theology itself. My contention is that Balthasar is not just a theologian who writes about prayer but one whose theology is a form of prayer. This claim can be substantiated by showing that for Balthasar both prayer and theology arise from the same source and aim at the same end—in other words, they could be said to be coextensive. In short, this source is the eternal Trinitarian life, and this end is the eschatological re-rendering of the world. These arguments will be advanced in the chapters that follow, but the point at the moment is simply that Balthasar is a particularly important theologian to engage with if one wishes to understand how theology might be done as prayer. The second reason to take a wide view of Balthasar's theology of prayer is in order to better see how revisionist his aims were on various questions of theological method and substance. Several of Balthasar's most stimulating polemics are underwritten by his account of prayer in ways which I will highlight in this book. Some examples of these topics include the possibility of positive Trinitarian speculation; the existence of real faith in Christ; the inadequacy of manual theology; the proper disposition for liturgical worship; and the distinctiveness of Christian spirituality, especially when compared to Eastern alternatives. Balthasar's positions on any of these issues are, of course, open to debate, but it is important to grasp them in their full depth if they are to be debated in good faith. Focusing on the question of prayer, therefore, not only helps to foreground certain of the most distinctive aspects of Balthasar's theology, but it, therefore, also helps to expose the contours of his overall theological vision.

---

2. My reference to prayer as a "dramatic interaction of freedom" draws on the definition of prayer put forward by Prevot (see *Thinking Prayer*, 1–3 especially). I will have the opportunity in a moment to clarify more fully my working definition of prayer. Of course, both Prevot's and my own definitions of prayer are distinctly Balthasarian.

The third reason to take Balthasar's account seriously is because he grasped an essential fact, which is that a fuller and more robustly theological notion of prayer is necessary if it is to plausibly be claimed that prayer is a central aspect of the Christian existence. Balthasar was so preoccupied with prayer, in other words, not because he judged the average Christian to have a deep and adequate sense of prayer's importance but rather the opposite. Lauren Winner has written recently of what she calls "damaged" Christian practices (including prayer) that have, through abuse, neglect, or their entanglement with violent structures, ceased to "foster intimacy with God and growth in Christlikeness."[3] Although Winner's term is not Balthasar's and although anyone should pause before labeling another's prayers as "damaged," Winner's concept is helpful inasmuch as it captures a very real sense that prayer's common practice does not generally seem to reflect its true theological depths. Prayer often does not seem to be credible as an expression of faith in a God who saves, a God who collaborates with the praying person in order to bring about a promised future. Rather, prayer is often seen to be a burden, an embarrassment, or a nuisance. Balthasar was particularly concerned with the ways in which prayer is made into a pious abstraction that serves to keep God at arm's length. It does not seem unreasonable to call these prayer practices "damaged" in Winner's sense of the word, or at least to acknowledge the need for some standard of healthy prayer, such as Balthasar's account attempts to provide, lest the one who sets out to pray immediately be discouraged by the various difficulties inherent in prayer. Balthasar's understanding of prayer as a lived reality, something that matters in the life of the praying person and indeed something that matters to the God to whom they pray, is an understanding of prayer that still has the power to provoke today.

Already I have invoked a number of physical metaphors (referring to prayer's "shape" or "structure," for instance) to describe what is essentially a metaphysical reality—after all, prayer is not simply the act of praying but refers to the comprehensive interaction of finite and infinite freedoms that plays out when and as one goes about praying. For this reason, Balthasar's preferred metaphor of prayer as a dialogue[4] is not at all inadequate since the notion of a dialogue refers to much more than the literal words which pass between interlocutors. A dialogue includes not just flat words but pregnant pauses, meaningful glances, tonal and rhythmic patterns as well as shifts, reference to third parties, and the like. It is this sort of living reality that Balthasar thinks of prayer as. (Of course, as Balthasar is quick to add, prayer is no simple dialogue among equals: God both speaks first and indicates the proper creaturely response in the Son who is the eternal Word

---

3. Lauren Winner, *The Dangers of Christian Practice: On Wayward Gifts, Characteristic Damage, and Sin* (New Haven: Yale University Press, 2018) see 4 and the chapter on prayer 57–93.

4. The notion of prayer as a dialogue is a common motif in Balthasar, and one to which I shall refer repeatedly throughout this work; see, for example, *Prayer* (H), 14–17 or TD.2, 24ff., .

in human form.) Thus, prayer is properly speaking a dynamic *process* in which the praying person is implicated, more than it is a discrete *action* of the praying person. Explicit verbal prayers like the Our Father operate synecdochically to express the general sense of faith which is operative for the one who lives a life "in Christ." The alternative to this view—an alternative which seems to me plainly untenable—is that the words of prayer themselves operate magically as invocation and can do so over against the intention or will even of the praying person. God does not will to be God over God's people, but to be God with God's people (*Immanuel*)—prayer is thus a process of freedom coming to fruition. This is not to deny, of course, that prayers themselves do shape the praying person even as they are being made; this is the point of Paul's claim that it is not we who pray but the Spirit who prays in us (cf. Rom. 8:26). Creaturely prayer on this understanding can thus be said to be a mode of incorporation in God, of the praying person's relocation within the eternal rhythms of divine love and freedom which characterize the Trinitarian life. Another way of putting this is to say that prayer is a certain kind of relation, specifically the kind of relation that God intends to have with God's creatures (because it is already the kind of relationship that pertains in the Trinitarian life). When I speak of prayer's shape or structure, it is in reference to this relational incorporation into God (even if this claim still remains necessarily abstract at this point). For his part, Balthasar represents this structure with a diagram (Figure 1).

Although the diagram is not sufficient on its own, it does succeed in capturing several key features of Balthasar's account of prayer which will reappear in the following chapters. If we take the double-sided arrows which connect the hypostases to indicate some kind of dynamic mutual relation, then this is or includes what Balthasar will refer to as the inner-Trinitarian prayer (cf. Chapter 3 *infra*). Such a prayer cannot be definitively known (thus, the hard semicircle separating it from

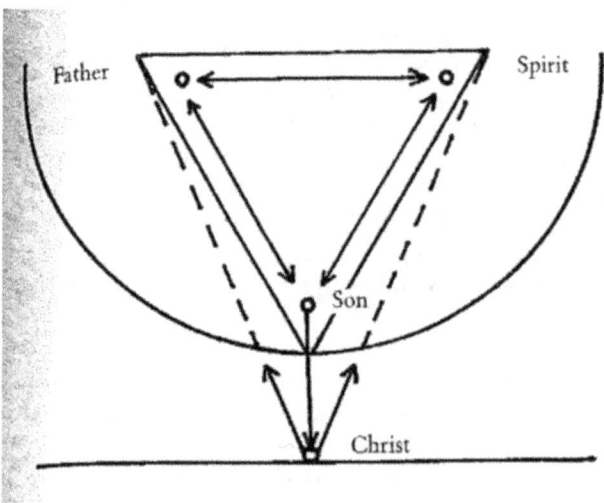

Figure 1 Balthasar, *Das Betrachtende Gebet* (Einsiedeln: Johannes, 1955), 162.

the creaturely plane) but it reveals itself in the world in the person of Christ, who participates in this inner-Trinitarian dialogue while simultaneously opening it up to the creature. The dotted lines going from Christ on earth "up" to the Father and the Spirit represent a prayer relation, one in which the Son models Sonship precisely through dynamic obedience in mission: It is this filial relation that the creature can likewise participate in through prayer. The life and mission of Christ is, therefore, the connecting point (*Anknupfungspunkt*) between the creaturely plane and the Trinitarian life, and it is through Christ that prayer introduces genuine verticality into the horizontal plane. (My decision to put the chapter on the Trinitarian dimensions of prayer before the Christological dimensions therefore reflects the correct ontological priority, even if epistemologically the creature has no suitable concept of Trinitarian prayer outside what is revealed in the Son.) That it is a specifically Trinitarian dynamic which the praying person is invited to participate in (indicated in the diagram by the revolving triangle shape) suggests that the process of prayer is ongoing and, in this sense, future-oriented; in prayer God's future becomes our future. These and various other essential aspects of prayer will be developed at length in the following chapters.

Having introduced my guiding questions, briefly indicated why they are relevant, and sketched in very broad terms the approach that Balthasar will take, it is time now to turn to the relevant arguments involved in this book. Chapter 1 will present a roadmap to the various waves of Balthasar readers and the categories of Balthasar texts, thus providing a service to future students of Balthasar's theology regardless of their research interests. Chapter 2 goes further in establishing prayer's role. This will involve looking at some of the major trends within modern theology against which Balthasar set himself, and how prayer figured into those polemics. Following these first two chapters, the subsequent chapters will go through the various "dimensions" of prayer as they feature in Balthasar's theology. Chapter 3 deals with the Trinitarian foundations of prayer. Balthasar is (in)famous for his daring Trinitarian speculations, and prayer is no exception inasmuch as he posits the existence of prayer "in" the Trinity. Chapter 4 considers the all-important Christological dimensions of prayer. Not only does Christ make all creaturely prayer possible, as I have already suggested, but prayer figures into Balthasar's revisionist mission-Christology in surprising ways, so that it is prayer which (at least within the context of mission) becomes the substance of Trinitarian solidarity between Father and Son. The ecclesial mediation of prayer is treated as part of the Christological approach, since the head should never be separated from the body; at the same time and for the same reason, the church itself is shown to be constituted by prayer. Chapter 5 concerns the anthropological effects of prayer, which flow from the Christological basis. Personhood "in Christ" is discovered, confirmed, and continually reenacted in prayer, such that the creature is essentially *homo orans*.[5] Chapter 6 looks ahead to the eschatological dimensions of prayer.

---

5. The apt phrase is Victoria Harrison's, from "*Homo Orans*: Von Balthasar's Christocentric Philosophical Anthropology," *Heythrop Journal* 40 (1999): 280–300.

Since in prayer the creature gains a unique share in the saving mission of Jesus Christ, prayer's fruits are always judged by the extent to which they build up the Kingdom. Finally, Chapter 7 considers prayer's critical dimensions that emerge more clearly when Balthasar considers how prayer functions vis-à-vis the powers of the world. Summary conclusions follow.

Chapter 1

MAPPING BALTHASAR STUDIES

Before taking up the substantive arguments I wish to make in this book, it is necessary to devote some attention to questions of method and reception history, since the figure with whom we will be working presents challenges to the reader that are arguably unique within the context of twentieth-century theology.

1.1 Which Balthasar?

It has become commonplace to acknowledge at the outset of books like this one just what an unconventional theologian Balthasar is. His style is eclectic, his sources seemingly endless, and his tone often more poetic or discursive than strictly systematic. Junius Johnson rightly notes that Balthasar's thought presents a twofold challenge to any potential interpreter, both in its ambitious scope and in its tendency to be most stylized or speculative at particularly those moments where precision would seem to be most called for.[1] Many have noted Balthasar's education (he boasted that he did not hold formal degrees in theology), professional status (he turned down every professorial chair that was offered to him and instead operated as a semi-independent writer and publisher for much of his life), and personal associations (most of all with the mystic Adrienne von Speyr) as contributing factors. To these I would add two more, which are less often mentioned: first, Balthasar's theology is deeply metaphysical inasmuch as it is preoccupied with the relationship of the finite to the infinite.[2] Ultimately, the "task" of Balthasar's theology is an "affirmation of Being" that he takes to be distinctive to the Christian worldview.[3] Thus, to the extent that postmodern theology after Heidegger has sought to avoid the charge of ontotheology by largely disavowing

---

1. Junius Johnson, *Christ and Analogy: The Christocentric Metaphysics of Hans Urs von Balthasar* (Minneapolis: Fortress, 2013), 18.
2. Cf. John O'Donnell, *Hans Urs von Balthasar* (Collegeville: Liturgical Press, 1992), 7–8.
3. See the famous passage at GL.5, 648. I will return to this point in Chapter 3 *infra*.

metaphysics, Balthasar's theology has paid a price.[4] Second, Balthasar's theology is (in ways which this book will help make clear) well understood in terms of prayer—that is, not just as a theology which happens to take prayer as one of its particular theologoumena, but a theology which is offered *as* prayer and derived *from* prayer. This fact is often paid lip-service but is not often shown to really affect a given reading of Balthasar, or, if it does, it does so in such a way as to render his theology, therefore, less precise. My contention, on the other hand, is that Balthasar's theology is prayer, but that Christian prayer for Balthasar bears a specific shape and rhythm. Accordingly, understanding the shape and rhythm of Christian prayer as Balthasar sees it helps us to better adjudge his entire project, and to locate it within the field of modern Catholic theology.[5]

But already we have a sense of the complexity of the task confronting any would-be reader of Balthasar. In praise of Maximus the Confessor, but using lines which might as well describe himself, Balthasar observes, "The freedom of the mind proves itself not least in one's unshakeable ability to change perspective, to see things at one time from behind, at another from below or from above. It also consists in the possibility of changing one's mode of expression, of saying the same thing in different ways."[6] Certainly, in his long career of publishing, writing, translating, transcribing, preaching, and editing, Balthasar showed a particular genius for "saying the same thing in different ways." This leads Oakes and Moss to conclude with some understatement that Balthasar's theological "positions cannot be easily categorized."[7] Indeed, even with the aid of the veritable trove of secondary literature that is available today, consensus among commentators remains elusive. Balthasar is represented at various points as a Romantic dilettante, an arch-conservative, a dangerous radical, and a modern-day Church Father.[8] The question of "Which Balthasar?" is thus pressing in a way that it is not with other comparable twentieth-century theologians.

A preliminary schema, then, is to help us come to grips with the task at hand. Broadly speaking, Balthasar's major works can be divided into three categories.[9]

---

4. Cf. Thomas Carlson, "Postmetaphysical Theology," in *Cambridge Companion to Postmodern Theology*, ed. Kevin Vanhoozer (Cambridge, Cambridge University Press, 2006), 58–75.

5. In an attempt to present Balthasar's account of prayer as clearly as possible, I will often take up engagements with secondary literature in footnotes, which may sometimes be quite extensive. Footnotes are therefore a vital part of the progression of my overall argument in this book.

6. *CL*, 57.

7. "Introduction," in *The Cambridge Companion to Hans Urs von Balthasar*, eds. Edward Moss and David Oakes (Cambridge, Cambridge University Press: 2004), 1–8, here 2.

8. See the extensive bibliography of recent secondary literature maintained by Johannesverlag at http://www.johannes-verlag.de/jh_huvb_sekund.htm.

9. In a 1984 address upon the occasion of receiving the Paul VI Prize, Balthasar divided his work into three "stages": (1) the practical work involved in launching and supporting

First ("Category 1"), and most widely known to academic theologians, are the so-called systematic works—that is, the fifteen-volume triptych comprised of *Glory of the Lord*, *Theo-Drama*, and *Theo-Logic* (first published between 1961 and 1987) as well as the speculative essays collected as *Explorations in Theology* Volumes 1–5 (1960–86). To this group we could also add a number of the more significant essays, such as "The Fathers, the Scholastics, and Ourselves." This is of course vital material, but it is not on the whole where the beating heart of Balthasar's theology is to be found. Second ("Category 2") are the polemic works (*Streitschriften*) like *The Moment of Christian Witness* (1966) and *Dare We Hope That All Men Be Saved?* (1986), as well as thin programmatic volumes like *Razing the Bastions* (1952) and *Love Alone is Credible* (1968) and essays like "*Communio*—A Programme" (1972). These works are often devoted to a particular question and often assume as background a good deal of the material found in the systematics. At the same time, they often represent programmatic statements that undergird much of the constructive theology in the first category. In a third category ("Category 3") are what we might call devotional or pastoral works, which would include the prayer-poem *Heart of the World* (1954), personal prayers (some of which are recorded in English in *The Von Balthasar Reader*), and the numerous sermons published in English as *You Crown the Year with Your Goodness*. *Our Task* (1984), the highly important volume in which Balthasar outlines an objective account of Speyr's mysticism and sets forth the structures of the Johannesgemeinschaft, also belongs to Category 3. These works often represent the most vital and the boldest material in the Balthasarian *oeuvre*, since they emerge more or less directly out of his life, work, and prayer.[10] The sermons, in particular, contain a vast amount of rich material which could be considered Balthasar's "theology in action," arising as they do from direct pastoral duties. And for that same reason, these Category 3 works reveal intuitions that animate all his other reflections. For my best attempt to divide Balthasar's major works among these three categories, see the Appendix.

Of course, these should not be taken to be strict divisions—there are moments in the systematics (the reflections on death in *Theo-Drama* Vol. 4, for instance) that display a depth of feeling which borders on the existential, just as, in the

---

the Johannesgemeinschaft; (2) the extensive program of translating and compiling works from other authors in the tradition; and, lastly, (3) his own original written work or positive theology (see "Address of Hans Urs von Balthasar," in *L'Osservatore Romano* July 23, 1984). These "stages" are not unhelpful, but the "categories" proposed by me here are more concerned with the written work as such and have the advantage of already accounting for variances in style and genre (original written work, sermons, translations, etc.).

10. More than anyone else, Manfred Lochbrunner has mined the available archival and epistolary resources to assemble a remarkably comprehensive picture of Balthasar as a thinker and a person. See, for example, *Balthasariana: Studien und Untersuchungen* (Münster: Aschendorff, 2016); *Hans Urs von Balthasar und seine Theologenkollegen: sechs Beziehungsgeschichten* (Würzburg: Echter, 2009); *Hans Urs von Balthasar und seine Literatenfreunde: neun Korrespondenzen* (Würzburg: Echter, 2007); and *Hans Urs von Balthasar und seine Philosophenfreunde: fünf Doppelporträts* (Würzburg: Echter, 2005).

devotional writings Balthasar is often wont to slip into a magisterial tone (as in one of his Ascension sermons titled, "The Threefold Presence of Christ").[11] And there are early studies on particular thinkers (from Origen to Thérèse of Lisieux to Karl Barth) that straddle both the first and second categories, but which largely appear *before* the productive period starting in 1959 and thus can be said to form more thematic overtures to a subsequent positive theology.[12] His translations (of Claudel or Ignatius, for instance) tend to reflect his programmatic aims but obviously do not present the same opportunity for explicit argumentation, so they should generally be seen as background material.[13] It is also worth noting that across the three categories Balthasar is remarkably consistent in his concerns. There is no explicit *Kehre* in his thought (the postconciliar move toward conservatism was more a question of appropriation than of any conscious alignment on Balthasar's part; see Section 1.2.1 *infra*). Sachs is right to suggest that Balthasar's themes "deepened" over time but did not necessarily undergo "development" in ways that

---

11. Indeed, as Stephan Van Erp argues, the "systematics" should perhaps not even be considered as such, inasmuch as their method is often eclectic and, at times, self-contradictory (see *The Art of Theology: Hans Urs von Balthasar's Theological Aesthetics and the Foundations of Faith* [Leuven: Peeters, 2004], 84 n.42). Sachs likewise notes that "Balthasar himself never tires of emphasizing the non-systematic nature of his theology" (see "Spirit and Life: The Pneumatology and Christian Spirituality of Hans Urs von Balthasar" [PhD diss., University of Tübingen, 1984], 25–6).

12. Balthasar's translators have often noted how when he undertakes to present a given thinker, he is as likely to tell us as much about himself as the thinker in question; see, for example, Daley's foreword to *CL*, especially 17–21, and Martin's foreword to the section on Elizabeth von Dijon in *2SS* 365–7. Oakes comments, "I have often discovered that Balthasar frequently gives an unconscious portrait of himself when he is ostensibly describing another theologian" (*Pattern of Redemption*, 5). That being said, Balthasar was clearly capable of producing works of "pure patristics" which proved adequate to the standards of philological and historical scholarship; see, for example, "Das Scholienwerk des Johannes von Scythopolis," in *Scholastik* 15 [1940]: 16–38), which Daley claims is still authoritative today (see Brian Daley, "Balthasar's Reading of the Church Fathers," in *Cambridge Companion to Hans Urs von Balthasar*, 187–206, here 205–6 n.29).

13. For helpful comments regarding Balthasar's many translations, see Aidan Nichols, *Divine Fruitfulness: A Guide to Balthasar's Theology beyond the Trilogy* (London: T&T Clark, 2007), 3–4 as well as Antonio Sicari "Hans Urs von Balthasar: Theology and Holiness," in *Hans Urs von Balthasar: His Life and Work*, ed. David L. Schindler (San Francisco: Ignatius, 1991), 121–32, 126–7. Balthasar himself claimed in 1975 that the translations he undertook on behalf of the Johannesverlag of de Lubac, Bouyer, Blondel, John of the Cross, and others were "dearer and more important to me than my own books" (Balthasar, "Another Ten Years," in *The Analogy of Beauty: The Theology of Hans Urs von Balthasar*, ed. John Riches [Edinburgh: T&T Clark, 1986]). This remark shows further just how decentralized Balthasar's conception of his own creative output was.

would contradict his earlier work.¹⁴ So the point of this proposed schema is not to introduce rigid distinctions where there are none, merely to suggest that Balthasar varied style and form to suit his particular needs, and that any conscientious reader should be aware of how these levels relate and interact. We could expect a theme from a Category 3 work to be tested in a Category 2 work and perhaps treated definitively in a Category 1 work. But we should not mount a systematic challenge to Balthasar on the basis of a comment or digression in a Category 3 work, for instance. Nor should we insist on reading an argument that appears in a Category 1 work against those basic sentiments which are expressed with more simplicity in Category 3 works. Accordingly, I will attempt to proceed in a balanced way and whenever possible to corroborate my more significant claims with citations from at least two of the three proposed "Categories."

But we might return at this point to the initial observation regarding the difficulty of interpreting Balthasar today. In some ways, the challenges of intelligibility have only grown in the three decades since his death. The fact (already mentioned) that Balthasar never worked as a university professor and thus occupied something of an outsider role vis-à-vis the academic mainstream means that his legacy is particularly susceptible to politically motivated interpretations. There is no generation of students who can be counted on to translate and comment on such a vast body of work in a spirit more or less faithful to the master. But, as at least the contributors to one seminal volume understood, this distance may be fruitful in its own right, especially if it allows us to see the full ambition of Balthasar's project from our own position "at the end of modernity" and to then, in turn, perform our own "giddy synthesis" upon it.¹⁵ Indeed Balthasar welcomed such creative engagements, describing his systematics in particular as merely an "apparatus [which has been erected] so that gymnasts may eventually exercise upon it."¹⁶ This is part of what I mean when I describe Balthasar's theology *as* prayer. It is offered up to the church for the sake of engendering further contemplation—and ultimately action—and is willing to be judged as to its usefulness by that measure, not as a freestanding ideational structure or as a construct of pure reason.

As an ecclesially situated prayer, Balthasar's theology (whatever category we are dealing with) will naturally bear the stylistic markers of prayer as he understands it. One of the most important of these markers is an emphasis on *parrhesia*, which Balthasar considers a distinctive feature of Christian prayer. Mature prayer dares to speak plainly, even boldly, before God as the praying person realizes that it is not their own heroic virtue that enables them to speak but the grace of the Spirit who prays in them. I will have several opportunities to discuss the notion of *parrhesia* in more detail in other portions of this book; for now, the point is stylistic and hermeneutical. If prayer does indeed undergird so much of Balthasar's theological

---

14. Sachs, "Spirit and Life," 129.

15. See Kerr's Foreword in *Balthasar at the End of Modernity*, Lucy Gardner, David Moss, Ben Quash, and Graham Ward (Edinburgh, T&T Clark, 1999), 1–13.

16. TD.1, 9.

approach, and if prayer is marked for him by a certain parrhesiastic privilege, we have here already some indication of why Balthasar's theology is often as bold as it is. (It should go without saying that this does not therefore imply that Balthasar's bold theology is always necessarily correct; parrhesiastic theology will by definition remain open to being confronted and corrected by alternative versions of the same.) What I am suggesting is that to understand Balthasar's theology as prayer ought to reorient the way in which we receive it and to do so in a way that alerts us to precisely that feature of it that his critics so often express their bewilderment over, namely his tendency toward daring speculation and idiosyncratic expression. It is this bold Balthasar that I am particularly interested in entering into dialogue with here and who, I believe, has the most to teach us still today.[17]

If I have just given some indication of "Which Balthasar?" I will be concerned with in this study—namely, the bold thinker who approaches questions repeatedly from different angles—we still have the rather more vexing question of "Whose Balthasar?" to consider. What I called earlier the "trove" of secondary literature can often prove as bewildering for a would-be reader as Balthasar's own body of work. It is, therefore, worth charting the major fault lines of the debate(s) over Balthasar's legacy.

1.2 Whose Balthasar?

There are, I propose, three "waves" of Balthasar reception that we would do well to keep in mind as we make our way among the vast secondary literature. Such a schema has not yet been seriously attempted.[18] Again, as with the previous schema, these categories are not meant to introduce artificial distinctions, but to draw out differences in the main interpretive trends within contemporary Balthasar Studies, especially in English. Without wishing to push the parallel too far, one might say that the three waves, and thus the three major phases of receiving Balthasar's thought, correspond to the three stages of his trilogy—that is, perceiving (aesthetics), acting (dramatics), and integrating (logic).

1.2.1 The First Wave: Seeing the Form

Hans Urs von Balthasar died suddenly at home in June of 1988.[19] Up to that point, a handful of students and scholars had shown an interest in his work, but he

---

17. Accordingly, Category 3 works like *Heart of the World* deserve to be taken seriously as substantial *sources* of Balthasar's theology.

18. Part 3 of Lochbrunner's *Balthasariana* offers a survey and assessment of the secondary literature up to 2005 and reviews of some major works, but it is by now dated and is not thematically arranged.

19. For my purposes here, it is not necessary to enter an extended biographical discussion. For useful treatments, see Elio Guerriero, *Hans Urs von Balthasar: Eine Biographie*

remained, in the main, a subject of non-English-language dissertations and niche journal articles. To be sure, his own vast output during his life ensured Balthasar a certain degree of celebrity and, eventually, official vindication (in 1969, for instance, he was appointed a member of the Vatican's International Theological Commission). Nevertheless, his major works did not start to appear in English until 1982. He thus retained a status as something of a fringe figure among the theological establishment; it is often mentioned, for instance, that Balthasar was not invited to participate as a *peritus* at the Second Vatican Council.[20] To be sure, this certainly does *not* mean that Balthasar was obscure in his time or that his influence (even at the Council) was merely marginal, as O'Meara has it.[21] But it does mean that his legacy during these years was largely under the guardianship of his unofficial disciples and devotees.[22]

(Einsiedeln: Johannes, 1993); Philipe Barbarin, *Théologie et sainteté: Introduction à Hans-Urs von Balthasar* (Paris: Parole et Silence, 1999); or Peter Henrici "Hans Urs von Balthasar: A Sketch of His Life," in *Hans Urs von Balthasar: His Life and Work*, 7–45, especially 7–28.

20. Lochbrunner suggests that this may have been a blessing in disguise, since it allowed Balthasar to focus attention on developing his own positive theology (see *Balthasariana*, 246ff.)

21. See Thomas O'Meara *Erich Przywara, S.J.: His Theology and His World* (Notre Dame: University of Notre Dame Press, 2002), 133–9. O'Meara judges Balthasar to be a theologian "of the era before Vatican II" who "had removed himself from exercising theological influence by leaving the Jesuits, by affiliating himself with a group around a private mystic, and by writing little of service to the Council" (139). Since he presents this picture of Balthasar's work and legacy without any critical comment, one has to assume this is O'Meara's settled judgment. For an opposing view on this last point in particular, see Steffen Lösel, "Conciliar, Not Conciliatory: Hans Urs von Balthasar's Ecclesiological Synthesis of Vatican II," *Modern Theology* 24, no. 1 (2008): 23–49.

22. See "The Achievement of Hans Urs von Balthasar," *Communio: International Catholic Review* 2, no. 3 (Fall 1975) and "Hans Urs von Balthasar Symposium," *Communio: International Catholic Review* 5, no. 1 (Spring 1978). The role of *Communio* in Balthasar's *oeuvre* is complex, not least of all due to the fact that it was not merely his own initiative but a collaborative, international undertaking. It is fair to say that Balthasar always considered the journal a means to an end, and Nicholas Healy is right to note that for Balthasar, "*Communio* the review was meant to be an instrument of *communio* the theological reality" (Healy, "*Communio*: A Theological Journey," *Communio: International Catholic Review* 33 [2006], 117–30, 127). That is, Balthasar's involvement in the journal should not be understood as an effort to institutionalize his legacy or—as has often been suggested—as a "conservative" reaction to the launch of the more "liberal" *Concilium* in 1965, but rather as an extension of his own constructive theological project. For Balthasar's inaugural essay explaining his concept of *communio* see Balthasar "Communio—A Program," *Communio: International Catholic Review* 33 (2006): 153–69 (originally published as "Communio: A Programme," *International Catholic Review* 1 [1972]).

By the 1990s, then, the effort of bringing Balthasar into the English-speaking context seemed well overdue. The project was taken up by a small group of editors and translators—including Rowan Williams, Andrew Louth, Erasmo Leiva-Merikakis, and Brian McNeil—who by 1991 had brought out the full seven volumes of *Herrlichkeit* in English. Thus, with the arrival of the aesthetics Balthasar became something of a fashionable figure in the Anglophone academy. The 1990s saw a veritable explosion of Balthasar scholarship, mainly carried out by sympathetic parties and mainly (though by no means exclusively) focused on the aesthetics.[23] Louis Dupré famously declared *Herrlichkeit* to be "among the foremost theological achievements of our century,"[24] a view also shared by Donald MacKinnon, himself notable as one of the earliest and most perceptive English-speaking readers of Balthasar's *oeuvre*.[25] As Davies notes, much of the initial interest in Balthasar may have been motivated in part by the thrill of novelty—Balthasar's recourse to a long tradition of continental literature, philosophy, and drama, combined with his discursive, often biting style lay in stark contrast to an English-language professoriate trained in the ways of systematic rigor, clarity of thought, and economy of expression.[26] More importantly still, Balthasar appeared to offer an alternative to the transcendental Thomism of Karl Rahner at a time when that theological approach seemed so dominant in Catholic circles. This seemingly new way of doing theology was precisely one of the things most attractive to these first-wave Balthasarians, and, accordingly, a number of competent but essentially introductory *vade mecums* began to appear in English in the years around and following Balthasar's death.[27]

---

23. Harrison notes how Riches' seminal volume likely overdetermined the aesthetics' importance in subsequent Anglophone scholarship (see Victoria Harrison, *The Apologetic Value of Human Holiness: Von Balthasar's Christocentric Philosophical Anthropology* [London: Kluwer, 2000], 5–6).

24. Louis Dupré, "The Glory of the Lord: Hans Urs von Balthasar's Theological Aesthetic," in *Hans Urs von Balthasar: His Life and Work*, 183.

25. See MacKinnon reviewing O'Hanlon in *The Philosophical Quarterly* 42, no. 169 (1992): 517–19, here 518. See also MacKinnon "Some Reflections on Hans Urs von Balthasar's Christology with Special Reference to *Theodramatik* II/2 and III," in *Philosophy and the Burden of Theological Honesty: A Donald MacKinnon Reader* (London: Bloomsbury, 2011). MacKinnon's influence is particularly noteworthy as an early teacher of other important Balthasarians including Williams and John Milbank.

26. See Oliver Davies "The Theological Aesthetics" in *The Cambridge Companion to Hans Urs von Balthasar*, 131–42, 131–2.

27. See, for instance, John O'Donnell, *Hans Urs von Balthasar* (London: Continuum, 1991); *Hans Urs von Balthasar: His Life and Work*; Angelo Scola, *Hans Urs von Balthasar: A Theological Style* (Edinburgh: T&T Clark, 1995); *The Analogy of Beauty: The Theology of Hans Urs von Balthasar*; or *The Beauty of Christ: An Introduction to the Theology of Hans Urs von Balthasar*, eds. Bede McGregor and Thomas Norris (Edinburgh: T&T Clark, 1994). An example of a more recent first-wave work is Rodney Howsare, *Balthasar: A Guide for the*

Early Balthasarians were on the whole more adulatory of than critical toward their subject, often casting him as a stand-in for orthodoxy and a bastion of "authentic" Catholic thought. Leiva-Merikakis, for example, declares Balthasar to be "one of the scant few thoroughly reliable teachers and pathfinders in the thicket of late-twentieth-century life."[28] These strained readings are often further marked by a certain sectarian triumphalism; so Saward, for instance, emphasizes how Balthasar's theology supposedly reflects the "unity of the faith[,] the God-given whole" that belongs "to the Catholic Church *alone*."[29] For Saward, Balthasar's aesthetic turn to the form (*Gestalt*) of theological content, namely the figure of Jesus Christ, serves to ground theology on a "concrete and objective" basis.[30] In this Saward and others see a tool for combating what they take to be the formless relativism of modernity, which has (on their telling) triggered an epistemological crisis of meaning.[31] Theological aesthetics, in particular, are enlisted as a kind of trump card against modern relativism.[32] To be sure, Balthasar exhibited genuine misgivings about the modern era—especially as a young man (consider his association during his student years with members of the arch-conservative George-Kreis, especially the eccentric Ludwig Derleth).[33] Liberalism's tendency to degenerate into a "decadent individualism" was certainly a cause for concern in

Perplexed (London: Continuum, 2009), thus suggesting that these categories are not strict chronological divisions as much as thematic groupings.

28. *GW*, xi.

29. John Saward, *The Mysteries of March* (London: Collins, 1990), xvii–xviii (italics mine). It is noteworthy that Saward eventually soured on Balthasar's theology, writing critically of him later in life.

30. Saward *op. cit.*, xix. Conspicuously, Saward does not note here the rather decisive influence of Goethe on Balthasar's *Gestalt* theology (cf. Balthasar's address upon the occasion of receiving the Mozart Prize in 1987, quoted by Guerriero, *Hans Urs von Balthasar*, 420). D. L. Schindler makes a more extended attempt to explain the "catholicity of reason" and theology's legitimate claims to include the insights of philosophy in *The Catholicity of Reason* (Grand Rapids: Eerdmans, 2013).

31. Bernard Lonergan identified the crisis of modernity as the struggle to come to grips with the seemingly endless multiplication of meaning brought about by the turn to historicity and empirical sciences. Lonergan called this the problem of the "mediation of meaning" (see the essay "Dimensions of Meaning," in *Collection: Papers by Bernard Lonergan*, Crowe ed. [London: Darton, Longman & Todd, 1967], 232–45, especially 244).

32. See a typical example of this maneuver by Robert Barron, *Exploring Catholic Theology: Essays on God, Liturgy, and Evangelization* (Grand Rapids: Baker, 2015). Barron also draws on Balthasar in *The Priority of Christ: Toward a Postliberal Catholicism* (Grand Rapids: Baker, 2007).

33. See Paul Silas Peterson, *The Early Hans Urs von Balthasar: Historical Contexts and Intellectual Formation* (Berlin: De Gruyter, 2015), 120, 250ff.

the young Balthasar.³⁴ But it was Balthasar's mature judgment that the modern period represented a pivotal opportunity for a certain integration of the patristic and scholastic insights, and thus ultimately held the promise of theological *"progress."*³⁵ He was also an avowed enemy of integralism (of the sort advocated by the Action Française, for instance),³⁶ and should not be considered a "reactionary" in the political sense of that term.³⁷ We would thus do well to follow Henrici here, who helpfully notes that the *Gestalt* of Balthasar's theology is not so much a hard and unchanging "form" but rather a relatively stable "frame" (also *Gestalt*) within which a unique drama can be seen to unfold.³⁸ In this way, Balthasar's theological imagination is in fact much more experimental and flexible than his appropriation by the first wave would seem to suggest.

Nevertheless, this picture of a conservative Balthasar remains a widely influential one. Tina Beattie was right to argue in 2005 that "a growing number of conservative Catholics" had begun to appropriate Balthasar's legacy, especially as a way of buttressing the papacy of John Paul II.³⁹ This was also Medard Kehl's earlier judgment from beyond the Anglosphere.⁴⁰ This is due in no small part to the influence of the American publishing house Ignatius Press, which has been

---

34. Peterson, *The Early Hans Urs von Balthasar*, 94. Peterson generally oversells Balthasar's devotion to George, however, and is especially strained in tying whatever admiration Balthasar did have for the "conservative revolutionary" to a nascent crypto-fascism (see 161ff.)

35. See "FSO," 389 (my italics).

36. See GL.1, 451: "[Absent Christ, the Church] would be plausible neither as a religious institution [. . .] nor as an historical power for order and culture in the sense of the Action Française and of the German Catholic Nazis. On the contrary, seen in this way [the Church] *loses all credibility.*" See also Balthasar's remarks against integralism in "Kirche Zwischen Links und Rechts," *Civitas* 24 (1969): 440–64; *CL*, 31–4; *WiC?* 105–6; and *VBR*, 372.

37. Thus, van Erp's labeling of Balthasar as a "reactionary" (*The Art of Theology*, 88) is misleading. Van Erp means by this that Balthasar "responds strongly to the developments [within theology] of his time" (*loc. cit.*) but then it would have been clearer to describe Balthasar as an "engaged" thinker and so on. Mark Lilla usefully distinguishes between the conservative and the reactionary in *The Shipwrecked Mind: On Political Reaction* (New York: New York Review of Books, 2016), ix–xxi. In Lilla's sense, the "theocons" among the first wave are *reactionaries*, and merely use Balthasar as a weapon in their struggle against relativism.

38. See Peter Henrici, "The Philosophy of Hans Urs von Balthasar," in *Hans Urs von Balthasar: His Life and Work*, 149–68, 155.

39. Tina Beattie, "Sex, Death, and Melodrama: A Feminist Critique of Hans Urs von Balthasar," in *The Way* 44:4 [2005]: 160–76. Beattie's point is buttressed by the fact that many first-wave Balthasarians were clerics who numbered among the hierarchy and who had usually been promoted by John Paul II (Scola and Barbarin, for instance).

40. See Medard Kehl, "Hans Urs von Balthasar: Ein Porträt," in *In der Fülle des Glaubens: Hans Urs von Balthasar-Lesebuch*, ed. Werner Löser (Freiburg imBreisgau, 1980), 13–60.

responsible for translating the majority of Balthasar's work into English.[41] Ignatius' founder Joseph Fessio knew Balthasar personally, and in 1975 wrote a doctorate on Balthasar's ecclesiology under the supervision of Joseph Ratzinger at Regensburg.[42] A controversial figure in his own right, Fessio is not as much a scholar as he is a facilitator of Balthasar's legacy.[43] Other American scholars of Balthasar have tended to reinforce this right-wing association. For instance, D. L. Schindler is usually grouped with the so-called Communio School of theologians and philosophers;[44] likewise, the late Oakes, while easily one of the most rewarding first wave thinkers, is fairly considered one of the conservatives Beattie was speaking about.[45] American Catholic journals like *First Things* have also at times

41. In the Preface to GL.1, Riches explains that by 1978, when he was first approached by T&T Clark to undertake a translation of *Herrlichkeit*, the newly founded Ignatius Press "was already engaged" in the same project (GL.1, 13). All seven volumes of *Glory of the Lord* were thus produced as joint ventures of T&T Clark and Ignatius, but then Ignatius took sole responsibility for subsequent translations of the *Theodramatik* and the *Theologik*, as well as four volumes of the collected essays entitled *Skizzen zur Theologie* and forty-three of Balthasar's monographs. For a list of Balthasar's books published by Ignatius, see http://www.balthasarbooks.com/books/#books-by (last accessed July 6, 2019).

42. Cf. Lynn Garrett, "Ignatius Press' Papal Connection," *Publishers Weekly* 252:17 (2005): 7.

43. Aside from his unpublished 1974 doctoral dissertation, Fessio is the author of no significant monographs or essays on Balthasar or his thought. His energies have gone instead into launching schools, institutes, or publishing houses that advance his particular brand of American postconciliar conservatism. In 2002, Fessio and others founded a two-year liberal arts college in San Francisco as a protest against what they perceived to be the doctrinal abuses and administrative "constraints" of the existing Jesuit University of San Francisco (see http://www.campion-college.org/about/history.htm). In response Fessio was removed from San Francisco by his Jesuit superiors (see George Neumayr, "Jesuits Implode," *The American Spectator* from March 13, 2002; accessible online at https://spectator.org/52958_jesuits-implode/). Fessio went on to become chancellor and provost of Ave Maria University in Florida, a school consistently identified as one of the "most conservative colleges in America" by the *U.S. News and World Report*'s annual rankings. Fessio was subsequently fired—twice—from his posts at Ave Maria after disputes with the administration over the school's financial management. Today he still serves as an editor for Ignatius Press. For a sense of Fessio's legacy among theological conservatives, see the contributions to the recent *Festschrift* in his honor, *Ressourcement after Vatican II: Essays in Honor of Joseph Fessio, S.J.*, eds. Matthew Levering and Nicholas Healy (San Francisco: Ignatius, 2019).

44. See, for example, "Schindler, David L. (1943–)," in *American Conservatism: An Encyclopedia*, eds. Bruce Frohnen, Jeremy Beer, Jeffery Nelson (Wilmington, Delaware: ISI Books, 2006). Other members of the Anglophone Communio School include Michael Hanby, Tracey Rowland, and Nicholas Healy.

45. In any case, Oakes' *Pattern of Redemption* remains an invaluable treatment.

enlisted Balthasar to anti-modern, anti-liberal ends.[46] The interest in Balthasar among American conservatives is all the more noteworthy when one considers that before the Second Vatican Council Balthasar had often been named as one of several noteworthy young progressives of European theology.

Balthasar, for his part, never accepted the label of "conservative" and insisted as late as 1984 that it was not his positions that had changed but the orientations of those around him.[47] This statement followed earlier entreaties (in 1978 for example) that his work be seen as "not traditionalistic, not progressive, but simply Catholic!"[48] While it is certainly the case that Balthasar held any number of conservative positions on questions of church policy (his opposition to women's ordination, for instance),[49] on other issues his sympathies were clearly with more progressive strains in the church (his support for lay youth movements, for example, or his qualified endorsements of communism). It must be said that first-wave Balthasarianism, whatever its merits, has often been overdetermined by a style of postconciliar politics that has wreaked so much havoc upon the American and European theological academy. Thus, McIntosh was able to note correctly as early as 1996 (less than a decade after Balthasar's death) that the "categorizations and compartmentalizations of [Balthasar's] achievements are already hardening, threatening to obstruct an unprejudiced, wide-ranging perspective" of his work.[50] To be clear: my intention is not to read Balthasar *against* these first-wave interpreters but rather *beyond* them. Affecting this maneuver means moving in two seemingly opposite directions at the same time. On the one hand, I clearly agree with the first wave that Balthasar is a thinker worth taking seriously. And, even further, I will posit with them that he must be approached on his own terms—that his theology has a certain *Gestalt* through which it must be viewed lest it be badly misinterpreted. As Davies notes: "The perception of a work of art has to do with taste and enjoyment, but it is also in fact a form of cognition."[51] In this sense, the

---

46. See Murphy, "Is Liberalism a Heresy?" in *First Things* (June 2016). Accessible: https://www.firstthings.com/article/2016/06/is-liberalism-a-heresy (accessed July 14, 2019).

47. In response to a question about where the "turn" came between the publication of his 1952 book *Schleifung der Bastionen* and his so-called conservative phase in the 1960s, Balthasar responds: "There was *no* turn. It is as I said about Rahner: We [i.e., Rahner and I] did not change, but the people who had set us on the Left now set us on the Right because they themselves had become the Left. In fact we always wished to be in the middle" (see "Last Interview with Hans Urs von Balthasar" accessible online at https://www.youtube.com/watch?v=ygKIWUa-iLM; accessed online February 3, 2021). Balthasar also rejects the label "conservative" in writing as well (see, for example, *DWH?*, 20).

48. Balthasar, "Zur Überwindung der kirchlichen Flaute," *Vaterland* 150 (1978): 3.

49. See, for example, Balthasar, "Women Priests?" in *New Elucidations* (San Francisco: Ignatius, 1986), 187–98.

50. Mark McIntosh, *Christology from within: Spirituality and the Incarnation in Hans Urs von Balthasar* (Notre Dame: University of Notre Dame Press, 1996), 2.

51. Davies, "The Theological Aesthetics," 133.

first wave of Balthasar Studies represents a necessary prethematic experience of the source material upon the basis of which further critical discussion can unfold.

Left as it is, however, the first wave declines to engage Balthasar's thought in favor of reifying it. Such an approach to the Balthasarian corpus risks setting it up as a kind of twentieth-century Scholasticism—a system to be maintained and expanded but never fundamentally challenged.[52] Such a reification would be ironic (at the very least), given that this was precisely the attitude toward Thomas among the modern theological establishment that Balthasar so bitterly resented. This tendency toward reification is all the more regrettable since some of Balthasar's more adventuresome speculations need to be moderated or recapitulated in order to bear fruit.

A second, more critical wave of interpreters has submitted Balthasar's thought to a higher degree of scrutiny, thus moving from perception to contestation and thereby helping to uncover certain fundamental themes in Balthasar's theology. It is to them that we now turn.

1.2.2 The Second Wave: Characters in Conflict

If the first-wave Balthasarians were mostly sympathetic clerics engaged in translating and summarizing Balthasar's project as they saw it, the second wave was made up of more critical scholars—usually laypeople and especially laywomen—trying to evaluate rather than assert Balthasar's central role in modern theology. The friendly studies into the theological aesthetics continued to appear, of course, and in particular Aidan Nichols released six noteworthy volumes summarizing various aspects of Balthasar's theology—not just the aesthetics,[53] but the dramatics,[54] the logic,[55] and the later writings.[56] In 2006, Kerr was still (somewhat belatedly) able to observe that "[Balthasar] is by far the most discussed Catholic theologian at present."[57] On the whole, however, this second phase was marked by a hermeneutics of suspicion, and even sometimes outright hostility, regarding the Balthasarian project. Now, the second wave's occasional hostility to

---

52. William Portier recognized this danger of a Balthasarian Scholasticism in an exchange with D. L. Schindler in a 1996 meeting of the Catholic Theological Society of America (see *CTSA Proceedings* 51 [1996]: 297–305, 298).

53. See Aidan Nichols, *The Word Has Been Abroad: A Guide Through Balthasar's Aesthetics* (Edinburgh: T&T Clark, 1998).

54. Ibid., *No Bloodless Myth: A Guide Through Balthasar's Dramatics* (Edinburgh: T&T Clark, 2000).

55. Ibid., *Say It Is Pentecost: A Guide Through Balthasar's Logic* (Edinburgh: T&T Clark, 2001).

56. Ibid., *Scattering the Seed: A Guide through Balthasar's Early Writings on Philosophy and the Arts* (London: T&T Clark, 2006); *Divine Fruitfulness*; and *A Key to Balthasar: Hans Urs von Balthasar on Beauty, Goodness, and Truth* (Grand Rapids: Baker Academic, 2011).

57. Fergus Kerr, *Twentieth-Century Catholic Theologians* (Oxford: Blackwell, 2006), 144.

their subject no doubt came in part as a reaction to the first wave's enthusiasm. But it also represented a conscious effort to put Balthasar's style to the test—to see if in fact he was the model of theological thinking that he had been presented to be by his boosters in the first wave. It is important to note, however, that despite the generally critical tenor of these engagements, second-wave Balthasarians still (often) admitted the creativity and ambition of Balthasar's efforts. George Pattison perhaps speaks for the group when he describes the "infuriating combination of often startlingly original flights of thought, insightful textual comments [. . .] and a complacent Olympian (or should it be 'Goethean'?) elevation that collectively characterize [Balthasar's] sprawling theological achievement."[58]

As Michelle Gonzalez rightly noted in a 2004 article in *Theological Studies*, first-wave works tended to ignore Balthasar's gender theology, thus delaying a fruitful dialogue with feminist theology.[59] Feminist theologians who have engaged Balthasar on this front have often adopted a highly critical judgment of him and his influence. To name a representative example, Beattie's 2004 book *New Catholic Feminism: Theology and Theory* takes up the case against Balthasar as part of her larger campaign against a wave of traditionalist "new feminism" embodied by Catholic thinkers like Michele Schumacher, Mary Ann Glendon, and Prudence Allen.[60] Balthasar is for Beattie "one of the primary sources" for these "neo-orthodox" feminists, especially inasmuch as they take their lead from the gender theology of John Paul II (itself heavily influenced by Joseph Ratzinger and—Beattie alleges—Balthasar).[61] For Beattie, these new feminists ultimately serve to reinforce the hierarchic and androcentric presuppositions of Catholic theology as she sees them. To be sure, there is space to question Beattie's assertion that these neo-orthodox (anti-)feminists are best understood as a class of

---

58. George Pattison in *Reviews in Religion & Theology* 24:1 (2017): 147–50. What Pattison means here by referring to Balthasar's "Olympian elevation" is related to what Kilby has in mind when she accuses Balthasar of standing "above" his sources. I will return to this criticism momentarily.

59. See Michelle Gonzalez, "Hans Urs von Balthasar and Contemporary Feminist Theology," *Theological Studies* 65 (2004), 566–95, 567. Gonzalez's effort in the article is to engage in such a dialogue, in particular stressing that both Balthasar and feminist theology posit a robustly *relational* anthropology, even if Balthasar's apparent belief in gender complementarity often proves unpalatable to feminist readers.

60. Beattie, *New Catholic Feminism: Theology and Theory* (London: Routledge, 2006). In particular Beattie is responding to a seminal collection of essays edited by Schumacher and published in 2004 under the title *Women in Christ: Toward a New Feminism* (Grand Rapids: Eerdmans, 2004). For Beattie's discussion of the volume, see Beattie, *New Catholic Feminisms*, 23–6.

61. In her introduction to *Women in Christ*, Schumacher acknowledges this influence explicitly, citing §99 of John Paul II's 1995 encyclical *Evangelium Vitae*. But as Schumacher also notes, the call for a "new feminism" was at least as old as Mary Aquin O'Neil's 1975 article, "Toward a Renewed Anthropology," *Theological Studies* 36 (1975): 725–36.

Balthasarians,⁶² but her association of them with the Balthasarian legacy as it was transmitted through the papacies of John Paul II and Benedict XVI is apt enough. In particular Ratzinger, both as prefect of the Congregation for the Doctrine of Faith and as pope, advanced a certain sort of Balthasarianism largely indebted to first-wave readings.⁶³ According to Beattie, this tradition, despite the many women theologians who sustain it, hides "violent sexual undercurrents" which must be identified and unraveled.⁶⁴ And these violences are disclosed most tellingly, for Beattie, in the relationship between Balthasar and Speyr, a relationship that Beattie considers a "disturbing" icon for the Swiss theologian's overall untrustworthiness.⁶⁵ Notice that this association of Balthasar's thought with late twentieth-century papal conservatism trades on precisely the reputation of Balthasar that the first wave had aimed to cultivate. Against the first-wave interpretations, Beattie

62. As Graham Ward does in his review of Beattie's book, see *Theology & Sexuality* 15:2 (2009): 251–3, 252.

63. Thus, Joshua Brotherton was able to write as recently as 2015 that, "The formative influence of the thought of Hans Urs von Balthasar on the theology of Joseph Ratzinger is common knowledge" (see Brotherton, "Damnation and the Trinity in Ratzinger and Balthasar," *Logos: A Journal of Catholic Thought and Culture* 18, no. 3 [2015]: 123–50, 123). Brotherton cites the by-now well-known remark by Ratzinger that "meeting Balthasar was for me the beginning of a lifelong friendship [that] I can only be thankful for. Never again have I found anyone with such a comprehensive theological and humanistic education as Balthasar and de Lubac, and *I cannot even begin to say how much I owe to my encounter with them*" (see Ratzinger, *Milestones: Memoirs 1927–1977* [San Francisco: Ignatius, 1998], 143, italics mine). Nichols calls Ratzinger a "disciple" of Balthasar and notes in particular the influence that Balthasar seems to have exerted on Benedict XVI's first encyclical as pope, *Deus Caritas Est* (see Nichols, *Divine Fruitfulness*, 25–6). The extent to which a new Balthasarianism, closer to the one I am advocating in this study, is present in the current pontificate of Pope Francis is something that remains to be seen, though there is reason to believe that several of the current pope's philosophical and theological intuitions are deeply informed by his early readings of Balthasar (see Massimo Borghesi, *Jorge Maria Bergoglio: Una Biographia Intellettuale* [Milan: Jaca, 2017]).

64. Beattie, *New Catholic Feminisms*, 3–4, 13.

65. Ibid., 13. The role of Speyr is one of the major fault line in Balthasar Studies: first-wave works tend to either ignore or downplay her influence (cf. Oakes) or else to valorize the pair's "symbiotic" relationship (cf. Johann Roten, "The Two Halves of the Moon: Marian Anthropological Dimensions in the Common Mission of Adrienne von Speyr and Hans Urs von Balthasar," *Communio* 16 [1989]: especially 421). Second-wave critiques often follow Beattie in considering the relationship suspect. The most sustained and illuminating treatment of the relationship between Speyr and Balthasar remains Schumacher, *A Trinitarian Anthropology: Adrienne von Speyr and Hans Urs von Balthasar in Dialogue with Thomas Aquinas* (Washington, DC: Catholic University of America Press, 2014), but see also Kerr, "Adrienne von Speyr and Hans Urs von Balthasar," *New Blackfriars* 79, no. 923 (1988): 26–32.

intends to render a new Balthasar, one seen through the lens of the psychoanalytic approaches of Lacan, Kristeva, and Irigaray. While these resources provide the basis for a sharp rereading of the Balthasarian *oeuvre*, it must be said that Beattie's critique sometimes degenerates into bald polemic, as when she accuses Balthasar's project—and indeed *all* traditional Catholic soteriology—of amounting to a kind of gay pantomime where the male theologian yearns "to be fucked by Christ."[66] Beattie even accuses Balthasar of sexual "self-loathing" over the shame he allegedly felt in his (seemingly chaste) relationship with von Speyr.[67]

Such accusations—diverting as they may be—seem to me not merely uncharitable but, what is worse, fruitless, since they cannot possibly be verified. Did Balthasar really (i) secretly lust after his married spiritual mentee, such that (ii) he internalized feelings of antagonism toward all women and (iii) ontologized this antagonism in his theology? To answer all these questions in the affirmative requires a degree of psychoanalytic insight into Balthasar's inner life that simply cannot be gleaned from available sources. But even if Beattie's rhetoric often runs ahead of her argumentation, the force of her criticism is clear, and it nevertheless raises certain fundamental questions not only about the dramatic viability of Balthasar's imaginary but also about the largely unchallenged first-wave appropriations of it. Importantly, while first-wave appraisals tended to ground themselves in the theological aesthetics, Beattie sets a precedent for second-wave critiques by engaging primarily with the theological dramatics.[68] Not only is the *Theo-Drama* the place where Balthasar spells out his own account of human sexual difference,[69] but, more importantly, it represents the point at which Balthasar's theology shifts from "seeing the form" to "creat[ing] a network of related concepts and images that may serve to hold fast, in some fashion, in what we think and say, to the singular divine action."[70] The contention of Beattie and others is simply that Balthasar's "network of related concepts and images" obscures more than it clarifies, in particular by what they perceive to be its elision of the feminine into the masculine.[71]

It is also worth mentioning here Linn Marie Tonstad's trenchant queer-feminist critique of Balthasar (alongside Graham Ward and Sarah Coakley) as a zero-sum kenoticist whose Trinitarian imaginary commits him to a problematically gendered

---

66. Beattie, *New Catholic Feminisms*, 196.

67. Ibid., 170 (see also 163–7).

68. Beattie announces her intention to perform a "parodic feminist staging of [. . .] Balthasar's idea of theo-drama" at *New Catholic Feminisms*, 9.

69. See TD.2, 335–430 and in particular the famous passage on 365.

70. TD.1, 17.

71. For other feminist critiques, see Lucy Gardner and David Moss, "Something like Time, Something like the Sexes—an Essay in Reception," in *Balthasar at the End of Modernity*, 69–138 or Corrinne Crammer, "One Sex or Two? Balthasar's Theology of the Sexes," in *Cambridge Companion to Hans Urs von Balthasar*, 93–112.

hierarchy in the creaturely realm.⁷² Tonstad's deconstruction of the Balthasarian *Gestalt* is undoubtedly indebted to, but arguably proves itself more theologically constructive than, Beattie's psychoanalytic critique. In particular, Tonstad assails what she considers Balthasar's "masochistic" Trinitarian taxonomy, in which the Persons are defined by their (revolving, primordial, eternal) self-sacrifice.⁷³ This critique builds on earlier versions of the same by, for example, Kathryn Tanner.⁷⁴ This alleged masochism reaches a climax in Balthasar's account of a divine "superdeath [*Übertod*]," upon the basis of which the divine Persons' self-gift becomes not simply what they give, but what they are.⁷⁵ Tonstad sees in this trajectory a dangerous tendency toward death worship, and as a solution she tries to develop an alternative Trinitarian imaginary which stresses friendship instead of sacrifice.⁷⁶ Tontsad's engagement with Balthasar is perhaps one of the most subtle and serious of the second wave, but it essentially amounts to a confrontation of theodramatic repertoires: where Balthasar speaks of mutual sacrifice, Tonstad speaks of mutual enjoyment; where Tonstad emphasizes (arguably one-sidedly) Balthasar's account of *kenosis*, she prefers to speak of superabundance; and instead of a masculine penetration by Christ, the believer seeks to enjoy the feminine "light caress" of the Holy Spirit.⁷⁷ Obviously, one could as easily reject Tonstad's imaginary as Balthasar's (if indeed it is Balthasar's). But the relevant point for my immediate argument is that critical readers like Beattie and Tonstad push the Balthasarian material further than it ever would have gone in the hands of the first-wave interpreters.⁷⁸

72. See Linn Marie Tonstad, *God and Difference: The Trinity, Sexuality, and the Transformation of Finitude* (London: Routledge, 2016), 27–58. See also idem., "Sexual Difference and Trinitarian Death: Cross, Kenosis, and Hierarchy in the Theo-Drama," *Modern Theology* 26, no. 4 (2010): 603–31.

73. Tonstad, "Sexual Difference and Trinitarian Death," 613.

74. See Kathryn Tanner, *Christ the Key* (Cambridge: Cambridge University Press, 2010), 212.

75. See GL.5, 84ff.

76. Tonstad, "Sexual Difference and Trinitarian Death," 613; see generally Part III of *God and Difference*.

77. Tonstad, *God and Difference*, 276. Tonstad's alternative imaginary brings out many features of Balthasar's system that could be fruitfully appropriated by a queer theory in need of an ideational apparatus with which to justify kenotic self-donation. However, I think she overreacts by rejecting *kenosis* as thoroughly as she does. Furthermore, as I will discuss below, *kenosis* in Balthasar is always rhythmically accompanied by a subsequent moment of *pleroma*, and it is this *combined* emphasis which should be considered the controlling factor in Balthasar's theology.

78. Tonstad's book engendered many responses, both critical and appreciative. Among the most illuminating are those in a symposium organized by the journal *Syndicate*, "God and Difference: Trinitarian Theology, Theological Method, and Sexual Difference," ed. Brandy Daniels (May 14, 2017); accessible online at https://syndicate.network/symposia/

In addition to queer and feminist attacks, Balthasar's project faced notable challenges from its right flank as well. For instance, Alyssa Pitstick accuses Balthasar of heresy over his controversial account of the *decensus Christi*, building on a line of attack that had been developing within the German scholarship for years.[79] Pitstick construes the "traditional doctrine" of Christ's descent in such a way that excludes Balthasar's admittedly inclusivist account of eschatological grace. As O'Regan notes, Pitstick is engaged in "nothing less than [an attempt to] vitiate Balthasar's entire theological enterprise."[80] While the first wave took Balthasar almost as a stand-in for the Tradition, Pitstick sees the Swiss theologian standing squarely against the established magisterial teaching of the church.[81] Pitstick's study is a dogged and carefully researched polemic against what she considers a serious threat to the orthodox doctrine of hell and salvation; in this way her subject matter is substantively different than the feminist critics I have just discussed. But she shares with them a strong, almost visceral, sense that Balthasar's theology is essentially dangerous. However, Pitstick's polemic, though widely noted, has yet to effect quite the sea change in Balthasar Studies that she would have hoped for. In particular, a leading member of the first wave enlisted Newman's *Essay* in order to suggest that Balthasar's *decensus* Christology constitutes a "legitimate and logical development of church doctrine" on hell,[82] and David Lauber offered a Barthian defense of Balthasar, noting that both the Swiss theologians stressed the pro nobis

theology/god-and-difference/ (last accessed February 7, 2021). In the *Syndicate* symposium, Tonstad's arguments are evaluated by Kilby, Gerard Loughlin, Eboni Marshall Turman, Coakley, and Paul DeHart, with responses from Tonstad to each.

79. See Alyssa Pitstick, *Light in Darkness: Hans Urs von Balthasar and the Catholic Doctrine of Christ's Descent into Hell* (Grand Rapids: Eerdmans, 2007). For German sources, see Johannes Rothkranz, *Die Kardinalfehler des Hans Urs von Balthasar* (Durach: Anton Schmid, 1989), 47–50, 379–81 and David Berger, "Woher kommen die Thesen Hans Urs von Balthasars zur Hölle? Oder: hatte 'Theologisches' doch recht?" *Theologisches Katholische Monatsschrift* 31 (2001): 267–8.

80. See Cyril O'Regan reviewing Pitstick in *Religious Studies Review* 34:3 (2008), here 177.

81. According to Pitstick, Balthasar "sets Scripture against that very Tradition and ends up concluding something contrary to the Tradition he received and in which he claims to stand" (*Light in Darkness*, 337).

82. See Oakes, "The Internal Logic of Holy Saturday in the Theology of Hans Urs von Balthasar," *International Journal of Systematic Theology* 9, no. 2 (April 2007): 184–99, 184. Pitstick responded in turn to Oakes' article, doubling down on her claim that Balthasar's Christology constitutes a "corruption" of the traditional teaching (see Pitstick, "Development of Doctrine, or Denial? Balthasar's Holy Saturday and Newman's Essay," *International Journal of Systematic Theology* 11, no. 2 [April 2009]: 129–45, 130). The debate also raged in the popular Catholic press, with Pistick and Oakes both making their cases in the pages of the conservative American journal *First Things* (see "Balthasar, Hell, and Heresy: An Exchange" [December 2006]). It is worth noting here that Pitstick's arguments

character of Christ's passion, which must constantly amplify the question of what God is willing to do "to seek out and to save the lost" (Lk. 19:10).[83] For my part, I agree with McIntosh's assessment that Pitstick's study wrongly insists on reading Balthasar within "the approved sheepfolds of normative dogmatic language and neo-scholastic rigor," without apparently realizing (or caring) that to do so is to engage in a "very serious sort of genre mistake."[84] In any case, Pitstick's efforts have succeeded in shifting the conversation around a figure many first-wave readers considered to be "a bastion of theological orthodoxy"[85] and thus constitute an important part of the second-wave project.

One more important second-wave critique is worth mentioning before moving on: Karen Kilby gave voice to a widespread sentiment when in her 2012 monograph on Balthasar she expressed serious reservations over his voice and style.[86] For Balthasar's first-wave boosters, his grand cadence and sweeping view of the Western intellectual tradition proves an attractive—even necessary—feature of his theology, showing as it does the interconnectedness of his themes and thus performing the *perichoresis* of transcendentals for which his great trilogy seeks to argue. But for Kilby these same tendencies within Balthasar's writings betray a hubris which leads him to write "as though from a position above his materials [. . .] above tradition, above Scripture, above history—and also, indeed, above his readers."[87] She notes not only the "difficulty of finding one's way around Balthasar"—which nearly everyone acknowledges—but the related "difficulty of *criticizing* Balthasar"—which she considers a result of various factors (notably his persistent, if by-now counterintuitive, status as a theological underdog and the lack of a single clear idea upon which the rest of his *corpus* might rise or fall). Though Kilby examines various specific points within the Balthasarian *oeuvre* (his Trinitarian thought, for instance, which she finds moderately useful, or his gender theology, which she finds much more problematic), the lasting effect of her book has been to suggest that the whole Balthasarian approach is essentially unstable and "unfettered"—not least because of the influence of Speyr (who Kilby clearly holds in some suspicion).[88] Kilby acknowledges that Balthasar wrote for most of

---

did convince some first-wave Balthasarians, notably Saward (see Saward, *The Sweet and Blessed Country* [Oxford: Oxford University Press, 2008], 99–100).

83. See David Lauber, "Response to Alyssa Lyra Pitstick, *Light in Darkness*," *Scottish Journal of Theology* 62, no. 2 (2009): 195–201.

84. McIntosh reviewing Pitstick in *Modern Theology* 24:1 (2008): 137–9, 138. There are also the textual critiques, for instance to do with Pitstick's reading of Maximus, that are raised by Mark Yenson, *Existence as Prayer: The Consciousness of Christ in the Theology of Hans Urs von Balthasar* (Oxford: Peter Lang, 2014), 186–7.

85. O'Regan reviewing Pitstick (*op. cit.*), 177.

86. Karen Kilby, *Balthasar: A (Very) Critical Introduction* (London: Eerdmans, 2012).

87. Ibid., 13.

88. Ibid., 38. For Kilby's discussion of Speyr, see *Balthasar*, 24–6. Her reservations aside, Kilby represents what might be considered a pragmatic approach to the "Speyr Problem"

his career from a position on the periphery of the theological establishment but does not see this fact alone exonerating him from what she considers his repeated offenses against acceptable academic style. Since, according to Kilby, Balthasar "asserts too much [and] argues too little," his usefulness for Catholic theology must be fundamentally called into question; indeed, "the one thing [. . .] one ought *not* to learn from [Balthasar] is how to be a theologian."[89] Kilby's book set off a number of debates, with D. C. Schindler and Mongrain, for instance, both coming to Balthasar's defense[90] while others lauded Kilby's boldness in challenging this most bold of modern theologians.[91] Even if the picture of Balthasar's theology I want to present is in many ways inconsonant with Kilby's own, she has furthered the discourse by raising certain fundamental questions to do with theological method and the use of theological language. For now, I need only note Kilby's critique as part of the broader second-wave reaction against the interpretive hegemony established by first-wave readers.

My dissatisfaction with the second wave has to do not so much with any of their specific criticisms of Balthasar's admittedly adventurous theologoumena; rather, I submit that in their rush to correct the overwrought and politically motivated interpretations advanced during the first wave, they often misrepresented the particular sort of theological performance that Balthasar's writings represent. I have already raised this point in Section 1.1 *supra*, but it bears repeating that Balthasar never intended to preside over a "system" which might be subject to cadaverous dissection; rather, he only intended in his writing to give rise to genuine contemplation of the central Christian mysteries. Ultimately, he wanted his work "to become superfluous," as he wrote at the outset of the book on prayer.[92] Thus, many of the second-wave critiques can be said to miss the forest for the trees inasmuch as they set out to show that Balthasar was not the great system-builder

---

inasmuch as she acknowledges Speyr's obvious influence on Balthasar, but likewise recognizes the complexity and even "undecidability" that would confront anyone intent on "teasing out" exactly where Speyr ends and Balthasar begins (see Kilby, *Balthasar*, 100).

89. Kilby, *Balthasar*, 167. Kilby's view here is echoed, perhaps surprisingly, by the conservative editor of *First Things* Russell Reno, who calls Balthasar "largely unusable" for the purposes of theological education (see Reno, "The Paradox of Hans Urs von Balthasar," in *How Balthasar Changed My Mind: 15 Scholars Reflect on the Meaning of Balthasar for Their Own Work*, eds. Rodney Howsare and Larry Chapp [New York: Crossroad, 2008], 172–90, here 177, and see also 180).

90. See D. C. Schindler, "A Very Critical Response to Karen Kilby: On Failing to See the Form," in *Radical Orthodoxy: Theology, Philosophy, Politics* 3, no. 1 (September 2015): 68–87; see also Mongrain's entry in, "Review Symposium: 'Balthasar: A (Very) Critical Introduction': Four Perspectives," *Horizons* 40, no. 1 (2013): 91–113, 96–100.

91. See, for instance, the generally appreciative (if brief) reviews by both Peter Maican (in *Theology in Scotland* 22, no. 1 [2015]: 65–8) and Mark McInroy (in *Theology* 116, no. 6 [November 2013]: 436–7).

92. *Prayer* (H), 8.

or mastermind that his first-wave readers had made him out to be. Indeed, he was, as Rahner recognized, a fundamentally profligate thinker, one who had sown his seeds far and wide and whose full importance would need time in order to come to fruition.[93]

The real danger of certain second-wave approaches, then, is that they risk short-circuiting the necessary process of engaging Balthasar constructively in favor of barring him outright from the guild of acceptable theological discourse (whatever that is taken to be). Of course if, as some of the second-wave critics allege, Balthasar is truly a dangerous thinker whose theology—as it was intended—represents a tool of oppression or a degradation of doctrine, then perhaps my call for patience and flexibility in reading him will seem naïve. I have little recourse here but to declare that I do not judge Balthasar to be dangerous in this way. But *even if he were*, the vehement rejection of Balthasar from the realm of acceptable discourse would consign his legacy entirely to those who would enlist him as a conservative hero—it would thus have the effect of reinforcing the very reading of Balthasar it sets itself against.

As it was with the first wave, my own reading of Balthasar is not simply against these critics but is meant to coexist alongside them. In a typically Balthasarian way, we should attempt today to synthesize everything in their approach which can be put to constructive use. What they have achieved in responding so forcefully, even iconoclastically, to our author is a real dramatic confrontation of theological imaginaries and vocabularies. In carrying out this confrontation, they have rendered a service to Balthasar's vision, if not always his substantive project, by lending their own voices to the cloud of witnesses attempting to sustain the Christian theological tradition.

A third wave of readers have generally succeeded in treating the Balthasarian material as just this kind of generative resource. They have undertaken to understand Balthasar without lionizing him, to critique him without muting his particular theological voice. It is to these readers that we now turn.

1.2.3 *The Third Wave: Integration*

The task of reading Balthasar today is the task of coming to grips with a particular theological "style," one which, as all great theological styles must, "overflows what a doctrinal approach [alone] can achieve."[94] Balthasar gave pride of place to style,

---

93. See Karl Rahner, "Hans Urs von Balthasar," *Civitas* 20 (1964–5): 601–4.

94. See Christoph Theobald, "Le christianisme comme style: Entrer dans une manière d'habiter le monde," *Revue d'éthique et de théologie morale* 251 (2008): 235–48, 242. Theobald begins in this article to develop an account of theological "styles," which is highly useful. I am content to agree with him that the multiplicity of Christian experience will necessarily multiply the legitimate styles of Christian proclamation: "L'approche stylistique permet de tenir ensemble l'absolue singularité de l'événement eschatologique et sa présence dans l'histoire, selon une variabilité étonnante de formes ou de figures, expression d'une

even at the expense of systematic consistency: "The truth of all great things rests less in the *what* than in the *how*; the spirit of the whole gives sense and unity to the whole."⁹⁵ What I am calling third-wave readers have developed an ear for the particularly Balthasarian style—his rhythms of thought and speech—and are able, therefore, to integrate that style into any number of other complimentary (or competing) approaches. They can synthesize the great synthesizer. This most often involves, as Derek Brown has forcefully argued, "recontexutaliz[ing] but never decontextualiz[ing]" Balthasar's theology.⁹⁶ These readers are united by their conviction that Balthasar is a *source* of theology, as opposed to its *end*. Both the first- and the second-wave position Balthasar as a kind of terminus ad quem—the first wave because Balthasar has apparently summed up the fullness of Catholic thought so completely, the second wave because no defensible theology can continue further down the same path with him. Third-wave thinkers view him closer to his own description as that "apparatus" which is useful for the sake of "further exercise."⁹⁷ The task of "integration" is the highest work of logic, and so this third wave could be said to represent the most mature efforts to think *with* Balthasar.⁹⁸ Thus, Kilby may be right, in a certain sense, that Balthasar represents a dangerous example of the theological method for beginner students; however, for the same reasons (his boldness, his loose approach to voice, even his lack of clarity) he proves an especially generative partner for the theologian who seeks to test and combine his insights with their own critical projects, or who seeks to be pushed further than they would be within the confines of a purely academic style.

---

prodigieuse créativité qui ne cesse de déborder toute tentative de réduire celles-ci à une structure unique" (244).

95. *OSF*, 4.

96. Derek Brown, "Kneeling in the Streets: Recontextualizing Balthasar," *New Blackfriars* 99 (2018), 788–806, here 794. Brown's provocative essay takes important steps toward "liberating Balthasar" from his conservative legacy. It has also been the task of the third wave to recontextualize Balthasar in terms of his own intellectual history and context, as Jonathan King has done in an important study of Balthasar as a Germanist ("Theology under Another Form: Hans Urs von Balthasar's Formation and Writings as a Germanist" [PhD diss., St. Louis University, 2016]). King's approach usefully shows that Balthasar's methods and patterns of thought were formed by hermeneutical debates proper to twentieth-century *Germanistik* scholarship before they were influenced by his formal theological education. Specifically, Balthasar was indebted to the so-called New Germanists like Cysarz, Castle, and Kluckhohn, who stressed a "bold, *geistesgeschichtlich*, and synthetic" approach to texts rather than the "cautious, historical, and text-critical" method of the traditional school (see King, "Theology under Another Form," 298–303, here 298). King shows how these hermeneutical impulses heavily colored Balthasar's early engagements with the Fathers, for instance, but appear still in *A Theology of History* and persisted as late as *Theo-Drama*.

97. See again TD.1, 9; cf. the remarks by Matthew Moser, *Love Itself Is Understanding: Hans Urs von Balthasar's Theology of the Saints* (Minneapolis: Fortress, 2016) 271 n.3.

98. On integration cf. TL.1, 15.

As Peter Casarella puts it, "Balthasar raises rather than lowers the bar for expertise in a specialized field."[99] A number of such works have appeared in recent years, and it is worth pointing to a few of those which are genuinely generative in their own right.

The sort of creative, integrative undertaking was arguably inaugurated with a collection of essays assembled by a small group of Anglo-Catholic theologians in 1999.[100] Though the three main contributions to that volume all stand on their own as distinct entries into to the secondary literature on Balthasar, they evidence a willingness to take certain Balthasarian themes (namely kenosis, gender, drama) further than they had been pushed up to that point. So Gardner and Moss, for instance, read Balthasar alongside Irigaray; Ward does so alongside Kristeva; and Quash does so alongside a number of Radical Orthodoxy thinkers like Pickstock and Milbank. The volume is also noteworthy for promoting a "serious re-engagement with metaphysics" not just among Balthasar scholars but Catholic theologians generally.[101]

Anne Carpenter further contributes to the development of a constructive Balthasarian grammar by showing the extent of Balthasar's efforts to keep theology, art, and metaphysics in a proper balance. Her book, *Theo-Poetics*, argues for an integration of the poetic style itself into the systematic form and distinguishes several apparent advantages to such a move.[102] Carpenter's account is distinct from the older theopoetics movement,[103] and in part for that reason it is significant that she looks to Balthasar as a resource when assembling a new critical-imaginative

---

99. Peter Casarella, "Foreword," in Anne Carpenter, *Theo-Poetics: Hans Urs von Balthasar and the Risk of Art and Being* (Notre Dame, Indiana: University of Notre Dame Press, 2015), ix–xiii, here ix. Henri de Lubac expresses something of the same sentiment in "Un témoin du Christ dans l'Église: Hans Urs von Balthasar," in *Paradoxe et mystère de L'Église* (Paris, 1967).

100. *Balthasar at the End of Modernity* (*op. cit.*). Though this book appeared quite early in the timeline of Balthasar scholarship as I have been sketching it, its full critical impact is still being felt.

101. Kerr, "Assessing this 'Giddy Synthesis,'" 13. Michael Murphy likewise attempts to reconcile Balthasar with postmodernism, but his treatment is overdetermined by a literary approach and less metaphysically probative than the essays by Gardner, Moss, Quash, and Ward; see Murphy, *Balthasar, Postmodernism, and the Catholic Imagination* (Oxford: Oxford University Press, 2008).

102. Among the advantages Carpenter claims in favor of a "theological poetic" are the following: an increased sensitivity to thematic *resonance*; a more *flexible* mode of expression which nevertheless need not sacrifice specificity of reference; and a sensitivity to *hierarchies of meaning* which fit well with a metaphysical approach (see *Theo-Poetics* 155 and Chapter 4 generally).

103. Cf. Amos Wilder, *Theopoetic: Theology and the Religious Imagination* (Philadelphia: Fortress, 1976). Cf. Casarella "Foreword" in Carpenter, *Theo-Poetics*, xiii n.6, for references to Balthasar's treatment of Wilder and Wilder's novelist brother Thornton.

language. Finally, Carpenter rightly notes Balthasar's "fundamental confidence in language's ability to express metaphysical reality," a confidence grounded in Christology.[104] This confidence—a confidence Balthasar repeatedly identifies with *parrhesia*—is a point to which I will return in what follows.

John Cihak rehabilitates a bygone theme in modern theology by asking what Balthasar can teach us about the phenomenon of human anxiety.[105] Starting with the insights found in the Category 2 work, *Der Christ und die Angst*, Cihak accomplishes an impressive task by combining scripture, phenomenology, and psychology to render a deeply theological account of anxiety and fear—something hinted at by the Magisterium in several of the documents of Vatican II, even if it has been left largely unaddressed by theologians since.[106] Cihak also brings Balthasar into close dialogue with Kierkegaard on the issue. In these ways Cihak's study *deploys* Balthasar to new and creative uses in an exemplary way. We will return to the question of anxiety in Christ's prayers in Chapter 4.

Morrison performs another such creative combination by reading Balthasar's trilogy in light of the ethical thought of Levinas.[107] Both Levinas and Balthasar are engaged in efforts to maintain the organic connection between metaphysics and ethics in the wake of Heidegger's ontotheological critique. And both personalize reflection on Being through the face of the Other (Balthasar most famously in his analogy of the loving gaze between mother and child). Helpfully for our purposes, Morrison also draws out how, for Levinas, thought and discourse in light of the Other naturally issues in prayer, though he is relatively less clear on how this is also true for Balthasar.[108]

Raymond Gawronski's comparative study of Balthasar and Eastern spirituality attempts to address a notable lacuna within Balthasariana, but, for the reasons listed by Oakes, tends rather to replicate the intuitions of Balthasar more than to accomplish the promised "encounter between East and West."[109] Balthasar

---

104. Carpenter, *Theo-Poetics*, 3–4.

105. John Cihak, *Balthasar and Anxiety* (London: Continuum, 2009). Cf. Jörg Splett, "Der Christ und seine Angst erwogen mit Hans Urs von Balthasar," in *Gott für die Welt: Henri de Lubac, Gustav Siewerth und Hans Urs von Balthasar in ihren Grundanliegen* (Mainz: Matthias-Grünewald Verlag 2001), 315–31.

106. See, for example, *Gaudium et Spes* and cf. Cihak *Balthasar and Anxiety*, 8 n.28. For one twentieth-century treatment, see Rahner, "Anxiety and Christian Trust in Theological Perspective," in *Theological Investigations*, vol. 23: *Final Writings*, trans. Joseph Donceel and Hugh Riley (London: Burns and Oates, 1992): 3–15.

107. Glenn Morrison, *A Theology of Alterity: Levinas, von Balthasar, and Trinitarian Praxis* (Pittsburgh: Duquesne University Press, 2013).

108. See Morrison, *A Theology of Alterity*, 33, 162–3, 189–91.

109. Raymond Gawronski, *Word and Silence: Hans Urs von Balthasar and the Spiritual Encounter between East and West* (Kettering: Angelico, 1995). See Oakes review in *The Journal of Religion* 78:2 (1998): 283–4.

himself admitted[110] that his work did not, in the main, treat the East with the depth and nuance it deserves, but in the intervening years since his death this route has not been sufficiently developed.[111] More promising is Jennifer Martin's monograph, which undertakes to trace out the "subterranean" lines of influence, overlap, and creative tension between Balthasar's thought and that of various Orthodox figures such as Berdyaev, Bulgakov, and Soloviev.[112] Other works in this mold have similarly uncovered the full depths of Balthasar's theology by focusing on a previously underexplored topics within his writings, such as his teaching on the spiritual senses[113] or eschatology.[114] Several works have succeeded in considering Balthasar's relationship to Protestant sources, especially Karl Barth, in a constructive and non-polemical way.[115] In addition, a handful of noteworthy studies have explicitly concerned themselves with topics that Balthasar did not treat at length, such as ethics[116] or a theology of God the Father.[117] The aesthetics

---

110. GL.1, 11: "The overall scope of the present work naturally remains all too Mediterranean. The inclusion of other cultures, especially that of Asia, would have been important and fruitful. But the author's education has not allowed for such an expansion, and a superficial presentation of such material would have been dilettantism. *May those qualified come to complete the present fragment.*"

111. A notable exception is Hohyun Sohn, "Hans Urs von Balthasar and the East: Identity or Dialogue," *Heythrop Journal* 59, no. 3 (2018): 573–85. Sohn's article is, ironically, not only a more compact but also a more comprehensive introduction to the theme than Gawronski's scrupulously footnoted book, inasmuch as Sohn proves himself to be a good deal more critical toward Balthasar and seems to have a firmer grasp on Eastern thought than Gawronski.

112. See Jennifer Martin, *Hans Urs von Balthasar and the Critical Appropriation of Russian Religious Thought* (Notre Dame: University of Notre Dame Press, 2015); more work deserves to be done uncovering these important sinews of influence, though Martin's book will clearly set the standard for any that follow her lead.

113. Mark McInroy, *Balthasar on the Spiritual Senses: Perceiving Splendour* (Oxford: Oxford University Press, 2014); cf. Stephen Fields, "Balthasar and Rahner on the Spiritual Senses," *Modern Theology* 57 (1996): 224–41.

114. Nicholas Healy, *The Eschatology of Hans Urs von Balthasar: Eschatology as Communion* (Oxford: Oxford University Press, 2005).

115. See Rodney Howsare, *Hans Urs von Balthasar and Protestantism* (London: Bloomsbury, 2005); Stephen Wigley, *Karl Barth and Hans Urs von Balthasar: A Critical Engagement* (London: Bloomsbury, 2007); and D. Stephen Long, *Saving Karl Barth: Hans Urs von Balthasar's Preoccupation* (Minneapolis: Fortress, 2014).

116. Christopher Steck, *The Ethical Thought of Hans Urs von Balthasar* (New York: Crossroads, 2001).

117. Margaret Turek, *Towards a Theology of God the Father: Hans Urs von Balthasar's Theodramatic Approach* (Oxford: Peter Lang, 2001).

have also come in for reevaluation in light of more recent scholarship.[118] Todd Walatka produced one of the most important third-wave works with his lucid and compelling study of the significant (if often underappreciated) overlap between Balthasar and liberation theology.[119] And a number of Balthasarians have again taken up the theme of metaphysics, though these works do not always capture the connection between metaphysics and prayer in Balthasar's thought.[120]

Regardless of whether any of these particular experiments completely succeeds or fails they represent a much-needed return to Balthasar's *generative* theological material. The wide scope of themes and topics covered in the third wave is enough to set it apart from the previous two, but it is also distinctive in the way its members typically relate to the Balthasarian material. The operative hermeneutic is one of *critical generosity* which seeks to learn from Balthasar when it is possible to do so and correct him when it is necessary. Such is the general approach to his own sources that Balthasar often displayed in his writings, so in this way the third wave represents not only a more fruitful but also a more faithful method.

1.3 Reading Balthasar Today

This survey of Balthasar scholarship is not intended to be an exhaustive review, nor is it meant to definitively resolve all of the prevailing debates within the field. It is, rather, offered as a map for making one's way within the sprawling realm of Balthasar Studies. We can sum up the key insights of these proposed schemas with a few general observations.

First, adequate Balthasar scholarship today should strive to exhibit the sensitivity to sources and levels of meaning that Balthasar's *oeuvre* actually calls for. Second

---

118. See *Theological Aesthetics after von Balthasar*, eds. Oleg Bychkov and James Fodor (Burlington: Ashgate, 2008).

119. Todd Walatka, *Von Balthasar and the Option for the Poor: Theodramatics in the Light of Liberation Theology* (Washington: Catholic University of America Press, 2017). Another notable experiment in Balthasarian political theology is Stephen Waldron, "Hans Urs von Balthasar's Theological Critique of Nationalism," in *Political Theology* 15:5 (2014): 406–20. Cf. again Brown, "Kneeling in the Streets." If it is perhaps still too early to claim the mantle of a "Balthasarian political theology," contributions like Brown's, Walatka's, and Waldron's nevertheless go some way toward mitigating the charge of Dalzell that Balthasar's theology is primarily interpersonal at the expense of the social or political (see Thomas Dalzell, *The Dramatic Encounter of Divine and Human Freedom in the Theology of Hans Urs von Balthasar* [Berlin: Peter Lang, 2000]).

120. Most significant here are Johnson, *Christ and Analogy*; D. C. Schindler, *Hans Urs von Balthasar and the Dramatic Structure of Truth: A Philosophical Investigation* (New York: Fordham, 2004); Prevot, *Thinking Prayer*; and O'Regan, *The Anatomy of Misremembering: Von Balthasar's Response to Philosophical Modernity*, Vol. I: *Hegel* (New York: Crossroads, 2014).

and relatedly, due to the fact that there is an underlying *unity* among Balthasar's various works, readers should take care to maintain a sense of that cohesion. This means that the influence of Speyr, for instance, should not be merely bracketed out as an aspect of his style which is "not essential" to understanding his overall vision.[121] Of course, not every book on Balthasar needs to deal with every aspect of his thought—but it is necessary to have a sense of the whole before engaging in either appropriation or critique. As Balthasar was fond of saying, quoting an old German axiom, "*Wer mehr Wahrheit sieht, hat mehr recht.*"[122] Third (and this point has been made before) Balthasar should not be judged primarily as an interpreter of texts, but as a creative thinker in his own right (albeit one who necessarily argues *through* the texts and authors he is reading). Johnson remarks: "If the task is to understand von Balthasar, it is only marginally interesting whether or not his reading of Hölderlin [e.g.] gets the poet *right*; what is much more important is that von Balthasar thought that *this* type of material could be drawn from *this* type of poet."[123] A related fourth point would be that efforts to identify the most decisive "sources" of Balthasar's theology should be taken with a heavy dose of salt.[124] He is always, in the end, his own thinker. From these follows a fifth and final point, which seems at first counterintuitive: canonicity functions for Balthasar as a kind of license, rather than as a constraint. If (theological) truth is symphonic, according

---

121. See van Erp's hasty judgment to this effect (regarding the influence of Speyr) in *The Art of Theology*, 81 (following the earlier judgment of Mongrain in *The Systematic Thought of Hans Urs von Balthasar: An Irenaean Retrieval* [New York: Herder, 2002], 11–2).

122. "Whoever sees more of the truth is more right" (see e.g. *Epilogue* 15).

123. Johnson, *Christ and Analogy*, 17. Balthasar himself wrote in an undated letter to Josef Pieper that he (i.e., Balthasar) had "no historical intentions" but that his "entire work consists in this making-present" of the Tradition as an ever-new, living reality (quoted by Lochbrunner, *Philosophenfreunde*, 18).

124. Several works make various (and sometimes incompatible) claims of influence: See, for example, Mongrain, *The Systematic Thought of Hans Urs von Balthasar*; Martin, *Hans Urs von Balthasar and the Critical Appraisal of Russian Religion Thought*; Katy Leamy, *The Holy Trinity: Hans Urs von Balthasar and His Sources* (Eugene, Oregon: Pickwick, 2015); Sachs, "Spirit and Life," 20–3; or Gill Goulding, "The Jesuit Imprint: Ignatian Insights into the Theology of Hans Urs von Balthasar," *Ultimate Reality and Meaning* 32, no. 1 (2009): 75–89. My point is not to deny that certain figures command a particular influence upon Balthasar's thought (by my lights the most important are Ignatius, Maximus the Confessor, and Speyr), but that one should not undertake to trace out these lines of influence in a straightforwardly causal way. Johnson's discussion of Balthasar's sources (namely Plato, Aquinas, Hegel, Heidegger, and Bonaventure) is a good example of how to approach the question of sources in general—not least since it captures the often-undervalued role of Bonaventure (see Johnson, *Christ and Analogy*, 10–17). For Balthasar, as Johnson argues, "It is precisely because he believes that the best way to *replace* a system of thought is by showing that its insights have *already been included*, but with a broader vista, in the new system of thought" that he undertakes to renarrate such wide swaths of metaphysical history (11).

to Balthasar's famous metaphor, then even the virtuoso is never merely a soloist.[125] This implies an implicit (theological) account of tradition itself, inasmuch as it is God (and we might say the Holy Spirit in particular) who guarantees the "unity of the composition."[126] Notably, Balthasar thinks that this pluralism within tradition will have to go on increasing.[127]

With these points in mind, then, we can look ahead to our substantive undertaking—namely, Balthasar's theology of prayer itself. As has already been indicated, prayer is of central importance to Balthasar's entire theological project. He theologizes *from* prayer and *for the sake* of prayer. Indeed, his revolving style, which "says the same thing in different ways," can be thought of as a kind of meditation or chant, reflecting again and again on the central mysteries of the Christian faith in the hopes of rendering a more-adequate sense of the real. Furthermore, prayer itself is, quite simply, a great mystery, one that resists simple definitions. Accordingly, in treating prayer, we will find ourselves treating a number of other fundamental topics in a similarly revolving style, approaching the same basic phenomenon from different angles in order to uncover more fully prayer's true depths.

---

125. Kilby accuses Balthasar of usurping the role of conductor and ultimately "writ[ing] from a position, with a perspective, which on his own account ought not to be possible" (Kilby, *Balthasar*, 96). This criticism confuses style for substance: Balthasar's "extraordinary intellectual ambition" does not in itself prove disqualifying, but rather constitutes the form of his particular theological performance. To the extent that Balthasar sacrifices his own speculative idiosyncrasies in the interest of an approach that works within an historically and dogmatically grounded tradition, he remains a member in good standing of the theological symphony. Elsewhere Balthasar makes his aversion to idiosyncrasy explicit (this is a running theme of *2SS* and the reason for supplementing Thérèse with Elizabeth of the Trinity). This point is well made by O'Regan in *The Anatomy of Misremembering*, 79. If Kilby were to argue that Balthasar's theology actually constituted a breach of dogma (as, for instance, Pitstick does), then her criticism would have greater purchase; as it is, however, Kilby punts on that question (see Kilby, *Balthasar*, 17–8).

126. Cf. *TS*, 9.

127. Ibid.

Chapter 2

PRAYER'S ROLE

2.1 Theology and Prayer

If some unfortunate student were suddenly asked to identify *the* defining feature of Balthasar's theological project, they would not be far off base to point to his dogged insistence on the inseparability of theology and spirituality. It is a theme that occupied Balthasar since the 1940s,[1] and one which is often enough noted by commentators.[2] However, it is also the case that Balthasar tended to conceive of the relationship between theology and spirituality in more radical and thoroughgoing ways than has often been admitted.

2.1.1 The "Contemplative Style" of Theology

A representative example of an arguably flawed approach to the question occurs in Gerard O'Collins' recent handbook on fundamental theology, which distinguishes between "three styles of theology," which he names as the academic style, the practical style, and the contemplative style.[3] Each style is said to have its advantages and its disadvantages: the academic style can speak precisely about texts and concepts, but risks degenerating into abstraction and even a churlish refusal to grant assent; the practical style stands in considerable solidarity with the poor and suffering, but risks turning into mere activism that does not do justice to the full scope of a properly theological vision; and the contemplative style grows out of organic patterns of common life within the church, but risks neglecting both intellectual rigor and a social consciousness. Balthasar is cited as a classic example

---

1. The famous Category 1 essay "Theologie und Heiligkeit," which appeared in the first volume of *Skizzen zur Theologie* in 1960, was originally published in 1948 in *Wort und Wahrheit* 3 (1948), 881–96. Cf. later *Convergences,* 14.

2. For example, see Sicari, "Theology and Holiness," 121–32. More recently, see Gardner, "Hans Urs von Balthasar: The Trinity and Prayer," in *A Transforming Vision: Knowing and Loving the Triune,* ed. George Westhaver, *God* (London: SCM, 2018).

3. See Gerard O'Collins, *Rethinking Fundamental Theology: Toward a New Fundamental Theology* (Oxford: Oxford University Press, 2011), 323–5.

of a Western theologian who fits squarely in the third category, which is formed in the context of "prayer and worship" and which takes "persons at prayer" as its main sources of authority.[4] At first blush, Balthasar would presumably not object to this rough schema, nor his being categorized as one of O'Collins' contemplative theologians—recall, for instance, his famous insistence that theology be done "on one's knees."[5]

But upon consideration it becomes necessary to point out that for Balthasar, the value of a kneeling theology was not just as *one more way* of doing theology, but as the method most appropriate to theology's basic task (i.e., to account for "God and all things in relation to God").[6] The contemplative style of theology is the "form of theology that is indispensable for all succeeding forms," Balthasar writes.[7] The "structure [and] pattern" of this form of theology is set forth by Revelation, especially the revelation in Christ, who, therefore, makes theology possible.[8] Indeed, the exhortation to a kneeling theology first arises in a discussion of biblical interpretation—a task which O'Collins reserves to the "academic theologian" but which Balthasar claims cannot be done adequately without the "conviction that the written word has within it the spirit and power to bring about, in faith, contact with the infinity of the Word."[9] O'Collins' admirable commitment to Irenicism thus risks obscuring the rather stronger claim that Balthasar wants to make about theology's essential nature. The much-decried divorce of theology and spirituality under discussion in the essay "Theology and Sanctity" is not to be overcome by balancing various approaches to the theological material in question, nor is the tension to be resolved by token acknowledgments of prayer's place in a well-ordered systematics.[10] Rather, Balthasar is calling for a new (yet old) method of doing theology as such, wherein understanding itself participates in the reality that the theologian seeks to understand. "What is lacking" in modern theology, Balthasar writes, "is not just a piece of material that can be easily incorporated into the existing structure, or else a sort of stylistic quality to be reproduced anew," but, rather, a whole "atmosphere" in which theology can operate according to what we might call the logic of prayer, in constant dialogue with the Word (on prayer's Christological basis, see Chapter 4).[11] This approach also implies that the church is the necessary space in which theology is to be done, since the "atmosphere"

---

4. O'Collins, *Rethinking Fundamental Theology*, 324–5. Although I hope to show how Balthasar avoids the dangers of the "contemplative" approach.
5. "The Place of Theology" at ET.1, 150.
6. Cf. Thomas Aquinas, *ST* I.1.7.
7. *VBR*, 357.
8. "Theology and Sanctity," at ET.1, 196.
9. Ibid.
10. A tokenism which seems to be on display in O'Collins' own treatment (see *Rethinking Fundamental Theology*, 340–1).
11. "Spirituality" at ET.1, 214.

that gives rise to it is no individual achievement of the theologian (on prayer's ecclesiological dimensions, see Chapter 4).[12]

O'Collins goes on to suggest that this logic of prayer finds a "natural home" in Eastern Christianity,[13] and Orthodox theologians are often eager to claim the advantage over their Western counterparts on precisely this point.[14] And while it is certainly the case that Balthasar's reading of Bulgakov in particular helped confirm his views on the necessity of prayer in theological thinking, especially as a way of guarding against an overweening gnosis,[15] here again we have reason to think that his turn to prayer is stronger than O'Collins would lead us to believe. For Balthasar, it is no special virtue of the East to carry out theology in the necessary atmosphere of prayer—as the example of Anselm (for one) suggests. And indeed, the value of Anselm's theology (to remain with that example) is not that it merely gives prayer pride of place and then proceeds according to an essentially rational-philosophical method, but that it operates at all times with a "praying reason [*betenden Vernunft*], which only hopes to find insight in dialogue with the eternal truth."[16] The Cartesian reduction is, therefore, precisely the opposite of theology properly understood.[17] To be sure, kneeling theology is not therefore condemned (again *pace* O'Collins) to sacrifice precision (as the example of Anselm amply suggests!): "Prayerful theology does not mean 'affective' theology," and the need for an "exact [and] realistic" language is still paramount.[18] But the exactitude and realism of the language in question will be judged with reference to those living forms of sanctity in the world that provide the ultimate test case for all theology— that is, the saints, whose lives are "doctrine put into practice."[19] The saints—and

---

12. Cf. the remarks at *VBR*, 356–9.

13. O'Collins, *Rethinking Fundamental Theology*, 324.

14. For a representative example, see Thomas Hopko, "God and Man in the Orthodox Church," in *God and Charity: Images of Eastern Orthodox Theology, Spirituality, and Practice*, ed. Francis Costa (Brookline, Massachusetts: Holy Cross Orthodox Press, 1979): 1–32.

15. See Martin, *Hans Urs von Balthasar and the Critical Appropriation of Russian Religious Thought*, 198–200.

16. GL.2, 212 (H.2 218); see the whole section on Anselm 211–59. Anselm is something of a norm for Balthasar regarding theological method; see also "Theology and Sanctity," 206 and "The Fathers, the Scholastics, and Ourselves," 380–6.

17. Cf. "Theology and Sanctity," 206. Cf. Balthasar, "On the Concept of Person," in *Communio* 13 (1986): 18–26, 23–4. Emily Crosholz has identified a "spiritual oneness" which characterizes Descartes' speculative thought (see "Descartes and the Individuation of Physical Objects" in *Individuation and Identity in Early Modern Philosophy: Descartes to Kant*, ed. Kenneth Barber and Jorge Garcia, [Albany: State University of New York Press, 1994], 55).

18. "Theology and Sanctity," 206–7; see the following section for Balthasar's reservations regarding mysticism.

19. "The Place of Theology," at ET.1 158. The *Catechism of the Catholic Church* often employs saints as the illustrations of dogmatic teaching; see, for example, the reference to

especially Mary—will thus reemerge as touchstones and icons of the various dimensions of prayer under consideration.[20]

Now here Kilby's critique comes back to the fore, since in appealing to the authority of prayer and in particular the saints as sources of theology, is not Balthasar claiming too knowing a perspective? She argues that he fails to pay sufficient attention to the real historical lives of the saints, and that, inasmuch as he does, his view remains overdetermined by Speyr's mystical experiences. When Balthasar speaks of the authority of the saints, is he not just speaking of his own authority (intellectual, spiritual, and ultimately theological) in another voice?[21] Besides, does not an appeal to the saints in their historical specificity threaten to confuse as much clarify, given the many vagaries of their lives and the politically fraught process of canonization?[22] Kilby is certainly right that Balthasar uses the saints in an unusual way, but her critique arguably undersells the value of such an approach. A few points in response, then. First, it must be said that when Balthasar speaks of the saints, he is hardly only interested in those public and canonized persons proclaimed by the hierarchical church. Indeed, in 1961 he worried publicly about the proliferation of canonizations (a trend which would only accelerate under John Paul II), writing that, "Nowhere so much as here is quantity the enemy of quality."[23] Closer to his heart are those many "invisible" saints who impress by their largely "anonymous" forms of witness.[24] (Balthasar seems to have considered his mother to be one such witness.[25]) The church does

---

Thérèse of Lisieux in the heading to the chapter on prayer (see 2558).

20. On the role of the saints in Balthasar's theology, the two most useful studies are Moser, *Love Itself Is Understanding* and Pauline Dimech, *The Authority of the Saints: Drawing on the Theology of Hans Urs von Balthasar* (Eugene: Wipf and Stock, 2017). See also Patricia Sullivan, "Saints as the 'Living Gospel': Von Balthasar's Revealers of the Revealer, Rahner's Mediators of the Mediator," in *Heythrop Journal* 55 (2014): 270–85.

21. Cf. Kilby, *Balthasar*, 96–101. See Moser's discussion of Kilby's critique at *Love Itself Is Understanding*, 270–7.

22. Kenneth Woodward provides a politically sensitive treatment of the question of canonization in *Making Saints: How the Catholic Church Determines Who Becomes a Saint, Who Doesn't, and Why* (New York: Touchstone, 1990).

23. "The Experience of the Church," at ET.2, 26.

24. Cf. TD.3, 29 and *MCW*, 137. For this reason, the designation "holy person" may be a less confusing term here. The anonymity of witness was an important feature of the Johannesgemeinschaft; see the discussion of "Discretion" at OT, 146–7.

25. Balthasar speaks of his mother, Gabrielle Pietzcker, in an interview toward the end of his life, in which he calls her quiet commitment to her faith "an extraordinary image [*ein unvergleichliches Bild*]" that would continue to inspire him for his entire life. See also the remarks at OT, 35. A committed organizer of lay Catholic causes, both spiritual and humanitarian, Pietzcker died as Balthasar was finishing his thesis on German apocalypticism, and her death seems to have pushed him to enter the Jesuits. For biographical background, see Henrici, "Hans Urs von Balthasar: A Sketch of His Life"; Elio Guerriero, *Il Dramma*

not create saints, it only recognizes them, and accordingly their authority is not ultimately dependent upon the church's institutional integrity.[26] This leads on to a second consideration: Balthasar's appeal to the saints is not meant to harken back to an "unctuous, platitudinous piety" characteristic of, say, the sixteenth and seventeenth centuries.[27] The saints are by no means perfect models for life or virtuous exemplars to be emulated in all ways—indeed, it is one of Balthasar's more deeply revisionist aims to disturb this sentimental picture of sanctity.[28] Nor is it merely a question of repristinating certain historical facts of a given saint's life. Rather, the "new theological hagiography" that Balthasar proposes at the start of *Two Sisters* seeks to draw the objective content (which is always Christoform) out of particular subjective missions, and to do so in a way that is always responsive to a given historical context.[29] The saints *say something* with their lives, their prayers, and—often in the last instance—their writings; it is the task of the theologian to hear these messages "from God to the Church" and to attempt to give them an adequate expression.[30] Of course, in undertaking such an attempt, the theologian themself will have to address their own particular historical and intellectual contexts. This speaks to the dynamic and ongoing understanding of grace that Balthasar is operating with. Revelation (in this case the revelation that the particular saint's life is) is never merely a "past event" but is rather "something always happening," a constant work of the Spirit which adjusts itself to different times and places.[31] The saint thus becomes something of a "storehouse" of grace to be drawn upon by future generations (we will see this idea reemerge in the discussion of intercessory prayer in Section 6.2.2 in this volume).[32] So for instance, Elizabeth of the Trinity's reflections on the infinity separating God from humanity are enlisted in Balthasar's

---

di Dio: letteratura e teologia in Hans Urs von Balthasar (Milan: Jaca, 1999), 13ff.; and the illuminating remarks by King at "Theology under Another Form," 101–4 and 147–9. That Balthasar and his sister Renée both entered religious orders the same year, just months after Pietzcker's death, while their brother Dieter would go on to become a Swiss Guard, suggests just how effective their mother's witness was for the young Balthasar children (see here King *op. cit.* 104).

26. Cf. the Apostolic Constitution *Divinus Perfectionis Magister* (1983).

27. Cf. ET.1, 208. For Balthasar's critique of the Baroque, which always risks slipping into religious chauvinism, see *Convergences*, 34–5.

28. He goes as far as to write at one point that "[moral] perfection is not in itself self-sufficient and purposeful" (*CSL*, 82). See also the harsh remarks at *LAC*, 97–8, against identifying "absolute love [itself with] those pointing towards it."

29. *2SS*, 37–8.

30. GL.1, 165. Howsare discusses the role of theological discernment in *A Guide for the Perplexed*, 34.

31. ET.1, 205; cf. *TH*, 110. See Patricia Sullivan, "Saints as the 'Living Gospel': Von Balthasar's Revealers of the Revealer and Rahner's Mediators of the Mediator," in *Heythrop Journal* 40 (2014): 270–85.

32. *Prayer* (H), 106.

running effort to think difference after Heidegger. McIntosh aptly describes the process as one of "hagio-theological *extrapolation*" that never claims to be a simple restatement of a particular saint's own self-understanding.[33] It is in this process of extrapolation that the fruitfulness of a given saint's mission is tested.[34]

We ought not to worry, then, if we find much of Balthasar in his saints. Of course, Balthasar's own theological adequacy can and should likewise be tested; but the standard for such a test should emphatically not be whether or not the saint upon whom Balthasar seeks to draw has had a wholly authentic vision/"experience," nor whether or not Balthasar perfectly transmits that vision/"experience," but instead whether or not the teaching he draws from a given source gives rise in turn to further contemplation in the reader—that is, whether it bears ecclesial fruit.[35] Admittedly, this process of extrapolation can result in a certain "exploitation" of the saint's (and the theologian's) personality by the church.[36] This is arguably what Speyr has demonstrated with her *Allerheiligenbuch*, a remarkable work in which she seeks to illuminate an inside view of the prayer lives of various saints and other figures.[37] The point of such a work is not to make historical claims (that Jerome "fights with God" in prayer, for instance) but to *deploy* the saints as icons of this or that style of prayer in the church, such that more and more perspectives are able to be arrayed in light of the one common identity "in Christ." Some might consider this a bald appropriation of the actual saints in question, but if Speyr and Balthasar are

---

33. See Mark McIntosh, "A Hagio-Theological Doctrine of God: Hans Urs von Balthasar on Three Carmelites," *Irish Theological Quarterly* 59 (1993): 128–42, here 140 (italics added). Dimech's discussion (3–6) is also useful.

34. Marie-Dominique Chenu arguably oversimplifies, then, when he describes "theological systems [as] simply the expressions of a spirituality" (see *Une École de Théologie: La Saulchoir* [1937]; cited in Matthew Ashley, "The Turn to Spirituality? The Relationship between Theology and Spirituality," *Minding the Spirit: The Study of Christian Spirituality*, eds. Elizabeth Dreyer and Mark Burrows [Baltimore: Johns Hopkins University Press, 2005]: 159–70; see note 15). The theologian's task is in fact more dynamic than this, even if they are ultimately attempting to gain a view to the same mystery as the saint.

35. See a concurrent opinion by Gardner in "The Trinity and Prayer," 200. Balthasar's admiration, especially later in life, for lay movements such as Communion and Liberation, suggests the extent to which he was willing to judge in terms of visible fruits. Apparently in response to Luigi Giussani's effusive praise of his scholarly work, Balthasar responded almost impatiently, "Yes, yes, but *you* have created a people" (the exchange is noted by John Allen Jr. in "Musings on Guissani, von Balthasar, and the Creation of a 'People'" in *Crux* [March 17, 2019]; accessible online at https://cruxnow.com/news-analysis/2019/03/musings-on-giussani-von-balthasar-and-the-creation-of-a-people/). Balthasar's 1971 book *In Gottes Einsatz leben* is dedicated to Giussani.

36. GL.1, 342.

37. See Speyr, *The Book of All Saints* (San Francisco: Ignatius, 2008); see also Balthasar's introduction to that work.

right about the overriding priority of mission, then it is an appropriation the saints would welcome as the necessary consequence of an ecclesial existence. I will discuss further what an ecclesiology that presupposes the church's prayer-constitution would look like in Chapter 4 (cf. Section 4.3 *infra*), but for now I merely mean to indicate the essential point, namely that genuine Christian prayer always takes place against the ecclesial horizon—and not just emerging out of it but returning to it, so that the praying person (paradigmatically the saint) becomes a kind of resource for the church and for theology which seeks to express the ecclesial faith. There is in a real sense no such thing as a private prayer (a point which will be echoed in the discussion of mysticism at Section 2.3 *infra*). All this suggests the radical decentering of self that Balthasar considers a distinctive feature of Christian sanctity.

Third and finally, then, the whole way in which the relationship between theology and sanctity is generally conceived of remains arguably too schematic. This is due in no small part to Balthasar's own schematic approach in the "Theology and Sanctity" essay and the insistence of subsequent commentators to focus on that Category 1 work. If, however, one considers "Theology and Sanctity" alongside *Heart of the World*—perhaps the Category 3 work par excellence—then Balthasar's novelty here becomes more apparent.[38] To speak broadly, *Heart* expresses the "inside view" of the theodrama which is presented more systematically elsewhere (especially TD.4) similarly to the way in which the *Confessiones* express Augustine's "inside view" of the doctrine of God put forth in *De Trinitate*. Read together, these works represent simultaneous expressions of theology as prayer, effectively transcending O'Collins' strict divisions between three apparently separate ways of doing theology. So when Kilby worries that Balthasar "[is doing] his theology in part on the basis of information not available to the rest of us, and information whose nature and value we cannot independently judge," she does not seem to appreciate the extent to which Balthasar has made his (and Speyr's) "inner" experience available for all to see.[39] Of course, one is not compelled to find *Heart* credible, but its mere existence does seem to me to go quite a ways toward discrediting the idea that Balthasar is dealing in bad faith. Matthew Ashley notes that, "Most theologians are now comfortable with the recognition that theology [. . .] cannot authorize [its results] simply on the basis of logical coherence and argumentative precision."[40] But if this recognition is to go beyond lip-service, then

---

38. Originally *Das Herz der Welt* (Zurich: Arche, 1945). Andrew Louth argues for the programmatic role of *Heart* within Balthasar's *oeuvre* (see "The Place of *Heart of the World* in the Theology of Hans Urs von Balthasar," *The Analogy of Beauty*, 147–63, especially 147–8). Of course, in order to mitigate against the "schematic" approach to the question, one must not fail to consider also the biographical studies of the saints.

39. Kilby, *Balthasar*, 99. Moser notes that Kilby does not cite *Heart of the World* in her critique (see *Love Itself Is Understanding*, 276 n.16).

40. Ashley, "The Turn to Spirituality?" 163.

space needs to be made for Balthasar's particular blend of traditional sources, speculative argumentation, and mystical experience.[41]

2.1.2 Balthasar's Personal and Polemical Resonances

I have been discussing how Balthasar's understanding of theology as prayer reorients a critical evaluation of his thought in general. In these considerations a word should be spared to highlight how Balthasar's approach to prayer fits within his early polemics and eventually led on to the more mature position that predominated later in his life.

In this regard it is important to recall the early studies of the Fathers—particularly the Origen compilation in 1938, the article "The Fathers, The Scholastics, and Ourselves" in 1939, and the important book on Maximus in 1941. A theme in all these works is that the Patristic period managed to maintain the essential unity of theology and prayer better than the Scholastic or modern periods.[42] It is interesting, however, to consider just what the difference to their theology the Fathers' prayer is to have made. In each case, Balthasar suggests that the integrity of prayer-theology made possible more daring, more synthetic, more "brilliant [and] edifying" experiments than those which would be undertaken by a Scholasticism of the schools.[43] Reading *Cosmic Liturgy*'s introductory chapter on Maximus' method and intellectual style, one cannot help but notice just how taken the young Balthasar apparently was with the Confessor's (and Origen's) intellectual ambition and their "freedom" of mind, which Balthasar took to be hallmarks of distinctively Christian thought.[44] For Maximus, "spirituality and genius, freedom and boldness are never separate from each other," just as for Origen it was the "tender love" for Christ which led him to construct a system of such "passion [and]

---

41. Another sign of Balthasar's partial vindication can be seen with reference to the 2011 document of the International Theological Commission, "Theology Today: Perspectives, Principles and Criteria" (November, 2011): especially 86, which is largely content to echo the Balthasarian idea that "spiritual experience and the wisdom of the saints" must figure in the theologian's method as legitimate sources of insight.

42. As Daly notes, there is a danger of anachronism in Balthasar's reading the Fathers in this way, inasmuch as they could not even have conceived of theology as a rationalistic enterprise wholly divorced from spiritual practice (see "Balthasar's Reading of the Church Fathers," 186). But for reasons that have been under discussion throughout this chapter, this concern need not detain us now.

43. Origen is the foremost example of this for Balthasar; see *SF*, 10. Likewise Maximus' flexibility of thought is accredited to his being "sunk in pure prayer" (*CL*, 30). Cf. "FSO," 391. Cf. Catherine Lacugna's remarks about "theological speculation" being the "fruit of contemplation" (*God for Us: The Trinity and Christian Life* [San Francisco: Harper, 1973], 366–7).

44. *CL*, 34.

breadth."⁴⁵ (As it happens, this was also the feature of Karl Barth's theology that most appealed to the young Balthasar.) To underline the point: when prayer is integrated with a systematic approach, it tends, on Balthasar's account, to produce a theology which is bolder than it otherwise would be. This is because, as we will see at more length later in this study (cf. Sections 5.3.1 and 7.2 *infra*), prayer's purest form is the parrhesiastic dialogue wherein God gives the praying person the (W/w)ord with which to speak back.

Surely Balthasar is right to have noticed the apostolic boldness that marked the first several centuries of Christian thought. But his reasons for emphasizing the boundless freedom of prayer-theology as one of the first major themes of his work also has to do with a number of contextual reasons particular to his upbringing and outlook as well. First there was the broader cultural situation in his native Switzerland, which Balthasar judged to be afflicted by a bloodless, bourgeois mentality and in desperate need of spiritual renewal.⁴⁶ Then, later, as a Jesuit novice Balthasar was so deeply alienated by the dry manualism which he was confronted with in the classroom that he wrote of an impetuous desire to "[lash] out with the fury of Sampson" and "rebuild the world from its foundations," something he later attempted to do in his first major work, *Apokalpyse der Deutschen Seele*.⁴⁷ His disaffection during this time was considerably more than anodyne anecdotes about wax in the ears tend to suggest. The political experiments that Peterson focuses so much attention on should be seen against the backdrop of this youthful disaffection.⁴⁸ But so too should his notion of prayer. In these early works, prayer is presented as something that *disrupts*, giving rise to new possibilities of life and thought, as it did for the Fathers.

As the years went on, however, Balthasar grew in spiritual maturity, not least due to his ever-deeper practice of the Exercises, which, by the time he had arrived

---

45. *CL*, 30 and *SF* 10.

46. See Balthasar, "Realisticher Blick auf unsere Schweizer Situation," *Timor Domini* 7:2 (1978) as well as the remarks at *YCYYG*, 263, 300ff. and ET.2, 327 n.2. See the discussion by Nichols at *Divine Fruitfulness*, 12–4.

47. Letter to Przywara qtd. by Moser, *Love Itself Is Understanding*, 3–4.

48. And yet it is also necessary to point out, as Gawronski does in a review of Peterson's biography, that Balthasar himself, even during his youthful "Samson" period, "*never* became a member of any political party and *never* advocated anything like violence against any community" (see review of Peterson in *Journal of Jesuit Studies* 3:4 [2016], 679–89). Balthasar's refusal of Nazism would have to have been a considered judgment on his part, given just "[how] many Germanists became involved with the National Socialist regime" during the 1930s and 1940s (686). Indeed, though Peterson imports the worst of motives to the fact that Balthasar knew and studied with some men who would go on to become Nazis, he resolutely ignores the various explicit denunciations of Hitler and Nazism that Balthasar puts into print (see, e.g., TD.5, 212 or TL.3, 264).

in Basel in 1940, he was regularly engaged in giving to students.⁴⁹ Reflecting back on an epiphanic prayer experience he had undergone himself before entering the Jesuits, Balthasar was able to admit that the peace of mission came from true indifference: "You have no plans to make," he recalls being told by God while at prayer, "you are just a little stone in a mosaic which has long been ready."⁵⁰ This later perspective is not as much a repudiation of his youthful desire for bolder, more daring theological method than it was a recognition that such boldness is always most fulsome when it takes the form of the Son who makes himself available for whatever the Father asks. For it is through those individuals dispossessed of their own grasping "plans" that God does the most unexpected work. Balthasar's intellectual work remained ambitious his whole life, of course, but the boldness of his kneeling theology came to prove itself more, to his eyes, in practical works like the Johannesverlag and Johannesgemeinschaft than in his own searching studies. To build these communities and sustain these ministries, which Balthasar always considered ecclesial missions, required not his youthful desire to tear down like Samson, but the patience to build up. Such patience—or hope—was seen to be nurtured most of all in prayer. Even by the time he wrote *Prayer*, then, Balthasar was in a position to praise contemplative "sobriety" as one of the most essential missionary virtues.⁵¹ To be sure, there was still room in this vision to resist and protest—his 1953 book on the anti-Nazi poet Reinhold Schneider attests to this at length, especially with recourse to the example of Joan of Arc—but such *parrhesia* would, like all authentic prophetic witness, have to be grounded in the depths of contemplation.⁵² These observations also suggest some of the reasons why Balthasar's explicit political activity during the tumultuous period of his most intellectually productive years was seemingly so modest.

---

49. For a useful discussion of Balthasar as a spiritual director, see Servais' "Editor's Introduction" in *Hans Urs von Balthasar on the Ignatian Spiritual Exercises: An Anthology* (San Francisco, Ignatius, 2019). Balthasar was innovative for his time in that he offered Ignatian retreats to lay men and women, and his effectiveness as a director was testified to by the popularity of his ministry and the large number of vocations that resulted from it.

50. Cf. Balthasar, "Pourquoi Je Me Suis Fait Prêtre," in *Pourquoi je me suis fait prêtre: Témoignages recueillis*, ed. Jorge et Ramón Sans Vila (Tournai, 1961). Balthasar repeats this advice years later in a letter to a young man who had written to him seeking spiritual advice: "You must get beyond this [anxious tendency to turn-in-on-yourself]: It is not important what happens to me personally ([i.e.] whether I build 'myself' up or I be undone): as long as I do the objective will of God" (letter quoted by Servais at *loc. cit.*). I will discuss the "objectivity" of mission-consciousness as the foundation of personal identity in Chapters 4 and 5 (see especially Section 5.4 *infra*).

51. *Prayer* (H), 138.

52. Brown clearly grasps this point in his lucid discussion of this infrequently cited work (see Brown, "Kneeling in the Streets," 804–5). Cf. *RB*, 23. I return to *Tragedy under Grace* in Chapter 7 *infra*.

In light of the preceding considerations, it is now possible to summarize and say that for Balthasar, theology is not just *supported* by prayer, not just *complemented* by the "spirituality" genre—it is rather a simultaneous exercise with prayer, coterminous with it and aimed at giving rise in turn to new prayer and work. As Graham Ward has written, "*Lex credendi* cannot be separated from *lex orandi*; nor [. . .] is *lex credendi* a 'second order' reflection upon *lex orandi*."[53] Rather, they mark two aspects of the same movement of the creature towards God and thus implicate one another and stand in a unity of purpose. This unity must be maintained if one is to make sense of Balthasar's theological vision, at the heart of which prayer provides the "vital force."[54]

2.2 *Placing* Das Betrachtende Gebet

I have made much of the different "levels" of Balthasar's written work. And while my point about the need to see his various enterprises as one cohesive theological performance still stands, this study puts a special emphasis on Balthasar's one book-length treatment on prayer, *Das Betrachtende Gebet* (1955), and so a word should be said to place it. A relatively early work, it initially appears some six years before the first volume of *Herrlichkeit*. It comes between two other slim Category 2 titles, both of which were more explicitly practical, even polemical in nature: *Schleifung der Bastionen* (1952)[55] and *Die Gottesfrage des Heutigen Menschen* (1956).[56] It is echoed in later years by the even smaller volume, *Christlich Meditieren* (1984),[57] and its specifics are nowhere fundamentally altered in the various discussions of prayer in the trilogy.[58] At first glance, the prayer book's initial placement might seem conspicuous—especially when compared to *Bastionen*, which Balthasar would describe in 1965 as an "impatient trumpet blast" calling for "a Church which was no longer barricaded against the world."[59] When seen alongside that heady manifesto, does not a book on contemplative prayer give the impression of retreat? To the contrary, in the same 1965 retrospective Balthasar goes on to suggest that the full import of *Bastionen* actually only becomes clear in light of what is said in *Betrachtende Gebet*: "The last ten years have shown inexorably that [. . .] whoever desires greater action needs better contemplation; whoever wants to play a more formative role must pray [. . .] more profoundly; whoever wants to achieve additional goals must grasp the uselessness [of] the eternal love in

---

53. Ward, *How the Light Gets In*, 26 (but see in general Chapter 1).
54. "Theology and Sanctity," 193.
55. ET = *Razing the Bastions: On the Church in this Age* (San Francisco: Ignatius, 1993).
56. ET = *The God Question and Modern Man* (New York: Seabury, 1967).
57. ET = *Christian Meditation* (San Francisco: Ignatius 1989).
58. Cf. GL.7, 134ff.; TD.4, 159ff., 420–2; TD.5, 95–8, 400–1; TL.2, 114, 245–6, 286ff.
59. Cf. *MWiR*, 51.

Christ."⁶⁰ Even later, in his end-of-life "résumé," he likewise emphasizes the prayer book as one of those which is necessary in order to keep the trilogy from becoming "too abstract."⁶¹ The substantive relationship between prayer and action will be considered explicitly in Chapters 6 and 7, but at the moment it is simply important to note how Balthasar himself ascribed a certain programmatic significance to his early work on prayer.

Das Betrachtende Gebet (translated simply as *Prayer*)⁶² was also strategically released in relation to two other major figures in Balthasar's personal and intellectual life. Between 1947 and 1949, Karl Barth gave a series of lectures in Neuchâtel on the topic of prayer and in particular the Our Father; these lectures were quickly published in French in 1949 as *La Prière*.⁶³ This material was important in the development of Balthasar's approach to the same topic. Later, in the 1961 "Afterword" to *The Theology of Karl Barth*, Balthasar admits that he was decidedly "Barthian" when writing *Prayer*, and indeed, several features of Barth's treatment will reappear in Balthasar's own: prayer's basis in Christ; prayer's role as a bulwark against ideology; and prayer's eschatological dimensions.⁶⁴ But Barth's Neuchâtel account does not sufficiently develop the Trinitarian dimensions of prayer and arguably performs a certain compression of prayer's breadth by insisting univocally that prayer is always petition.⁶⁵ No doubt in response, two

---

60. *MWiR*, 52.

61. "Résumé," 1.

62. There are two English translations of *Das Betrachtende Gebet*: One by A. V. Littledale (Geoffrey Chapman, 1961) and one by Graham Harrison (Ignatius, 1986), both entitled *Prayer*. The simplified English title is a curious choice, in that it risks leaving out a certain existential dimension that the German suggests, but, on the other hand, it is arguably necessary to avoid the confusions (to do with formal technique, etc.) that the word "contemplative" conjures in English. Often the Littledale edition captures more of Balthasar's meditative rhythms of speech than the Harrison edition, though there are certain issues of translation present in both editions. The Ignatius edition includes a brief Preface, which the Chapman edition excludes (pp. 7–9 in Ignatius edition). I follow Victoria Harrison in referring to the Harrison translation as "*Prayer* (H)" and the Littledale translation as "*Prayer* (L)." When I give the German in brackets, the text comes from the Johannesverlag original.

63. Karl Barth, *La Prière* (Neuchâtel: Delachaux and Nestlé, 1949). ET = *Prayer* (London: Westminster John Knox, 1951). For the best recent treatment of Barth on prayer, see Ashley Cocksworth, *Karl Barth on Prayer* (London: Bloomsbury, 2015).

64. See *TKB*, 400.

65. See Migliore's critical essay in Barth *Prayer: 50th Anniversary Edition* (London: Westminster John Knox, 2002): 95–113. Cocksworth locates the Neuchâtel seminars in relation to the concomitantly drafted *Church Dogmatics* III/3 in *Karl Barth on Prayer*, 11–5; see especially note 81. As Cocksworth argues, the Neuchâtel material is clearly an important indicator of Barth's developing thought on prayer, but the most mature treatment does not appear until IV/2 (1955) and IV/3 (1959), by which time the concerns about prayer's petition-constitution are addressed in part.

years after Barth's book, Speyr produced a monograph on prayer entitled *Die Welt des Gebetes*, a book which Balthasar himself edited and published.[66] Like practically all of Speyr's published works, the material from which it is drawn was scattered and unsystematically arranged until Balthasar gave it a more definite shape.[67] It is therefore telling when in Speyr's book's foreword, Balthasar explains that he chose to place the section on "Prayer in the Trinity" at the beginning of the book, even though it constitutes more demanding theological content than what follows; clearly, the "trinitarian basis of prayer" was what Balthasar saw as crucial in Speyr's approach, especially as a corrective to Barth's treatment.[68] Speyr's book describes prayer as the creature's "participation in the center of [God's] being" and, therefore, a sanctifying mystery at the very heart and summit of the Christian life.[69] These are key features of Balthasar's account as well. But there was work still to be done. Balthasar ultimately describes Speyr's reflections in *Die Welt des Gebetes* as a "powerful *impetus* to the [development of a] theology of prayer," a theology he would attempt to deliver four years later with *Das Betrachtende Gebet*.[70]

In terms of my proposed Categories, *Prayer* is a standout work that combines aspects of all three. It arises out of the everyday experience of prayer (Category 3) and claims, rather coyly, "simply to provide stimuli, perspectives and possible starting points for personal and individual contemplation" in order to eventually make itself "superfluous."[71] At the same time, as I have already said, Balthasar repeatedly named it as one of his programmatic works that held the key to ideas found elsewhere in the trilogy (Category 2). And yet, finally, the book is in fact a dense and even systematic treatment of prayer in its own right (Category 1), which presupposes a certain amount of dogmatic infrastructure. Balthasar does not set out to offer a generic description of prayer nor—much less—trace the historical development of a particular prayer practice. Rather, he is concerned to reflect on the "depth and splendor of [contemplative prayer] *within the whole context of Christian revelation*."[72] In this sense, one "might do worse" than to approach Balthasar's dogmatic material through the route of the prayer book, as Nichols

---

66. Speyr, *Die Welt des Gebetes* (Einsiedeln: Johannesverlag, 1951). ET = *The World of Prayer*, trans. Harrison (San Francisco: Ignatius, 1985); hereafter "*WP*." Speyr's book on prayer was published the same year as Balthasar's groundbreaking book on Barth.

67. For insight into their working relationship, see Maximilian Greiner's illuminating interview with two founding members of the Johhanesgemeinschaft in *Life and Work*, 87–101

68. *WP*, 10.

69. Ibid., 13.

70. Ibid., 11; see also the relevant parts of the trilogy where Balthasar draws heavily on *Die Welt des Gebetes*, especially TD.5 (*passim* but especially 50–1, 87–8, 273–94) or TL.2 (e.g., 288–9).

71. *Prayer* (H), 8.

72. Ibid.

suggests.[73] Still, if pressed, I would place *Prayer* in Category 2. In fact, there is a way in which, when set between "Theology and Sanctity" and TD.4 (Category 1) on the one hand and *Heart of the World* (Category 3) on the other hand, *Prayer* constitutes something of a connecting bridge such that we could even speak of these works forming a miniature prayer "triptych."

Though *Prayer* has been praised as a spiritual resource by first-wave Balthasarians,[74] it has largely been neglected within the secondary scholarship. Victoria Harrison is the one English-language commentator who gives the most sustained critical treatment to the text, in her 1999 article "Homo Orans"[75] and her 2000 monograph *The Apologetic Value of Human Holiness*.[76] Harrison is concerned to give an account of how the person animated by prayer makes with his or her life an effective apologia for faith in God.[77] These are indeed central themes to Balthasar's own approach (he says at one point that, "The 'perfect' Christian is also the perfect proof of the truth of Christianity")[78] but it is also the case that Harrison's account is more concerned with philosophical theology (her main interlocutors are epistemologists like Putnam) than this book is. She is right, however, to highlight that "human holiness is portrayed by von Balthasar as a dynamic and transformative process," and it is as an attempt to understand the particular rhythms of that process that subsequent chapters of this book are best understood.[79] I will also make a turn to eschatology and political theology that Harrison largely declines to pursue. Cyril O'Regan, on the other hand (although he oversells the extent to which Balthasar's account developed between *Prayer* and the later systematic works), is right to highlight the political dimensions of Balthasar's notion of prayer: "Prayer is essentially an ecclesial act which defines itself against the speculative hubris [. . .] of modernity."[80] Prevot continues

---

73. Nichols, *Divine Fruitfulness*, 263.

74. For example, see Oakes, "What I Learned about Prayer from Hans Urs von Balthasar" in *America* (August 1, 2005); accessed online at https://www.americamagazine.org/faith/2005/08/01/what-i-learned-about-prayer-hans-urs-von-balthasar. Nichols spends some time on *Prayer* (in *Divine Fruitfulness*, 259–87) but his account is generally expository.

75. Victoria Harrison, "*Homo Orans*" (*op. cit.*). Gawronski ably incorporates *Das Betrachtende Gebet* into his argument in *Word in Silence* (see, e.g., *op. cit.* 228–69).

76. Victoria Harrison, *The Apologetic Value of Human Holiness: Von Balthasar's Christocentric Philosophical Anthropology* (London: Kluwer, 2000). See also *idem*, "Human Holiness as Religious *Apologia*," *International Journal for Philosophy of Religion* 46 (1999): 63–82, though this treatment draws more heavily on the trilogy than on *Prayer*.

77. Cf. Harrison, *Apologetic Value of Human Holiness*, 2–3.

78. GL.1, 229.

79. Harrison, *Apologetic Value of Human Holiness*, 13. Harrison also rightly notes that it is one of Balthasar's "major achievement[s]" to present a "model of holiness that is especially consistent with the New Testament" (14); the truth of this claim will be borne out in the various discussions of "mission" that follow.

80. O'Regan, *Anatomy of Misremembering*, 453.

in this vein in his important study by appealing to the "doxological character" of prayer (drawing explicitly on *Prayer*), arguing that for Balthasar prayer is a form of knowledge (*theoria*) that takes as its object the free manifestation of the divine *Logos* in Christ.[81] Of course, this particular object cannot be "objectivized" as in the usual processes of knowing, so prayer requires the prior action of God in order to be effective. If prayer is a dialogue in which the creature finds itself already addressed by God, the form of that prior address is the Word and thus creaturely prayer is always (i) Christologically grounded and (ii) revelatory.[82] Prevot also usefully argues that inasmuch as prayer is Christologically grounded it is also therefore eschatologically oriented—as Balthasar writes, prayer is "situated between two *parousias* of the Lord" and simultaneously anticipates and contributes to the Kingdom to come.[83] Mark Yenson's groundbreaking study also does well to highlight the role that prayer plays in Balthasar's mission-Christology, such that the mutual coinherence of "prayer and action" in Christ sets a template for all subsequent theological anthropology.[84] Harrison, O'Regan, Prevot, and Yenson thus point to some of the key features of prayer that I will build upon later in the text, but for now we still only want to judge the status of *Prayer* among Balthasar commentators. And on that front, it is fair to say that apart from these particularly creative third-wave works, the text remains an underutilized resource. There are even instances of commentators whose specific critiques would be ameliorated by more thorough recourse to this particular text.[85] Without wishing to overstate my own indebtedness to this particular text, I will say this study follows *Prayer* in both its spirit and structure by seeing prayer as a central mystery of the Christian life through which any number of other dogmatic questions can be pursued. The 1955 book is thus something of a "key" to Balthasar's sprawling *corpus*, but also an "icon" for the sort of flexible yet deeply interconnected sort of theology he was capable of.

2.3 Mysticism Considered

I have earlier made reference to the role of Adrienne von Speyr's mystical experiences, and thus far I have been talking about prayer in a rather general

---

81. See Prevot, *Thinking Prayer* (*op. cit.*) 83–6; cf. TL.3 369ff.
82. See Prevot, *Thinking Prayer*, 84; cf. *Prayer* (L), 9–14 and TD.2, 24ff.
83. *Prayer* (H), 142.
84. Yenson, *Existence as Prayer*, 132.
85. For instance, Dalzell's charge of a certain sort of individualism is hard to square with Balthasar's relentlessly ecclesial picture of prayer (especially over against the dialogists) and underestimates the extent to which Balthasar's turn to prayer was intended as a deconstruction of the solipsistic self so prevalent in much modern spiritual writing.

way, so some terminological disambiguation is likely in order. While the status of "mysticism" in theological discourse is naturally a large and hotly debated topic, it is nevertheless possible to focus more narrowly on the status of mysticism in Balthasar's approach, and in particular how it relates to his notion of prayer.[86] On this count, a certain balance must be maintained. Balthasar clearly sees fit to appeal to the authority of mystics (who he appears to consider a subset of saints)[87] as generative sources of theological renewal, especially over against the desiccated neoscholasticism that had so upset him as a student. From among the forms and images of mystical experience, the theologian can (attempt to) render an account of the faith of which those forms and images are but expressions. Note already that this means for Balthasar there is a "radical homogeneity" between mysticism and faith *simpliciter*.[88] Kilby, as we have seen, objects to this kind of source material since it is by its nature not "publicly available" and therefore not liable to final verification.[89] But in addition to pointing out that *Kilby's*, not Balthasar's, might in fact be the minority position here,[90] it is also the case that her concerns on this point seem to posit theology as a kind of natural science which must satisfy general laws of replicability. Whatever the merits of this notion of theology might hold, it is clearly not the one Balthasar was operating under.[91]

86. The authoritative treatment of the general theme is still Bernard McGinn, *A History of Western Christian Mysticism*, Vols. 1–5 (London: SCM, 1992–2016).

87. Dimech's distinctions here are sound: For Balthasar, there is "mysticism in a general sense" that can be said to include all those "experience[s] for which the gifts of the Holy Spirit are responsible," and there is, as a subset of this, "mysticism in its narrow sense" (see *Authority of the Saints*, 150). As Dimech notes, "saint" and "mystic" are "not univocal" for Balthasar (ibid., 153), but "those who above all have undergone and enjoyed such [mystical] experience [i.e., those conventionally known as 'mystics'] have in every age been the saints" (Balthasar, "Tradition," 125). In other words, not every saint is a mystic, but every mystic has been a saint.

88. GL.1, 300–1. Cf. Dimech, *Authority of the Saints*, 151. As Balthasar writes, "faith in Christ is *already* a genuine and objective encounter of the whole man with the incarnate God" (GL.1, 309; qtd. by Dimech *loc. cit.*).

89. See Kilby, *Balthasar*, 99.

90. For a recent argument in favor of a liberal approach to theological sources (including nontextual happenings, group experience, and popular arts), see the editors' "Afterword" in *Minding the Spirit*, 363–72, here 365–6.

91. For a stimulating argument about the possibility and desirability of replicability in the humanities, including theology, see Rik Peels, "Replicability and Replication in the Humanities," *Research Integrity and Peer Review* 4:2 (2019). Peels makes a strong case for something like what I am characterizing as Kilby's position here—that is, that theological arguments should be based on publicly available data and aim to arrive at a workable overlapping consensus. But, while this may suit the task of certain "para-theological" undertakings (scriptural analysis, hermeneutics, even philosophical theology), it is harder to assume the same empirical basis for what Balthasar would have considered the more

If mystics are acceptable theological sources, according to Balthasar, it is still not the case that any given mysticism is as legitimate as any other. Indeed, there are several chief dangers that must be avoided if the mystic perspective is to contribute to a genuinely theological approach (Balthasar calls the theology of mysticism a "minefield" filled with dangers of psychological and sociological reductions).[92] On the one hand, it is necessary to emphasize that since "God is not just one being among others encountered in this world," *experience* itself is an ambivalent category in this context.[93] Even the disciples who enjoyed direct interaction with Christ "did not yet really see and hear at all" (as evidenced by their repeated lack of faith); it was only after Easter, when Christ withdrew from the world ("It is good for you that I go"), that their experience of him is effectively realized among the community. So mystic experience is, at least, never a solitary achievement or a private insight, but an ecclesially situated and Christologically oriented event: "Every true mysticism, however rich it may be in visions and other experiences of God, is subject at least as strictly to the law of the Cross— that is, of non-experience—as is the existence of someone apparently forgotten in the desert of secular daily life."[94] On the other hand, if the genuine mystic must by rights renounce "every autocratic attempt" to impose their own form and image on God, this does not mean that they are ultimately left without the forms or images which God avails Godself of in revelation.[95] Indeed, Balthasar often appears to have little patience for those world-denying or purely apophatic modes of mysticism that dissolve into nothingness through a relentless technique of "unsaying."[96] The language of unsaying such as it has developed within these strands of mysticism may in fact be the highest expression of what Balthasar calls the natural religious impulse, which is prepared to acknowledge the profound fact that the creature is not God, but it falls well short of the truly dialogical potential of Christian prayer, which is "quite different from that of other mystical" models in

fundamental type of theology, which necessarily involves giving a particular view of the personal Christ-form. The "data" that Balthasar *would* point to would be the "fruit" of the particular theologian or mystic (as I have argued earlier), which can certainly be weighed and tested by certain standards; but, then, at this point the authenticity of the given mystic in question becomes something of a secondary question.

92. ET.4, 309.

93. See the essay "Experience God?" *NE*, 20–45, here 21. Something of this same ambivalence is on display in Balthasar's essay "Understanding Christian Mysticism" in ET.4, 309–35.

94. *NE*, 44.

95. *NE*, 26; Balthasar identifies the autocratic impulse to impose one's own form on revelation as the essence of pharisaism (see *YCYYG* 44–5).

96. For thorough accounts of "unsaying" in a number of mystic writers, including Plotinus and Eckhart, see Michael Sells, *Mystical Languages of Unsaying* (London: University of Chicago Press, 1994).

that it posits the possibility of genuine dialogue between God and man in Christ.[97] When insisted upon without the sufficient Christological modulation, a negative mysticism is "always in danger of losing both the world and God."[98] Such was often Balthasar's concern with Patristic sources, marked as they were by a lingering Platonic residue,[99] but it is also a feature of certain modern accounts of mysticism such as W. T. Stace's so-called vacuum plenum.[100] Both these tendencies—a mute mysticism and an escapist mysticism—forget Christ. This is because it is Christ who "returns [to the Father] from the world accessible to our senses and mind [. . .] and [thus] for the first time, opens the true way to contemplation."[101] After the Incarnation, every genuine mysticism must stand within the space opened up by Christ, for he has inhabited the rhythms of divine love more deeply than any creature could ever hope to achieve:

> No mystic of the negative theology has ever traversed the" dark night of the senses and the mind" [. . .] so completely as Christ in the terrible desolation of the cross, in which not only the world sank away before his dying eyes, but God himself withdrew and abandoned him. Neither has anyone experienced the movement from appearances to reality in more blessed fashion than he did in his ascension from the world to the Father [. . .]. But this death was no turning

---

97. *Prayer* (L), 44; cf. "FSO," 354, *NE*, 150, and *TuG*, 22. This is a delicate point: Of course, Balthasar acknowledges the importance of "silence" even in the active process of prayer (see the discussion at TL.2, 107–15, to which we will return later), but this silence can never be taken to be a terminal perspective. A purely "negative mysticism [. . .] entails of necessity a profound and wrongful disparagement of the world and all creation" (*Prayer* [L], 44). For Balthasar, the ultimate orientation of Christian mysticism is cataphatic. See Section 5.3.2 for more on silence in prayer. Gavin Flood has argued that genuine "verticality" applies to a religious experience (such as prayer) "in so far as it [i.e., the religious experience] becomes *narratable* and brought into the realm of *language*" (italics added). For humans, Flood writes, "vertical experience [. . .] becomes inwardness through its articulation and narratability" (see Flood, *The Truth Within: A History of Inwardness in Christianity, Hinduism, and Buddhism* [Oxford: Oxford University Press, 2013], 244). For Balthasar, then, prayer or contemplation in the Christologically cataphatic mode amounts to a process of articulating and narrating faith in Christ that lies at the core of the Christian identity.

98. *Prayer* (H), 54; indeed, such a view can even give rise to "great *injustice* [towards] our fellow creatures" (emphasis mine). The relationship between prayer and justice will be pursued later in the text.

99. See the critique of Origen and Evagrius, for example, at GL.1, 315, 551; cf. *Prayer* (L), 215–6.

100. Stace describes mystical experience as entry into undifferentiated singularity—the "Vacuum-Plenum"—where all subjectivity and particularity give way to a nonspatiotemporal or "nonsensuous unity in all things" (see Stace, *Mysticism and Philosophy* [London: Macmillan, 1960], 14–5 and 153–4).

101. *Prayer* (L), 44; cf. *CM*, 7–8.

from the creature to gain God [n]or was the ascension a turning away from the world, whether from indifference or revulsion, to possess God alone; it was [rather] a beneficent departure with a promise of return before long, a departure to prepare a place with the Father to be occupied by men and the world as a whole, changed, indeed, and purified, but not repudiated or destroyed. And as a sign of his fidelity to the world, Christ, in leaving it, promised to send the Holy Ghost from heaven, who, now that the Son's contemplation is finally perfected, is to sow its fruits in the hearts of those who believe.[102]

We will have to wait until Chapter 4 to deal with the Christological dimensions of prayer in earnest, but for now we can see clearly enough how prayer's Christological basis works to mitigate—or contextualize—the effect of mystic experience as that term is often understood. A mysticism of pure experience neglects Christ's definitive self-expropriation to his community (in the form of the Spirit "breathed out" [Jn 20:22]) and thus engages in ahistorical abstraction. And likewise a mysticism of merely "negative concepts" ignores the explicit public ministry of Jesus Christ—in which signs, images, and parables were a constant feature.[103]

This suggests a third criteria for judging genuine Christian mysticism. Inasmuch as such a mysticism will be marked in the Christoform way (which is cruciform) and grounded in the embodied gifts of the Spirit (of which the greatest corresponds to the virtue of charity), the mystic will by no means refrain from active involvement in the world.[104] On the contrary, the mystic embraces the world—and above all his fellow man—all the more closely as the site of encounter with God.[105] For the person who knows Christ in prayer, "*everything* human is sacramental."[106] Balthasar often argues that full witness to this form of love finds its natural end in suffering for and with others in true imitation of Christ.[107] The universal scope of

---

102. *Prayer* (L), 45. This passage, as well as the aforementioned critiques of "natural mysticism" and the insistence that "God speaks first" in prayer all speak to Balthasar's pronounced Barthianism at the time he wrote *Prayer* Cf. also *MiH*, 282: "Therefore, all Christian mysticism of the 'bright darkness,' of the failure of words before the majesty of God, of falling silent after everything that can be said in Church teaching—all this mysticism of the 'abyss' and the 'desert of God' is seen inevitably as true *mysticism of the cross*, as mysticism of a sharing in the helplessness of the Word of God. *Only as seen in this way can mysticism have a place in the Church*" (italics mine).

103. GL.1, 551.

104. On the correspondence of charity and wisdom, cf. Thomas, *ST* II.II q.45 a.6.

105. *Prayer* (L), 171–3, 177. Cf D.L. Schindler, *Heart of the World, Center of the Church: Communio Ecclesiology, Liberalism, and Liberation* (Grand Rapids, Michigan: Eerdmans, 1996). Related to this is the danger of what Thomas Merton called a "Promethean mysticism" which seeks selfishly to assert itself and therefore fails in charity (see Merton, *The New Man* [London: Burns & Oates, 1962], 15ff.).

106. *Prayer* (L), 161 (italics mine).

107. Cf., e.g., *NE*, 44–5.

neighbor-love (established in the universal mission of Jesus Christ) overpowers any schematic approach to mystical experience: "Nowhere in the behavior of Jesus is there to be found even the least trace of a technical instruction for meditation."[108] Rather, mystic "credibility" is only established in the form of an active love in and for the world.[109] Crucially this also grounds Balthasar's account of mysticism in an ecclesial perspective. There is no purely private experience that can only bear on the mystic alone: "Nothing in the structure of the Church is secret," and even the darkest night of the soul is an "ecclesial event."[110] In TL.3, Balthasar describes this in terms of Paul's preference for prophecy over tongues (1 Cor. 14:5): Experience of "ecstasies" can be "fruitful" for a particular person's "spiritual development" but unless they "bring forth fruit for his practical apostolic life," such ecstasies are not genuine works of the Spirit who underwrites all prayer.[111] As Dimech notes, this conviction was what led Balthasar to work so tirelessly to "integrate" Speyr's perspective into the wider ecclesial horizon, especially through the practical work of the Johannesgemeinschaft.[112]

Genuine Christian mysticism, then, will be, according to Balthasar, dialogical with the Word, attentive to the world, and ratified in love alone. If this seems an idiosyncratic understanding of "mysticism," it is not wholly inconsistent with the contemporary *ressourcement* position.[113] It is also a perspective deeply underwritten by Balthasar's Ignatian background (cf. Section 5.4 *infra*). It is worth emphasizing that this missionary sense of prayer is in its own way a profound political statement: I said earlier that *Prayer* must be read alongside *Razing the Bastions* as complementary work, providing the "how" (i.e., prayer) to *Bastions*' "what" (i.e., a more active love of the world). The horrendous moral failures of the twentieth century urgently called for a different mode of witness than a mysticism of silence or pure experience, and it was toward this new notion of sanctity that Balthasar was attempting to build; it would be a mistake to see Balthasar's

---

108. Cited by Nichols at *Divine Fruitfulness*, 286. Balthasar has in mind here a critique of the Spanish style of mysticism—exemplified in Teresa of Avilà or John of the Cross—with its focus on "levels" of mystical experience. See Harrison, *Apologetic Value of Human Holiness*, 70 n.51 for a necessary caveat regarding the accuracy of Balthasar's charges against John in particular.

109. Cf. *LAC*, 125.

110. *OT*, 146 and *Prayer* (H), 272.

111. TL.3, 375–6.

112. Dimech, *Authority of the Saints*, 151. Whether or not Balthasar was successful in this endeavor is a separate question entirely.

113. Cf. De Lubac, *Catholicism: Christ and the Common Destiny of Man*, trans. Sheppard (London: Burns & Oates, 1962), 101 or Jean Daniélou, *Prayer: The Mission of the Church*, trans. Schindler (Edinburgh: T&T Clark, 1996), 10. In a Foreword to Daniélou's book, Balthasar approvingly quotes the former's sentiment that, "There is *no difference* between contemplation and mission. It would be absurd to have to choose between the two. Mission is nothing other than the self-unfolding of contemplation" (xiv).

reflections on sanctity apart from this historical context. By 1961, this notion of engaged sanctity would sharpen further still, such that Balthasar could declare that "for the first time" the "form of sainthood [is] the *layman in the world*."[114] It would be less than three years later that *Lumen Gentium* would expound upon the "universal call to holiness," according to which prayer is a constitutive aspect of the charity which is the "bond of perfect unity" (Col. 3:14) among the people of God, no matter their ecclesial rank.[115] In contemplation, the one who prays meets the Lord who "challenges" with a mission. Accordingly, "every [act of] contemplation (*theoria*) contains the element of conversion (*praxis*)."[116] It is the task of the theologian, in turn, whether lay or ordained, to express something of this same simultaneity (of contemplation and conversion, *theoria* and *praxis*) in a way that likewise constitutes a witness to and for the world. Against the occasional characterizations of Balthasar as a conservative aesthete sunk in abstraction, then, texts such as these reveal a desire to meet the challenges of the modern era with an adequate and engaged form of sanctity (and to tie this notion of engaged sanctity to the theological task itself). He does this in part by reorienting mysticism around the core concept of mission. To be sure, Balthasar admits that conventional mystics (those who undergo ecstasies, visions, and the like) can still exist: they are to be considered "extraordinary" characters in the church.[117] But it is primarily the "ordinary" praying person who Balthasar is most interested in, and in whom he believes the Spirit is accomplishing the most work in the world today.[118]

It is thus to Christian prayer—in its simplicity and yet its mysterious depths—that we now turn in earnest. By examining prayer's Trinitarian, Christological, anthropological, eschatological, and critical dimensions according to Balthasar, I hope to show not only the comprehensive view he had of prayer but also prayer's centrality to the Christian "task" in the modern world.

---

114. ET.2, 457 (my italics), cf. ibid., 33.
115. See *Lumen Gentium*, 39–42.
116. *CM*, 38.
117. 2SS, 40; cf. *Prayer* (H), 92.
118. ET.4, 330; *Das Betrachtende Gebet*, 81: "Mystical prayer is only an awareness, at the level of experience, of the same mysteries of faith which the ordinary person lives out under the veil of faith" (the Littedale edition mistranslates the word "experiential" [*erfahrungshaftes*] as "experimental" at 75).

Chapter 3

PRAYER'S SOURCE

Trinitarian Dimensions

I explained earlier my intention to undertake engagement with a more daring Balthasar than we often meet in the pages of books like this one. It is in considering and responding to Balthasar's speculative thought that we are confronted with the full creative potential (and perils) of his theology. Perhaps chief among the areas which make up this "daring" realm of speculative theology are Balthasar's reflections on the Trinity. In this chapter I would first like to show the implications of one such instance of Trinitarian speculation: namely, Balthasar's identification of something like prayer in the Trinity. This prior Trinitarian prayer, in turn, grounds all subsequent creaturely prayer. However, as often as Balthasar's daring Trinitarianism is remarked upon, it is equally regarded with suspicion for arguably speaking with *too much* "confidence [and] ease" about the inner workings of the Godhead.[1] From where does he get "the right to such a vivid picture of the eternal life of God" as seems to emerge from his work?[2] Thus, in this chapter I would like to argue that an answer to this charge has to do with prayer's Trinitarian source. The question of epistemic limits (which is, at heart, the question of theological style around which so many questions of interpretation turn) is shown to bear upon the question of (Trinitarian) prayer in a particular way.

3.1 Positing Trinitarian Prayer

Whatever it is that creaturely prayer essentially is already finds a Trinitarian referent in God's imminent patterns of relation. In one typical formulation, Balthasar observes that, "Prayer [is] not only [. . .] something that ascends from man to God, but, more profoundly, what descends from God to man."[3] Elsewhere Balthasar describes how "the Son, as man, continues the *eternal dialogue of prayer*

---

1. Kilby, *Balthasar*, 74.
2. Ibid., 64.
3. *TE*, 89.

[among] the Divine Persons in heaven."[4] Or yet again, we are told that prayer has a "trinitarian structure" because prayer is itself not something alien to the divine nature.[5] Nor is it the case that the hypostases simply pray in an undifferentiated way; rather, each Person is said to pray in a way befitting their role in the order of procession (more on this in a minute). Certainly, if one's intention is to take prayer seriously, then reading prayer into the very life of God provides a solid basis upon which to argue for prayer's centrality to the Christian life. But equally obviously, since what can definitively be said about the immanent life of God is limited by very real epistemological constraints, and since any apparent similarity between God and creature should be seen in the light of an "ever-greater dissimilarity" (Lateran IV), we cannot understand Trinitarian prayer in exactly the same way as creaturely prayer. Balthasar is careful (although sometimes less careful than others) to present the idea of inner-Trinitarian prayer as a *postulate* ("It is not difficult to think")[6] that exists primarily in order to ground "our modes of prayer" in certain "archetypes," which can then in turn prove dispositive.[7] Furthermore, the postulate regarding Trinitarian prayer serves as a good illustration of one of Balthasar's foundational exegetical principles. The economic Trinity appears as the immanent Trinity's definitive self-interpretation in history (see discussion at Section 3.2 *infra*). Let us consider some advantages and disadvantages to this way of proceeding.

First, some advantages. By speaking of Trinitarian prayer, Balthasar immediately undercuts any anthropocentric account of prayer that might otherwise be offered. Not, again, as merely "something that ascends from man to God" but as a *grace by its very nature* is a prayer of interest to the theologian. Strictly philosophical accounts of prayer typically start off on the wrong foot, then, when they conceive of it as involving a "subject" (the praying person) and an "object" (the thing prayed for), as if the praying person were the originator of prayer.[8] Rather, Trinitarian prayer is something in which the praying person participates.[9] Related to this first danger is a second, namely that prayer comes to be seen as a kind of conversation with oneself. This was Kant's[10] disparaging conclusion, for instance, but it is also present (although judged altogether more positively) by those who see prayer as a form of therapeutic introspection. Balthasar's Trinitarian postulate sidesteps

---

4. TD.5, 122; cf. Speyr, *World of Prayer*, 28ff.

5. *Prayer* (H), 137. Indeed, in Chapter 2 of *Prayer* Balthasar proceeds by treating the distinct "roles" of the three Persons in prayer (see 38–82).

6. TD.5, 122.

7. *TE*, 89.

8. Cf. Scott Davison, *Petitionary Prayer: A Philosophical Investigation* (Oxford: Oxford University Press, 2017), 24.

9. Cf. *TE*, 89; *Prayer* (H), 38, 70; TL.3, 371.

10. See Immanuel Kant, *Religion within the Boundaries of Mere Reason and Other Writings*, trans. Allen Wood and George di Giovanni (Cambridge: Cambridge University Press, 1998), 188.

these interpretations since it emphasizes that prayer is ontologically prior to the individual praying person—in prayer the creature is addressed and invited into an existing dialogue. Third, among more properly theological accounts of prayer, there is often the danger of conceiving of prayer primarily in terms of petition; in Chapter 2, I noted this as a potential weakness of Barth's account (at least in the Neuchâtel lectures). Balthasar, on the other hand, stresses that petition (though a central aspect of creaturely prayer, especially liturgy) does not exhaust prayer's essence.[11] As a warrant, Balthasar points back to Christ, who, though he is constantly petitioning the Father in a beggarly way, does so always on the strength of a prior Trinitarian intimacy: "*Abba* is not, first and foremost, a cry of petition; rather, it is the cry that understands itself as a child, its whole existence dependent on another; it is the sound made by *self as gift*."[12] Absent this deeper understanding of mutual life, an overemphasis on Christ's petitions might risk modalist or subordinationist interpretations.[13] Finally, if prayer is properly thought of as a Trinitarian grace, then it implies a whole range of attendant dynamics—such as mission, sacrifice, and resurrection—which might then bear upon the creature caught up in the Trinitarian action. In other words, by grounding prayer in the Trinity, Balthasar signals that prayer must be truly transformative—"not only [. . .] correct, but *useful*," as he puts it in the famous "Theology and Sanctity" essay.[14] Here Barth's influence is more positive, since it is as a consequence of an "actualistic" ontology that prayer's basis in the Trinity must necessarily give rise to newness in the person who prays.[15]

I have just given several reasons why one might want to base a notion of prayer in the Trinity. At the same time, there are apparent dangers to speaking of prayer in the Trinity. First of all, there is Kilby's charge of hubris. Why bother with *any* kind of description about the inner-Trinitarian life, speculation which Balthasar himself admits often gives rise to "mathematical concepts or vague speculations."[16] This raises the related but distinct concern that to speak of Trinitarian prayer

---

11. On petition and liturgy, see *Prayer* (H), 108.

12. TL.3, 370 (internal quotation marks omitted, italics mine).

13. The depths of this mutual life are made explicit in Christ's high-priestly prayer, wherein petition and Trinitarian consubsistence (Jn 17:23!) are shown to be in perfect alignment.

14. "Theology and Sanctity," 196 (italics mine). Cf. Herbert McCabe, *God Matters* (London: Mowbray, 1987), 220-1.

15. In other words, if "God's being is event" (CD II/1, 271), and prayer is grounded in God's being, then prayer is likewise an "event" in which the praying person is moved to new life. On Barth's actualism and the legitimate possibility of Trinitarian speculation, see Justin Stratis, "Speculating about Divinity? God's Immanent Life and Actualistic Ontology," *International Journal of Systematic Theology* 12, no. 1 (2010): 20-32. However, as Schumacher rightly notes, Balthasar is also surely influenced here by Thomas's notion of God as "pure act" (see Schumacher, *A Trinitarian Anthropology*, 312).

16. *Prayer* (L), 84.

collapses the immanent into the economic Trinity. A third concern might be that on this question Balthasar proves himself too tethered to the perspective of Speyr, who devotes significant attention to the idea of Trinitarian prayer in her writings[17] and from whom Balthasar often quotes liberally when discussing this idea. Fourth, despite what I have said about a certain understanding of Trinitarian prayer guarding against subordinationism, some critics worry about the possibility of "tritheism" in Balthasar's Trinitarian writings; the question of Trinitarian prayer could potentially be fodder for this charge, if one were to conceive of the Persons as discrete wills reaching out to one another in prayer.[18] It is, after all, one of the basic facts of creaturely prayer that the praying person is separate from—is *not*— the one to whom they pray.

Exhaustively resolving each of these concerns (and others that might arise besides) need not be the primary task of this section. There is no point denying that Balthasar's Trinitarian language carries certain theological risks with it. But I would suggest some possible ways forward given the apparent tensions between the advantages and disadvantages that have been mentioned. First, it is worth noting that the Trinitarian solecisms, whose specters have been raised (tritheism on the one hand and subordinationism on the other), depend on other discrete questions of how Balthasar approaches issues related to divine freedom, will, and decision. For instance, the idea that the Persons pray to one another need not be interpreted as tritheistic if Balthasar understands prayer in such a way as to overcome (or at least decisively reorient) the creaturely understanding of relation itself. It is my contention that Balthasar's concept of prayer operates precisely in this way, and so to fault him on this basis at this point would be to preempt the full extent of his argument. Likewise, although the usual theological controls (analogy, dissimilarity, scriptural warrant, etc.) must be applied to what can be said about Trinitarian prayer, we need not thereby surrender to total apophaticism (or what Rahner called an "anti-trinitarian timidity")[19] on this front. Indeed, it is another of my central contentions that Balthasar's account is noteworthy for what it allows the person to *say* in prayer, precisely as a participation in the prior Trinitarian dialogue which is revealed, above all, in the life of Christ.[20] Recourse to the notion of analogy in particular seems to recommend, rather than discredit, Balthasar's confident language about Trinitarian prayer. If the creaturely experience of intersubjective "word and response" *does* express something real about the creature's capacity to know God (and therefore if Christ's prayers on earth are not

---

17. Speyr, *World of Prayer*, 28–74, for example.

18. Cf. Bertrand de Margerie, "Note on Balthasar's Trinitarian Theology," *The Thomist* 64 (2000): 127–30, here 128.

19. Rahner, "Remarks on the Dogmatic Treatise 'De Trinitate,'" in *Theological Investigations*, Vol. IV (London: Darton, Longman & Todd, 1966), 81 (qtd. in Steck, *The Ethical Thought of Hans Urs von Balthasar*, 38).

20. For the finite creature, this dialogue must often avail itself of the *positive words* of Scripture; cf. Dalzell, *Dramatic Encounter*, 191.

meaningless instances of play-acting), then the referent for this form of love must be found "in" the Trinitarian life.[21] Understanding more clearly how the creature is formed by these Trinitarian dynamics will be the task of Chapter 5, but it is enough now to say at this point that this will depend upon what Balthasar calls the "Christological *transpositions*" that ground creaturely prayer in the Trinity.[22]

3.2 The Spirit's Role

Already we have a sense of the extent to which Balthasar bases his postulate about Trinitarian prayer on the picture of Christ at prayer in mission. In a pithy form of what we might call Balthasar's own *Grundaxiom*, he writes, "The economic Trinity assuredly appears as the interpretation of the immanent Trinity," though he is quick to add that the two cannot simply be "identified" with one another since the immanent "grounds and supports" the economic.[23] Steck calls this Balthasar's "resolute commitment to the *noetic* point of [Rahner's] axiom": in the form of historical revelation—paradigmatically Christ at prayer—the believer has a reliable view (albeit through the "dark glass" of analogy and fallen forms of knowing etc.) to the *true* life of divine love.[24] What is more, the same believer has in Christ an open path toward that triune life. While I will avoid preempting the full discussion in the following chapter regarding the Christological dimensions of prayer, I should give some attention to the pneumatological dimensions at play here.[25]

---

21. Cf. Steck, *The Ethical Thought of Hans Urs von Balthasar*, 38.
22. TD.5, 122.
23. TD.3, 508 (Balthasar endorses Rahner's Rule at note 3 *loc. cit.*); cf. *TH*, 56.
24. Steck, *The Ethical Thought of Hans Urs von Balthasar*, 36. Cf. *Prayer* (H), 193 and *passim*.
25. The Spirit is not properly speaking a subject of systematic attention, on Balthasar's understanding, since it is in the Spirit's nature not to draw attention to itself but to point always to the Father through the Son: "He will not speak on his own" (Jn 16:13). On the Spirit's "invisibility," see GL. 7, 389ff., ET. 3, 111, ET. 4, 11, and TL. 3, 13. In this last citation from the *Theo-Logic*, Balthasar directs the reader to a contemporary study that offers a critical assemblage of his pneumatology, such as it is: Kossi Tossou, *Streben nach Vollendung: Zur Pneumatologie im Werk H. U. v Balthasars* (Freiburg: Herder, 1983). See the concurrent opinion by Killian McDonnell, who says, "One respects [the pneumatological] horizon not necessarily by making the Spirit the specific object of theological reflection, or by continual talk about the Spirit, but by recognizing [pneumatology's] role of point of entry and contact and its consequences for the whole theological process" (McDonnell, "The Determinative Doctrine of the Holy Spirit," *Theology Today* 39:2 [1982]: 142–61, here 153). My decision not to devote a separate chapter to the "pneumatological dimensions of prayer" reflects this insight, though I will highlight the Spirit's role at various points as needed.

The impression from the section in *Prayer* on "the Holy Spirit's Role" is clear: it is the Spirit who "makes prayer possible"; who "draws us into" prayer; who impregnates our hearts with Christ; who "incorporates" us into the Word; who "opens up the depths" of God to the praying person; who "unfolds" God's Word to the listening church; who serves as "vehicle and interpreter" of the incarnate Word; who "shows the way" to prayer; and who "places the contemplative in the closest intimacy with divine truth."[26] It is precisely the Spirit's role to lead the praying person to the Father along the path of prayer. This is certainly true of human prayer but also (and this is another fairly original feature of Balthasar's account) for the Son at prayer: "The Son never encounters the Father, and the Father never encounters the Son, except in the Holy Spirit. So no prayer of Jesus is made to the Father except in the Holy Spirit."[27] The famous "Trinitarian inversion" from the third volume of the *Theo-Drama* is but the most explicit form of this teaching, but it is already present in *Prayer* when, for instance, Balthasar calls the Spirit "architect of the Son's return to the Father" (for further discussion of the "inversion," see Section 4.2.3 *infra*).[28] The Spirit is thus positioned as the one who makes all prayer possible and who reveals prayer's Trinitarian underpinnings.[29]

Prayer is thus presented as the creature's share in Trinitarian indwelling, an "abiding in the truth" of God's love (cf. Jn 8:44; 17:17, 19; 1 Jn 2:21; 2 John 3; 3 John 4, etc.). Christ is "the way" to this truth (indeed *is* this truth), but it is the Spirit who must act as its "vehicle and interpreter."[30] Thus, Balthasar often refers to the Spirit as the "Exegete."[31] There is an interior, ontological level on which this is true: "The same Spirit who brings the Son to men from the Father has also prepared their hearts to receive him."[32] But the Spirit also continues to carry out this task in the visible structures of the church, through "sacraments, scripture, liturgy and

---

26. *Prayer* (H), 67–82.

27. TL.3, 370. Cf. TD.3, 185ff., and *FGAS*, 60. McDonnell discusses the fact that, since at least the time of Ignatius of Antioch, "there was the recognition that every Christological statement had its pneumatological counterpart," but that nevertheless within the tradition there is "a tendency to make pneumatology subject to Christology in an unacceptably subordinationist manner" (McDonnell, "The Determinative Doctrine of the Holy Spirit," 153–4). Balthasar's heavy accent on the Spirit thus has the effect of binding his undoubtedly Christocentric approach to a concomitant (if largely implicit) pneumatocentrism.

28. See TD.3, 183–91, and 515–23. *Prayer* (H), 74. Mention of the "inversion" appears throughout the Balthasarian corpus (see, e.g., CSL, 190ff.). See the discussion by Matthew Sutton, "A Compelling Trinitarian Taxonomy: Hans Urs von Balthasar's Theology of the Trinitarian Inversion and Reversion," *International Journal of Systematic Theology* 14:2 (2012): 161–76, as well as McIntosh's summary observations at *Christology from within*, 49.

29. *Prayer* (H), 67. "The very possibility of Christian contemplation is founded entirely on the doctrine of the Trinity" (76).

30. *Prayer* (H), 74; cf. TD.3, 38–9.

31. See e.g. Balthasar, "God Is His Own Exegete," *Communio* 4 (1986), 280–7.

32. *Prayer* (H), 71.

preaching."³³ Thus, prayer under these conditions is an especially integrated type of prayer, one which demonstrates the plausibility of my claim that there is properly speaking no private prayer in the church (cf. Section 2.1.1 *supra*).³⁴ That the Spirit works through the visible ministries of the church (although not only through them) also suggests some of the ways in which the Spirit prays in us even when our own words fail (Rom. 8:26). The pneumatological-ecclesial perspective acts here as another check on unfettered mystical "experience."³⁵ The final confirmation of this perspective, for Balthasar, is prayer's necessary issuance in charity and mission, such that prayer-as-indwelling is decidedly not another form of mystic escape or quietism: "Contemplation may enable man to plumb other depths and abysses, but unless they are explicitly or implicitly depths of the triune, human-divine and ecclesial life, they are either spurious or demonic."³⁶ Prayer is the site of the ongoing work of the Spirit-as-Revealer-of-God, and in bringing us into the "heart of God" the Spirit (thereby) brings us into the "heart of the world."

There is a "thoroughly practical" intent to Balthasar's grounding prayer in the Trinity in this way.³⁷ First, if we can expect the Spirit to bring us to the Father in a similar way that the Spirit brings the Son to the Father (i.e., in mission), then we need not fear any form of self-annihilation in prayer. Unity in the Spirit does not require the overcoming of personality. Indeed, one's "own energy and personal quality [are] *affirmed* and taken up" in the work of the Spirit.³⁸ Again, this is to do with the Spirit's Trinitarian role in itself, which is to "express the unity and union of Father and Son" as loving unity-in-difference and as infinite affirmation of the Other.³⁹ We might wish to say that it is the particular genius of the Spirit to construct a "unity [that] does not destroy distinctions—neither

---

33. *Prayer* (H), 74; cf. "God Is His Own Exegete," 287.

34. Drawing on Elizabeth of the Trinity, Balthasar describes contemplation as participation in the common adoration of the church, in which "there can be no solitary self with a private, distinguishable destiny" from the rest of the Body (Balthasar's words, see 2SS, 461). Balthasar defends this notion of "ecclesial predestination" if it is understood in the Pauline, Trinitarian manner (see the whole discussion 438–62). Balthasar identifies the source of this teaching in the pattern of "mutual interdwelling of persons" in God who in turn "interdwells all [that is]" (2SS, 462). Thus, even the truly solitary vocations in the church (anchorites or Trappists or the isolated layperson, for instance) participate in the common life of prayer. I will return to the idea of prayer as the substance of ecclesial solidarity (cf. Sections 4.3.1, 6.2.2, and 7.2.2 *infra*).

35. Cf. *Prayer* (H), 78.

36. *Prayer* (H), 74. Grace Jantzen argues, with reference to the medieval mystics, for a similarly positive understanding of the divine abyss, especially as opposed to the nihilistic *Abgrund* of postmodernity (see Jantzen, "Eros and the Abyss: Reading Medieval Mystics in Postmodernity," in *Literature & Theology* 17, no. 3 [2003]: 244–64).

37. *Prayer* (H), 76.

38. Ibid., 77.

39. Ibid., 74.

the personal distinctions in God nor the differences of nature between God and the creature."[40] If the chief metaphysical difficulty of prayer is to bring the finite creature and the infinite God into "dialogue" with one another, the Spirit ensures that such an undertaking need not require the creature's absolute "absorption."[41] This is not to say that the creature merely comes as it is. Inasmuch as the method of this integration is Christoform, it will likewise be cruciform. Inevitably a certain confession (Section 5.2.2 *infra*) is necessary in order to resolve oneself to mission. But even here the creature can never "get behind" its own identity in order to "put on Christ" (Rom. 13:14, Gal. 3:27, etc.). Second, the Spirit's role in prayer overcomes what is often felt to be one of the persistent difficulties of prayer—that is, merely making a start. Rather than the "tentative efforts" at prayer, which "start with a kind of aloofness" or an "uninvolved objectivity," prayer should be entered into simply and with the confidence that we have an advocate before the Father (cf. Jn 14:16-17).[42] This implies that a certain spiritual maturity is required to pray as one ought to—we cannot bring every doubt or "belated denial" that springs to mind into the context of prayer.[43] And yet, it is precisely this maturity which takes the form of the "defenseless child" who is ready to give assent ("*Ecce ancilla Domini!*") as the one necessary thing.[44] From this assent, the Spirit has all it needs to accomplish its work. As always, this work is proven by its fruits; charity is the offspring of the union of prayer and Spirit. Thus, Christian "ecstasy [is] not [one] of inebriation but of service."[45]

The work of the Spirit *ad extra* (in the life of Christ and in the church and in the prayer of the individual Christian) interprets the role of the Spirit *ad intra*. In both cases, the Spirit proves itself to be the one who upholds the unity born of love and who in turn plays midwife to the new birth of love. I want to emphasize that this thoroughly Trinitarian vision is expressed with such force in a book that Balthasar wrote, as I said in Chapter 2, very much with Barth in mind; the charge of "christomonism" that Balthasar would take up in earnest in *The Theology of Karl Barth* was thus already taking shape by 1955. More broadly, we can clearly see how Balthasar rescues himself from any possible charge of pneumatological neglect which could otherwise be so easily leveled against his—and our—contemporaries.[46] And quite apart from the specifics of pneumatology, we already

---

40. Ibid., 75.

41. Ibid. Incorporation in Christ is thus a form of *integration* rather than *absorption* (see also ibid., 58).

42. Ibid., 7, 78, 79.

43. Ibid., 78.

44. Ibid., 80; cf. ET.1, 72.

45. *Prayer* (H), 79; the aversion to "experience" was one of the things Balthasar found most attractive in the spirituality of Thérèse of Lisieux, who preferred "the monotony of sacrifice" (see McIntosh, *Christology from within*, 101).

46. Steck notes how the Spirit is often only tasked with "tidying up [the] loose ends that remain after christological reflections have come to an end" (*The Ethical Thought of*

have a sense of how prayer operates within Balthasar's general approach as both a wide frame within which to view other theological debates and as one through which we gain a view to the central mysteries of the Christian faith. In this way, we can already see that Leiva-Merikakis was right to call prayer the "life-blood" of Balthasar's entire theology.[47]

3.3 Characterizing Trinitarian Prayer

It is clear *that* the Trinitarian relations can be understood in terms of prayer for Balthasar, but *how* does he characterize the Trinitarian prayer life? Obviously, this is delicate theological ground. But when Balthasar warned against the danger of "mathematical concepts or vague speculations" in attempting to think of the inner-Trinitarian reality, however, he did not mean to suggest that the theologian should simply not attempt to do so. On the contrary, the point is that any such speculations should be vivid (i.e., not "mathematical") and objectively grounded in revelation (i.e., not "vague") enough to in turn give rise to contemplation in the believer. Under these conditions, one might very well arrive at some productive reflections on the Trinitarian prayer life (where "productive" is taken to mean giving rise to genuine contemplation). Broadly, Balthasar describes the patterns of Trinitarian relation as follows: *The Father* gives an "initial" blessing, speaking with a *parrhesia* that conceals nothing;[48] *the Son* receives this blessing eucharistically and "returns" it to the Father tenfold (cf. Mt. 25:14-30);[49] while *the Spirit*, as we have seen, both is and bears witness to the love between Father and Son, "searching the depths of God" (1 Cor. 2:10) for ever-new ways to bring this exchange to fruitful expression.[50] These characteristics of Trinitarian prayer (the Father blessing, the Son giving thanks, the Spirit confessing) can be thought of in terms of what Thomas called the "appropriation" of certain divine attributes to particular Persons (*"manifestatio personarum per essentialia attributa"*).[51] To be sure, this is analogical language, but it is an analogy that Balthasar hopes serves to highlight the relational, and thus loving, constitution of God's very

---

Hans Urs von Balthasar, 48). Steck refers to the arguments against pneumatological neglect advanced by Lacugna, McDonnell, and Walter Kasper (*The God of Jesus Christ*, trans. Matthew O'Connell [New York: Crossroads, 1992], 198).

47. *3FG*, 8.
48. *Prayer* (H), 45ff.
49. Cf. *Prayer* (H), 67.
50. Cf. *Prayer* (H), 72. Cf. TD.4, 323–4 and *YCYYG*, 170. On these characterizations, see also Gardner, "The Trinity and Prayer," 195.
51. Cf. *ST* I.39.7 and discussion on TL.2, 134. Balthasar comments: "This [method of identifying 'appropriations'] is justified because of a certain intrinsic affinity [between the Persons and their attributes], and it serves to point, in a more than accidental way, to something truly present in the Person in question."

being—*and thus* the relational, loving constitution of created Being as such.[52] Speyr describes these same dynamics in terms of "believing, beholding, and loving," language which Balthasar adopts at certain points.[53] Speyr goes as far as to describe an "element of [. . .] faith" in God, which she admits is "unsatisfactory [yet] indispensable" language to describe the mutual constitution of Trinitarian life in terms that are somewhat "accessible to us."[54]

For his part, Balthasar describes this Trinitarian dynamic with reference to two concepts—one primarily philosophical and one primarily biblical—which manifest as much as we might hope to know about how God prays.[55]

3.3.1 Aletheia

More than one commentator has noted that for Balthasar the very structure of truth is a combination of *aletheia* (unveiling, revelation) and *emeth* (steadfastness and, especially in the Hebraic understanding, fidelity).[56] In other words, the pattern of truth is to announce itself and then to remain faithful to that which has been revealed; this suggests truth's freedom (to reveal itself as it will) and truth's relational constitution (since fidelity is always ordered toward another—to be "true to oneself" is simply to be). Such is the pattern of Trinitarian prayer. By starting with *aletheia*, Balthasar sounds a Barthian note regarding the "sovereign" prerogative of God to "shine forth [cf. Ps. 79:2] in complete freedom," a prerogative the Son embodies in a unique way appropriate to his place in the *ordo processionis* (cf. Jn 1:5, etc.).[57] God's sovereign freedom is a key theme in *Prayer*.[58] But the alethic perspective also represents a conciliatory gesture to Heidegger, for whom

---

52. "Any other explanation of the divine Persons than a relational one would be inconsistent with the divine life of love" (ET.1, 225). The talk of prayer in the Trinity, then, is a chief instance of Balthasar's notion that "the highest instance of the *analogia entis* is the *analogia personalitatis*" (*Prayer* [H], 23). In the *analogia pesonalitatis*, "the infinite and finite subjects do not simply remain alongside each other; they live in a 'fluidity' flowing into one another, something for which there is no further example on earth" (ET.2, 301). Cf. discussion by Angelo Scola at *The Nuptial Mystery*, trans. Michelle Borras (Cambridge: Eerdmans, 2005), 235–6.

53. See Speyr, *World of Prayer*, 33ff.

54. Ibid., 35.

55. Cf. *Prayer* (H), 136–7.

56. See Aidan Nichols, "The Theo-Logic," in *Cambridge Companion to Hans Urs von Balthasar*, 158–71, 161. See also John O'Donnell "Truth as Love: The Understanding of Truth according to Hans Urs von Balthasar," in *Pacifica* 1 (1988), 189–211. On the relationship of the two terms, see TL.1, 35ff.

57. Cf. *Prayer* (H), 20–1; cf. *TH*, 56.

58. See *Prayer* (H), 19–21, 40–1, 160–1, 188–9, 231.

the appearance of Being is the "privileged happening" of metaphysics.⁵⁹ However, by identifying Christ so strongly with the "event" of divine love, which undergirds but does not thereby reduce the "event" of Being, Balthasar attempts to guard against what he sees to be the impersonal and sphinxlike form that Being comes to take on in Heidegger.⁶⁰

But the initial "appearance"—the alethetic event—does not exhaust the subject's powers of self-disclosure. There will always be an aspect of the thing that does not appear as the thing appears.⁶¹ This does not mean the un-appeared aspects of the thing are not properly part of it—indeed, they are constitutive. Instead, just like the skin covers the organs and thereby expresses the form of a body without revealing every part of the body all at once, there is a certain form of revelation that must include both unveildedness and veiledness.⁶² Now, if this dynamic clearly pertains, according to Balthasar, to the creature's relationship with other creatures, with Being, and with God (in the form of Christ),⁶³ it cannot be said to apply straightforwardly to God in Godself. The consubstantial Persons encounter no true "veiledness" among one another, at least none born of misperception, misunderstanding, secrecy, or deception (the commonest sources of confusion for finite creatures). However, Balthasar does affirm the speculative possibility of something like "surprise" (*Überraschung*) in the Trinity, by which he means to

---

59. Martin Heidegger, *An Introduction to Metaphysics*, trans. Raply Manheim (New Haven: Yale University Press, 1959), 4. For Heidegger on truth as *aletheia*, see "On the Essence of Truth," in *Basic Writings* (New York: Harper, 1977), especially 137 and the discussion by Richard McDonough, *Martin Heidegger's Being and Time* (Bern: Peter Lang, 2006), 44. Balthasar's interest in Heidegger dates to his student days in Munich. Seventeen years later, in 1946, Balthasar was insisting that scholasticism had neglected any meaningful "confrontation with Heidegger," which would require reckoning with the problematics of time and difference ("Task," 184–5). And by the time of *Herrlichkeit* 5 in 1965, Balthasar is undertaking this confrontation himself, with a sympathetic but ultimately critical section of that work devoted to Heidegger (cf. GL.5, 429–50). For specific discussions of the relationship, see Davies, "The Theological Aesthetics" in *Cambridge Companion to Hans Urs von Balthasar*, 131–42; Prevot, *Thinking Prayer*, Part I; Carpenter, *Theo-Poetics*, 30–1; and Anneliese Meis, "El Ser, Plenitud Atravesada por la Nada, según Hans Urs von Balthasar," *Teología y Vida* 50 (2009): 387–419, especially 387–8.

60. Inevitably, for Balthasar, Heideggerian Being becomes a "fixed [. . .] form [. . .] before which and for which man cannot live and love" (GL.6, 643). On the sphinxlike status of Being in Heidegger, see William Horosz, *Search Without Idols* (Leiden: Nijhoff, 1987), 301–33.

61. Cf. *TKB*, 60. Here again the dialogue with Heidegger is implicit. That Christ alethetically reveals the God beyond Being does not mean that he thereby commits a violent ontotheological reduction of Being. Indeed, there are still yet unexplored depths of existence even for the one who lives "in Christ."

62. Cf. TL.1, 208.

63. Cf. *Prayer* (H), 62.

emphasize the fact that God discloses Godself as love.⁶⁴ There is "surprise" in God to precisely the same extent that love freely given does not proscribe the form of its response (we might say surprise is the positive valence of freedom while disappointment is the negative valence). Accordingly, since God is pure love, God's capacity for surprise is constitutive of Trinitarian mutuality, such that Balthasar goes as far as to refer to the Trinity as a "community of surprise."⁶⁵ In a strictly logical sense, there is little conceptual tension between the (uncontroversial) affirmation of immanent "unveiledness" among hypostases and their capacity to surprise one another. A key feature of alethetic truth is that it shines forth unreservedly and uncalculatingly—to be unable to be surprised by the other would require one to have made provisions ahead of time. Divine love is altogether more spontaneous and unable to be thought of ahead of time (*Unvordenklichkeit*), and so surprise, in this sense, is a confirmation of its purity.⁶⁶

Looking ahead to the Christological "transposition" of this principle to creaturely prayer, we can say that prayer in the Trinitarian mode will not hold anything back. A perfect "transparency" should pertain to the prayer dialogue. That God allows for such alethetic transparency—which as creatures we can simply call honesty—is itself one of the fundamental graces of prayer (John even appears to elide *aletheia* and *charis*, for instance at Jn 1:14, 17).⁶⁷ We can also say that this kind of honesty is the exact opposite of the "refusal of [. . .] self-surrender" that is characteristic of human sin.⁶⁸ And further, we can see how inasmuch as prayer implies a process of

---

64. See *Prayer* (H), 189, TD.2, 258, or TD.4, 69 n.54. See the discussion by Antonio Lopez, "Eternal Happening: God as an Event of Love," *Communio* 32 (2005), 214–45, 241–2. This "surprise" does not imply a deficiency in God's knowledge, but rather the full depth of divine creativity, which includes but is not limited by time (see D. L. Schindler's discussion of time and surprise in the Trinity at "Time in Eternity, Eternity in Time: On the Contemplative-Active Life," *Communio* 18 [1991]: 53–68, 55–60).

65. TD.5, 54.

66. See TL.2, 135ff.

67. Cf. TL.2, 17.

68. TL.1, 211. Kilby notes that this kind of move—looking to the Trinitarian modes of relation as a "model" for human action—puts Balthasar in the company of the so-called social theorists of the Trinity like Moltmann (Kilby, *Balthasar* 69). However, the usual problems associated with social Trinitarianism (namely, exactly how to apply abstract concepts of Trinitarian relationality to the organization of human society) do not pertain as powerfully here, since precisely what Balthasar is suggesting is that both the Trinity and the creature pray—although obviously not in exactly the same way. In other words, it is not a matter of arriving at some understanding of how the notion of *perichoresis*, for instance, bears upon the seemingly unrelated question of economics (as Boff is concerned to do, for example, in *Trinity and Society* [New York: Orbis, 1988]) but rather it is a matter of rendering an account of creaturely prayer which derives from the prior Trinitarian version of the same. Thus, the "transposition" is more focused and ontological than conventional social Trinitarianism.

coming-to-know Christ, who is the form and summit of Being, prayer functions as a mediational structure between existent beings and Being itself.

3.3.2 Emeth

Aletheia is thus the defining characteristic of truth, but this immediately "provokes the question" of relation: "*To whom* is [truth] being revealed"?[69] It is in the nature of unconcealedness to appear, to make itself known to any "conscious mind" with eyes to see (which can include the other or the alethetic subject itself).[70] But in this unconcealedness, the spirit of truth cannot possibly engage in "illusion [or] deception," lest it not in fact be true.[71] Thus, *aletheia* "entails analytically" the "second" property of truth which is *emeth*, that is, "fidelity, constancy, reliability."[72] *Emeth* is what personalizes the truth of being, making it something "firm, sure, reliable," and therefore worthy of the assent of faith.[73] Again, Balthasar means to deploy the deeply biblical notion of *emeth* as a defensive flank against Heidegger here, suggesting that the distinctively Christian contribution to metaphysics is to render a conception of Being not just as something before which the existent being should display wonder, but as something which proves to be "*worthy* of wonder."[74]

But it would ultimately be reductive to view Balthasar's position here primarily in terms of Heideggerian debates. What is really at stake is the effort to give voice to the unique biblical perspective, the "fundamental attitude" of faith in God's covenantal *emeth*.[75] From Adam to Noah, Abraham to Moses, and finally in a "definitive" way in Christ, "covenant is the objectivity of the love between God and the man he loves, and only in this setting can love be fully lived out."[76] For Balthasar, the entire biblical perspective is "summed up in Yahweh's fundamental assurance: 'I will betroth you to me in *faithfulness*; and [thereby] you shall know the

---

69. TL.1, 37–8.
70. Ibid., 38.
71. Ibid.
72. Ibid.
73. Cf. GL.6, 161. See the summary discussions by O'Regan, "Martin Heidegger and Christian Wisdom," in *Christian Wisdom Meets Modernity*, ed. Kenneth Oakes (London: T&T Clark, 2009), 37–57, 50–3, or D. C. Schindler, *Hans Urs von Balthasar and the Dramatic Structure of Truth*, 52–6).
74. GL.5, 615 (italics mine). Cf. Prevot, *Thinking Prayer*, 96–7. In this regard, Balthasar is likely influenced in a decisive way by Karl Löwith, as O'Regan rightly notes (see "Martin Heidegger and Christian Wisdom," 52, and the explicit citation of Löwith at GL.5, 440). Löwith was concerned to counter Heidegger's "nihilism," which involved finding a way of "soldering" together "truth and goodness." *Emeth* provides this connecting link.
75. GL.7, 87; also GL.6, 161–3, and 173ff.
76. *Prayer* (H), 137. Cf. Gen. 9:12–6; 15:13ff.; 24:27; Jer. 10:10; Isa. 16:5.

Lord' (Hos. 2:20)."⁷⁷ To be sure, this constitutes no curtailment of divine freedom. Precisely *as* the one who makes himself known in sovereign covenant, God's perfect commitment to the covenant is the fullest expression of God's freedom.⁷⁸ But covenant fidelity also ratifies human freedom as being involved in the sort of relationship God wants to have with God's creatures.

Notice how this establishes a reciprocal relationship between faith and trust. Etymologically, the term *emeth* belongs to a family of words derived from the Hebrew *'mn*, which becomes *amen*, the verbal sign of the creature's steadfast belief in the steadfastness of God's love: "*Amen* recognizes the absolute validity of God's fidelity, and it affirms the absolute resolution of man to stand by it."⁷⁹ God's faithfulness itself comes through a process of metonymy to refer to the creature's faith in God, expressed above all in prayer. And so by one more further logical step, we can say that it is *emeth* which undergirds and encourages the creature's prayerful transparency before God—generally, one discloses more of oneself in proportion to the ability another shows to reliably receive what is offered. *Emeth* in the lover gives rise to a confidence in the beloved as they learn that their reciprocations will not be mishandled or misunderstood. This progressive deepening of the trust dimension in prayer does not come naturally to the fallen creature—it is precisely one of the primary graces of prayer in the Trinitarian mode that it trains the praying person in this form of self-gift. Thus, why, in *Heart of the World*, speaking in the ironic voice of a tempter (a la C. S. Lewis' Wormwood), Balthasar warns the praying person that it is much easier to keep God at a distance in prayer, "so that the boundaries [between God and the creature] won't be blurred."⁸⁰ But genuine trust knows no boundaries; it is a love that goes "to the end" (Jn 13:1) to prove itself.⁸¹ It is this love that Balthasar takes to be at the source of Christian prayer, and thus why prayer in turn is the necessary school for enabling the creature's total "Yes"—their genuine *amen*—which is the affirmation of Being.⁸²

The combined *aletheia* and *emeth* features of God's revelation can be seen quite clearly in Christ's encounter with the Samaritan woman at the well (Jn 4:1-26).⁸³ In this episode, which Balthasar calls the "classic example" of divine encounter, Jesus makes no effort to hide himself from the woman, to deceive her as to his true nature. Indeed, it is Christ's plain unveiledness that proves so confusing to the woman, who distrusts Jesus as a Jew and as a stranger. But Christ proves himself to the woman by the reliability of his speech ("Sir, I perceive that thou art a prophet" [v. 19]), speech that could only come from an intimate love that

---

77. Paul maintains this perspective, even while putting it in Christological terms (e.g., Gal. 2:20); see discussion at TD.5, 409–10.
78. Cf. TD.2, 256.
79. See the discussion in "Fides Christi," at ET.2 48ff.
80. *HW*, 121.
81. Cf. the remarks by Healy, *Eschatology as Communion*, 117.
82. Cf. GL.6, 162–3.
83. Cf. discussion in *Prayer* (H), 252.

precedes all calculating knowledge. Importantly, however, Christ's appearance to the woman does not impose itself against her will; he does not absorb her will into his but rather provides her the basis upon which to enter into a relationship of abiding trust with him. Her confession to him regarding her own past serves as a kind of mirrored *amen* to Jesus's own confession of his true nature. The dynamic of trust (a result of *emeth*), then, works to reinforce the dynamic of assent (a result of *aletheia*) in a kind of circular motion. It is *aletheia* that makes *emeth* credible and *emeth* that makes *aletheia* attractive. Balthasar notes that subsequent to the genuine encounter between the two, "Everything else, including the woman's 'apostolate' [she confesses Jesus publicly at verse 28], is simply the radiation of her adoration"—that is, her prayer.[84] For the one who has made themselves transparent to grace in this way, as Balthasar says elsewhere, their whole life is a prayer.[85]

It is no violation of the epistemic distance between creature and creator to say that these same dynamics apply to God, though not, admittedly, as a sequenced happening within the economy of salvation (as with the Samaritan woman who encountered Christ and was then converted) but as an eternal "ever-greater" event.[86] If the Trinitarian prayer is characterized by this eternal coincidence of unveiledness and constancy—of honesty and trust—this is simply another way of saying that God is love. If these concepts seem somehow "too human" to be plausibly located in the divine life, this in fact suggests that the Trinitarian prayer is itself a grace which aims from the beginning at reconciling the world in its otherness: "If God wishes to reveal the love that he harbors [in himself] for the world, this love has to be something that the world can recognize, in spite of, or in fact *in*, its being wholly other. The inner reality of love can be recognized only by love."[87] Crucially for our purposes, then, Balthasar is presenting prayer as that bridge between God and the world that is both the invitation to and the method of incorporation into the divine life.

Now this raises certain ontological questions about the relation of finite to infinite. Here, as ever, Balthasar's intentions were decidedly revisionist, especially in light of Heidegger's emphasis on the absolute ontological difference. We might draw comparisons with some of Balthasar's contemporaries for a sense of how

---

84. *Prayer* (H), 253.
85. Cf. the essay "Characteristics of Christianity," in ET.1 (161–80), here 167.
86. Balthasar places a heavy emphasis on the "ever-greater" quality of God's essence-as-love (see, e.g., *Unless* 46 or TD.5, 54) for which the influence of Przywara should of course be noted (cf. Przywara, *Deus Semper Major: Theologie der Exerzitien* [Munich: Herold, 1964]) but also, more fundamentally, Ignatius of Loyola. As Löser notes ("The Ignatian Exercises in the Work of Hans Urs von Balthasar," in *Hans Urs von Balthasar: Life and Work*, 103–20), Balthasar considered Ignatius' repeated use of the "open comparative" ("*semper maior*," etc.) to be the "spiritual password of the *Exercises*" for what it reveals about the ever-ascending quality of divine love.
87. *LAC*, 75.

he handled these questions of distance and difference, which lie at the heart of a notion of Trinitarian prayer.

3.4 Contemporary Perspectives on Distance

Balthasar quotes approvingly from a *Communio* colleague Claude Bruaire, who approached the question of ontological difference thus:

> Talk of the "ontological difference" undergoes a radical transformation [in light of an account of Trinitarian difference]: being does not differ *from* the supreme Being, but *in* him, since there is the Spirit *in* God, as the difference between the hypostases in himself [. . .] The ontological difference is null if it [merely] signifies the being that God is not.[88]

The whole trajectory of post–Heideggerian metaphysics is to a certain extent preoccupied with this question of how to understand the difference between finite and infinite being. Balthasar's originality emerges from contextualizing this difference (i.e., the God-world difference) within the Trinitarian difference (i.e., between Persons). Famously, Balthasar puts the Trinitarian difference in strong terms, calling it an "infinite [. . .] distance [*unendlich . . . Distanz*]" between Persons.[89] As we have seen, the Trinitarian method for holding this latter distance in productive (i.e., loving) unity is something like prayer, which emerges from and expresses the depths of the divine attributes (rooted as they are in the common essence); it may be helpful to think of Trinitarian prayer as the substance of divine unity-in-difference. So too can we expect prayer to express something of the underlying unity between God and world, as well as the underlying unity among the multiplicity of created beings. Balthasar's thought on this point can perhaps be seen more clearly in the light of comparable projects by Marion and Siewerth.

The lines of influence between Balthasar and Marion are such that more of the former is to be found in the latter, even if Marion is eager to draw certain distinctions between his project and Balthasar's.[90] In approaching the challenge of thinking the Absolute, for instance, Marion takes from Balthasar a methodological

---

88. Claude Bruaire, *L'Être et l'esprit* (Paris: Presses Universitaires de France, 1963), 190; quoted at TL.2, 135.

89. TD.5, 245; cf. TD.3, 228; TD.4, 323, 362; TD.5, 125; and TL.2, 223.

90. For Marion as a(n idiosyncratic) Balthasarian, see the discussion by Tasmin Jones, "Dionysius in Hans Urs von Balthasar and Jean-Luc Marion," *Modern Theology* 24:4 (2008): 743–54, especially 747–9 and 753 n.21–2. Marion acknowledges Balthasar's influence in the Foreword to *The Idol and Distance*, trans. Thomas Carlson (New York: Fordham University Press, 2001), xxxviii.

commitment to starting with what God has revealed about Godself,[91] though Marion's further commitment to a thoroughly phenomenological approach will obviously lead him down different avenues than Balthasar's more explicitly theological approach.[92] Marion would have no insurmountable objection, however, to seeing in Christ at prayer the "icon" of God's self-interpretation in history.[93] And if, for both, there is a genuine iconicity to the Son's mission (and especially to the Son on the Cross), then the fact of distance must be taken seriously as a feature of God's own self-interpretation.[94] In Marion's terms, distance is the means by which God establishes an icon of "the gift of Being" itself.[95] That is, distance becomes the precondition of gift (which Marion often posits in the form of *kenosis*), and it is gift that is the characteristic feature of Being itself. Trinitarian difference thus preserves creaturely difference as something that has a place in the economy of love—here Marion explicitly appropriates Balthasar.[96] Jones notes that for Marion, distance's "primary purpose [. . .] is to conceptualise the possibility of an infinite and eternal gap between God and God's creation which nonetheless enables relation between the two," just as for Balthasar the point of talking of an inner-Trinitarian distance is to indicate the space in which creaturely distinctions can be taken up and reread in light of a prior Trinitarian unity-in-difference.[97] For Marion, notably,

---

91. Compare *The Idol and Distance*, xv, for instance, with GL.2, 171 (see discussion by Jones, "Dionysius in Hans Urs von Balthasar and Jean-Luc Marion," 747).

92. For instance, in order to accomplish the necessary "phenomenological reduction" Marion is forced to de-emphasize the role of prayer. Prevot sees this, however, primarily as a feature of Marion's pivotal middle period (*c.* 1989–2003), which after 2008 comes to be replaced by a more explicit interest in prayer as a method of resisting "conceptual idolatry" (see Prevot, "The Gift of Prayer: Toward a Theological Reading of Jean-Luc Marion," *Horizons* 41 [2014]:250–74).

93. Cf. Marion, *The Idol and Distance*, 172. For an account of Christ as the "saturated phenomenon *par excellence*" in Marion, see Brian Robinette, "A Gift to Theology? Jean-Luc Marion's 'Saturated Phenomenon' in Christological Perspective," *Heythrop Journal* 48 (2007): 86–108.

94. Henrik Frandsen identifies distance as the "key to Marion's phenomenology," since the appearance of a given phenomenon requires a "coming-from-elsewhere" which is by definition not constituted by the subject (see Frandsen, "Distance as Abundance: The Thought of Jean-Luc Marion," *Svensk Teologisk Kvartalskrift* 79 [2003]: 177–86, here 185).

95. Cf. Marion, *The Idol and Distance*, xxxvii. Cf. Frandsen, "Distance as Abundance," 182.

96. See Marion *Idol and Distance*, 155 n.32 where Marion refers to *Cosmic Liturgy*. Cf. also GL.3, 142–3: "The distance of persons in God [within] the womb of substantial unity is the presupposition of all love both eternal and created."

97. Jones, "Dionysius in Hans Urs von Balthasar and Jean-Luc Marion," 748. Marion is also happy, in another significant appropriation of Balthasar, to read Dionysius as a prayerful reflection on the positive "content" of the divine abyss (compare Marion's reading

"prayer performs distance" by keeping this space—the space between God and the creature—open and, in light of the recognition of the gift of Being, eucharistic.[98]

For Marion, this insistence on distance stands against an assimilationist metaphysics where the finite is merely absorbed into the infinite. As Marion puts it, "*incommensurability* alone makes intimacy possible" since "only he can become my neighbor who remains forever outside of me."[99] But at the same time, and more pressingly, Marion means to resist the Heideggerian charge of ontotheology. It is precisely the idolatrous tendency in metaphysics that Marion seeks to preempt with his account of the icon.[100] Marion aims to show that a Christian philosophy can succeed in being properly "post-metaphysical" while still speaking in a distinctively theological (which is to say prayerful) tone.[101] This involves locating "God beyond being" as the Absolute Other of the ontological difference, who can only be spoken of in the self-subverting language of theology. But it is precisely here that Balthasar faults Marion for conceding too much to Heidegger.[102] There is a concern, in other words, that Marion's distance does less to safeguard God's transcendence than to prevent a meaningful account of divine involvement in the world (an account which it is, after all, theology's task to render).[103] Balthasar

---

of Dionysius with Balthasar's treatment in GL.2, 144ff.; see the discussion by Prevot in "The Gift of Prayer," 262).

98. Marion, *The Idol and Distance*, 162. For Marion, like Balthasar, theology is to be characterized by this same open stance (see Marion, *God Without Being: Hors-Texte*, trans. Thomas Carlson [Chicago: the University of Chicago Press, 1991], 1). Prayer thus resists what Frandsen calls a "domesticating hermeneutics" in metaphysics ("Distance as Abundance," 178).

99. Marion, *The Idol and Distance*, 198, 95; Marion also defines "di-stance" as that "duality [which] allows recognition." See also *idem.*, *The Erotic Phenomenon*, trans. Stephen Lewis (Chicago: University of Chicago Press, 2007), 105 ff. Cf. Werner Jeanrond, *A Theology of Love* (London: T&T Clark, 2010), 155-7. For a critical comparison of Marion's and Levinas' accounts of the Other, see Christina Gschwandtner, "The Neighbor and the Infinite: Marion and Levinas on the Encounter between Self, Human Other, and God," *Continental Philosophy Review* 40 (2007): 231–49.

100. See Brian Shanley, "St. Thomas Aquinas, Onto-Theology, and Marion," *The Thomist* 60, no. 4 (October 1996): 617–25, 622.

101. Cf. Brett David Porter, "Image and Kenosis: Assessing Jean-Luc Marion's Contribution to a Postmetaphysical Theological Aesthetics," *International Journal of Philosophy and Theology* 79:1–2 (2018): 60–79.

102. TL.2, 135.

103. Johnson considers the disagreement between Balthasar and Marion in terms of Balthasar's rejection of (what Johnson calls) the "Pure Difference Thesis" in metaphysics, of which Marion's insistence on "ontological difference" between God and world is but one sort (see Johnson, *Christ and Analogy*, Chapter 2.II.B but especially 60–1). Porter has suggested that Balthasar's critique is "premature" ("Image and Kenosis," 60) in light of Marion's developing project, but, as Johnson points out (*Christ and Analogy*, 29), the

for his part is more "unashamed" of the Christian metaphysical tradition than Marion and seeks to establish that Christian thought, *as* Christian thought, can carry out a genuinely theological engagement with modernity without writing off all that comes after Thomas as hopelessly ontotheological.[104] For one thing, as the aforementioned quote from Bruaire suggests, Balthasar goes further than Marion in providing a specifically Trinitarian basis for the sort of unity-in-difference which is to characterize love. For Balthasar, the Spirit is the one who navigates and bridges distances par excellence, who knows its way through the abyss that the divine infinity is (thus the Spirit's special role in prayer, as we have already seen), and who "regulates the distance" between God and world.[105] If Marion's account of the open stance of praise-at-a-distance proper to reflection on Being arguably risks an overemphasis on receptivity at the expense of mission and (as Robinette argues) prophetic witness, Balthasar's Trinitarian perspective provides a helpful supplement inasmuch as it grounds the possibility of creaturely action in the Spirit (as the one who navigates distance and *makes it fruitful*).[106] In this, Balthasar aligns himself with an alternative trajectory in post–Heideggerian thought, one represented mainly by Siewerth and Ulrich, which sought to give a more explicitly theological (read: Trinitarian) account of the "absolute positivity of difference" and the eternal event-quality of God.[107]

In particular, Siewerth's contribution was to expand upon the multivalent dimensions of properly Trinitarian thinking on difference. That is, it is not simply

---

point is to understand Balthasar's thought *as it developed* and to identify the salient points in Marion's early works that Balthasar aligned his metaphysics against. In other words, if, as Prevot suggests, Marion's more recent study of Augustine does indeed constitute his definitive "return to theology," this still does not mitigate against Balthasar's critique of the more limited phenomenological approach that predominates in *The Idol and Distance* and *God without Being*.

104. Johnson, *Christ and Analogy*, 29. For a survey of the so-called Catholic Heidegger school (Pryzywara's term), see Michael Schulz, "Beyond Being: Outline of the Catholic Heidegger School," *Studia Teologii Dogmatycznej* 3 (2017): 177–92.

105. See ET.3, 167; cf. GL.1, 255, TD.4, 324.

106. See Robinette "A Gift to Theology?," especially 100. See also critique of Robinette's critique by Joseph Rivera, "The Call and the Gifted in Christological Perspective: A Consideration of Brian Robinette's Critique of Jean-Luc Marion," in *Heythrop Journal* 51 (2010): 1053–60.

107. Gustav Siewerth, *Der Thomismus als Identitätssystem*, 2nd ed. (Frankfurt: Schulte-Bulmke, 1961), 104; see, for example, TL.2, 185, where four different works of Siewerth are cited on a single page. For background on Siewerth, see also Cabada Castro, *Sein und Gott bei Gustav Siewerth* (Düsseldorf: Patmos, 1971). For a typical example of Balthasar's recourse to Siewerth, see TL.2, 181, see especially n.14. Balthasar often cites Siewerth and Ulrich as stand-ins for fuller metaphysical arguments that he is unable to carry out at any given time (see, e.g., TL.2, 225 n.7 or 306). Balthasar acknowledges the deep debt to Siewerth again in *MWiR*, 90–1.

the case, *pace* Marion, that there is a difference between God and world into which God can project an icon of kenotic love, but that the difference pertains in God Godself in an ontologically prior and deeper way.[108] In the Barth book, for instance, Balthasar suggests the freedom of God to give as total self-gift is properly part of God's essence in itself (i.e., not just as the free response to an external world).[109] Balthasar draws this notion explicitly from Siewerth, as when he argues in the *Theo-Logic* that divine self-subsistence means that "the absolute Divine Being [contains] the relative oppositions of the divine hypostases *in itself*."[110] Otherwise relation in God would always stand in danger of collapsing into disunity. Balthasar presents this as a traditional trajectory in Christian metaphysics, pointing out (explicitly against Marion) that "even Thomas" describes the good (bonum) as being's (esse) natural self-transcendence (the Thomistic-Platonic doctrine of *bonum diffusivum sui*).[111] God as *purus actus* necessarily is a God in relation. Siewerth reinforces this trajectory and argues further that creaturely nonsubsistence is the worldly "likeness" of divine mutuality.[112] That is, the sheer givenness of existence evokes analogically the infinite distance between hypostases which is always being bridged and made fruitful in love. The self-subsistent divine life *and* nonsubsistent creation both attest to the fact that being does not accrue to itself but exists in order to be given. Balthasar's ontology is thus grounded in the rhythmic interplay of being

---

108. See the discussion by Schindler, *Hans Urs von Balthasar and the Dramatic Structure of Truth*, 69–72.

109. *TKB*, 111.

110. TL.2, 134 (italics in original). Cf. TL.2, 170; Siewerth, *Das Schicksal der Metaphysik* (Einsiedeln: Johannes, 1959), 289.

111. TL.2, 135; Balthasar does not cite any passage from Thomas here but cf. *De Virtu.* 2.2.c Thomas's notion of esse is fundamentally dynamic, drawing on a Neoplatonic tradition that emphasized the productivity of goodness. There is some ongoing debate among Thomists as to whether or not this teaching constrains God's transcendent freedom: see the argument in favor of an orthodox interpretation by Norris Clarke, "Person, Being, and St. Thomas," in *Communio* 19 (1992), 601–18, and compare it to the critical interpretation by Norman Kretzmann, "A General Problem of Creation: Why Would God Create Anything at All?," in *Being and Goodness: The Concept of the Good in Metaphysics and Philosophical Theology*, ed. Scott Macdonald (Ithaca: Cornell University Press, 1991), 208–28. Grasping Balthasar's position here does not require resolving these debates entirely, only to show that divine being is a being-in-relation in which Trinitarian love is expressed precisely through, not in spite of, difference (a position both Kretzmann and Clarke could affirm). The principle of *bonum diffusivum sui* arguably undergirds a notion of Trinitarian prayer, since it suggests how one can speak of petition, praise, thanksgiving, and so on, not as anthropomorphic projections but as expressions of an absolute goodness. For a general approach to the question, see Bernhard Blankenhorn, "The Good as Self-Diffusive in Thomas Aquinas," *Angelicum* 79, no. 4 (2002): 803–37.

112. Cf. Siewerth, *Das Dien als Gleichnis Gottes* (cited by Balthasar at TL.2 135 n.10)

and gift (being-as-gift).[113] It is only in light of such an understanding of Trinitarian mutuality that the biblical insistence on the identity of poverty and richness (2 Cor. 8:9, Rev. 2:9, etc.) comes more clearly into view: "The nonsubsistence of being, which is its self-dispossession, seems to be sheer poverty. And yet, it reveals that this poverty (as such!) is the plenitude of God's self-giving in essences."[114] Love is thus "more comprehensive than being itself"—it is "the transcendental *par excellence*" since it is the fundamental reality, the basis of all that exists.[115] The highest form of love, and thus also the fullest expression of reality as such, is the kenotic love which gives everything up for the other.[116]

3.5 Consolidation

We only have access to the Trinitarian life through Jesus Christ. But in Christ, and specifically in prayer, we *really do* have access to the same dynamics of reciprocity and mutuality which pertain in the triune God.[117] Such access, if it cannot be said

---

113. See Davies, "Von Balthasar and the Problem of Being," *New Blackfriars* 79:923 (1998): 11–7; Davies comments: "[In order to avoid both the nominalist and pantheist errors], Being therefore needs to be held distinct from God, neither confused with him, nor detached from him, but reconciled with him through the proportionalism (or analogy) of divine creation" (12). Cf. also Lexi Eikelboom, *Rhythm: A Theological Category* (Oxford: Oxford University Press, 2018).

114. TL.2, 183, cf. Ferdinand Ulrich, *Homo Abyssus: The Drama of the Question of Being*, trans. D.C. Schindler (Washington: Humanum, 2018).

115. Siewerth, *Metaphysik der Kindheit* (Eisiedeln: Johannesverlag, 1957), 63; qtd. by Balthasar at TL.2, 176–7.

116. Ulrich therefore emphasizes that the Cross—the final vindication of God's *kenosis* in Christ—is fundamentally congruous with Creation as such (see Stefan Oster "The Metaphysics of Being as Love in the Work of Ferdinand Ulrich," *Communio* 37 [2010]: 660–700, here 672). Balthasar affirms this argument in GL.3.

117. The analogical dimensions must be kept clearly in mind. So while in God the Trinitarian prayer—as the "dialogue" of Father, Son, and Spirit—is intelligible on the basis of the uncreated divine essence common to each Person, the creature who participates in the Trinitarian prayer does so still (and always) as a contingent created being. In other words, the creature at prayer participates in the Trinitarian dialogue not literally as God but *in proportion* with his or her faith in Christ. In this sense, there is a clear "analogy of proportion" rather than a straightforward "analogy of being." Balthasar's position is that Christ (as hypostatic person) is himself the "final proportion" between God and creature in that he enables creaturely participation in God (cf. TD. 3, 221). In this Balthasar is influenced by Przywara, who sees in the Son's descending to human form the basis of all theological analogy, and who defines "participation" as "con-formation to the Son" (see discussion by Jonathan Ciraulo, "Divinization as Christification in Erich Przywara and John Zizioulas," *Modern Theology* 32, no. 4 [2016]: 479–503, especially 488–9).

to establish a direct and unmediated path to the Father, does nevertheless unite the creature and God in a common form of love, when this love is understood as a whole way of life lived in light of the other. In turn, this open disposition, this life lived toward the other, is for Balthasar equivalent to prayer, which is seen to be a form of relation rather than a discrete act.[118] Prayer as a mutually determined life-in-view-of-the-other is the creaturely form of indwelling—the analogous participation in the ongoing event of love in God. True, in Balthasar's theology (and Speyr's) this vision of Trinitarian life finds a particularly vivid expression; but theirs is not properly speaking a private theology, inaccessible to those who would seek to understand it apart from a given experience. It is, rather, best characterized as an attempt to describe the process of incorporation (or divinization) in terms of a central Christian practice—that is, prayer. The Trinitarian dimensions of Balthasar's account reveal an original feature of his approach, which is one of my main tasks to illuminate. Spirituality is not an afterthought to doctrinal work but a deeply Trinitarian mode of reflection on the central aspects of Christian existence.

We must now push ahead into the other dimensions of prayer in order to determine how this process of incorporation in God takes shape. The Trinitarian discussion has indicated prayer's basis in God, but the definitive *Gestalt* of prayer is to be found in Christ, who appears to us both as and at prayer. The Christological dimensions of prayer (Chapter 4), which are so pivotal to Balthasar's overall account, will in turn become the basis for a consideration of the anthropological dimensions (Chapter 5) of prayer; and, inasmuch as prayer's grace is to conform a person more and more to Christ and thus overcome creation's alienation from God, this indicates the eschatological dimensions of prayer (Chapter 6) as well. However, at no point will this journey of prayer take us further than the lengths to which God has already gone in the eternal event of love that characterizes God's inner life. Thus, prayer, as I said at the outset, constitutes a uniquely compact way of understanding Balthasar's theology and, by nature of that fact, renders a view to the innermost Christian mystery.

---

118. Cf. *Prayer* (H), 48.

Chapter 4

PRAYER'S SHAPE

CHRISTOLOGICAL DIMENSIONS

In the course of the last chapter, it emerged that prayer is a prior Trinitarian activity characterized by superabundant patterns of disclosure and fidelity. This Trinitarian perspective is, according to Balthasar, the "indispensable background" for a workable doctrine of the Incarnation.[1] That is why it was necessary to treat the Trinity first before turning to an explicit Christology. Even while Christ is always the creature's entry point into the divine prayer life, there is no Christology that stands wholly apart from its Trinitarian foundations (i.e., ontology precedes epistemology). In a play of German syntax typical of Balthasar's way of thinking, the perichoretic Trinitarian infolding (*Einfaltung*) grounds the Son's outwardly oriented mission, or outfolding (*Entfaltung*), which, in turn, shows the creature the proper posture (*Haltung*) to take in prayer. The danger of a Christomonism or of an individualism in prayer is mitigated by this Trinitarian background, as well as by the emphasis Balthasar places on the ecclesial dimensions of prayer that flow from its Christological basis (accordingly, the ecclesial dimensions will be treated here rather than in a separate chapter). While the Trinitarian discussion could be characterized as speculative, the Christological discussion will be where specific features and operations of prayer come more clearly into focus. Certain distinctive features of Balthasar's Christology are directly related to his theology of prayer, such that he conceives of Christ both as the expression of the Trinitarian prayer in history (i.e., the eternal Word of blessing) and sees in Christ at prayer the redeemed and redeeming instance of finite freedom (i.e., "firstborn of all Creation" [Col. 1:15] and "pioneer of faith" [Heb. 12:2]). That is, both Christ's identity and Christ's mission are indicated by his prayers. Christ's prayers—paradigmatically the High Priestly Prayer of John 17—express and reveal his most profound intimacy with the Father (Jn 17:21), while simultaneously showing how that intimacy issues in action and mission on behalf of the community of believers present and future (Jn 17:17, 20). Given that the unity of mission and identity is such a central theme to Balthasar's Christology and therefore also to his anthropology, my contention is

---

1. GL.1, 437. Cf. Kasper's judgment that Jesus at prayer provides the "clearest New Testament basis for a doctrine of the Trinity" (*The God of Jesus Christ*, 303).

that prayer is an essential aspect of personhood on this account. Indeed, Balthasar navigates some of the classic issues of hypostatic metaphysics with recourse to the notion of prayer. I aim to draw out these distinctive features in what follows.

Jesus' "twofold motion [. . .] to the Father and from the Father" is a central theme in the Christological passages of *Prayer*.[2] This twofold motion has always been the most distinctive, and the most bewildering, feature of Christ's mission, one which Balthasar reflected upon in a homily on the Bread of Life discourse from John 6. After describing the dynamics of Trinitarian prayer in which the Son expresses "the Father's eternal 'Thou'"—a "Thou" which is witnessed to and embraced by the "Spirit of Love common to them both"—Balthasar considers the "very strange" fact that this "Thou" stands in relation to the world, too:

> But now, Listeners, something very strange happens: we have spoken of the Father's "Thou" which he [now] *addresses to us* and by which he draws us to him: this "Thou" can be nothing other than the Son, Jesus Christ. Anyone who knows that he is addressed by the Father's love is standing in the very place of the Son, who is the eternal "Thou utterance" of the Father [. . .]: "Everyone who has heard and learned from the Father comes to me" [Jn 6:41]. But does this not mean that we arrive at the *wrong place*, at the Son instead of the Father? Does not the Son somehow screen the Father from view? Is he not a kind of penultimate station, stopping us from arriving at our final goal? This would indeed be the case if Jesus were only the Father's vice-regent or executive in the world. (This is liberalism's view of Jesus.) All of a sudden we see how indispensable the ancient [Chalcedonian] dogma is: Jesus is a man like us, of course, revealing and interpreting the Father to us in human terms, but at the same time he is God from God, Light from Light, eternal Word from the Father's eternal source, and as such he provides total accessibility to the One who speaks in and through him: "I am the way" [Jn 14:6] [. . .] What then can we say of his Eucharist, in which he gives us his Flesh and Blood to nourish us? What does this have to do with our being drawn to the ultimate Source? Does it not enclose us once and for all in something worldly? Jesus does something quite beyond the grasp of our minds: He identifies the Word uttered from God to us, and that promises us eternal life in God, with his own corporality: "The bread [from heaven] that I shall give for the [eternal] life of the world is my Flesh" (Jn 6:51).[3]

From the prior Trinitarian dialogue, the faithful are addressed and invited in as participants in full standing. The Son is simultaneously this Word of invitation and the Word by which the faithful make themselves heard. The Son brings the fullness of the Father's Word with him in mission, and through the ongoing work of the Spirit deposits that same fullness in the midst of the world in the form of

---

2. *Prayer* (H), 51–67, here 53. Elsewhere: "Jesus exists in *no other way* than in this double movement" (*CM*, 52–3).

3. *YCYYG*, 170–1 (italics added).

the sacraments, especially the Eucharist.[4] Prayer is the form and method of God's closeness to the world, as Christ reveals in a unique way in his mission-identity as/at prayer. Let us look more closely at each aspect in turn.

4.1 Christ as Prayer

4.1.1 "Christ As the Language of God"[5]

In Balthasar, one finds what can be described as a prayer Christology. By this I mean that Balthasar views prayer not only as one activity among others that make up the essential aspects of Christ's mission (i.e., prayer is not simply something he *does*) but as a constitutive aspect of his Sonship as such (i.e., prayer is what he *is*). To a large extent, the coherence of this approach depends on what was said earlier about Trinitarian prayer understood as eternal patterns of disclosure and fidelity in and by God. But in the Son, whose unique role it is to receive the Father's Word of blessing and to return it eucharistically, Trinitarian prayer becomes realized in history in a decisive and particular way. If prayer is dialogue, and the Son is the eternal Thou of the Father, then prayer subsists in the Son, who provides a "concrete vision of the life of the Trinity" as one of prayer.[6]

The metaphysical background is important here. "In giving himself [to the Son], the Father does not give something (or even everything) that he *has* but all that he *is*."[7] Inherent to Sonship, in turn, is the total receptivity of the Father's blessing, which enables the Son to express that same love in a total way (in the Spirit). There is no essential heteronomy between the Father's outpouring of himself into the Son (begetting) and the Son's outpouring of himself, with the Father, into the Spirit (procession).[8] In other words, the Son's *amen* both recognizes and repeats the Father's blessing. In considering how this Sonship exhibits itself in the economy of salvation, Balthasar relies heavily on Bonaventure's doctrine of expression, according to which Christ is the complete expression (*expressio expressa*) of the triune God—containing nothing that is not of God and leaving out nothing

---

4. As we will see later in the text, Balthasar's approach here helps to overcome the persistent polarization between "word and sacrament" that has long been an obstacle to dialogue with the East. See Paul McPartlan, "Who is the Church? Zizioulas and von Balthasar on the Church's Identity," *Ecclesiology* 4 (2008): 271–88, especially 275.

5. See *MiH*, 275ff.

6. *Prayer* (L), 154.

7. TD.5, 84.

8. Though the language here may give the false impression of a mythological sequence of events, the point of orthodox Trinitarian grammar should always be to underline how these "moments" of love constitute one coherent unity. Such is already the point of naming the Persons as we do (i.e., a father is not a father outside of his relationship to a son).

that is.⁹ At the same time, Christ is also, for Bonaventure, the precise expression (*expressus expressivus, ausdrücklich ausdrückend*) of the Father, meaning that the specific ways in which Christ points to the Father are not accidental or arbitrary, but "uniquely and definitively" indicate the creature's proper posture toward God.[10] This perspective suggests the necessity of maintaining the unity of mission and identity in Christ, and indeed this is one of Balthasar's most consistent and distinctive Christological commitments.[11] Prayer is a primary way in which Balthasar dramatizes this unity of expression. In prayer the Son both exhibits and enacts his Sonship.

> The Son does not contemplate the Father for a while and then pause in order to imitate in his own activity what he has seen the Father do. Even while he is active, he keeps his gaze fixed steadily upon the Father in order not to lose a moment's direction from him. But he is not inactive while he is contemplating. He understands his contemplation so entirely as service and mission that he translates into action and reality all that the Father shows him.[12]

In expressing God fully *of course* Christ prays, for "prayers are words in the language of God."[13]

But the Father and the Son cannot help "transcending themselves in embracing the other."[14] The *amen* which resounds at the most intimate level of being between them does not remain a self-enclosed secret or a private prayer—"What you have whispered in the inner rooms will be proclaimed from the rooftops" (Lk. 12:3). This is the natural form of the (W/w)ord according to Balthasar: "Even in human relations, speech is never separable from turning toward the respective person; it seeks self-expression, to be perceived and noticed."[15] All the more, then, for God's

---

9. See GL.2, 292ff.

10. GL.2, 287ff. Cf. also GL.1, 447. Johnson argues that Bonaventure is "the most important of all von Balthasar's sources," and this is "to a large extent [because of] the robust Christology" that marks Bonaventure's system (see Johnson, *Christ and Analogy*, 10–16).

11. On the unity of mission and identity see, for example, TD.3, 149–253. Maintaining the unity of identity and mission in Christ is a central aspect of what Yenson has called Balthasar's "Neo-Chalcedonian" Christology (see Yenson, *Existence as Prayer* but also *idem*, "Making a Difference: Implications of Hans Urs von Balthasar's Neo-Chalcedonian Christology for Creation," in *To Discern Creation in a Scattering World*, eds. Frederiek Depoortere and Jacques Haers [Leuven: Peeters, 2013], 367–80). In particular, Balthasar's reclamation of Maximus the Confessor grounded his arguments about the hypostatic synthesis (see *CL*, 207, e.g.), from which the notion of mission-identity flows.

12. *CSL*, 81; cf. GL.2, 169.

13. *3FG*, 122.

14. *YCYYG*, 170.

15. Balthasar's notion of speech as such—hinted at in several places but made explicit in the essay "Implications of the Word," at ET.1, 47–68—derives analogously from a Trinitarian

eternal Word of blessing, which seeks to expand the Trinitarian dialogue to include the creature. This foregrounds prayer's *reconciling* function, which we will see more clearly in Chapters 5 and 6. Focusing for the moment on the Christological aspects at work here, we can say that Christ seeks to elevate the dialogue between God and creature to the realm of the Trinitarian dialogue. Previous attempts at establishing a dialogue set the contours of salvation history: in the promise to Noah; in the call of Abraham; in the revelation on Sinai—again and again God exhibited the Trinitarian prayer and invited the creature into its rhythms. That this dialogue which God seeks has been repeatedly degraded (indeed, deformed) by the exigencies of human freedom is a tragic fact that Balthasar refers to as the "fundamental theodramatic law of world history[:] the greater the revelation of divine (ground-less) love, the more it elicits a groundless (Jn 15:25) hatred from man."[16] (I will have occasion to cite this "fundamental theodramatic law" again in subsequent chapters.) In response to this ever-escalating drama, it is the Incarnate Son who decisively expresses God's prayer within the context of salvation history.[17] And at the same time Christ locates us in the Trinitarian dialogue, such that through him "the Father contemplates us [. . .] and is well pleased."[18] The Word of blessing at the heart of Christ's mission-identity thus proves to be both one of election *and* of glorification.[19] In doing so, Christ transforms the barren distance between God and creature from one in which contradiction reigns (*Wort-Unwort*) to a fruitful distance in which the free dialogue of love can participate in the

perspective. According to this perspective, all authentic speech must be true (i.e., it actually discloses something of the speaker), free (i.e., it is expressed by the speaker themself), and relational (i.e., it is aimed at being heard by others). This ontology of the word could be usefully compared to certain prevailing philosophical versions of the same. Caseralla makes the first steps toward such an undertaking in "The Expression and the Form of the Word: Trinitarian Hermeneutics and the Sacramentality of Language in Hans Urs von Balthasar," *Renascence* 48, no. 2 (1996): 111–36. Caseralla notes that "Balthasar would agree with J. L. Austin that human speech is a mode of expression in which the utterer can perform as well as describe what is being said" (Caseralla, "The Expression and the Form of the Word," 132). But this is only so, for Balthasar, due to the creature's participation in the eternal Word's expressive flexibility—the Word who performs (*expressus expressivus*) as well as describes (*expressio expressa*) the truth of God. Thus, why Balthasar parts ways with the so-called ordinary language philosophies in the wake of Wittgenstein as just so many "sterile forms of functionalism" (TL.1, 14; cf. the essay "God's Speech" in ET.5).

16. TD.4, 338. Cf. *TuG*, 25.
17. Cf. GL.7, 265, *Prayer* (H), 51, 53, *Prayer* (L), 154.
18. *Prayer* (H), 51.
19. *Ibid*. The emphasis on election is a point that resonates with Barth, for whom "election is the sum of the gospel" (CD II/2, 3). See Balthasar's discussion of this point at *TKB*, 121–5.

Trinitarian exchange (*Wort-Antwort*).[20] Every creaturely prayer thus takes place in the space opened up by Christ.[21]

This "expressive" Christology (another clearly Barthian[22] feature of *Prayer*) has specific advantages. Perhaps most importantly, it assumes a profound coherence to Christ's mission-identity, and so immediately guards against certain Christological errors. It is not, for instance, that Jesus is a particularly gifted praying person who thereby manages to find favor with God (i.e., Adoptionism).[23] Rather, only the preexistent Son could pray in the way Jesus does, as one who calls God "*Abba*."[24] As a result of this, creaturely prayer "in Christ" does not lead merely to a "penultimate station" somewhere short of the Father but constitutes genuine creaturely participation in the self-expressed "language of God."[25]

4.1.2 God's Language in Historical Form

However, the expressive Christology being described here can seem to come too much "from above," and indeed Balthasar's approach has been criticized for existing "up in the clouds."[26] Therefore, it is important to stress the necessarily historical nature of Balthasar's argument here. First of all, when seen within the overall context of covenant history, Christ's arrival as the definitive Word of blessing affirms, rather than diminishes, God's commitment to the concrete reality of covenant. Earlier (cf. Sections 3.3.1 and 3.3.2 *supra*) I described the Trinitarian prayer in terms of a combination of *aletheia* and *emeth*—if Christ is clearly the "unveiling" of the triune God (*aletheia*), he is also necessarily an affirmation of God's ongoing commitment (*emeth*) to the covenant, even to the point of fulfilling both sides of it. We will see this more clearly in a moment when we turn to

---

20. Cf. TL.2, 107–15, 122. Joshua Furnal is thus wrong to allege that in Balthasar distance is univocally a negative consequence of human sin, experienced by the creature as anxiety (see Furnal, *Catholic Theology after Kierkegaard* [Oxford: Oxford University Press, 2015], 153). Distance, as we saw in Chapter 3, is a feature of Trinitarian love itself. Christ comes not to collapse the distance between God and man but to make it a *productive* distance in which prayer can occur (cf. also ET.2, 63).

21. Cf. *WiC?* 62: "[Christ] gives us the 'space' in which to live a life of faith, but he does it by making himself the first and model act of faith."

22. Cf., for example, Barth, CD.III/4, 94 and CD.III/3, 274ff. Cf. also Herbert McCabe, who, following Barth, holds that Christ "is not just the one who prays, not even the one who prays best, *he is sheer prayer*" (McCabe, *God Matters* [London: Continuum, 1987], 220, italics mine).

23. Cf. *PT*, 172.

24. Balthasar's basic hermeneutical principle when considering Christ is, "Who must he be, to behave and act in this way?" (GL.2, 149).

25. Cf. *Prayer* (H), 51.

26. Gerard O'Hanlon, "The Jesuits and Modern Theology: Rahner, von Balthasar and Liberation Theology," *Irish Theological Quarterly* 58, no.1 (1992): 25–45, 34.

consider Christ *at* prayer, but it is already indicated, for instance, by the way in which Christ insists on praying from within the covenantal faith, repeatedly even using the exact words of the psalms (e.g., compare Ps. 118:22 with Mt. 21:42, Mk 12:10, or Lk. 20:17; or compare Ps. 31:5 with Lk. 23:46). "The Old Testament is not past for [Jesus]" but rather "contains a definite pattern, as it were, for his earthly life, [and] lays down certain points from which he cannot depart, and [. . .] which create a unified course in his life."[27] Jesus invokes the faith of Israel not only as a way of establishing his own authority publicly (e.g., Jn 5:46) but also in his private communication to the Father (e.g., Mt. 27:46). That the Son prays in this way is no incidental feature of his mission. The form of covenant is never superseded: "God has *no other* relationship with his creation, no other way of bringing the world back to him [than in covenant]; [likewise] man has no other access to God than this."[28] The covenant form does not just *contain* grace, according to Balthasar—it *is* grace.[29] Christology therefore gains nothing if it forsakes the picture of faith found in the Old Testament in favor of a hermetically sealed Christomonism; indeed, such a Christology would lose what is necessary for making sense of the Christ who actually appears in history.[30]

By giving a new force and vividness to the covenant faith, Christ not only ratifies its actual historical development in Israel, but also "elevates and translates" the words and concepts—and therefore expands the confines—of covenant in a way which is decisive for the future trajectory of humanity's development toward God.[31] It was precisely this elevation of the historical which was what "Moses could not do."[32] To be clear, what Christ accomplishes is no simple negation (of

---

27. *TH*, 54. That his words of prayer are frequently taken directly from the prior prayers of Israel suggest the extent to which Jesus' own self-consciousness is rooted in the historical reality of Covenant faith. Still, from the Christian point of view, this salvation history flows proleptically *from* Christ as "an account *of him*, not preceding him" (*TH*, 55).

28. *Prayer* (H), 37.

29. Ibid., 37–8; cf. Speyr, *World of Prayer*, 80.

30. See the section on Irenaeus at GL.2, 31ff. for discussion of this point. We will see in the next section the extent to which Balthasar's conception of the *fides Christi* is decisively shaped by certain Old Testament notions of faith and sight. Charges of supersessionism in Balthasar (such as those made, for instance, by Daniel Rancour-Laferriere in *Imagining Mary: A Psychoanalytic Perspective on Devotion to Mary* [London: Routledge, 2017], 71) therefore seem to me difficult to sustain. Indeed, by integrating the Old Testament perspective so thoroughly into his Christology, Balthasar appears to me to be resisting any easy dichotomy of "law" and "faith" (a dichotomy he rejected as characteristic of an early-modern form of Protestantism). Anthony Sciglitano pursues the question fruitfully in *Marcion and Prometheus: Balthasar Against the Expulsion of Jewish Origins from Modern Religious Dialogue* (Freiburg im Breisgau: Herder, 2014).

31. See *Prayer* (H), 54; cf. *WiC?*, 64–5: "[Christ] is the continuance of the covenant [. . .]. He *is* the covenant because his humanity is lived in complete obedience to his divinity."

32. GL.7, 91.

the particular, the historical), but a reintegration in a higher register, which is the contemplative register. This is nowhere else as obvious as in the Ascension, which Balthasar says "eternalizes everything about Christ that is of time and place and offers it to *contemplative eyes*."[33] In taking leave of the world, Christ in fact penetrates ever more deeply into its structures of existence and thus allows for further and more profound forms of closeness to his people: "I have many things yet to say to you" (Jn 16:12). Crucially, however, after the Ascension it is prayer which becomes the believer's method of participating in the ongoing dialogue with God. In handing over his mission to the Spirit, the Son relocates the word of prayer deep within our own "wordless groans" (Rom. 8:26). The great Pauline theme of spiritualization should be understood along these lines—that is, as an inhabiting of the given structures of reality (sensory, epistemic, even rhetorical) but now on a level of meaning beyond the literal.[34] We have already touched upon this point in Chapter 2 when we saw how Balthasar insists on grounding "authentic" mysticism in the Christ form. Christ progresses beyond the negative language of unsaying by presenting the Father in "forms of this world." What is relevant at this point is to note how Balthasar's expressive Christology does decidedly *not* come at the expense of the specific historical forms—indeed the exact words and images—inhabited by Christ at mission.[35]

Far from devaluing history, then, Balthasar's heavy emphasis on Christ as the prayer of God realized in the world provides the basis upon which to affirm both the historical form of covenantal faith and God's ongoing involvement in the world. That God speaks is sheer grace. That God speaks in the form of the Son who enables us to speak back suggests the radical depths of even the simplest prayer—*amen*.

4.2 Christ at Prayer

But this question must be approached from another angle as well, lest it give the impression of univocity to Christ's mission-identity. It is perhaps easy enough to understand Christ as prayer, given Balthasar's characteristically strong Christology. But as soon as one grants the point, the really relevant questions emerge: *What is*

---

33. *MiH*, 298; cf. *Prayer* (H), 69, and *TuG*, 202–3.

34. Cf. *Prayer* (H), 54. Likewise Christ's body and blood persist in the form of the Eucharist—a simultaneous inhabiting-of-while-transcending the forms of this world. See the following text for discussion of the sacramental dimensions of prayer.

35. Since Incarnation is in essential continuity with Creation, certain forms and images exist in the world which Christ can avail himself of in explaining his mission (like the parables of the mustard seed or the grain of wheat, for instance); but these "likenesses" always need the Son's explicit word in order to fully "develop" into the fullness of revelation (cf. *MiH*, 287–8). There is also the issue of Christ's *silences*, which are also part of his expressive character in mission (this point regarding silence will be taken up in Chapter 5).

God saying in prayer, and *how* is God saying it? If one of the virtues of Balthasar's account of prayer is that it arguably rescues us from many of the abstractions and generalities of "natural" spiritualities, in favor of grounding Christian prayer in the specific form of Christ, it becomes of decisive importance what we see when we look at Christ at prayer. Here is another spot at which Balthasar's approach takes a significant turn, and we see him resisting two distinct yet related tendencies prevalent in the theological debates of his time. In the first instance, Balthasar was resisting the traditional argument, usually traced to Aquinas, that Christ had no faith, but rather an "immediate vision" of the Father and of the plan which would fulfill his mission while on earth. For reasons I will expand upon later in the text, Balthasar is unsatisfied by this argument, primarily for what it does to the efficacy and depth of Sonship: "If [Christ] knows everything better than other men, if he decides everything on the basis of total insight, how can he be open at every moment to the inspiration of the Holy Spirit, in order at all times to be doing not his own will but the Father's?"[36] Christ must be more than a prophet in possession of a certain vision; he must, rather, existentially perform a new mode of faith and open it up to the faithful in turn if his mission is to be a success. Christ at prayer is therefore evidence, for Balthasar, that Sonship involves decision, a decision which those "in Christ" can likewise make. In both cases (i.e., for Christ and for the creature), the realm of this decision is prayer. Related to the extrinsicist Christology of immediate vision was a certain conception of church as a self-contained society; this was the second contemporary perspective Balthasar sought to undermine with his account of prayer as a dynamic, dramatic state of being in which the one who prays becomes more and more aware of their mission and therefore their identity. It is this outfolding of mission-consciousness that Balthasar believes the church must learn from the example of Christ at prayer.

Let us consider these points in more detail, starting with the question of how prayer relates to Christ's unique mission-identity.

4.2.1 Mission-Consciousness and Prayer

Christ's identity is always coterminous with his mission; this is what defines the Son's unique theodramatic efficacy.[37] Accordingly, his prayers cannot be considered discrete or separable aspects of his personhood; indeed, they are described by Balthasar as "*the* integral part [of his] earthly work."[38] Certainly Christ was a man who prayed abundantly. Scripture records significant moments of prayer at the beginning (e.g., Mt. 4:1-11), the middle (e.g., Lk. 9:18, Mk. 8:6), and the end (e.g., John 17) of his public ministry. Luke in particular emphasizes the place of prayer at each of the "great events of [Christ's] mission" (Lk. 3:21; 9:18, 28; 11:1; 22:42; 23:34), not to mention the "frequent" retreats into the wilderness

---

36. YCYYG, 317–18.
37. Cf. TD.3, 149.
38. TD.3, 110 (my italics); cf. GL.2, 170.

to pray (Lk. 5:16).[39] In order to really be considered "integral" to mission, however, these must not just be exemplary instances of prayer to be imitated—indeed, the many prayers in the wilderness can hardly be imitated!—rather, they must themselves actually *accomplish* something new.[40] What they accomplish, according to Balthasar, is nothing less than the reconciliation of infinite and finite freedom.[41] In Christ at prayer, Monophysitic and Adoptionist metaphysics are both rendered untenable in equal measure inasmuch as we see two wills—a divine and a human—conformed ever more closely in the execution of mission. It is in this sense that prayer can be considered "integral" because it was in prayer that Christ integrated his life and his mission so thoroughly as to make them effectively indistinguishable: "[Christ] is not an 'autonomous' person who subsequently undertook, as a service to the Father, to transmit the Father's message to the world, [in fact] He [i.e., Christ] cannot possess the Father more perfectly in himself than by letting himself be 'missioned' by the Father."[42] In other words, Christ's awareness of mission is primarily his awareness of being sent (the German *Sendung* signals both meanings), and it is this characteristic that marks Jesus' prayers.[43] In short, "the Father is not addressed in isolation from the mission" of the Son, and, in turn, "prayer is essential to the One who is sent" as the method of sustaining him in mission (Balthasar even describes prayer at one point as the Son's "food").[44]

Seen in light of what we have already said about the Trinitarian background of prayer, the aforementioned points follow on naturally enough. But this constant

---

39. See discussion at GL.7, 244–50. In the fact that Christ turns to the Father in prayer at every key moment of his mission, Balthasar detects a "practical teaching" with regard to creaturely prayer: "[Prayer] cannot, it must not, be self-contemplation. On the contrary it must be a devotional attention to what is essentially the non-I" (*Prayer* [H], 115). We will return to this point—prayer as a method of expanding one's I-consciousness—in the following chapter.

40. John McDowell is right to note how *imitatio Christi* can easily become "too formal and external" if it is divorced from an awareness of the sheer grace that Christ accomplishes on our behalf (see McDowell, "'Openness to the World': Karl Barth's Evangelical Theology of Christ as the Pray-er," *Modern Theology* 25, no. 2 [2009], 253–83).

41. Dalzell's otherwise competent study on this topic suffers from a noticeable lack of attention to prayer. When he does mention prayer (*The Dramatic Encounter of Divine and Human Freedom*, 55–6, e.g.), it is simply as one of the capacities that finite freedom has to dispense with itself in obedience. Though it would be unwise to read too much into such a passing reference, there is reason to think prayer figures more significantly into Balthasar's understanding of freedom—finite *and* infinite—than Dalzell seems to suggest.

42. CSL, 186.

43. A typical prayer of thanksgiving (Mt. 11:25, for instance) is never made without an accompanying acknowledgment of having been sent (Mt. 11:27). Even the HPP of John 17 must be understood as a prayer of mission ("Glorify your Son, *that your Son may glorify you*").

44. TD.3, 170.

prayer relationship between Father and Son nevertheless proceeds according to a dramatic rhythm that can be characterized in terms of *kenosis* and *pleroma*. (These terms bear a relation to the combined *aletheia* and *emeth* constitution of Trinitarian prayer discussed in the previous chapter. If *aletheia* is a kind of *kenosis* in which the person pours themselves forth in a moment of total self-disclosure, then *emeth* is a kind of *pleroma* in which that fullness subsists faithfully with the one for whom it has been poured out.) In mission, the Son is formed by these rhythms, as we see, for instance, in three key moments when Christ receives words of affirmation from the Father in response to prayers of self-abandonment on his part: at the baptism in the Jordan, when Jesus "consented" and the voice from heaven said, "This is my beloved Son, with whom I am well pleased" (Mt. 3:15-17); during the transfiguration on Tabor, when at prayer before God Jesus is again likewise affirmed (Mt. 17:5); and in the lead-up to the Passion, when Jesus' soul is "troubled" and he is told, "I have glorified [my name], and I will glorify it again" (Jn 12:28).[45] In other words, the Son has to trust the Father regarding the successful execution of mission, a trust he exhibits again and again in prayer.

Although this point mitigates the concern that Balthasar's account of the *fides Christi* risks undervaluing the legitimate exercise of human freedom, a distinction is in order. Whereas the creature (as we will see further in the next chapter) relies on prayer in order to receive his or her mission and therefore identity, the Son is aware of his mission-identity but relies on prayer in order to sustain him "to the end."[46] In this sense, we could put the point in strong terms by saying that prayer is the substance of Sonship while Christ is at mission on earth. The Son knows perfectly from the start that his mission is to represent the Father, to "give them the words you gave me" (Jn 17:8). The ends of the Son's mission are not obscure to him, as is so often the case in the creature. However, the Son's perfect foreknowledge in regards to the ends of his mission does not guarantee him a specific vision of how that mission will be carried out: "About that day or hour no one knows, not even the angels in heaven, *nor the Son*, but only the Father" (Mt. 24:36). Commenting on this passage, Balthasar observes: "Certainly [Christ] was always accompanied by an implicit knowledge of an hour appointed by the Father and known only to him; [but] *what* this hour would bring was not to be anticipated."[47] Balthasar presents this nescience in mission as a logical (if mysterious) consequence of Incarnation itself, in which the Son "'emptied himself' of his divine form (Phil. 2:7) precisely

---

45. See discussion at *CSL*, 187–8. In *Engagement with God*, Balthasar evokes a musical metaphor, comparing the Son's consent to the Father as it is expressed especially in prayer to a "pedal note, sounding beneath all the intricacies of the fugue of his actions" (*EG*, 50).

46. McIntosh comments: "Whereas other human beings are already conscious subjects who struggle in various ways to uncover the truth of their identity, Jesus simply *is* the personal mission (the Person) of the Son and his fully human identity is given in and with his obedience to the filial relationship with the Father that this mission enacts" (see *Cambridge Companion to Hans Urs von Balthasar*, 33).

47. TD.3, 181.

so that he could be humanly obedient unto death."[48] It is only by doing so that Christ can be said to truly take on the form of human freedom and, by taking it on, redeem it (Nazianzen's dictum: "That which has not been assumed has not been redeemed").

Prayer is thus an actualization of freedom, not a passive surrender. It is the Son's form of continual (re-)commitment to the task of mission. As Yenson notes, "Prayer and action do not exist in juxtaposition in Jesus' life but mutually inhere."[49] This can be thought of in terms of receptivity (*Empfänglichkeit*) but again a distinction must be drawn. Although the Son's eternal "form of existence" is total receptivity vis-à-vis the Father, his is, as a consubstantial freedom, an *active receptivity* which also gives back fruitfully and eucharistically what it has received.[50] In prayer, the Son exercises this active receptivity in a way that is inclusive of humanity (as we can clearly see in the High Priestly Prayer). It is essential that in actualizing this freedom, the Son be confronted with the full range of human possibilities, which come to him in the form of the many instances of faithlessness (e.g., Mk 8:14-21) or outright rejection (Lk. 22:54-62) that Jesus is subjected to in mission. If Christ is sent as prayer in response to the "ever-escalating drama" of salvation (i.e., word and un-word), then at prayer Christ must confront those same dynamics in particular, historical ways.[51] Each instance of resistance on the part of sinful humanity suggests to the Son more and more of the truly universal scope of his mission. In other words, confronting the worldly "No" subjectively prepares the God-*man* to give the objective "Yes" as the *God*-man. Balthasar thus takes the lived history of Jesus very seriously as a key aspect of the dramatic unfolding of his mission: "Jesus undergoes a historical learning process with regard to his fellow humans."[52] As true human himself, Christ must be susceptible, at whatever

---

48. *YCYYG*, 319.

49. Yenson, *Existence as Prayer*, 132. The unity of contemplation in action among the faithful is often noted as a feature of Balthasar's thought, but what is less often noticed is how this unity is grounded in the prior unity of identity and mission in Christ—a unity that (in both cases) expresses itself in prayer.

50. *TH*, 26. For this reason, a better translation of *Empfänglichkeit* would be "responsiveness" than "receptivity," which regrettably invokes a sense of passivity. The notion of responsiveness or "active receptivity" lies at the heart of Balthasar's much-debated ontology of gender, according to which it is proper to the Son's "(super-)feminine" constitution vis-à-vis the Father to receive everything that he is, even as he simultaneously stands in a "(super-)masculine" relation to the Spirit who proceeds from the Father and the Son together (cf. TD.5, 91). In turn this pattern sets the stage for anthropology: humanity in relation to God is essentially feminine (cf. TD.3, 288) and so on. There are of course fierce debates as to the adequacy of the sexual metaphors, which I referred to in Chapter 1. Without minimizing the subtlety of those debates, it is worth stressing here just how *active* this "feminine" responsiveness is.

51. Cf. TD.3, 181.

52. TD.3, 179; cf. ibid., 182, *Unless*, 30ff., and *YCYYG*, 318–9.

general level of logical necessity, to the same "No" against which he sets himself. Thus, the possibility of Jesus being tempted, to which Balthasar ascribes particular significance (and thus also why the seriousness of the devil's temptations escalate in correspondence with the stages of Jesus' mission).[53] In any case, prayer is always implicated in this "learning process" as the indispensable activity through which the Son "matures" into the fullness of mission.[54] Prayer is the site of Sonship coming to earthly fruition.

Maximus the Confessor (*c.* 580–662) similarly saw Christ's temptations as theaters of instruction in which his finite freedom came to embrace its infinite source. Balthasar's Maximian *ressourcement* (though a highly significant historical undertaking in its own right) bears on our current argument inasmuch as Balthasar appeals to Maximus for an account of what is happening when Christ prays. Certainly, the interactions of freedoms (creaturely and divine) in Christ were a central occupation of Maximus, especially during the height of the Monothelite controversy in the seventh century.[55] In particular, the Gethsemane scene becomes important as a dramatization of the interaction of Christ's two wills. According to Maximus, the agony in the garden displays not a *conflict* of divine and human wills in Christ, but evidence of a necessary *alignment* of Christ's human will to his heavenly mission. The two wills are "different" but not in disagreement.[56] Here,

---

53. "The highest work between Father and Son is accomplished while the devil's highest work is also accomplished" (TD.5 209); though Balthasar is quick to add, "But [. . .] internally they [i.e., Satan's highest work and God's highest work] have *no point of contact*," and in the Cross, Satan's highest act is shown not to outpace God's. Cf. also TD.3 168, as well as the discussion of the dragon's rage at TD.5, 210ff.

54. Cf. *Unless*, 32 and *MCS*, 103.

55. Cf. Paul Blowers, *Maximus the Confessor: Jesus Christ and the Transfiguration of the World* (Oxford: Oxford University Press, 2016), 156–65. For historical background, see Paul Verghese, "Monothelete Controversy: A Historical Survey," *Greek Orthodox Theological Review* 13, 2 (1968): 196–208.

56. Maximus, *On the Cosmic Mystery of Jesus Christ: Selected Writings from St. Maximus the Confessor*, trans. Paul Blowers and Robert Louis Wilken (Crestwood, New York: St. Vladimir's Seminary Press, 2003), 174. Maximus' technical discussion of this point is extensive and focuses specifically on the *gnomic* will of Christ, understood as the volitional, self-interested aspect of finite rationality involved in decision-making. "Most simply put, gnomic will is free will as we rational creatures actually experience it, comprising deliberation and subsequent choice over the proper course of action toward a perceived good" (Blowers, *Maximus the Confessor*, 122). It was the gnomic will in Christ that was harmonized in prayer and obedience (at least according to Maximus' early position, before the polemical confrontation with Pyrrhus caused him to deny a Christic *gnome*). Léthel summarizes, in a view Balthasar endorses: "The human will that Christ has for our salvation reveals itself then at Gethsemane in the *supreme engagement of its human freedom*" (*Théologie de l'Agonie du Christ: La Liberté humaine du Fils de Dieu et son importance sotériologique mises en lumière par Saint Maxime le Confesseur* [Paris: Beauchesne, 1979], 98; cited at TL.2, 70 n.6).

as Marcel Doucet suggests, Maximus follows Gregory Nazianzus, for whom, there is an "*alterity*" of divine will and the divinized human will in Christ "but *no contrariety* in the object shared respectively by each will"—that object being the mission proper to Sonship.[57] Elsewhere, Maximus likens the alignment of finite and infinite freedom to "someone rowing a boat downstream and [thereby increasing] the intensity of its movement," an image Balthasar borrows at one point.[58] So Christian prayer in the mode of Christ is for Maximus no "serene contemplative vision uplifting the mind beyond the fray of materiality" but a truly dramatic-dialogue relationship with the Father that gives rise to action.[59] It is this account of alterity but not contrariety that Balthasar endorses, believing it provides a satisfying view of the "dynamic relationship between the Divine Person of Christ and his divine nature."[60] It is Maximus' achievement, in Balthasar's view, to "supersede in advance all Christologies that would speak of Jesus as the 'empty' vessel of the divine will—or at least [to give] them their correct interpretation as describing an active operation of the man Jesus that remains [. . .] even in his *kenosis*."[61] That is, even the prayer of complete self-emptying ("Let this cup pass from me, yet not as I will but as You will" [Mt. 26:39]) is a prayer of mission, a prayer of "decision."[62]

4.2.2 The "Pistis Christou" and Prayer

Notice that in the previous paragraph I have cited *Cosmic Liturgy*, *Prayer*, and the *Theo-Logic*: that Balthasar was willing to insert himself into (indeed, to launch) technical patrological debates in the 1940s in pursuit of a notion he would expand upon in *Prayer* in the 1950s and later revisit and restate in a systematic form in the 1980s not only shows the revolving nature of his thought on prayer but also suggests how he tends to think through his own positions

---

For background, see Peter Karavites, "*Gnome's* Nuances: From Its Beginning to the End of the Fifth Century," *Classical Bulletin* 66 (1990), 9–34, and for Balthasar's discussion, see *CL*, 266 ff.

57. Marcel Doucet, "Est-ce que le monothélisme a fait autant d'illustrés victimes? Réflexions sur un ouvrage de F.-M. Léthel," in *Science et esprit* 35 (1983): 53–83, here 55.

58. See *CL*, 145.

59. Blowers, *Maximus the Confessor*, 117. Balthasar aligns Maximus against the hesychastic tradition, saying that for him the "quieting of the heart's urgent quest does not at all have the character of self-abandonment" but rather a progressive, dynamic aspect (*CL*, 142).

60. *CL*, 145.

61. TL.2, 70.

62. *Prayer* (H), 148. The decision aspect of prayer is "vital" for Balthasar, and will reemerge in Chapter 6 on eschatology, since it is the decision aspect which shows prayer to be a dynamic act across time which can thereby contribute to the building up of the Kingdom.

with reference to the prevailing theological discourse. This tendency is on display again in the question of Christ's faith, a hotly debated topic during the middle of the twentieth century that bears upon the notion of Christ's prayers in a rather direct way. I have said that for Balthasar Christ at prayer both exhibits a genuine faith and even displays nescience—these judgments indicate just how progressive Balthasar was during this period, since in the schools in which he was trained, it would have been highly unusual to "even raise the question of the existence and nature of faith exercised by Jesus during his earthly life."[63] The idea of a faithless immediate vision in Christ was challenged in the modern era, however, with Sobrino and Rahner, for instance, both raising critical questions about "the faith of Jesus."[64] Rahner in particular questioned the usefulness of the very concept of a beatific vision,[65] a position with which Balthasar was inclined to agree.[66] Specifically, Balthasar argues that the faith of Christ (*pistis Christou Jesou*) referred to throughout the Pauline corpus (cf. Gal. 3:25; 5:6 Col. 1:15; 1 Tim. 1:14; 3:13; 2 Tim. 1:13; 3:15) cannot be understood simply as an objective genitive (i.e., faith *in* Jesus Christ); this reduces Christ merely to a receptacle for human faith, an option that we have already seen is precluded by the strong Christology of expression and the active dynamic of Sonship in mission. But neither can these Pauline phrases be simply understood as subjective genitives (i.e., referring to "the act of faith of Christ himself").[67] This would risk positing a univocal identity between human faith and Christ's, thus upending Balthasar's

---

63. Gerard O'Collins and Daniel Kendall, "The Faith of Jesus," *Theological Studies* 53 (1992): 403–23, here 403. The traditional teaching derives from Thomas (see ST-III 7.3; cf. Peter Lombard, *Sent.* 3, 26, 4).

64. See Jon Sobrino, *Christology at the Crossroads* (New York: Orbis, 1978), 79ff, as well as Karl Rahner and Wilhelm Thüsing, *A New Christology* (London: Burns & Oates, 1980): 143–54.

65. Rahner, *Theological Investigations* Vol. I: *God, Christ, Mary and Grace* (London: Darton, Longman, and Todd, 1961), 170ff.

66. Cf. TD.3, 195.

67. See the essay "Fides Christi" in ET.2, 43–80, here 57 (see 64ff. for Balthasar's arguments against the Thomistic trajectory). Richard Longenecker claimed the authority of consensus in 2011 when he argued that "from the late nineteenth century to the present" the subjective genitive interpretation has been the dominant one among biblical scholars and theologians (Longenecker, *Introducing Romans: Critical Issues in Paul's Most Famous Letter* [London: Eerdmans, 2011], 318). But Benjamin Schliesser ably challenges the strength of this assertion, especially by uncovering more nuanced and participatory senses of the phrase advanced by Barth and Haußleiter (Schliesser, "'Exegetical Amnesia' and ΠΙΣΤΙΣ ΧΡΙΣΤΟΥ: The 'Faith *of* Christ' in Nineteenth-century Pauline Scholarship," *The Journal of Theological Studies* 66, no. 1 [2015]: 61–89). Balthasar's essay in *Explorations* is thus prescient.

entire analogical approach.[68] He suggests instead, following Gustav Deissmann, a "mystical genitive" that implies a participatory dynamic: "Christian faith means, then, faith *within* the reality of Christ, faith that as such shares in the fullness of the truth, the love, the action, the suffering, and the Resurrection of Christ and in all the other aspects of his reality and indeed is made possible by them."[69] Prayer is the essential mechanism here as both the method by which Christ expands the "acting area" available to finite freedom and the means of creaturely entry into it.[70]

Christ's faith exhibits a unique view of the Father befitting the Son's unique mission-consciousness. In prayer we see how this faith incorporates but goes beyond the straightforward Old Testament ideal of a "direct seeing of God"—it is rather the Son's unity in love with the Father who sends him.[71] Before he is (or as the condition of his being) the one who "sees" God perfectly, Christ is the "Beloved" (Mt. 3:17; 17:5). And in love, the freedom of the other is never "swallowed up" by stale foreknowledge; rather, it is given abundant space to play out.[72] This relates to the point about "Trinitarian surprise" first discussed in Chapter 3 (cf. Section 3.3.1 *supra*). Thus, Balthasar speaks of a "dimming, a non-use of [. . .] divine vision" on Christ's part, but always as an aspect of Christ's overall performance of Sonship.[73] Certainly Speyr is an influence here but no more than Siewerth, for whom love is the overarching transcendental that ultimately only proves itself in the full kenotic self-dispossession of death.[74] In addition to taking the historical faith of Christ

---

68. For a more recent position that risks this same sort of univocity, see James Mackey, who reads Galatians 2 as an exhortation to exactly the same faith as Jesus (Mackey, *Jesus the Man and the Myth* [New York: Paulist, 1979], 163, 188).

69. ET.2, 58; Balthasar then quickly distances himself from Deissmann's related assertion that the faith of Jesus is therefore "identical with" the faith of Abraham, but nevertheless the essential "direction" of Deissmann's gloss is endorsed. And to the aforementioned point regarding charges of supersessionism, Balthasar is clear here that Abraham's faith is fundamentally consistent with and oriented toward Christ's.

70. TD.3, 51.

71. ET.2, 73.

72. TD.5, 96; cf. WiC? 61.

73. TL.2, 288.

74. Cf. TL.2, 187, for example. McIntosh renders a concurrent opinion at *Christology from within*, 48–9: "Any awareness Jesus has of the uniqueness of his filial relationship with the Father is not an innate theoretical knowledge but is progressively discovered in practice as Jesus becomes painfully familiar with the alienation from God in which others live." Some of Balthasar's critics take issue with what they consider his perilous position on the Son's imperfect vision of the Father during mission. See, for example, Pitstick, *Light in Darkness*, 166–90 or Matthew Levering, *Scripture and Metaphysics: Aquinas and the Renewal of Trinitarian Theology* (Malden: Blackwell, 2004), 132, or Berger, "Woher Kommen die Thesen Hans Urs von Balthasar zur Hölle?" Oakes responds to Pitstick directly in "The Internal Logic of Holy Saturday in the Theology of Hans Urs von Balthasar," *International Journal*

seriously, this approach also lends credence to a central claim of this chapter that Christ's prayers open up the space in which creaturely prayer can acquire Christological depth; this is because Christ's "dimming" of vision resonates with the human experience of faith (cf. 1 Cor. 13:12!). Indeed, it is soteriologically necessary that this "dimming" occur, if Christ is to truly show "how man comes to terms with God."[75]

4.2.3 Trinitarian Inversion

But again I must stress that Christ is not capable of this reconciliation as a man of heroic faith but as a consubsistent preexistent Person of the Trinity who undertakes to pray in and through history. I have already said (Section 3.2 *supra*) that the Spirit plays a vital role as the "architect of the Son's return to the Father" precisely as the driving force behind every genuine prayer.[76] All that has been said here about prayer as the process of the Son's mission-consciousness coming to fruition, therefore, cannot for a moment be separated from the necessary Trinitarian infrastructure, which Balthasar describes in terms of the "Trinitarian inversion."[77] Christ experiences the Spirit as not just the medium but the substance of intimacy with the Father who sends him: "The Son *never* encounters the Father, and the Father never encounters the Son, except in the Holy Spirit."[78] Of course, the Spirit's role here is not heteronomous to Christ's own mission-consciousness: "Jesus obeys the Spirit, not as one alien to our outside himself (any more than a religious does when he obeys his rule), but as the bearer of God's will."[79] That is to say, obedience is the economic, historical form of eternal Sonship that seeks to eucharistically

---

of *Systematic Theology* 9 (2007): 184–99, and Pitstick replies in kind with "Development of Doctrine, or Denial? Balthasar's Holy Saturday and Newman's *Essay*," *International Journal of Systematic Theology* 11, no. 2 (2009): 129–45. For another contemporary version of the debate over Christ's earthly vision of the Father, see Thomas Joseph White, "The Voluntary Action of the Earthly Christ and the Necessity of the Beatific Vision," *The Thomist* 69 (2005): 497–534, especially 497–98, and Thomas Weinandy, "The Beatific Vision and the Incarnate Son," *The Thomist* 70 (2006): 605–15. For a constructive treatment of Balthasar's approach to the problem, see Randall Rosenberg, "Christ's Human Knowledge: A Conversation with Lonergan and Balthasar," *Theological Studies* 71 (2010): 817–45.

75. TL.2, 288.
76. *Prayer* (H), 74.
77. Again, the main discussions of the inversion occur at TD.3, 183–91 and 515–23, although other references abound (see, e.g., TL.3, 308). The "inversion" refers to the fact that the Spirit appears to have a clear biblical role in "driving" the Son in mission and thus in a sense stands *over* him (e.g., Lk. 1:35; Mt. 3:16; Mk 1:12), despite being said (in the West) to "spirate" *from* the Father and the Son.
78. TL.3, 369 (italics mine). Consider Lk. 10:21 here (". . . full of joy *through the Holy Spirit*, Jesus said, 'I praise you, Father . . .'").
79. *CSL*, 190; the analogy to a religious rule comes from Speyr (cf. *FGAS* 60).

give everything it has and is to the Father.⁸⁰ In a similar vein, O'Donnell elaborates on the Spirit's role "in and over" Christ in terms largely resonant with Balthasar's account:

> The Spirit is in him (Jesus) divinizing his humanity and rendering him completely docile to the will of the Father. As such, the Spirit is always the Spirit of Jesus. But at the same time the Spirit is over him. The Spirit makes known to Jesus the will of the Father. Through the Spirit as a unique person or hypostasis Jesus comes to know the Father's will. The nature of his mission unfolds through the impulses of the Spirit which Jesus must follow in obedience even to the point of his death-cry on the cross. In this sense, the Spirit remains the Spirit of the sending Father. But the convergence between the Spirit of Jesus and the sent Spirit of the Father is precisely the Son's yes of obedience. The Son is nothing of himself. He is from the Father in the Spirit.⁸¹

If it is in the "Yes" of obedience to the Father (i.e., his total consenting to being sent) that the Son exhibits his ability to send forth the Spirit (as he does decisively at Jn 20:22), then it appears that the Spirit is working in two directions at once.⁸² This is consistent with Christ's twofold motion "to the Father and from the Father" as we already saw. Traditionally, the economic terms that have been associated with the two earthly "states" of Christ are the *status exaltationis* and the *status*

---

80. Compare McIntosh: "By placing himself at the disposal of the Father under the direction of the Spirit, Jesus accomplishes a kind of super-eminent act of loving, an enactment in human terms of the eternal Son's mode of existence" (*Christology from within*, 47).

81. John O'Donnell, "In Him and Over Him: The Holy Spirit in the Life of Jesus," *Gregorianum* 70, no. 1 (1989): 25–45, here 43. Balthasar's recourse to the notion of a "trinitarian inversion" constitutes a creative attempt to engage another one of the prominent theological debates of his time, regarding a so-called "Spirit Christology." While certain modern Western theologians argued for jettisoning the traditional understanding of spiration (Moltmann, for instance, at *Spirit of Life: A Universal Affirmation*, trans. Margaret Kohl [Minneapolis: Fortress, 1992], 306–8), others took the opportunity to emphasize the Spirit's preeminent role in sanctifying the Son's mission (see Kasper, *Jesus the Christ* [Mahwah: Paulist, 1976], 251). In a characteristic move, Balthasar amplifies the stronger position, claiming that the Spirit is not just the medium or guarantor of sanctifying grace in the Son's mission but the premise for its actualization: "It is the Spirit in [Christ] and over him who *makes [his] obedience possible*" (TD.3, 185, italics mine). In addition to taking the logic of the economy seriously, the inversion has the advantage of underlining the way in which the Spirit is responsible for relationship itself—an idea which is necessary to keep in mind if one is going to grasp what it means that "the Spirit prays in us." Whether or not one ultimately finds the inversion compelling, however, the essential point at the moment is that prayer is the means by which this Son-Spirit relationship plays out.

82. Cf. TD.3, 187.

exinanitionis, which correspond to what I have already identified as the rhythmic interplay between *kenosis* and *pleroma* that pertains to the Trinitarian relations as such.[83] We can also relate this distinction to the *aletheia-emeth* constitution of Trinitarian prayer (cf. Sections 3.3.1 and 3.3.2 *supra*), if Christ *as* prayer reveals God perfectly in time (*aletheia*) and Christ *at* prayer reveals God's steadfastness (to Godself, to humanity, to the covenant faith—*emeth*). Precisely as a mode of Trinitarian revelation, then, the Son's ability to share ("breathe forth") the Spirit stands in direct relation to his obedience to that same Spirit.[84] Since Christ's prayer is constant across these two states, and through the intermediary stages between them, Christology establishes the "concrete coordinates" of a creaturely theology of prayer.[85]

What the preceding discussion brings to the fore is that the objective basis of prayer is obedience—the attentive turning-to-God, the "Yes" which consents to being sent. Such prayer is "not servile, but filial," befitting not only the Son at prayer but also those adopted as God's children (cf. Gal. 4:6-7) who pray under the guidance of the Spirit.[86] Beyond this point, the subjective aspects of prayer will vary depending on the requirements of mission.[87] This objective "indifference is [itself] *always prayer*, prayer in the Spirit and to the Spirit, the prayer that asks to be able to receive the Father's will—or, what is the same thing, the Father's mission—in utter purity."[88] The only prayer that the Son ever prays, ultimately, is also the only essential one: "Not my will, but yours be done" (Lk. 22:42).

---

83. Cf. TD.3, 162ff. See useful discussion by Alberto Espezel, "La Cristología dramática de Balthasar," *Teología y Vida* 50 (2009), 305–18.

84. There is in Christ an "inner nexus binding his obedience with his glorification" (GL.7, 245). Cf. *Prayer* (H), 70. See also Barbarin, *Théologie et saintéte*, 88: "It is the obedience of the Son which reveals Trinitarian love."

85. TL.2, 406. This point was already discussed in Chapter 2 when I spoke of a Christoform mysticism which can go no further—either in ecstasy or in desolation—than the Son already has gone in prayer. Now the point acquires a fuller Christological basis as we see that the Son's "flexibility" in prayer is a necessary result of mission and is guaranteed by the Spirit who leads him in mission.

86. *CSL*, 191.

87. We will see this point reemerge in the following chapter: Balthasar attaches little importance to the subjective state of mind of the person who prays, provided they are praying in a genuine stance of obedience and "indifference" (see *Prayer* [L], 73). As regards Christ, this same point explains why Balthasar shows little interest in discerning a "psychology of Jesus" (see *YCYYG*, 315, e.g.).

88. TD.3, 521–2 (italics added). It is for this reason that Thomas calls the Lord's Prayer the "most perfect" prayer, in that it simultaneously expresses and forms the praying person in the open transparency that prayer most essentially is (ST II.II 83, 9 *respondeo*; cf. Augustine, *Ad Probam de Orando Deo*, cxxx 12).

4.3 The Ecclesial Dimensions

There is a further aspect of the "prayer Christology" I am developing here which must now be given some attention. For if one is inclined to take seriously the substance of Christ's prayers, then one cannot neglect consideration of the role of the church, understood as the community of faith established by Christ's prayers: "Christology cannot be separated from ecclesiology," and "there is no ecclesiology that is not, at its core, Christology."[89] In addition, the emphasis on the Trinitarian inversion underlines the way in which the Spirit, who was the active agent carrying the Son's prayers to the Father, is still responsible for those same prayers through the church and in history. At the same time, Balthasar admits, "nowhere except in the Catholic Church" can the contemplative task seem so hemmed in by "dogmas and institutions, definitions and paragraphs," which can appear "like so much barbed wire" for the one who desires only to look attentively at Christ and listen attentively for his Word.[90] There is always an ecclesial context to Christian prayer, then, but once the church starts to draw attention to itself, it shows it has misunderstood its role and deformed the overall rhythm of prayer. Indeed, the church "would not have the slightest plausibility [as] an autonomous form" apart from its basis in Christ.[91] Objectively speaking, however, the form of Christ in history that the contemplative seeks to gaze upon *is* the church (cf. Eph. 4:1-16), whose unity is constituted by the sacraments, especially the Eucharist ("this is my body . . .").[92] For the one formed by these objective rhythms (of sacrament, preaching, liturgy), their own prayer will likely not focus on the church at all but will still be born "from the very heart of the church."[93] That the church embodies its mission most completely when it shows itself to be wholly "transparent and transitive" to the Son is itself a proof of its Christological basis, since it is the Son's mission to be wholly transparent to the will of the Father.[94]

This last insight provides the basis for Balthasar's liturgical sensibilities, as well. He writes, "When the liturgy seems not to tolerate contemplation within itself

---

89. ET.2, 315, 22; cf. *TS*, 10-1: "We cannot wrench Christ loose from the Church, nor can we dismantle the Church to get to Christ." It is also the case that ecclesiology is one of the areas in which Balthasar proved to be at his most eclectic and unsystematic, writing at the start of the second volume of *Explorations in Theology* (on the church) that he was offering merely "a few building stones" for a future systematic account of the church (ET.2, 7), before admitting in ET.4 that he "mistrusts" any such attempt (11). Thus another reason why I have included the ecclesiological reflections in this current chapter.

90. *Prayer* (H), 53.

91. GL.1, 451; cf. ET.2, 27 and *Prayer* (L), 68-9.

92. Cf. *NE*, 87-103.

93. ET.2, 29; Balthasar identifies this experience especially with the Carmelite style of spirituality, mentioning Thérèse of Lisieux, John of the Cross, and Elizabeth of the Trinity specifically (*loc. cit.*).

94. ET.2, 36.

and alongside itself—especially through a busy activism, for example [. . .] then it degenerates into a worldly thing."⁹⁵ Prayer lies at the heart of liturgy, animating it and giving it is theological relevance.⁹⁶ This means that liturgy should never draw attention to itself but should always seek to point to the Son. Balthasar's polemic here is twofold: on the one hand, against those "activist" forms of liturgical experimentation that proliferated among certain quarters in the years after the Second Vatican Council; but equally against those performative and self-referential forms of worship which resemble more a stage play than anything else (Balthasar is impatient with the Baroque in this regard).⁹⁷ This claim mirrors the famous distinction in GL.1 between a theological aesthetics and an aesthetic theology; we might say that while there must be a liturgical aesthetics (which allow the Son to appear), there must never be an aesthetic liturgy (which points to itself). Existing as prayer and for the sake of prayer, liturgy is one of the chief ecclesial venues in which the Christ form appears. In other words, liturgy "does not replace" prayer, which remains the realm of personal encounter between the person and God, one in which the person has a positive duty to be attentive and to respond.⁹⁸

4.3.1 The Church's Prayer Constitution

Since the church exists in order to "transmit the voice of the Son," then the church is prayer at its source.⁹⁹ The individual who prays in the church is not engaged in a periphery activity but is participating "in the very being of the Church," in the "essential action" in which all the church's members are implicated.¹⁰⁰ This is indicated in what Balthasar identifies as the originary event of the church: the Marian "Yes" (whose "unconditional character" suggests the only true basis for claims of catholicity).¹⁰¹ "The dialogue which took place between the angel and Mary in Nazareth is continually being reenacted between God and the Church," Balthasar writes; in this exchange of freedom lies the "prototype" of every prayer in and of the church.¹⁰² To put the emphasis here implies no necessary Christological neglect, since it is precisely as "response" to the Word (who the Son is) that Mary gives her assent (this relationship is indicated dogmatically by the teaching on

---

95. Ibid., 30.
96. "Liturgical prayer that is Christian must be grounded in personal prayer and find its originating source there" (*VBR*, 328).
97. See the discussion at TD.4, 404.
98. ET.2, 30; cf. *VBR*, 326-8. The discussion of liturgy in the third chapter of *Prayer* resonates with these remarks
99. *Prayer* (L), 68.
100. Ibid., 72.
101. See *VBR*, 213-5, here 214. "Whoever posits the church's beginning later, say, with the calling of the Twelve or the bestowal of authority on Peter, has already missed what is essential" (*loc. cit.*). Cf. *MCS*, 141-4.
102. *Prayer* (H), 108-9, 195.

the Immaculate Conception, according to which Mary is declared spotless only "in view of the merits of Jesus Christ").[103] In this sense, Mary's Yes puts creation at the heart of the Trinitarian dialogue: "Mary's word of assent [serves as] the *reverberation* of the eternal word of assent which the Son gives in heaven to the Father's trinitarian decision to save mankind."[104] Mary's *fiat* is the Son's eternal *amen* on human lips.

That the church derives ontologically from Christ's prayers guarantees that it is also (therefore) a community of prayer in its own right. This is for Balthasar an aesthetic point, since the fuller unfolding of a given form never deforms the form itself.[105] It is also a hermeneutical point, since the narrative around which a community is constituted inevitably shapes the mode of the community's discourse. So if Christ is prayer, then "The narrative about [Christ] must also be received in prayer (of the community) and understood, mediated, and made one's own in the attitude of prayer."[106] If the Son is the Word of God spoken in history, the church is the historical interlocutor that receives that Word in the intended mode. Indeed, the church is *necessary* therefore as the condition of the "fulfillment" of Christ's purpose on earth through history.[107] His mission is the church's commission. Here Hanvey is worth quoting at length:

> Revelation cannot [...] occur without understanding; it does not occur, therefore, without the community. God does not will to be God without Israel nor Christ will to be the Saviour without his church. Indeed, history is presupposed not only as the medium in which the event of the incarnation-resurrection occurs

---

103. ET.2, 161; cf. *Ineffabilis Deus* (1854). See the pertinent remarks by Francesca Murphy, "Immaculate Mary: The Ecclesial Mariology of Hans Urs von Balthasar," in *Mary: The Complete Resource*, ed. Sarah Jane Boss (London: Continuum, 2007), 300–13, especially 307–8. As Murphy says, Balthasar sees the Immaculate Conception as the necessary "objective" ground of ecclesial sanctity (not as a "subjective" blessing or allowance pertaining merely to the Mother of Christ). Cf. the important study by Hilda Steinhauer, *Maria als dramatische Person bei Hans Urs von Balthasar: Zum Mari, anischen Prinzip seines Denkens* (Innsbruck: Salzburger Theologische Studien, 2001).

104. 3FG, 70. In his discussion ("The Form and the Drama of the Church: Hans Urs von Balthasar on Mary, Peter, and the Eucharist," *Logos: A Journal of Catholic Thought and Culture* 11:1 [2008]: 70–95), Robert Koerpel arguably misses the full depth of Mary's participation in the eternal dialogue, but his approach is still helpful for illuminating the essential points (see especially 82–5).

105. Specifically, this is a Goethean notion of form which impressed itself upon Balthasar from an early age. See the remarks by King ("Theology under Another Form," 300). Carpenter's discussion is also helpful (*Theo-Poetics*, 53–5). Elsewhere, Balthasar states the same principle formally: "That which gives measure takes rank over that to which it gives measure" (GL.4, 206).

106. GL.7, 266.

107. TS, 10-1; cf. *Prayer* (L), 68–9, and TD.3, 434.

but through which is it is operative. The community is not something apart from the economy of revelation but is already its effect and presence within the world. Thus history becomes part of the economy as the process of the community's understanding and witness. In this sense, revelation not only has a history[,] it creates it.[108]

The church is thus born of and formed as prayer. Due to space constraints, and since in this section it is not my intention to assemble a thorough systematic account of the church as such (but rather to illuminate the essential points regarding the church's "prayer constitution"), I will not seek to apply these insights exhaustively to the relevant areas of ecclesiology (such as missiology or ecumenical issues, say).[109] However, I will stress that this notion of a prayer constitution in the church serves to establish the church as an engaged presence in the world—and that, further, this was explicitly one of Balthasar's aims. A church of and at prayer will always seek to offer its cooperative "Yes" in new and constructive ways. In this sense, "Church" becomes a gerund: "One cannot be simply—today less than ever—the Church as a product; one must always be the Church producing."[110] This should be seen as of a piece with what I said in Chapter 2 about Balthasar's attempt to establish a more-adequate form of personal sanctity in the modern era, one which is responsive to the world.

The eschatological dimensions of this idea of church will be raised again in Chapter 6. In what remains of this current chapter, however, I want to consider how the Christological aspects of prayer that have already been raised relate to ministeriality in the church. The turn to sacrament and ministeriality follows on from the previous discussions in at least two ways: first, because I have already said that according to Balthasar the Spirit carries out its task of communicating the Father through the Son by making use of the visible structures of the church,

---

108. James Hanvey, "Tradition as Subversion," *International Journal of Systematic Theology* 6:1 (2004): 50–87, here 61; Hanvey refers to Thomas, *Commentary on 2 Corinthians* 12.1.422: "*Quando cum visione habetur significando intellectus eorum quae videntur, tunc est revelation.*" Cf. also Hanvey, "Healing the Wound: Discourse of Redemption," in *Challenging Women's Orthodoxies in the Context of Faith*, ed. Susan Parsons (London: Routledge, 2000), 205–22, at 214: "Grace itself needs a community of grace."

109. Although the possibilities are promising. For instance, consider the alternatives to the current method of "competitive ecumenism" which might apply to an approach that emphasized prayer as the shared source and substance of ecclesial unity; James Andrews makes some important steps in this direction with his attempt to assemble a "christological ecclesiology of prayer" (see "'That the World May Know': A Christological Ecclesiology of Prayer," in *Modern Theology* 30:4 [2014]: 481–99). Another constructive project is Eugene Schlesinger's *Ite, Missa Est! A Missional Liturgical Ecclesiology* (Minneapolis: Fortress, 2017), which ably refutes the now-seemingly axiomatic claim that "a missional church cannot be liturgical" (202).

110. ET.2, 30.

including the sacraments (cf. Section 3.2. *supra*); and second, because the person formed by these ecclesial rhythms of prayer is led on thereby to further prayer. In other words, prayer and sacrament stand in mutual reciprocal relationship to one another.

4.3.2 Prayer and Sacrament

The sacraments are of interest to our current discussion inasmuch as they are "Christ's guarantee that the grace of his Incarnation is always available."[111] On the broadest level, as I have been saying, and as the Second Vatican Council acknowledged in *Lumen Gentium*, the church itself is the sacrament of Christ's ongoing presence.[112] But this is true in a more particular and literal way in the Eucharist, which is the absolute meeting point "between the physical and the mystical body of Christ."[113] Each sacrament, for its own part, attests likewise to the same closeness between Bride and Bridegroom in the form (species) proper to it. That is, if Christ's prayer for his followers is to persist through history, it must do so from within the historical forms infused with grace which the church calls sacraments.[114] We have also seen how Christ's prayers involve a degree of faith that the Spirit will lead the way into the fullness of divine-human communion. The church makes this same prayer of faith in the epiclesis at each sacrament, so that every instance of sacrament substantiates the general "attitude of prayer" under which the church professes to live. (Thus, the sacraments offer the foremost vehicle of the participatory *fides Christi* discussed in Section 4.2.2 *supra*.) In fact, mention of the Spirit raises a vital point here. Inasmuch as the Son's obedience to the Spirit in prayer was a total act, it is therefore *only* in prayer to that same Spirit that the church can hope to enjoy the unity of love with the Son who has entrusted the fullness of his being to it.[115] The rhythmic interplay between *kenosis* and *pleroma* returns here again. Christ's kenotic self-dispossession in mission, to the point of death on the Cross, provides the (only) basis upon which the church can claim to be the "fullness of Christ" (Eph. 4:13). From these points, we can see why Balthasar says, "Prayer and sacrament form an indissoluble unity which is of the very nature of the Church," since both prayer and sacrament express the "pure

---

111. Cf. ET.2, 325.
112. *Lumen Gentium* (1964), 48.
113. TL.2, 304.
114. Cf. ET.2, 325; cf. the *Catechism of the Catholic Church* 1127. From here, it is not hard to see how "the [words of] the entire New Testament [also] have something of a sacramental character" inasmuch as it they "are not mere words in print but rather are testimony and transmission of a trinitarian Spirit and activity that are directed to the world" (*CM*, 78). Sacraments are to be distinguished from Scripture as deeds are to be distinguished from words, but in Balthasar it is an essential characteristic of the divine Word that it always implies a unity of word and deed. Cf. *LAC*, 62–3.
115. Cf. *Prayer* (H), 112–3.

mutual relationship of God and man, existing for one another, reflecting oneself in each other."[116]

That is not to say, however, that life in the church is simply coterminous with sacramental participation, or that such participation is without its own internal rhythms. In fact, Balthasar distinguishes "three levels" to ecclesial existence.[117] First is the *suprasacramental* (or *pansacramental*), which refers to historical roots of the ecclesial form itself: that is, the Incarnation and Mary's Yes. This level relates to the church's sacramental ministries as their premise and origin in ways that I have been discussing already in this chapter. It is also the level most clearly marked by prayer, understanding both the Word itself and Mary's response as prayers of the most profound sort. Second is the explicitly *sacramental* level, in which the visible "structure of the Church" is most apparent—what Balthasar elsewhere calls the Petrine office.[118] Here ministeriality must be put into practice, giving rise to a certain functional and "relative antithesis between priest and layman."[119] It seems important to stress that this "antithesis" is not an opposition. While Balthasar clearly sees ministeriality residing, by definition, with the ordained clergy, he emphasizes several ways in which the laity and the clergy are mutually constituted and even how the laity cooperate—including by prayer—in the sacramental ministry of the priest.[120] Following on from this is the third "level," the *subsacramental*, which

---

116. *Prayer* (H) 113, ET.2, 366.
117. See "The Layman and the Church," in ET.2.
118. Cf. *OPSC*, 154–71.
119. ET.2, 315.
120. See the discussion at ET.2, 319–25. First, Balthasar stresses that the laity's capacity to receive grace is not a passive form of being-acted-upon but "a particular form" of action—an active capacity which is itself first bestowed in the ministered sacrament of baptism (320). Second, the entire "matrix" of sacramentality is relativized against Christ's sovereign freedom (in this case, the freedom to establish particular forms for the transmission of grace on earth), and so any apparent hierarchy of ministeriality between lay and ordained Christians is seen to exist against the backdrop of a more fundamental equality as subjects "in Christ" (321–2). Third, Balthasar mentions those instances where laity are permitted to dispense sacraments themselves (lay baptism being the chief instance), which suggests that they participate in the "sphere governed by the hierarchy" not by dispensation but "by right as a Christian" (322; cf. Thomas' discussion of lay confession at *Sent.* 17.3.3). Balthasar also shows himself to be sensitive to the historical fact that laity have long shared in the threefold office established by Christ, in particular the "prophetic" or teaching office (see 322–3). Finally, Balthasar underlines the fact that although the laity should "look up with reverence" to the priestly *ministry* (note: not to any particular priest *qua* priest) as a necessary mediating structure of grace in the church, at the same time and for the same reason "the priest looks up with reverence to the layman, in whom he sees the purpose and the goal of his servant function" (325). These comments should be seen to balance the far-sketchier remarks concerning priestly ministry in *New Elucidations* ("A Note on Lay Theologians," 198–203) which, when read in isolation, might seem more disparaging of the

refers to the basic "sphere of life" within which each Christian functions on a day-to-day basis. All that can be said about ministeriality at the sacramental level must be related to this level as its proof and fulfillment: "The meaning of sermon and sacrament is attained *only* where the truth of the life of Christ is displayed in [the] life [of the Christian], in the millionfold variation of Christian existence."[121] It is at this level that the church's "innermost and necessary essence" subsists, and, for the same reason, it is at this level that prayer's particular rhythms are most immediately related to the life of the individual Christian.[122] We will see more clearly how prayer operates within the context of an individual life in the next chapter. What is important to underline at the moment is that prayer spans across these "levels" while at the same time binding them together and giving them their particular shape. The presacramental "Yes" is also the invocation of the Spirit to sanctify, in time and space, those visible signs of grace which in turn sustain the ongoing existence-as-prayer befitting a person in Christ. In this way, prayer serves as "the normal way [in the Church] to develop the resources of the sacramental life" and to "derive more fruit from the sacraments as time goes on."[123] Prayer is, in other words, one of the individual Christian's chief means of participation in what the *Catechism of the Catholic Church* refers to as the "sacramental economy."[124] That the sacraments are said to be effective *opus operatum* should not be taken to mean that they override the recipient's receptive "disposition," which is cultivated primarily through prayer.[125]

---

laity. (As it happens, we can see here the importance of reading a weak Category 2 work, in this case *New Elucidations*, in light of a more comprehensive treatment in a Category 1 text, *Explorations in Theology*.)

121. ET.2, 326 (my italics). Elsewhere Balthasar writes, "the sacramental element [on its own] *does not suffice*" (*CM*, 76). Balthasar considers it a particular advantage of the modern era that the church has come to reflect upon the importance of the everyday Christian existence, especially when compared to the apostolic era (which was overdetermined by the eschatological perspective) and the Medieval era (which proved to be "one-sidedly monastic") (ET.2, 327).

122. ET.2, 327.

123. *Prayer* (L), 97.

124. Cf. *Catechism of the Catholic Church* 1076ff.

125. "The *opus operatum* of the sacraments is effected or frustrated, is *more or less fruitful*, according to the dispositions of the individual [. . .]. There is no such thing as a disposition for grace in general or the sacraments in particular which can be considered apart from the individual; for that reason, all reception of grace within the Church includes some hearing of the word—of the word, that is, contained in the sacrament" (*Prayer* [L], 97, italics mine). Here, as is so often the case, Balthasar is waging a stealth war on two fronts: on the one hand, he means to oppose a rationalist/manualist tradition which was prone to see the sacraments as possessing an interior, almost imperious power and which ultimately risked seeing as irrelevant the subjective state of the recipient of grace. In this sense, he carries on Odo Casel's earlier revisionist project in, for instance, *The Mystery of Christian Worship*. However, with

4.4 Consolidation

We are in a position now to see how, according to Balthasar, the Trinitarian prayer announces itself in history as the Christ who speaks to man as and in the "language of God." Far from being a private language, Christ's prayers are Trinitarian events into which the faithful are explicitly initiated as legitimate participants. Christ's prayers are prayers in the Spirit, and it is the same Spirit who is responsible for underwriting the prayers of the church. The church, for its part, is shown to be born of prayer and formed in prayer. Its sacramental ministry is intended to instantiate the same love of God for God's people to which prayer, at its deepest levels, attests. In this sense there is a profound unity of life at the heart of the church, a unity that both flows from and attests to the Trinitarian communion of love which drove Christ in his mission.

I declared at the outset of this book my aversion to sociological or psychological answers to what is properly a *theological* question about the nature and effects of prayer within the overall economy of salvation. Precisely in pursuit of this theological account, however, we must turn now to consider how the person is implicated in these processes. One of the defining features of Balthasar's theological project, as I have argued, is that it is intended not as an exercise in abstraction but as a "thoroughly practical" unfolding of how God's Word reaches us in history; naturally enough, now that we have considered the Word in itself, we must turn to consider its effects on the praying person. Of course, much of what will be said in the following chapter will follow directly on from the Christological dimensions found in this chapter, since any theological anthropology that claims to be Christian must take its lead from the life of the God-man. And yet prayer lies at the very heart of Balthasar's theological anthropology in ways that are distinct from what has already been said and that prove to be enduringly relevant even today. It may be the case that God always speaks first—but each person, in answering, is obliged to find their own unique voice. Indeed, it is only by doing so, according to Balthasar, that they display the full depths of personhood.

---

reference to prayer as a form of "hearing the word," Balthasar is also implicitly responding to Rahner's notion of a "supernatural existential" (which first appeared in writing some five years before Balthasar's *Prayer*). Famously, the supernatural existential refers to the universal and constitutional capacity proper to each person as such to receive grace, a capacity which (in the stronger versions of the notion) itself amounts to a form of "transcendental revelation" (see, e.g., "Priestly Existence" in *Theological Investigations* Vol. III, 252). For Balthasar, prayer is perhaps the clearest indication that in the dialogue between God and man, God must be the one to speak first—and that, in speaking first, God establishes the mode of creaturely response in a way that goes beyond any existing "preapprehension." In this sense, Balthasar is aligning himself with the earlier Rahner of *Hörer des Wortes* (which he called Rahner's "most beautiful" book), whose emphasis was much more clearly on the particular and historical form of revelation (see, e.g., *Hearer of the Word*, 135). Kilby does an excellent job showing the relative "incompatibility of *Hearer of the Word* and the supernatural existential" in *Karl Rahner: Theology and Philosophy* (London: Routledge, 2004), 60–9.

Chapter 5

PRAYER'S EFFECTS

ANTHROPOLOGICAL DIMENSIONS

5.1 Against the Anthropological Approach

There would seem to be a danger implicit at the outset of this chapter—one which has already been hinted at in the course of the preceding discussions. Namely, in considering the "anthropological dimensions of prayer" how can we maintain the particularly *theological* nature of the account we are developing?[1] For Balthasar, prayer is not, as we have already seen, a human invention; it "descends from God to man."[2] And, on the human side of things, prayer is no therapeutic exercise in introspection: "Christian prayer is always addressed to the living God. It is never the search for one's own 'self' or for the transcendental ego."[3] Thus even as he

---

1. Bernard McGinn identifies three broad approaches to the study of prayer and spirituality: (i) the theological approach; (ii) the anthropological approach; and (iii) the sociological approach. Of these, the sociological approach stresses the cultural particularity or "lived experience" of a given spiritual practice, while the (largely prevalent) anthropological approach tends to consider prayer as part of a broader process of human self-realization. See McGinn, "The Letter and the Spirit: Spirituality as an Academic Discipline," 29. For the sociological approach, see, for example, Urban Holmes, *Spirituality for Ministry* (San Francisco: Harper & Row, 1982) or Sheldrake, *Spirituality and History: Questions of Interpretation and Method* (New York: Crossroad, 1992). For examples of the anthropological approach, see John Macquarrie, *Paths in Spirituality* (New York: Harper & Row, 1972); or Sandra Schneiders, "Spirituality in the Academy," *Theological Studies* 50:4 (1989): 676–97. McGinn calls Balthasar one of the twentieth's century's "most weighty" proponents of the theological approach.

2. Again, *TE*, 89.

3. *LLC*, 267 and *Prayer* (H), 56. Contrast this with Schneiders, who views prayer as "the experience of consciously striving to integrate one's life in terms not of isolation and self-absorption but of self-transcendence toward the ultimate value one perceives" (684). As McGinn notes, Schneiders' anthropological notion of prayer "leaves open the possibility for forms of non-religious or secular spirituality" (McGinn, "The Letter and the Spirit," 32), which, whatever else they are, cannot be considered properly theological.

insists that in prayer God really does meet humanity, Balthasar is nevertheless highly critical of what he considers anthropocentric approaches to the question. Balthasar's perspective here is explicitly presented as an improvement upon the account of the self given by philosophical dialogism (Buber, Rosenzweig, Marcel, etc.).[4] Dialogism maintains that the emergence of the "I" is decisively shaped by the "Thou," and second-wave dialogists in particular emphasized that God can feature in this relation in an utterly "transcendent" way.[5] Certainly, there is much in this general approach that Balthasar finds to be of "lasting validity," as can be seen from his subject-object discussion in TL.1.[6] But an anthropology based *entirely* on philosophical (or what Balthasar calls "horizontal") dialogism remains confined to an endless cycle of I-Thou reciprocity. Balthasar states the problem clearly:

> For however much a genuinely fulfilling encounter with a "thou" may seem to the individual, to have a quality of "destiny," it remains ultimately fortuitous [i.e., arbitrary] and is at most transitory. For one exclusive "I-thou" relationship can be followed by a second [. . .] and a tenth. In each of these, the "I" is endowed with a new and different name and nature.[7]

Such is the danger of dialogue as long as it remains confined to the "horizontal" axis.[8]

And yet it is not the case that Balthasar, therefore, simply dismisses as unimportant the questions about human nature raised by dialogism or depth-psychology—far from it. Rather, he simply believes that knowledge of one's mission is a surer form of insight about one's identity than abstract considerations of human nature as such.[9] "Only through the name that God uses to address the individual human being is he validly and definitely distinct from every other human being; only thus is he no longer simply an individual of a species but a

---

4. Cf. TL.2, I.B.b.

5. See Buber's response to Jaspers in *Werke*, Vol. I, ed. Lambert Schneider (Munich: Kösel, 1962), 300ff.

6. TD.1, 645.

7. TD.1, 628–9. Balthasar explains further at TD.3, 205: "Ultimately not even a fellow human being can tell another who the latter really is in himself. The most emphatic affirmation can only tell him who he is for the one who values him or loves him [. . .] Everything is stuck in a web of relative, reciprocal, provisional values and revaluations, in which recognition is now accorded and now withdrawn."

8. On "horizontal" versus "vertical" prayer see GL.1, 192 and *Prayer* (H), 195.

9. Balthasar reflects on the "ambivalence" of the classical (pre-Christian) philosophical attempts at self-knowledge and discounts the question, "What kind of creature is man?" in favor of the more personal, "Who am I?" (see TD.1, 481ff. and cf. the essay "Who Is Man?" at ET.4, 15–28). This is also a theme of his treatment of ancient myth—consider the illuminating discussion of Aeneas from the perspective of mission at GL.4, 267–79.

unique person."[10] In this sense the innermost truth of a person's life is to be found in their particular mission.[11] (There is an aesthetic parallel here to Hopkins, for whom the unique beauty and the full freedom of a given form lies in its distinction from other forms.[12]) In every instance, this disponibility for mission requires the personal dialogue-relationship of prayer in order to acquire texture and depth, in order for the praying person's personality to emerge more fully—crucially, however, this decisive dialogue is not one between creatures on the same plane, but rather between creature and creator (Balthasar does credit later dialogists like Rosenzweig for grasping this point "most clearly").[13] In prayer, one learns about oneself in ways altogether deeper (and, objectively, more important) than the sort of self-knowledge revealed through either pure introspection or reciprocal dialogue with another creature. Often this has the effect of surprising the praying person (and here it is worth recalling the discussion of Trinitarian surprise from Section 3.3.1 *supra*): "Simon the fisherman could have explored every region of his ego prior to his encounter with Christ, but he would not have found 'Peter' there."[14] Just as Christ was sustained in his mission by his prayer, so too for the individual person does prayer become a mode of uncovering their unique mission-consciousness and, consequently, their unique identity. More to the point, it is through the personal encounter with Christ in prayer that the creature receives a personalizing commission: "Come, follow me" (Mt. 4:19).[15] This is the creaturely share in Sonship that introduces genuine verticality to the individual life.[16] Introspection, which can too quickly become pathological, thus gives way to mission, which takes the form of service to the world. Using a metaphor borrowed

---

10. TD.1, 628.
11. Cf. Sachs, "Spirit and Life," 166.
12. See the discussion of "inscape" at GL.3, 377ff.
13. TD.1, 628. The limitation of dialogism at this point consists in its lack of Christological specificity, and, therefore (given the unity of identity and mission in Christ), its risk of remaining too abstract: "It only remains for us to indicate why, in that biblical realm in which [the dialogists] have achieved so much of lasting validity, the transition from the Old Covenant to the New appears necessary. In [Rosenzweig] we attain to the 'name,' that is, the individual's perfect definition as assigned by God. In [Buber] we also glimpse the world-fullness of the man who has been signed with a name. But only in Jesus Christ does it become clear how profoundly this definitive 'I'-name signifies vocation [and] *mission*" (TD.1, 645).
14. *Prayer* (H), 60.
15. *EG*, 38–9: "For the grace of God is fundamentally a call; it is being enlisted in God's service; it is being commissioned with a special task; and through all this there is bestowed upon us a unique personal dignity in the eyes of God."
16. This certainly implies a teleological view of human nature from Balthasar's perspective. If Christ is the Logos of creation, then a life "in Christ"—conformity to the idea of Sonship as it was modeled by Christ at mission—generally constitutes the *telos* of each created person (cf. Victoria Harrison, "Personal Identity and Integration: Von Balthasar's

from physics, Balthasar distinguishes between a false form of prayer which he calls "centripetal" (i.e., tending inward toward a center) and genuine Christian prayer, which is always "centrifugal" (i.e., tending outward).[17] And when a person lives completely in this centrifugal mode, that is, when their life is prayer, they themself become a site of revelation of God's love in and for the world.[18] Sainthood is no more than this effective transparency to mission-identity.[19]

If with Balthasar we understand the person at prayer as a real site of revelation in history, then we can understand better what he means by saying that spirituality is "the subjective aspect of dogmatic theology."[20] To be clear, "subjective" as it is used here has very little to do with a notion of self-subsistence; it is not that the holy person prays in the manner of Cartesian cogitation, as a method of extending oneself out to other freestanding objects (other people, God, etc.) that exist as discrete entities in the world alongside the thinking subject. Rather, Balthasar's meaning has more in common with the Heideggerian "subject" which is itself constituted by its prior relation to the object.[21] In this sense, sanctity is a given individual's cooperative assent to the God who sees that individual as a person of unique worth and purpose.[22] Of course, Balthasar's theological approach goes

---

Phenomenology of Human Holiness," *Heythrop Journal* 60 [1999]: 424–37). Each particular *telos* is unique, however, in that no two lives 'in Christ' are exactly identical.

17. *Prayer* (H), 54.

18. Cf. GL.5, 75.

19. This is well captured by Patricia Sullivan, "Saints as the 'Living Gospel.'" Sullivan notes rightly that Balthasar's approach has the advantage of taking the saint seriously as a real source of knowledge about God, knowledge which can then in turn be apprehended and disseminated within the church and among the wider world; piety and sanctity are rescued from individualism and put in an ecclesial context (see discussion at "Saints as the 'Living Gospel,'" 276–8). However, Sullivan worries that Balthasar's willingness to distinguish between "types" of saints based on the scope of their objective mission might diminish the importance of those whose task is deemed to be more modest (see "Saints as the 'Living Gospel,'" 278–9; Balthasar distinguishes between "customary" and "representative" sanctity at 2SS, 24). Although Sullivan's concern is pertinent, she may be placing too heavy an emphasis on canonization as the measure of a given saint's impact on the church. As I discussed in Chapter 2, Balthasar was less interested in canonization than in the fruits born by a given saint's life, and he considered the "large missions" of the great saints to be upheld and even tested by the ordinary lives of those countless invisible saints who occupy the spaces opened up by the former.

20. See the essay "Spirituality," in ET.1, 211; cf. GL.1, 231.

21. This is to put the difference between Heidegger and Descartes in very general terms; for further discussion, see Michel Henry, "The Critique of the Subject," *Topoi* 7, no. 2 (1988): 147–53.

22. Balthasar is fond of repeating Baader's reversal of the Cartesian maxim: it is not *cogito ergo sum* but rather *cogitor ergo sum* ('I *am thought* therefore I am'); see, for example, GL.1 439. For a thorough discussion of Baader's critique, see Joris Geldhof, "'*Cogitor Ergo*

further than Heidegger in what it is willing to say about the personal nature of the individual's relationship to the transcendent other: and inasmuch as prayer is the means by which Balthasar describes the individual person's coming-to-know their particularity vis-à-vis the transcendent God, then prayer functions as a means of making one's home in Being (i.e., personalization). Spirituality thus illuminates the "subjective aspect of dogmatic theology" in that it refers to the process of acquiring subjecthood as a creature known and loved. Absent this personalization in prayer, dogmatic teaching remains a "mere abstract principle" that has no place in the church.[23]

As it did for his understanding of the Trinity and of Christ, then, prayer plays a central role in Balthasar's understanding of the human person. Harrison's phrase, "*Homo Orans*," is an apt description of the human person according to Balthasar. The remainder of the current chapter will, therefore, consider this idea of personhood through prayer, exposing and testing some of its key points. As we will see, Balthasar's approach here is novel and presents what is in many ways a flexible notion of the person, which may prove surprisingly agreeable to contemporary theological sensibilities. Let us consider in turn: the creature's predisposition to prayer; the word of response; and the fullness of a creaturely life lived in and as prayer.

5.2 Predisposition

The point of the current discussion is not to present the act of prayer in an overly schematic way. There are as many different roads to prayer as there are persons who set out to pray. Nevertheless, there *is* what I am calling a certain rhythm to prayer which emerges from the objective theological structure of prayer—it is this rhythm that we are trying to catch.

5.2.1 Shame

The arguments of the previous two chapters, as well as the brief remarks mentioned earlier, make clear the fact that prayer precedes the praying person. From the creaturely point of view, as Speyr puts it, "Prayer has no beginning."[24]

Sum'": On the Meaning and Relevance of Baader's Theological Critique of Descartes," in *Modern Theology* 21, no. 2 (2005): 237–51.

23. "Norm," 20; cf. *TE*, 62–3. Holiness serves as a living expression of doctrine in a way that is essential to the church's witness: "The ecclesial magisterium can represent Christ's truth *only* from the standpoint of doctrine and *not* of life" (GL.1, 212–13, italics mine). The task of rendering a "living" witness belongs to the praying person possessed by a mission. Thus the plausibility of the central claim of Dimech's argument that in Balthasar "the Magisterium are there to serve the saints" (Dimech, *The Authority of the Saints*, 227).

24. Speyr, *The World of Prayer*, 28. See also comments by Prevot, *Thinking Prayer*, 110–1 and discussion by Quash, "Drama and the Ends of Modernity," in *Balthasar at the End of*

But of course, each person who eventually undertakes to pray has the experience of "beginning" somewhere, and usually this "beginning" is experienced with great difficulty. Spiritual "dryness" is a special concern for those attempting to grow in prayer. Balthasar opens the prayer book by acknowledging these difficulties, observing how "Many Christians are aware of the necessity and the beauty of contemplative prayer and have a sincere yearning for it. Yet, apart from tentative efforts soon abandoned, few [. . .] are really convinced and satisfied by their own practice of it."[25]

Yet beyond these introductory remarks, addressing directly the problem of difficulty in prayer is not, it must be said, one of Balthasar's explicit concerns either in *Prayer* or elsewhere (although there is a brief discussion in *Christian Meditation*).[26] Partly this reflects his commitment to rendering a theological account of prayer, as opposed to a manual on or a technical approach to pra*ying*. On a deeper level, however, the fact of difficulty in prayer need not detain Balthasar given what he understands prayer to be. As the creature's participation in the prior Trinitarian dialogue in which the praying person is rendered evermore transparent to mission, it is inevitable that the sinful ego-consciousness find this process difficult and resist it in various ways. As different as Trinitarian mutuality is from sinful self-centeredness, so much the same does prayer strike the person (especially at first) as a difficult undertaking.[27] We might put the point more strongly and say that difficulty in prayer is even a positive indication of its "Trinitarian background."[28]

What this point about difficulty in prayer further suggests is that the person is already imbued with a primordial call to prayer. Difficulty is only experienced because one has a sense, more or less strong, that prayer is something worth doing, but simultaneously that it is something one "does not know how to do as one ought" (Rom. 8:26).[29] This disconnect—between the natural desire to pray and the

---

Modernity, 139–72.

25. *Prayer* (H), 7.

26. See *CM*, 45–7, which will feature in what follows. Contrast this with Rahner, for instance, who devotes significant attention to the question of dryness (e.g., *Encounters with Silence*, trans. James Demske [South Bend, Indiana: St Augustine's Press, 1999], chapter 3).

27. See *WiC?* 68. In a discussion of the same phenomenon, Jos Moons argues that "transcendentality is difficult *per se*" (Moons, "The Difficulty of Prayer," *International Journal for Philosophy and Theology* 68, no. 2 [2017]: 162–84, here 176).

28. *Prayer* (H), 61; cf. *CM*, 47.

29. The sense that prayer is something worth doing in the first place derives from the creature's constitutional desire to be in dialogue with God. Riches rightly notes the influence of Blondel here. The human creature's orientation beyond itself is located so deeply within it as to seem natural but, precisely since what is being desired is engagement with the vertical axis of existence, the orientation is itself grace (cf. Riches, "Balthasar and the Analysis of Faith," in *The Analogy of Beauty*, 35–59). See also Henri Bouillard, *Blondel and Christianity* (Washington: Corpus, 1969), 18. Balthasar describes this prior orientation as conscience

perception that one is inadequate to the task—is a result of sin. Balthasar describes it as a "later encroachment" upon human nature (i.e., postlapsarian).[30] The effects of sin here are both ontological (the creature has been rendered "impure") and epistemological (the creature wrongly believes it is incapable of that which is in fact specifically intended for it by its creator). To be sure, sin does not wholly prevent the creature from praying, but it creates the false impression that to attend to God in prayer requires the neglect or indictment of oneself. It sets up a competition between the person and God.[31] Specifically, it is one of the chief effects of sin that the creature feels itself *ashamed* before God in prayer.[32] (Notice that the point here is not that shame in prayer is itself sinful, but that it is a kind of mistake of judgment which is attributable to the epistemological effects of sin.) It is as a form of entering into the fullness of sin that the Son takes on these feelings of shame in mission: "Let this cup pass from me . . ." (Mt. 26:39). In *Heart of the World*, Balthasar describes the Son's shame in the highly expressive language characteristic of that book: "Shame itself, shame-in-itself, that shame which none of us wants to taste or has ever tasted: what is it? You [i.e., Christ] will find out. You will be shamed before all the world, before the dead stones of the Mount of Olives, before every creature, and most of all, [even] before your Father."[33] Though Christ resolves himself to mission despite the feelings expressed at Mt. 26:39,

---

(*Gewissen*), which he calls the "organ capable of hearing" God's Word (cf. *Prayer* [H], 124; *Das Betrachtende Gebet*, 110). As a preecho of the Word which helps to prepare our hearts to receive him, Balthasar's notion of conscience conforms to Augustine's image of conscience as the "interior teacher" which is already a real instance of God's Word being present to man (cf. *Prayer* [H], 30).

30. *Prayer* (L), 64. See Harrison's discussion at "Homo Orans," 286–7, and Cihak's at *Balthasar and Anxiety*, 112–3.

31. *Prayer* (L), 21.

32. *Prayer* (H), 47. There is also what Paul refers to as the "godly grief [*lupē*]," which comes as a result of hearing the Word (cf. 2 Cor. 7:11); this can sometimes appear like a kind of shame in the praying person. However, this "godly grief" is distinct from shame in that it is no "mere resignation in the face of God's sovereign power" but rather a grief that "produces repentance" and leads to new life because crucially it already presupposes an existing love between God and creature (*Prayer* [H], 231–2).

33. *HW*, 108. More than that, the Son's shame is precisely that which, through a process of projection, sinful man finds most disgusting in him: "Everything base has entered you, and you are an aversion not only to yourself, but to all of us" (*loc. cit.*). On this latter point, the parallels with Girard's scapegoat theory are apparent, and explored explicitly by Paul Fiddes in "Sacrifice, Atonement, and Renewal," in *Sacrifice and Modern Thought*, ed. Julia Meszaros and Johannes Zachuber (Oxford: Oxford University Press, 2013), 48–65. See Balthasar's appreciative discussion of Girard at TD.4, 298–314, as well as the remarks at *YCYYG*, 82–3. The heart of Balthasar's critique of Girard lies in seeing that in Christ there is "Someone who is both ready and able" to take on the role of *universal* scapegoat (cf. *YCYYG*, 83).

many creatures who undertake to pray, feeling thus ashamed, often do so meekly or opt for a servile silence before the Father.

Properly speaking, however, shame has no place in Christian prayer, which is confident of being heard (cf. Mt. 18:19, 21:22, Mk 11:24, Jn 15:7, etc.). Growing in this confidence starts with recognizing that prayer is a natural activity of the creature, so much so, in fact, that, "There is in principle no need for any special way or effort in order to rise from nature to supernature" in prayer.[34] No need, that is, because prayer is already the realm of grace in which the creature finds itself addressed by God. Properly speaking the creature should never be ashamed to turn to God in prayer, even as (precisely as) a sinful creature.[35]

5.2.2 Confession

But the predisposition to prayer is still prethematic; it is not itself prayer. Adopting the proper disposition in prayer involves making oneself ready to receive the Word. Given the emphasis Balthasar places on prayer's naturalness to the creature, we ought not to expect this making-ready to involve "lengthy psychological adjustments" or a complex process of purification, as in some mystic schemas.[36] Balthasar appeals to the words of Jesus in the Farewell Discourse—"*Now* you are clean, by reason of the word I have spoken to you" (Jn 15:3)—to highlight that this purification is already (and only) accomplished in Christ.[37] Still, this readiness is not "automatic," even as a consequence of faith.[38] The only necessary

---

34. *Prayer* (H), 45.

35. Megan Loumagne discusses the dynamics of prayer and shame in broadly similar terms, concluding that "shame is not from God" but instead evinces the creature's "embarrassment in the face of one's [own] sinfulness" (see Loumagne, "Teresa of Avila on Theology and Shame," *New Blackfriars* 99:1080 [2018]: 388–402). However, Loumagne's account is arguably to be faulted for a certain sentimentality which believes "shame present[s] crucial opportunities for deeper union with God" (see *op. cit.*, 14). Balthasar would answer that shame is wholly exogenous to the sort of relationship God wants to have with God's creatures. At the very least, it is confusing to refer to two types of shame—that is, the kind that leads to union and the kind that does not—which is why Balthasar does not speak of "good" shame but rather "godly grief" (see footnote 32).

36. *CM*, 19.

37. *Prayer* (H), 123. As Harrison notes Balthasar's decision to read *katharos* at Jn 15:3 as "clean" is itself "not uncontroversial" ("Homo Orans," 287). However, neither is Balthasar's position an exceptional one; J. Ramsey Michaels likewise reads "clean" in verse 3, while pointing out how Jesus mixes moral terminology with agricultural metaphors ("pruning" or "trimming") to emphasize that it is ultimately God who readies the disciples to receive the word (Michaels, *The Gospel of John* [Grand Rapids: Eerdmans, 1971], 487). Michaels further notes the resonance of *katharos* with the earlier scenes of the washing of the feet (Jn 13:10–11).

38. *Prayer* (H), 123.

preparation for prayer, then, involves a simple but explicit "confession" in which we acknowledge "our sinfulness in the light of the word addressed to us."[39] Sacramental confession is an explicit form of this acknowledgment; however, every genuine act of contemplation implies the same moment of self-disclosure. Thus why prayer and penance are "connected" in a special way: confession is always an "element" of prayer because in genuine prayer we necessarily open ourselves to being seen and challenged by God.[40]

Such is one logical aspect of prayer's role in the constitution of mission-consciousness that (as we have seen) Balthasar stresses so consistently. As Christ made his "good confession" (1 Tim. 6:13) before Pilate as a way of resolving himself to his mission despite the resistance he faced, so too does the believer confess in spite of the resistance within himself or herself which prevents his or her full transparency to mission.[41] "Between the [. . .] confession of the 'I' struggling for the faith and that of the suffering and struggling Christ there exists [. . .] the closest bond, which is always an integral, integrating bond."[42] Through a regular practice of sacramental confession, then, an individual becomes "accustomed to looking in the mirror and seeing himself [sic] as God sees him," namely as *this* one and not another, guilty of *this* offense and not others but likewise called to *this* mission and not others.[43] Confession should be a method of personalization, preparing the

---

39. *Prayer* (L), 100.

40. *Prayer* (H), 123-4. Unsurprisingly, Speyr's account of the sacrament in *Confession: The Encounter with Christ in Penance*, trans. Littledale (New York: Herder, 1964) largely resonates with Balthasar's argument here.

41. *Prayer* (H), 124.

42. Cf. ET.2, 63-4. Here the principle of analogical dissimilarity must be kept very clearly in mind.

43. *Prayer* (H), 125. Of course, there is a "danger" of this practice becoming subject to a preening egoism, which precisely reverses the objective purpose of the sacrament (see *loc. cit.*). That confession may yield a certain amount of self-knowledge does *not* therefore recommend it as a form of therapy. While he is to be commended for realizing the danger of scrupulosity here, Balthasar regrettably obscures the issue with his intemperate views on psychoanalysis itself, going as far as to write at one point that therapy can in some cases become a "satanic caricature of sacramental confession" in which therapist usurps the role of priest (see *LLC*, 117 as well as discussion by Cihak at *Balthasar and Anxiety*, 103-8). It must be said that here Balthasar is not displaying either an abundance of charity nor any particular commitment to coherent argumentation, as the remarks come almost offhand and are not developed in any significant way. Cihak is right to point out that Balthasar's comments should be read against the backdrop of a much broader and generally more constructive polemic—whose theological depth we have been sounding throughout this chapter—against any purely "horizontal" anthropology such as the sort generally found in psychotherapeutic (especially Freudian) approaches. A more generous approach to the question than Balthasar's would be content to draw a distinction between the theological dynamics which are at stake in the sacrament, and the therapeutic processes which are

person to respond to the unique Word in their own unique voice (which is prayer). This helps clarify the claim in Section 4.3.2 that prayer and sacrament reinforce one another's fruitfulness over time. Nor should the claim regarding confession as a means of personalization be understood individualistically. Inasmuch as liturgy involves the same confession—in the form of the Penitential Act—it suggests the possibility of and the need for the community to seek reconciliation, with God and with one another, before endeavoring to pray *as* a community. Furthermore, in every good confession made from the perspective of personal mission-consciousness the person confessing will take account of the way in which he or she has failed others and will seek to reintegrate himself or herself among the community of those who pursue the common mission of the church.[44]

But, again, even explicit sacramental confession is properly speaking *preparatory*. If prayer is a dialogue, and God has spoken the initial word in Christ, confession is akin to the person's turning his or her gaze to acknowledge (*"confiteor"*) God so as to ensure he or she is properly attentive to the conversation that is about to unfold.

5.3 Response

Having turned their attention to God in prayer, the praying person now attempts to respond to the Word that confronts them there—this is the heart of creaturely prayer. This response is vital, lest prayer be a fruit that dies on the vine: "It is not

---

at stake in the psychological approach; however, there is no obvious basis upon which to then assert that the latter always come at the expense of the former, as Balthasar gives the impression of doing (indeed a certain amount of therapeutic introspection may conceivably *prepare* a certain individual for sacramental confession). An altogether more useful treatment of the question is to be found in Stephen Pattison's study, *Shame: Theory, Therapy, Theology* (Cambridge: Cambridge University Press, 2000).

44. In this sense, Joseph Martos confuses the issue with his allusive suggestions in *Deconstructing Sacramental Theology and Reconstructing Catholic Ritual* (Eugene: Wipf & Stock, 2015) that "rituals of genuine reconciliation" should emphasize communal healing and collective witness more than the private confession (see 265–7). Balthasar reflects on this precise question at *VBR*, 278–82, noting that "personal confession is not [. . .] something private in the church" inasmuch as each sin has a "social echo" that "must" be included in the penitent's confession (281). Indeed, collective "penance services" such as Martos suggests are seen by Balthasar to be capable of "uncover[ing] and bring[ing] to awareness many aspects of personal guilt which often escape those who are left just to their own examinations of conscience" (ibid.). But the "central point" of the sacrament "will always remain" the individual encounter between Christ and the person, in keeping with the "personal" nature of New Testament faith itself (ibid.). See also the comments at *WiC?* 99–101.

enough for the believer simply to 'listen'; unless his listening becomes an active response to the word, he will be found to have heard nothing."[45]

5.3.1 Parrhesia

God will not let the invitation to dialogue, once acted upon by the creature, go unanswered. The Word Christology, which I presented in Section 4.1, sets the outer limits of the divine-human dialogue.[46]

But in responding, the creature is obliged to conform to the fullness which the Son exhibited as the express Word of the Father. God has held nothing back in the dialogue with creation, and so the creature should endeavor to speak freely, to bring everything to God in prayer. Through Christ—who expresses the Father "in every conceivable way"—the Christian gains a "right to say everything" in prayer (*parrhesia* = *pan* + *rhema*).[47] The *parrhesia* that the praying person is to show in

---

45. *Prayer* (H), 99.

46. That is, Christ is the fullness of the Word that resounds as prayer between God and man. There is an implicit possibility of supralapsarianism here, since as the fullness of the divine Word, the Son's incarnation is arguably a completion of Creation and not just a mission made necessary by sin. At times, Balthasar appears to hint at this possibility—as he does, for instance, in an appreciative discussion of Maximus the Confessor's Christology in *Cosmic Liturgy*: "Maximus expressly says that the Incarnation—more precisely, the drama of Cross, grave, and resurrection—is not only the midpoint of world history but the *foundational idea of the world itself*" (*CL*, 134 italics added). To be sure, Balthasar formally rejected the idea of supralapsarianism out of a concern to safeguard God's ultimate freedom (cf. *CL*, 202). As Johnson notes in his discussion of the problem, "Balthasar believes that he has transcended the supralapsarian question" by building a system in which the pure spontaneity of God meets the pure receptivity of the creature living a life in Christ, and so any suggestion of necessity or obligation proves a "non-starter" (see *Christ and Analogy*, 128–32). Whether or not Johnson is right that Balthasar ultimately adopts the supralapsarian position (and I think he *is* right about that), the only essential point for us at the moment is that Christ plays this twofold role in the "dialogue-relationship" of prayer (i.e., its premise and its fulfillment).

47. *Prayer* (H), 48, 184; see generally 45–51. The term *parrhesia* is a prominent one in the Johannine and Pauline texts, and appears about twice as often in the New Testament overall as it does in the Septuagint. For illuminating surveys of the biblical usage, see William Klassen, "παρρησία in the Johannine Corpus" and David Fredrickson, "παρρησία in the Pauline Epistles," both in *Friendship, Flattery, and Frankness of Speech: Studies on Friendship in the New Testament World*, ed. John Fitzgerald (Leiden: Brill, 1996), 227–54 and 163–83, respectively. Though Balthasar uses the term exclusively in a positive sense, there is also a pejorative meaning ("idle chatter" or similar) which is sometimes attached to the word, especially by ancient authors (Plato considers *parrhesia* a negative feature of the democratic regime, for example: see *Republic* 577b). Although Foucault claims that early Christian sources regularly present *parrhesia* as a negative trait (one which is apparently

responding to the Word also involves a certain boldness since those who pray in this way

> come to [God] with their head held high, as those who have an innate right to be there and to speak. We may look into the Father's face without fear; we do not have to approach him as if he were an aloof monarch, with downcast eyes and obsequious gestures, within the confines of strict ceremonial and a prescribed form of address. The door stands open, [and] the door [. . .] is Christ [cf. Jn 14:6].[48]

Balthasar rather strikingly calls this *parrhesia* the "most important" trait of genuine Christian prayer—a claim which is not untouched by his ongoing polemic against Eastern spirituality.[49] But notice also how the emphasis on *parrhesia* follows logically from what was just said about confession and prayer: If sin deforms our prayer by introducing shame, and that shame is subsequently "cleansed" in the personal encounter of penance, then one has no reason to shrink or hide their face in prayer.[50] Indeed, for Balthasar at this point the whole Christian life is interpreted as a parrhesiastic prayer: In good conscience, the heart naturally seeks the "open path" to God, and "the heart [which is] advancing along this open path, is praying."[51]

Homo Orans is a parrhesiastes. That Balthasar characterizes the ideal creaturely response to the Word in terms of *parrhesia* also suggests how prayer can be a total

---

"*opposed* to silence as an [. . .] obstacle to contemplating God"), he does not argue the point and cites no direct examples (Michel Foucault, *Discourse and Truth and Parrhesia*, eds. Paul Fruchaud and Daniele Lorenzini [Chicago: University of Chicago Press, 2019], 41). One need only consider Chrysostom's generally positive understanding of the term to see the implausibility of Foucault's suggestion here (for a good discussion of the importance that Chrysostom attached to *parrhesia*, see Jirí Pavlík, "παρρησία in John Chrysostom's Homilies on the Gospel of Matthew," *Vigiliae Christianae* 73 [2019]: 1–15).

48. *Prayer* (H), 46.

49. See discussion at GL.7, 409ff. Balthasar poses Christian *parrhesia* especially against those forms of mysticism which emphasize self-annihilation or perfect stillness (see Section 2.3). In particular Balthasar seems to have in mind Eastern concepts like *nirvana* in Buddhism or *advaita* in Vedantic Hinduism (see *NE*, 150 or *Prayer* [H], 54 or *YCYYG*, 27–8). Balthasar's understanding of the East is arguably too simplistic, but it at least reveals significant features of what he takes to be distinctive about Christianity (i.e., Christian prayer's dialogical nature and the positive obligation for a word of response). In the Western traditions, this emphasis on *parrhesia* stands against Plotinian and gnostic strands of mysticism which leave behind the form of the word in the transcendent ascent to divine knowledge.

50. Cf. *Catechism of the Catholic Church* 2610, which likewise emphasizes the "filial boldness" befitting prayer in Christ.

51. *Prayer* (H), 48, 49.

life act and how, in turn, one can offer one's whole "existence as prayer." Since its earliest usage *parrhesia* has implicated the speaker completely with their words (this was what distinguished *parrhesia* from the rhetoric of the Sophists, whose words stood apart from what they themselves believed). Foucault observes: "[The *parrhesiastes*] emphasizes the fact [that] he himself is the subject of the opinion to which he refers."[52] The parrhesiastes, furthermore, knows that he is responsible for his words and is liable to be held accountable for them (as a trait of a royal adviser, for instance, *parrhesia* often involved the risk of punishment). When applied to prayer, *parrhesia* thus captures both the *aletheia* and *emeth* properties of prayer which emerged in Chapter 2. The person who prays with *parrhesia* holds nothing back in their discourse with God (*aletheia*), while at the same time resolving to abide by God's response (*emeth*), a response which comes in the form of a mission unique to each person. *Parrhesia* thus helps to fortify prayer as a "unity of life, love, and language" in the creature.[53]

5.3.2 Silence

It is essential to Balthasar's Christology that the Son be seen as the full express Word of the Father. This, in turn, undergirds the creaturely capacity for a prayer that transcends the purely horizontal level of existence. But at the same time, the Word that the Son is also includes silence. Though I did not stress it at any length in Chapter 4, Balthasar often speaks of Christ's silences at key moments in mission: leading up to the Transfiguration (and even the injunction to silence afterwards—Mt. 17:9); while standing before Pilate; in death on the Cross; and above all in the "great silence" of Holy Saturday.[54] Balthasar even refers to the thirty anonymous years of Christ's early life as a kind of silence in which the words of mission are not yet being spoken. Crucially, this silence is presented by Balthasar as an aspect of the overall Word that the Son is. Expressing the Father "in every conceivable way" means doing so "both actively and passively, with power and weakness, *in speech and in silence*, veiling and unveiling"[55]—"All of this is epiphany."[56] Expression includes silence not at the expense of its revelatory efficacy but precisely as an aspect of its fullness. Because the Son does not represent the Father in a merely procedural way (choosing this or that aspect of God's love to bring into the world) but rather shares "constantly" in God's very essence, Christ's silences speak as

---

52. Foucault, *Discourse and Truth and Parrhesia*, 123.
53. TL.2, 276, 278; cf. TS, 38. This unity of word and deed (*Tatwort* or *dābār*) is a running theme in Balthasar; see the discussion by Gawronski at *Word and Silence* 152-5 (unfortunately Gawronski does not consider the specific role prayer plays in instantiating this unity of word and deed). The *parrhesia* theme will reemerge in Chapter 7.
54. ET.5, 270.
55. *Prayer* (H), 184 (italics mine).
56. YCYYG, 33.

loudly as his words.⁵⁷ As Son, Christ is capable of uttering by being the "wordless but still resounding Word."⁵⁸

As I first discussed in Chapter 3, this notion requires a Trinitarian background in order not to see the Word's self-communication as a solitary action (in which case silence would indeed constitute a deficiency) but as revealing an ongoing dialogue (in which case silence finds a place in an overall pattern of relation). As any dialogue must, the Trinitarian one includes moments of pause, silent breaths which engender anticipation of the words to come.⁵⁹ A word not leavened by silence in this way quickly becomes "chatter" (and thus the opposite of *parrhesia*).⁶⁰ And on an even deeper level, the whole soteriological drama is implicated in the interplay between divine word and silence. On the Cross the Word has incorporated silence (by definition that which is not the Word) into itself without being overwhelmed: "[God] has drawn human death (separation from God!) into the relationship between the Father and the incarnate Son in the Holy Spirit, whom the Son breathes back to the Father in death, and [this means] that *this silence of death belongs to his mystery revealed to and for us*."⁶¹

If this relationship of silence and word pertains to the Trinitarian dialogue, then a stronger basis for speaking of silence within creaturely prayer emerges. Creaturely silence in prayer is for Balthasar a form of "positive readiness" that should never be considered meaningless; indeed, it models the disponibility which lies at the heart of the prayerful attitude as such.⁶² It is noteworthy that one of the few pieces of practical advice in *Prayer* is to seek a quiet, private room for contemplation in which one feels sufficiently "uninhibited," so that one might be

---

57. *Prayer* (H), 182; cf. *CM*, 14–15 and 40–6.
58. See *CM*, 40–1.
59. Properly speaking the Spirit is the "breath" between "the Utterer" and "the Word," who reveals that the fullness of divine essence consists in *going-out*. Ulrich's notion that the fullest expression of being consists in the self-emptying of love is crucial here (see, e.g., Balthasar's citation and discussion of Ulrich at TL.3, 227), as is Louis Bouyer's discussion of the Spirit as "breath of divine life" (see citation and discussion of Bouyer at TL.3, 54–5). With recourse to a typically Balthasarian neologism, the Son is described as "super-word" (*Uberwort*) which is *Wort + Nicht-wort* (but *not Un-wort*) (see TL.2, 122). On this view, the Son's "breathing forth the Spirit" thus constitutes his most expressive silence.
60. TL.2, 277; in this understanding of word Balthasar largely follows Max Picard, for whom "silence indwells the word" (TL.2, 113; cf. Picard, *Die Welt des Schweigens* [Zurich: Rentsch, 1948], 23). This incorporation of silence into word is also a way of ratifying Christianity's Jewish roots, since in the Old Testament God's silence or nonappearance is more often stressed as a feature of God's self-disclosure in history (cf. Exod. 33:20, etc.); on the "dazzling darkness" of God's revelation to Israel see GL.6, 39–41.
61. *CM*, 43 (italics mine). On this point, Balthasar often refers back to Ignatius of Antioch (see *CM*, 41 or TL.2, 122ff.)
62. *CM*, 18.

"totally awake" to the encounter with Christ.⁶³ Silence is a form of attention, then, which, crucially, must give way to the dialogue. It may be the case that the mature person of prayer can learn to draw out a certain amount of meaning from these silences themselves, as Thérèse of Lisieux seems to have done.⁶⁴ But this is always what we might call a missionary silence, searching for and expectant of the word of commission. Prayer as a mode of life is ultimately "more" than silence alone, and therefore any method of prayer which focuses one-sidedly on silent "space-making" threatens to deform the overall rhythm of mission.⁶⁵

63. *Prayer* (H), 94–5.

64. Balthasar reflects appreciatively on the fact that Thérèse distinguished her Little Way from its Carmelite antecedents by de-emphasizing the achievement of "sight" as the culmination of meditation; indeed, "Thérèse wishes *not* to see," since this allows her to live wholeheartedly in faith (see *2SS*, 335–6). According to Thérèse's own account, most of her time at Carmel was marked by this not-seeing, which she welcomed as a peaceful blessing (ibid., 291). Thérèse arguably pushes this perspective too far, however, when she claims that "on earth, one can *never* see heaven and the angels as they are" (quoted at *2SS*, 336). Balthasar rejects this conclusion ("Her opinion on this matter is mistaken") simply because it places limits on God's power to carry out the dialogue of prayer as God would (cf. also *Prayer* [H], 274). There is perhaps an overreaction to the Spanish tradition on Thérèse's part here, causing her to fail to grasp that "a person may be just as obedient in acknowledging a vision as in believing the truth by faith" (337).

65. Again, Balthasar's purpose here is implicitly polemical, especially against those strands of Quietism that consider silence a terminal position in prayer (Madame Guyon, for instance); for background see Elfrieda Dubois, "Fénelon and Quietism," in *The Study of Spirituality*, eds. Cheslyn Jones, Geoffrey Wainwright, and Edward Yarnold (London: SPCK, 1986), 408–15, 410. Of course, it would be inaccurate to characterize the whole of the French School in this way (for a balanced account, see Michael Buckley, "Seventeenth-Century French Spirituality: Three Figures," in *Christian Spirituality: Post-Reformation and Modern*, eds. Louis Dupré and Don Saliers [New York: Crossroads, 1991], 30–62). A latter-day version of the sort of spirituality that is being critiqued here is Sarah Coakley's account of prayer as a "silent waiting on the divine" (see Coakley, *Powers and Submissions* [Oxford: Blackwell, 2008], 34). Although Coakley rightly highlights the patient *askēsis* of "ceding and responding to the divine" as a necessary component of contemplative practice, prayer is not simply this "waiting," but the dialogue that the waiting invites. Coakley's emphasis also seems in the end to be too procedural, especially when she describes prayer arising out of "repeated phrase[s]" or the use of "quiet rhythmic tongues" (ibid., 34–5). Her apparent sympathy with Palamas' defense of hesychasm in the fourteenth century lends weight to this charge (ibid., 82–5). Another noteworthy example of a prayer practice arguably overdetermined by silence is Maggie Ross' "Rite for Contemplative Eucharist" (see *Silence: A User's Guide*, Vol. 2: *Application* [London: Darton, Longman, and Todd, 2017], 100–27), in which the *only* words that are spoken are a spontaneous epiclesis.

5.3.3 The Marian Word

More than any other person, Mary performs the appropriate response to the Word. In her perfect consent she incorporates both aspects of what I have been describing in this section: the silence which allows the Word to arrive uninterrupted and the parrhesiastic courage to respond (the dynamics of shame and confession from Section 5.2 do not apply to her in quite the same way). The American poet Denise Levertov captures the interplay of *parrhesia* and silence beautifully in her poem, "Annunciation."[66] Taking the familiar scene of Gabriel's appearance to Mary as a moment of prayer par excellence, Levertov observes that "we are told of meek obedience. No one mentions courage/The engendering Spirit did not enter her without consent/God waited." In fact, Thomas comes to the same conclusion, teaching that, "At the Annunciation, consent was awaited [*expectebatur*]."[67] This astounding moment of silence between the angel and Mary did not fall flat; it did not trail off into an uncertain response: it issued in the words of pure prayer—*Ecce, ancilla Domini*. In silence God shows God's respect for human freedom, and in silence human freedom resolves itself to the mission it has been given. Then, in turn, there is undoubtedly a boldness to Mary's response ("courage unparalleled," as Levertov describes it); in giving her Yes she makes "no stammering or approximate formulation, but an exact verbalization" which simply and powerfully expresses her total disposability before God.[68]

But even this "best answer" of the creature to the Word in prayer cannot anticipate its own "consequences" (a fact Mary is herself reminded of by Simeon's prophecy, Lk. 2:35).[69] Her disponibility to God will make her, at the foot of the Cross, "disponible to the new son John and thus [to] the Church" in an ongoing way.[70] As word lies beyond silence, so does life itself (i.e., mission) lie beyond the literal word.[71] It is to this lived mission, as the most comprehensive form of the life of prayer, that we turn now.

---

66. See Denise Levertov, *A Door in the Hive* (New York: New Directions, 1989), 86–8.

67. S.Th III 30.1 *respondeo* (cited at TD.4, 353).

68. GL.7, 112. Merold Westphal emphasizes the "shamelessness" of Mary's prayers in "Prayer as the Posture of the Decentered Self," in *The Phenomenology of Prayer*, eds. Bruce Benson and Norman Wirzba (New York: Fordham University Press, 2005), 13–31, here 24. On this point, Rachel Muers arguably undervalues the extent to which Mary's Yes is, for Balthasar, a positive response (see "The Mute Cannot Keep Silent: Barth, von Balthasar, and Irigaray, on the Construction of Women's Silence," in *Challenging Women's Orthodoxies in the Context of Faith*, 109–20, especially 115–16). Muers points to the familiar texts from the *Theo-Drama* concerning the "feminine" response in order to claim that "in Balthasar's Mariology and Ecclesiology [. . .] woman *is* the answer and does not *give* it" (115); however, the parrhesiastic aspects of prayer that have been under discussion here call this claim into question.

69. *CM*, 44–5.

70. ET.5, 145.

71. TL.2, 115.

5.4 Life and Mission

One key feature of the anthropological account so far is that it emphasizes how prayer is not a discrete or transactional exchange between God and the praying person. There is a genuine dialogue in prayer (*cor ad cor loquitur*), but a dialogue that implicates the *whole* of the praying person. It is also necessary to see all of these dynamics (of predisposition and response) in their proper ecclesial context: The praying community (and by extension the world) are implicated immediately in the constitution of selfhood. Thus, despite the language of dialogue—of word and response—I must emphasize again that these realities are holistic and social. In other words, prayer implicates the praying person at the level of *life itself*.

That prayer implicates the praying person at the level of life itself follows on from the objective definition of prayer as grounded in disponibility for mission. Availability is necessarily a maximal position—if one were to make oneself available only *to a certain extent*, one would not rightly be considered available.[72] Naturally enough, in normal circumstances one's subjective feelings of availability will ebb and flow; it is sometimes necessary to "recharge our batteries" (although it is important not to confuse recreation for prayer).[73] However, "spiritually and existentially [i.e., 'objectively'], this openness [to the Word] *has no limits*. The Christian must always be available, whether he is waking or sleeping, praying or working, speaking or being silent—because he has been made *in principle* available."[74] This is the meaning of the injunction to "pray without ceasing" (1 Thess. 5:17; Lk. 18:1), and constitutes creaturely imitation of Christ who expresses the Father at all times and "in every conceivable way." Central to Balthasar's dramatics is the idea that Christ opens an "acting area" in which the faithful "can become persons of theological relevance, coactors in theo-drama" to the extent that they live "in Christ."[75] My point here is that this mode of life-as-prayer constitutes the creaturely method of acting within the space opened by Christ. Obviously, imitation here cannot be understood as in any way "mechanical" but rather as a total life act—the Marian "Yes" in which one lays a claim even to one's own future.[76] There is thus a transtemporal aspect to prayer which clarifies how it can possibly be an existential disposition.

In addition to prayer's transtemporality, it is also an existential disposition in that it covers various subjective states of mind. Here Balthasar's notion of prayer

---

72. Cf. the remarks by Harrison "Homo Orans," 293–4.

73. *YCYYG*, 304; cf. *LAC*, 89.

74. *YCYYG*, 304.

75. TD.3, 263; see generally 263–82.

76. *Prayer* (H), 131. There is an allusive comparison to be drawn with the so-called method acting such as the kind taught by Stanislavsky, whom Balthasar discusses approvingly in TD.1. For Stanislavsky, there should be no essential distance between the actor and their role (*pace* the "rationalist" approach to acting from Diderot onwards, see TD.1, 288–9). Likewise, the theodramatic actor has to "commit" to their role entirely.

is most far removed from any kind of mystic "experience," if that is understood to mean an acute moment of ecstasy or the like. And it is here that his task, which I alluded to earlier, of upending a sentimental hagiography, is as clear as anywhere else. For the praying person to project their own "trivial emotional states in the same context as the vast mystery of redemption," Balthasar says, "is, frankly, kitsch."[77] In fact, Balthasar's emphasis on mission as the objective basis of personalization suggests to him that "personality" goes well beyond incidental questions of mood or emotion. What matters most is the "Yes," and God does not begrudge the inevitable variance in attitude or tone in which one is prone to give it: "It makes *no difference* whether the answer is given with repugnance, as Moses gave it; or generously and freely, as Isaiah gave it [. . .]; or reluctantly, as Jeremiah gave it, [etc.]."[78] Even a positive "No" such as Jonah's does not stop God from attempting a "second" call (Jnh 3:1). It is significant that this striking claim occurs in the middle of *The Christian State of Life*, a work which represents Balthasar's extended meditation on the Ignatian "Call of Christ" (*SpExx* 91–8). It is the essence of Ignatian *elección* to choose God's choice: "His [i.e., the one making an election] answer must be so absorbed into and enveloped by the word of his calling that it forms an indissoluble union with it."[79] "Indifference" is the term used to describe the proper attitude of the creature who seeks to make such a choice—nor is this "indifference" to be understood as simply "the extinction of the creature's function in favor of the divine function" but rather as the creature's seeking to place all it has, precisely as creature, in service of the divine task.[80] So an overemphasis on enthusiasm threatens to obscure the objective form of obedience, which is life itself. Indeed, the presence of reluctance or repugnance in making one's Yes may in fact signal the seriousness with which one is committed to the mission one has been given; it may signal, in other words, what Rowan Williams describes as the "decision not to escape" which lies at the heart of mission-consciousness (cf. Isa. 6:8 or Lk. 1:38).[81]

---

77. *Prayer* (H), 305.

78. *CSL*, 398, my italics. Elsewhere he calls such considerations ultimately "irrelevant" (*MCW*, 140). See also the remarks on mission at *TuG*, 20.

79. *CSL*, 399; in this sense it is not necessary to "divide the one act [of election] into its divine and human components" (ibid., 400). Cf. Balthasar's discussion of Ignatian prayer at *Prayer* (H), 130ff. And see as well the pertinent treatments by Löser ("The Ignatian Exercises in the Work of Hans Urs von Balthasar") and Servais (*Théologie des Exercices Spirituels: Hans Urs von Balthasar interprète saint Ignace*, [Paris: Culture et Vérité, 1996]).

80. *CSL*, 401; see Balthasar's discussion of the famous *suscipe* prayer, which expresses this indifference with a special clarity, at *MCW*, 140–1. One need not draw too sharp a distinction between prayer and discernment in this regard: To the extent that the praying person is willing to listen for and ultimately submit to the judgment of the objective Word which comes to them in prayer, then they are already engaged in an effort to discern effectively (Cf. *Prayer* [L], 158).

81. Williams, *On Christian Theology* (Oxford: Blackwell, 2000), 122.

Does this "objective" view of personality do violence to the concrete person who prays? On the contrary, it allows for the person to come to prayer as they are, and to commit their particular traits and gifts to mission. There are as many different ways of making one's Yes credible, ultimately, as there are personalities in the church. What has been said about the objectivity of mission-consciousness, therefore, must be seen in light of the church's claims to catholicity, which, in Chapter 4, I said were based on the unconditional nature of Mary's Yes (the infinite diversity of subjective states of mission mirrors the total open-endedness of her prototypical Yes). In this sense the communion of saints (understood minimally as all those who respond to the call to mission) serves to illustrate the substance of catholicity, "one thus and another quite differently" but all united under the one Spirit of prayer.[82] The objectivity of mission-consciousness must also be seen in light of the remarks in Chapter 2 about Balthasar's effort to establish an engaged model of sanctity in the midst of the modern world, since it foregrounds the extent to which prayer is an ongoing work carried out over the span of a lifetime. The life of prayer is

> perforce an everyday life, of small fidelities and services performed in the spirit of love [. . .]. It is a conversation in which we try not to be tedious, not to say and think the same thing day after day, but use our gifts of imagination or reason to offer God the little we can draw from our own resources.[83]

In other words, life itself is implicated in prayer since prayer ultimately has no other venue in which to occur than the life of the person who prays. We see here that the impossibility of an escapist mysticism (which I argued for in Section 2.3 *supra*) is borne out by the fact that prayer implicates the praying person at the level of daily action and "small fidelities." And finally, the objectivity of mission-consciousness once more indicates the pneumatological underpinnings of prayer, since it is only on the basis of the Spirit who holds unity-in-difference that each member of the body can be trusted to act in some sense in unison.

The ecclesial dimensions which (re-)emerge at this point indicate one final aspect of prayer's significance at the level of life itself: If prayer is this process of personalization in and through mission, then the picture of the person which thereby emerges is fundamentally oriented in two directions at the same time. This is because the church is most true to its unique essence, as we already said, when it points away from itself to the Son—and in turn the Son is most faithful to his unique mission when he demonstrates its basis entirely in the Father's love. So therefore, "Vocation to the Church and within the Church is both personalizing

---

82. Cf. TD.2, 50 and *TS*, 14: "The first thing presupposed by sanctity is the will to be a part of the Body, with its many counterpoised members."

83. *Prayer* (L), 111–2; cf. a similar sentiment at ibid., 246.

and socializing" for the individual person.[84] On the one hand, it is in prayer that the person comes to terms with their individual mission-identity; on the other hand, this mission-identity is never self-referential but always seeks to expand beyond itself through the other-oriented movements of love. Just as "God does not will to be God without Israel nor Christ will to be the Saviour without his church," so too the praying person does not want to merely be an autonomous person, does not wish to be "left alone" in prayer.[85] The ecclesial person's life is thus marked by a prayer that has the effect of "expand[ing their] 'I' to the limit [and] universaliz[ing their] own situation."[86] In the unique form of Trinitarian participation that prayer makes possible, the praying person's "I" is constituted within the ecclesial "We." The means of this ecclesial I-expansion are various but include everything from communal social practices to shared sacramental discipline.[87] But none of these means of I-expansion fundamentally go beyond that act of self-extension that one already undertakes in the simplest of prayers: *amen*. In these ways, one's very sense of self is "stretched" by prayer (as various scriptural citations suggest by describing prayer in terms of stretching: 1 Kgs 8:22, 54; 2 Chron. 6:13, 29; 2 Macc. 3:20; Mt. 12:49; etc.).[88] Ultimately the surest form of this I-expansion is the common

---

84. TD.2, 427–8. Cf. *VBR*, 369: "Election and choosing is a personalizing and at the same time a dispossessing of the person." O'Regan explains Balthasar's model of ecclesial sanctity further, emphasizing the "depersonalized" aspect of life in Christ: "[For Balthasar,] the saint is an ecclesial person whose aim is to excavate the unrepeatable call or mission that defines them and to which he or she bears witness. In this sense the less idiosyncrasy the better; for idiosyncrasy is what darkens the self that would be a mirror of Christ" (*The Anatomy of Misremembering*, 79). O'Regan perhaps overstates his point here, as it seems Balthasar leaves much more space for "idiosyncrasy" in the course of mission than O'Regan suggests. Even a cursory consideration of Balthasar's method in the first part of his trilogy—where he deploys various poets, philosophers, and theologians while allowing each to speak in his or her own unique, idiosyncratic voice—seems to mitigate against O'Regan's reading. Nevertheless, he is surely right that for Balthasar the essential thing is a total transparency to (Christoform) mission-consciousness and that, further, this transparency is ecclesially recapitulated as universalizability, thus the saint's role as a model for the *whole* church.

85. Hanvey, "Tradition as Subversion," 61.

86. *Prayer* (H), 89.

87. See *EG*, 54–5. See also the pertinent discussion by Schumacher, "Ecclesial Existence: Person and Community in the Trinitarian Anthropology of Adrienne von Speyr," in *Modern Theology* 24:3 (2008), 359–85.

88. Cf. TD.2, 181, 369; TD.3, 270; or *Prayer* (H), 142. This is also the essence of Paul's exhortations to the Galatians. Origen likewise describes prayer in terms of "stretching"—see *An Exhortation to Martyrdom, Prayer and Selected Word*, trans. Rowan Greer (New York: Paulist, 1979), 164–5.

participation in mission, to which each contributes in a unique way toward an end which belongs to none individually or in isolation.[89]

5.5 Consolidation

However, at this point we run up against the distinctively *eschatological* dimensions of prayer, since the collective striving toward that "end which belongs to none individually or in isolation" is nothing less than the work of building up the Kingdom of God. This collective striving toward the Kingdom involves prayer in ways that are decisively important to Balthasar's overall account. As prayer served to orient the anthropological discussion in a genuinely "vertical" direction, so too, as we will see, is it necessary in order to prevent Christian eschatology from becoming merely another ideology of progress. Prayer also undergirds Balthasar's notions of action and history in ways that are not always sufficiently appreciated. However, as it seems to me necessary to treat the distinctively eschatological aspects of prayer separately, since these are not simply reducible to what has been said already, it will suffice for the moment to conclude this current chapter by briefly recapitulating those essential points of the anthropological discussion.

Prayer itself performs the work of grace upon the creature by calling them out of their shame before God. Through confession the person begins to come into focus as a relevant theodramatic actor—as someone repentant of certain sins and resolved to certain missions. Having spoken one's sins plainly, one then learns to undertake the dialogue-relationship of prayer with a greater boldness and

---

89. Westphal's account is useful here ("Prayer as the Posture of the Decentered Self"). Westphal discusses, with reference to the prayers of Samuel (1 Samuel 3) and Mary at the Annunciation, the ways in which prayer puts the person in a position of simultaneous "belonging and disponsibility" (23), a simultaneity which is ultimately paradoxical (Westphal draws parallels with Kierkegaard, Derrida, and Marion). Prayer reveals that the self does not belong to itself, and thus only acquires the truth about itself when it allows itself to be given (cf. 30). However, Westphal arguably shows the limits of his phenomenological approach with his one-sided emphasis on the moment of reflection in which the self turns away from itself and from the world (!) in order to receive its truth—even if, as Westphal admits, this must then involve God "send[ing the praying person] *back* [into the world] with a task" (22). Without wishing to oversell the differences at work here, I note that there is nevertheless a subtle shift in emphasis precisely on the question of mission. For Balthasar, any attempt to conceive of this moment of prayer's decentering outside (or prior to) the realities of mission and world is fraught from the start. There is no theologically relevant sense in which the person is sent "back" into the world from prayer, since it is precisely in and through the structures of the world that prayer must take place and become real for the creature. Most of all this is borne out in one's love of others—others, after all, who are only ever encountered in the world. Thus, it is not that the self is decentered in the experience *being given* (which is an insight of reflection) but in *being sent* (which is a lived reality).

openness to mission; this dialogue-relationship spans across one's life and includes even the many and seemingly interminable silences that so often afflict prayer. On this basis, prayer can be seen as a mode of relation which implicates the person at the level of life itself—rather than a reflective drawing back from the world or a solipsistic turning inward. Prayer is on this telling a form of free exchange between God and creature which orients the person beyond themself in an open posture of love. Such a view is expansive enough to include the endless variety of emotions, states of mind, or impressions that are liable to be experienced in prayer.

To be clear, the point of the preceding is not to describe a form of prayer that *ignores* the legitimate diversity of experience but to render an account that can hope to explain what, in objective theological terms, is happening when we pray.

Chapter 6

PRAYER'S END

ESCHATOLOGICAL DIMENSIONS

6.1 Theocentric Eschatology

Balthasar opens a 1957 essay on eschatology by noting its revival as a major topic in twentieth-century dogmatics. Like a mighty thunderstorm, Balthasar says, eschatology bears down upon every major field of dogmatics, in many cases "reinvigorating their various growths" for the better.[1] In his more systematic handbook on the same topic, Joseph Ratzinger explains this "shift" in terms of a fateful combination of the historical-critical turn in biblical studies (which served in part to emphasize just how "soaked through with eschatology" Jesus' preaching was) and, more significantly, the rise of Marxism (which Ratzinger characterizes as an "anti-theistic [. . .] messianism").[2] There was also, as a noted historian of the period has put it, the general "mood of messianic expectation and world repudiation" that hung over Europe after the devastation of two world wars.[3]

However, if it was clear enough that modernity was giving rise to a renewed eschatological sensibility, Balthasar wanted to ensure that eschatology not, therefore, be carried out according to modernist assumptions. In other words, he insisted, "there is no 'system' of the last things," no "settled [. . .] structure," according to which one might scientifically determine the factors which move history forward

---

1. "Some Points of Eschatology" in ET.1, 255–77, here 255 (originally "Eschatologie" in *Fragen der Theologie Heute* [Einsiedeln: Benziger, 1957]). Balthasar's most mature attempt at a positive eschatology comes in TD.5.

2. Joseph Ratzinger, *Eschatology: Death and Eternal Life* (Washington: The Catholic University of America Press, 2nd edition 2006), 1–3; originally *Eschatologie—Tod und ewiges Leben* (1977). Balthasar characterizes Marxist eschatology similarly, referring especially to Bloch's notion of hope as a "radically secularized Messianism" (see TD.5, 170).

3. Anson Rabinbach, *In the Shadow of Catastrophe: German Intellectuals between Apocalypse and Enlightenment* (Berkeley: University of California Press, 1997), 2. For a concise account of Catholic intellectual history during the early interwar period, see James Chappel, *Catholic Modern: The Challenge of Totalitarianism and the Remaking of the Church* (Cambridge, Massachusetts: Harvard University Press, 2018), 22–59.

and, once having determined them, control them.⁴ Nor must eschatology collapse into mere apocalypticism, which likewise vitiates human agency in favor of vague ideas about a sudden deliverance. Rather, a distinctively Christian eschatology has always insisted not upon the foreclosure of human agency but that the "horizon [of history] is left *open*" to transformation by grace, grace which it is then incumbent upon the creature to assist cooperatively in building up.⁵ It is this eschatological sensibility that pervades all theology which remembers that God is God.

But it is also the case, and largely for the same reasons, that properly eschatological theology is fundamentally hopeful—that it expresses the fullness of the theological vision of history as the realm in which God makes God's love definitively and decisively known. "Almost more even than any other *locus theologicus*," Balthasar writes in the essay mentioned already, "eschatology is [. . .] entirely a doctrine of *salvation*."⁶ This follows on from a view of the person as fundamentally made in the image of and ordered toward God. If eschatology concerns "last things," then God *is* the *eschaton*, the end to which all life is ultimately directed: "God is the 'last thing' of the creature. Gained, he is heaven; lost, he is hell; examining, he is judgment; purifying, he is purgatory. He it is to whom finite being dies, and through whom it rises to him, in him."⁷ Here, as Healy notes, "the traditional themes of eschatology such as death, judgment, resurrection, purgatory, heaven, hell, etc. are considered first as christological and trinitarian events."⁸ In this sense, Balthasar's approach should be seen as part of the wider eschatological renewal that was underway within Catholic theology at the time, in reaction to the manualist tendency to confine the topic to the status of a "harmless appendix to the theological curriculum."⁹ His approach reflects what in TD.5 Balthasar calls a properly "theocentric, not [. . .] anthropocentric" eschatology.¹⁰ (My own decision to place the "eschatological dimensions of prayer" toward the end of this

---

4. ET.1, 255.
5. Ibid., 256.
6. Ibid., 261.
7. Ibid., 260; cf. *WiC?* 63: "God's kingdom is God himself."
8. Healy, *The Eschatology of Hans Urs von Balthasar*, 16. Healy continues: "This approach does not entail a disregard of the anthropological *eschata*—man's death, judgment, and final destiny—but a shift of perspective such that the latter are considered as occurring *within* the person and mission of Christ, and ultimately *within* the Trinity" (*loc. cit.*). See Healy's discussion from 13-8, which gives a helpful overview of Balthasar's eschatological writings—although unfortunately Healy neglects the rather significant eschatological section of *Prayer* from which I will be drawing in this chapter. In fact, Healy's otherwise thorough study commits almost no sustained attention to prayer's eschatological dimensions in Balthasar's thought.
9. Peter Phan, "Roman Catholic Theology," in *The Oxford Handbook of Eschatology*, ed. Jerry Walls (Oxford: Oxford University Press, 2008), 216-32, here 216. See the historical summary by Phan at 216-20.
10. TD.5, 57.

book reflects my view not that eschatology is a "harmless appendix" but more like something of a summit which can only be scaled after having made the necessary approaches.)

Seen from the perspective of this "theocentric" approach, eschatology's connection to prayer begins to come more clearly into focus. The expectant hope that characterizes eschatological reflection is essentially a prayerful stance. Again, prayer's *aletheia-emeth* rhythm recurs. The eschatological prayer occurs "after" the Incarnation, understood here as the central event of history in which God announces God's saving intention for the world (*aletheia*), but "before" that saving plan is yet fully realized within history, although God continues to honor the commitment and works to see it come to fruition (*emeth*). Thus, Balthasar describes all prayer as "situated between the two *parousias* of the Lord," a Johannine "abiding" with Christ, who is both the source and the end of faith (cf. Jn 15:4-11).[11] I have described prayer as that steady gazing upon the Father (cf. Sections 4.1.1, 4.3, and 5.2.2 *supra*)—now in the eschatological register we see prayer as the effort to *maintain* the gaze, to "watch" attentively even amid the confusions and concealments of history. Maintaining the gaze is no passive undertaking, but an act of endurance that calls for a certain conscious effort. Balthasar emphasizes this point so much that he apparently elides the dual injunctions of Lk. 21:36 ("Watch ye therefore and pray always") such that "prayer apart from watching [. . .] is not Christian prayer at all."[12] Christ is the focal point here, so that abiding-with-Christ is itself eschatologically significant.[13] Prayer's Christological basis implies its eschatological orientation. To take up the dialogue-relationship of prayer with Christ but to neglect the eschatological dimensions is to prove oneself less than totally invested in the dialogue, since it is not until the end of time that the Word attains finality.[14] This prayerful abiding-with-Christ is necessary if the "horizon [of history] is [to be] left open" and a crude apocalypticism is to be meaningfully resisted.

This approach also indicates prayer's soteriological function as a defense against sin. It is in this time of waiting and watching before the second *parousia* that "the dragon" rules the earth, and temptation therefore besets any fallen creature who attempts to keep watch, since "the dragon's wrath" increases as "he knows he has but a short time" left to reign (Rev. 12:12).[15] In other words, the fact that prayer always must operate from within the midst of history suggests it is subject to the same laws of fallenness that govern unredeemed history. Earlier in Chapter 4, I cited the "fundamental theodramatic law of world history[:] The greater the

---

11. *Prayer* (L), 115; cf. *EG*, 54.

12. *Prayer* (L), 119–20.

13. Cf. ET.1, 267. Rahner makes a similar assertion, writing that, "Christ himself is the hermeneutic principle of all eschatological assertions" (*Theological Investigations*, vol. IV, 342-3, qtd. by Balthasar at TD.5, 36 n.3).

14. Cf. *Prayer* (H), 150.

15. *Prayer* (L), 115; cf. the fuller discussion of this passage at TD.5, 210ff.

revelation of divine (ground-less) love, the more it elicits a groundless (Jn 15:25) hatred."[16] Here we see that this law persists even (or especially) in eschatological end time, and prayer is presented as a method of keeping faith despite the predations of "the dragon." Again, "watching" is the essential thing. It is when asked to "watch and pray" with Jesus through the night that the disciples prove themselves most faithless by succumbing to sleep (Mt. 26:40) and thereby letting the dialogue-relationship of prayer fall silent. Sin operates in this regard simply as the distraction—which of course can take an endless number of forms—that keeps us from prayer.[17] Interestingly, Balthasar notes how rote prayer can be its own form of distraction which is opposed to the true openness of the dialogue-relationship. The ironic tempter from *Heart of the World* "warns" against constant watchfulness in prayer, recommending a regimented approach instead (in which the person attempts to get in their "five minutes a day"), so as to effect a clean "separation of prayer and daily life."[18] In this way, prayer itself (or, rather, prayer of an inauthentic sort) can prove to be a distraction from prayer! True prayer, on the other hand, "never wearies," Balthasar writes, "it does not want to 'sleep' at the Beloved's side but to be wide awake."[19] To be "wide awake" with Christ in prayer involves a "decision" which "temporal man needs continually to reaffirm [. . .] and keep [. . .] fresh and new."[20] It is thus a dramatic decision, which is for the person a "constant struggle" to maintain—a life in "tension."[21]

All of this is consistent with the picture of prayer as existential mission-consciousness that I have been developing up to this point. Prayer here is seen to be the substance of faith, ratified across time and space in the context of a given life. To be clear: Prayer is not itself a perfect prophylactic against sin, but the attentive and responsive orientation to the Father which defines prayer is reparative of precisely the sort of inattentiveness that otherwise characterizes so well sinful humanity's relationship toward God.[22]

---

16. TD.4, 338.

17. Pope Francis often speaks of the devil—the dragon—as the facilitator of this kind of distraction. For a useful discussion, see Alan McGill, "What Does Pope Francis Mean by His References to the Devil as a Being? An Intratextual, Cultural-Linguistic Perspective," in *Heythrop Journal* 60 (2019): 769–82, especially 771–2, on "Francis' References to the Devil as a Facilitator of External Temptation."

18. *HW*, 125–6.

19. *Prayer* (H), 130; cf. *EG* 55.

20. Ibid., 148.

21. Ibid., 148, 150.

22. To describe prayer in terms of attentiveness in this way recalls Simone Weil's definition of prayer as "attention taken to the highest degree" (Weil, *Gravity and Grace*, trans. Emma Crawford and Mario von der Ruhr [New York: Routledge Press, 2002], 117).

6.2 Prayer and (Salvation) History

Earlier I described prayer as a process of "watching" from amid history for the final end of history—the *eschaton*. It is important to note, however, that this implies no degradation of history's status. Indeed, prayer works from within history in certain ways to sanctify it and to (re)orient it toward its final end.

6.2.1 Sanctifying History

As a "decision" ratified across space and time, prayer is profoundly active. Indeed, prayer of this sort constitutes eschatologically significant work in itself that contributes to the forward progress of salvation history. Perhaps the word "progress" here seems misplaced. Is not this attentive "watching" for Christ in prayer a regressive form of looking back, which "runs counter to the onward march of history"?[23] For the "merely historical man," Balthasar admits the answer to this question must be "Yes." But for the one who looks back upon Christ with contemplative eyes—that is, for the one who sees Christ as and at prayer—then this "looking back" is itself an individual share in the *fides Christi* which saves.

It was Christ's prayers that sustained him through the night at Gethsemane, and which expressed his commitment to the eschatological future: "Not my will but yours" expresses not immanence and consummation but expectation and hope. In his "watching" for the face of the Father, which seemed then so far and so hidden, Christ expressed "an openness of the heart towards God"— an openness into which God poured the guiding Spirit who drove him to the very ends of mission.[24] That is to say, the Son's action was made possible to the same extent that he made himself available in prayer. Christian hope after Christ likewise grows in the suffering expectation of the "not yet" and allows that distance from God to give us our bearings—it becomes the *distance that draws us closer*, a point Balthasar expands upon at length in the opening sections of TD.5.[25] All eschatologically significant prayer operates from within this distance that draws us closer. By "participat[ing] in Christ's vision" prayer turns our nescience into the very condition of our experience of God's presence.[26] For the person of prayer, formed by "the rhythm of Christ, and built up by his word, it is possible for our earthly existence's remoteness from God to be itself a form and an expression

---

23. *Prayer* (H), 143. This is essentially the Marxist critique; for discussion and comparison of Marxist and theological accounts of progress in history, especially as they relate to memory, see my "Competing Accounts of Progress: The Redemptive Purpose of Memory in J. B. Metz and Theodor Adorno," in *Heythrop Journal* 59:3 (2018): 544–60.

24. *Prayer* (L), 119.

25. See TD.5, 82–125, especially the pivotal pages included under the heading "The World is from God." This is a distinctively Speyrean theme, as Balthasar's frequent citations of *The World of Prayer* at this point suggest.

26. *Prayer* (H), 169; cf. ibid., 147.

of heavenly existence."²⁷ In this context, prayer serves as "the way in which faith can be transformed, to a certain extent, into insight."²⁸ This is the eschatological function to prayer itself. It is precisely by "looking back" to the Son and with him "watching" for the Kingdom to come that the Christian arrives at a distinctive view to the Father.²⁹

In fact, on this account it is prayer that quite literally gives a coherent shape to history. As Hanvey notes: "If history is the realm of our fall, the experience of our not knowing, then it is precisely in, and through, history that we come to be redeemed by the presence of Christ."³⁰ Indeed, as we have just seen, it is precisely "in and through the experience of our not knowing," when that not knowing is recontextualized within the loving dialogue-relationship of prayer, that the presence of Christ is most real for us. There is no prayer relationship between Christ and the individual outside of this historical reality, and it is only in history, "with all its drama, its judgments, rejections, redemptions and elections, [and] its obduracies" that one can learn "at long last [. . .] the lesson of prayer," which is mission.³¹ This sense that history "attains fulfillment" in the prayer relationship between God and creature gives rise in turn to a certain trajectory within history, a sense of how to move through history and toward what ends.³² As Christ's "not yet" drove him to activity in mission, "the Christian's activity [likewise] springs from the fact that he and the world in which he dwells have not yet attained the status made possible in principle by the redemption accomplished by Christ."³³ This is seen in a particularly clear way when one considers the forty days of the risen Christ, in which the temporal elements of Christ's (and the church's) mission

---

27. *Prayer* (H), 293.

28. Ibid., 145.

29. Tonstad argues that even this "looking backward is a gendered act" ("Everything Queer, Nothing Radical?," *Svensk Teologisk Kvartalskrift* 92 [2016]: 118–29, here 128), since after looking back the possibility of any subsequent futurity is usually denied to the feminine (Tonstad compares the stories of Lot's wife and Orpheus, 128–9). Tonstad's provocative proposal is to "stay with the Sodomites and accept the fixity of Lot's wife," thereby exposing (and thereby challenging) the deadly "stasis" which denies escape to those deemed damned (129). In this way, "looking back" itself becomes a form of protest, upsetting what Balthasar called "the onward march of history." That Balthasar himself would likely not have been deeply sympathetic to Tonstad's broader (explicitly anti-Balthasarian!) queer-feminist project need not prevent us from seeing the clear resonances between their accounts and the importance they both place on an attentive practice of "watching" which refuses to forget.

30. Hanvey, "Continuing the Conversation," *Radical Orthodoxy? A Catholic Enquiry*, ed. Laurence Hemming (Aldershot: Ashgate, 2000), 149–171, here 170.

31. *TH*, 61. See also *TuG*, 20: "But this utterly personal element remains inseparable from history in [the] man who has received the commission."

32. *TH*, 60.

33. *Prayer* (H), 142–3.

are arranged in a coherent way. That is, *past* events of the Passion are recalled and come into focus (Jn 20:27, e.g.), while the *present* time is rendered a sacramental vehicle of real presence (Mt. 29:18, e.g.), and the *future* is explicitly and repeatedly implicated as the realm of final consummation in the Spirit (Lk. 24:44-49, e.g.).[34] Pentecost thus "inaugurates" the particularly Christian sense of futurity—but it is a futurity, crucially, conceived of entirely in terms of mission. Just as Pentecost was fundamentally a commission, a sending-forth which implied concrete historical responsibilities for the disciples (the diversity of "tongues" suggesting where each was to go and preach), so too in prayer the individual person is to a certain extent made responsible for history, inasmuch as "mission implies responsibility."[35] Prayer understood in this way grounds Christian futurity, not despite but as a result of its "looking back" to Christ whose commitment to mission extends to the end of time.

This is prayer sanctifying history, an idea which can be traced through Balthasar's general account of God's appearance in history. In a discussion of Old Testament revelation toward the beginning of GL.6, Balthasar observes, "Like his word, God's holiness is active; it imposes itself and has an effect."[36] The proper creaturely response to this might be described in terms of "glorifying" God, or of giving him "praise" or "blessing," but such are not to be understood as activities of an exclusively otherworldly focus: "At the deepest level, it is by making room for grace that man obediently contributes to God's self-sanctification and self-glorification in the world."[37] In GL.7, Balthasar explains further that Christ brings this process (of glorification as sanctification) to its highest historical point, so that the holy person subsequently becomes the occasion of God's presence in the world to the extent that they embrace Christ's mission through the Spirit: "The act whereby God's justifying act in Christ takes possession of man is therefore at the same time also the sanctification of the man" as such.[38] And finally in *Prayer*,

---

34. See *TH*, 89–90.

35. TD.5, 179. A simple contrast is helpful here. If a person were to believe that history has no future, so to speak, or that whatever future is to come, must do so deterministically according to an impersonal set of rules, then it would simply make no sense to pray. At best, a prayer of this sort would be a display of momentary emotion (it is precisely this complaint that Balthasar lodges against German Idealism; see *Prayer* [H], 63, GL.5, 643 or TD.1, 588–9). Seen in this light, Christian prayer is an affirmation of human agency. It *matters* that the praying person prays, and in praying they help to bring about a future which might otherwise not have been thus. It is also important to stress that since the prayed-for Kingdom is eternal, the "future" in question here is thus not primarily temporal but refers to the fuller unfolding in history of the already-present reality (see *Prayer* [H], 104). Pannenberg's notion of salvation history as a proleptic structure is a helpful concept here.

36. GL.6, 59.

37. Ibid.

38. GL.7, 303.

Balthasar describes this act as prayer, wherein the praying person, as we have seen, becomes progressively better acquainted with the unique role they have to play as a fully formed person in Christ.[39] And to the extent that a given person comes to recognize the "truly historical and 'eventful' character" of their personhood in Christ, then they can be said to "contribute" to a concrete history of salvation.[40]

6.2.2 Intercession

What has been said here becomes clearer when one considers the case of intercessory prayer. In intercessory prayer, the petitioner prays in hopes that their own burden will be taken up by their advocates in heaven. That is to say, the community of praying persons on earth and the *Communio Sanctorum* in heaven intermingle—more than that, in prayer they "carry each other's burdens" (Paul's exhortation at Gal. 6:2 applies to both the earthly and heavenly church).[41] Prayers of intercession thus presuppose what Balthasar calls a "complete communism in all goods and graces," so that the praying person can dare to lay claim to a "double portion" of love enough to sustain them in their mission.[42] This request for a "double portion" was a common prayer of Thérèse of Lisieux.[43] This laying claim to a "double portion" is a good example of the *parrhesia* of prayer, which is not afraid to ask for what it needs. It is also, more fundamentally, a straightforward metaphysical consequence of love's source in the ever-flowing abundance of the prior Trinitarian life. Even the simplest form of petition thus participates in the open relations of mutual trust and availability which characterize God's inner life: "It is scarcely possible to have a deeper insight into the Trinitarian openness of Father and Son for one another in the Spirit," Balthasar says, than to enter into the perspective from which "asking and receiving flow into one another, and the fact of having [already] received does not exclude asking."[44]

---

39. Cf. *Prayer* (H), 186–7.

40. *Prayer* (L), 26. Graham Ward calls this "prayer's therapeutic action"—reconciling the praying person's sense of alienation from existence by acquainting them with the "wholeness that makes us whole" (Ward, *How the Light Gets In*, 174).

41. Dimech distinguishes between the *Communio Sanctorum* (capitalized) and the *communio sanctorum* (uncapitalized), the latter referring inclusivistically to "all of humanity" and the former to those explicitly named saints by the hierarchical church (see Dimech, *Authority of the Saints*, 11–2, especially Diagram 01). Dimech's distinction is plausible, especially given how often Balthasar's meaning seems to shift between the two types of "saints." My specific point here about prayer uniting the earthly church with the *Communio Sanctorum* does not preclude likewise describing prayer as the substance of unity among the broader *communio sanctorum*.

42. 2SS, 205.

43. See 2SS, 204–7.

44. GL.7, 410.

It is worth noting that there is a revisionist point here to do, again, with Christ's faith. Against Augustine, who explicitly taught that one can only have hope for oneself, Balthasar argues (with Thomas) that hope can properly also apply to those whom one loves as one's own.[45] Since Christ's love includes the whole world (cf. 1 Tim. 2:4), and since the whole world is made in Christ (cf. Eph. 2:10), his hope "on earth and even [. . .] in heaven" is for "the redemption of his *whole* Mystical Body."[46] Nor does the imputation of hope to Christ's mission imply any violation of his perfect foreknowledge: "Hope does not need to be uncertain," and Christ's "infallible hope" should be seen as a positive aspect of his mission that rightly includes all he was sent to save.[47] Consequently, the saints to whom intercessory prayers are directed, since each saint shares in their unique, historically specific ways in Christ's saving mission, continue to hope for, and therefore continue to work toward, the object of their hope (i.e., the ends of their particular missions).[48] Sanctity "in its essence is [. . .] the bringing to bear of Christ's influence on history," and as long as history carries on—that is, until the eschatological "last days"—the saints, who are above all *defined* by their sanctity, must likewise carry on their missions.[49] Thus, why it is right to pray to particular saints for particular purposes. Recourse to the saints in prayer—daring to draw a "double portion" from the heavenly reserves of grace—suggests a profound solidarity between members of the Mystical Body, whether living or dead. (Naturally, this solidarity works in both directions, so that the prayers of the living can also benefit the dead.[50])

In this way, the particular practice of intercessory prayer conforms to what was said in Chapter 4 about the efficacy of Christ's faith, reinforces the general teaching regarding Christ's universal saving mission, and lends a degree of specificity

---

45. See Augustine, *Enchiridion* 8, 3, and cf. Thomas, *ST* II-2, 17.3. See the whole discussion at ET.2, 64–73, and corroborative remarks at *YCYYG*, 261 and *Prayer* (H), 169.

46. ET.2, 67.

47. Ibid.

48. The theological virtues of faith, hope, and love *together* remain in heaven, as Paul clearly says (1 Cor. 13:13); what are predicted to "pass away" are the "gifts" of grace like prophecy, tongues, and *gnosis*. This is because the theological virtues spring forth from and naturally conform to God's own "event-character," rather than arising as (gracious and necessary) concessions to fallen creatures in mission, as the gifts do. That a "later theology" came to regard hope and faith as "essentially virtues of the pilgrim state," which will therefore likewise "perish" reflects more than anything else Scholasticism's insistence on philosophical dialectic over Paul's deeply biblical perspective. Ultimately, "The three concepts [i.e., faith, hope, and love] are *interpenetrating traits of a single basic attitude* of the man who has been drawn into the Covenant with God." See the discussion of all this at TD.5, 407–9 and cf. the remarks at *WiC?* 59–60. The critique of Augustine reappears at ET.1, 266–7.

49. *TuG*, 24.

50. See Paul Griffiths' useful discussion of ancient Christian prayer practices, "Purgatory" in *Oxford Handbook of Eschatology*, 430–4.

to the idea of creaturely (ecclesial) participation "in Christ." More broadly, intercessory prayer reveals the close nexus that exists between hope, prayer, and the eschatological progress of history.

What the example of intercessory prayer also brings to light is just how "realized" Balthasar's eschatology is. The hope expressed in intercessory prayer suggests the creature's willingness to relocate itself entirely within, and (therefore) see its end in, God.[51] In his own discussion of the eschatological significance of prayers to the saints, Ratzinger ventures as far as to say that in prayer, "the walls separating heaven and earth, and past, present and future, are now as glass."[52] In one of his most "programmatic" Category 2 works, *Razing the Bastions*, Balthasar goes even further than this, suggesting that in prayer these "walls" are not just rendered transparent, but collapse altogether.[53] For Balthasar, prayer describes to a very considerable degree the type of communion with humanity that God seeks to achieve in covenant, a type of communion in which "nature" and "supernature" stand not in tension but rather coinhere ("*inter-cedere*" literally means to "go between").[54] If those like Moltmann worry that this realized perspective robs Christianity of a genuine futurity, Balthasar's running emphasis on mission-consciousness can be seen to mitigate these concerns significantly (cf. Section 6.2.1 *supra*).[55]

---

51. Cf. *Prayer* (H), 169.

52. Ratzinger, *Eschatology*, 9.

53. *RB*, 102–3. Consider also these lines from a sermon Balthasar preached on the feast of the Immaculate Conception: "Man, even the man who is religious and righteous, sets limits, unconsciously, automatically, because that is his originally sinful nature [. . .] But God is limitless, and he aims to *abolish the boundaries* set or demanded by men. When he comes, it is not to draw a boundary between the pious and the godless [. . .] but, as Paul says, to 'break down the dividing wall' [Eph. 2:14]" (*YCYYG*, 266). As the occasion of the feast suggests, Mary is important here as the one necessary creaturely counterpoint to the perfect divine invitation to communion; hers is no sinful "Yes, but . . ." but rather a "whole [and] exact" "Yes" in which "the earth [. . .] accept[s] the arrival of grace so that it [i.e., grace] can really come to earth and carry out its work of liberation" (ibid., 267). As Gabriel suggests at the Annunciation, this process is already oriented to the eschatological end (Lk. 1:33). So the grace of the Immaculate Conception is, again, not a heroic achievement of the individual woman Mary, but the necessary preparatory aspect of God's furtherance of salvation history in Christ. Cf. *LAC*, 63–5 and *Prayer* (H), 214–15. This conforms with what was said about the Immaculate Conception in Section 4.3.1, but it also indicates Mary's special role in intercessory prayer as the one whose "portion" of grace can never be fully exhausted.

54. Recall the sentence quoted earlier in Chapter 5 that according to Balthasar, in prayer "there is in principle no need for any special way or effort in order to rise from nature to supernature."

55. See Balthasar's extended discussion of Moltmann's theology of hope at TD.5, 168–80. Balthasar endorses Moltmann's efforts to reintegrate the perspective of Old Testament

Intercessory prayer is not, in the end, best understood as merely petition for an immediate and limited purpose ("Dear Saint Anthony, please come around"), but rather the expression of a radical hope that the entire community of prayer, earth and heaven together, stands united in the one eschatological mission, a mission which was first given to the Son and now continues to be carried out in his name.[56]

6.3 Action

This unity in eschatological mission is what I meant in the last chapter by referring to "the collective striving toward that end which belongs to none individually or in isolation." The Kingdom is the work of no individual—not even of God "alone," inasmuch as God wills that the victory of the Kingdom be a collaborative effort with and for the world. Unity here is itself a sign of eschatologically significant progress in history, as the otherwise opaque biblical denunciations of "double-mindedness" suggest (Jas 1:8; 4:8).[57] But to be united in this way means to see oneself as part of a whole which actively works so that "thy Kingdom come." That is, precisely as the mission-consciousness that is founded in Christ, carried forth in the Spirit, nourished by the church, and lived out in the world, prayer gives rise to action.[58] This can be put conversely by saying that any "activity" that is to plausibly claim to be eschatologically relevant must always be founded on prayer, since prayer is the appropriate method of I-expansion (see Section 5.4) that allows one to recontextualize one's own life and mission within a larger eschatological drama.[59]

---

prophecy into a modern Christian theology, but faults Moltmann for largely neglecting the Johannine perspective (remarkably, the fourth Gospel is not cited once in *A Theology of Hope*) and for misunderstanding how eschatological futurity is not opposed to Christ's "presence" among his disciples but rather how the latter serves as the premise of the former. Healy also makes the pertinent observation that Moltmann's overpowering focus on the historical drama of the Cross, at the expense of any deeper or prior account of the immanent "drama" of love in Godself, risks degenerating into a "Hegelian and indeed ultimately mythological" picture in which "*God needs the world* to become fully God" (Healy, *The Eschatology of Hans Urs von Balthasar*, 131–2).

56. Vincent Brümmer's discussion of intercession is not unhelpful on these points, although unfortunately it neglects the Christological dimensions; see *What are We Doing When We Pray?* (London: SCM, 1984), 55–9.

57. Single-mindedness or "purity of heart" means transparency to mission in prayer. Kierkegaard's discussion is illuminating—see "Purity of Heart Is to Will One Thing," in *Upbuilding Discourses in Various Spirits*, trans. Howard and Edna Hong (Princeton: Princeton University Press, 1993).

58. See *LAC*, 88.

59. *Prayer* (H), 143.

It is in this context that one must understand Balthasar's comments on the "unity" of action and contemplation, a unity that is ontologically grounded in Christ and that paradigmatically in him "issue[s] finally in the Passion."[60] Christ's life was a perfect unity of contemplation and action, and the Passion, as the "ultimate aim" of his life, likewise expresses this unity in its fullness. On the one hand, "all [Christ's] works and achievements lead logically to their climax in the voluntary sacrifice of his life"; on the other hand, Christ's "abiding disposition [was] to let the Father's will work in him"—it was this he was always contemplating interiorly.[61] While in the *Explorations* essay on the topic Balthasar is happy to affirm the Greek (and therefore Medieval) priority of contemplation over action as far as it goes, he is quite clear that at the "deeper levels of philosophical or theological speculation" the antithesis does not hold.[62] "When talking about contemplative faith from a Christian viewpoint, it is not permissible to imply the validity of the Greek philosophical concept that accepts an unequivocal unilateral 'ascent' from the temporal to the eternal, away from the world to God."[63] Christ shows, rather, that the apparent opposition between God and world is reconciled in a unified reality which is prayer at the "hour" of the utmost decision.[64] Creaturely prayer, inasmuch as it is truly Christoform, takes place in that same "hour" of decision, when inaction is simply not an option.[65] Ultimately for Balthasar, "Nothing is more active than contemplation."[66]

Derek Brown is thus exactly right to see in Balthasar's treatment of Joan of Arc the icon of a creaturely "kneeling theology," which leads not further into the depths of introspection or abstraction but out "into the street" in order to resist specific historical forces of oppression.[67] Todd Walatka likewise opens his study of Balthasar and liberation theology by drawing attention to an infrequently cited sermon in which Balthasar exhorts his listeners that their proper place is "*on the streets* of the world," where they are to meet and "identify with [their] manacled

---

60. ET.1, 227–40, here 236. See also the discussion at *Prayer* (H), 104–7.

61. ET.1, 236.

62. ET.1, 237. Balthasar explicitly rejects the Greek antithesis ("that contemplation is focused on eternity and action on time") at *Prayer* (H), 104. See also *EG*, 52–3 as well as *TuG*, 109, where Balthasar cites a distinction, introduced by Schneider, that spirit is "*sent down*" into history—as opposed to having "*fallen* down" as "m[e]n of the classical period, from Plato to Origen and Augustine" would have held—thus emphasizing the role of mission and history in the soul's "return" to God.

63. *WiC?* 76.

64. See ET.1, 237. D. L. Schindler refers to the "anterior unity" that only becomes clear against the backdrop of revelation in Christ and that brings a Christian notion of action beyond that which is possible as long as Greek categories are taken to be determinative (Schindler, *Heart of the World, Center of the Church*, 221–2).

65. *Prayer* (H), 107; cf. ET.1, 237.

66. *TuG*, 189. On the basis of Christian action see also *WiC?* 40–50.

67. Brown, "Kneeling in the Streets," 805–6. See *TuG*, 185–205.

and poor brethren, [and with] all who suffer, hunger, and thirst."[68] Although these sentiments may seem surprising to those with only a casual idea of Balthasar's theology (or whose view of his theology is overdetermined by what I have been calling Category 1 works), everything I have been saying about prayer naturally leads in this direction. The dialogue-relationship of prayer involves the praying person's constant "attempts to make a complete and selfless answer, in order to show that he has understood the divine message."[69] This "answer" implicates the praying person's entire existence, and introduces certain responsibilities upon them, as we have seen. And the answer that is given, finally, is the life-affirming "Yes" which cannot help but stand against everything that sinfully insists on saying "No" to God.

It is important to note that this "No" is as often likely to come from within the church as from outside it. Brown notes how Joan's sacrifice was not just a protest against the English state, but against a church that was complicit in carrying out "inquisitorial" violence.[70] Joan burns, Balthasar says, *"for* the Church [and] *because* of the Church."[71] All that was said in Chapter 4 about the church as the objective historical form established in and by Christ's prayers need not be seen to be contradicted here. The church, precisely as the conduit of grace (grace which is, after all, directed at sinful creatures), is necessarily composed of sinners: "All Christians are sinners, and if the Church does not sin as Church, she does sin in all her members, and through the mouths of all her members she must confess her guilt."[72] This confession of guilt, as we have seen (Section 5.2.2 *supra*), is essential to prayer, and it is this complicity in guilt that the church must "constantly" acknowledge if it is to truly pray as church ("Forgive us our trespasses"; "Holy Mary, Mother of God pray for us sinners . . ."; *"Kyrie eleison"*; etc.).[73] No easy dichotomy

---

68. YCYYG, 277; see Walatka, *Von Balthasar and the Option for the Poor*, 1–4.
69. *LAC*, 89.
70. Brown, "Kneeling in the Streets," 805.
71. *TuG*, 192.
72. ET.2, 245. This remark comes about halfway through Balthasar's bravura essay on the church as "Casta Meretrix," in which he traces the "chaste whore" theme through its biblical, Patristic, and Scholastic iterations (see ET.2, 193–314). As Servais shows ("The Confession of the *Casta Meretrix*," in *Communio* 40:4 [2013], 642–62), Balthasar's important essay, which was republished in 1961 on the eve of the Second Vatican Council, "doubtless shares a certain affinity of spirit" with *Lumen Gentium*'s description of a church that "always follows the way of penance and renewal" (see Servais, "The Confession of the *Casta Meretrix*," 643 and *Lumen Gentium* 8). Brian Flanagan reflects on the "decline" of auricular confession as a "starting point for [reflecting on] renewed forms and theologies of ecclesial conversion" ("Reconciliation and the Church: A Response to Bruce Morrill," *Theological Studies* 75:3 [2014]: 624–34, here 634), though his approach suffers from some of the same dangers I identified in Martos' account (see Chapter Five, footnote 44 of this work *supra*).
73. ET.2, 243, 288.

between world and church can thus be maintained here, even (especially) at the eschatological moment of witness in which the saint acts in furtherance of mission.

As the example of Joan makes abundantly clear, this action in furtherance of mission often takes the form of sacrifice—or, at least, such action must not avoid sacrifice as something which lies opposed to mission.[74] It is important to be specific with one's claim at this point. Joan's "commission" is not to die, but to witness.[75] That as a witness (*marturion*!) she meets resistance enough to be killed is evidence of the "fundamental theodramatic law of world history" (which claims, again, that the world's hatred of God increases proportionately to the extent that God reveals Godself to the world). The dragon's rage against eschatological progress takes the form, within history, of what Balthasar calls the "superpowers of darkness": war, starvation, hopelessness, hatred, violence, and everything else that lies opposed to life.[76] As a real instance of God's revelation to the world (cf. Section 2.1.1 *supra*), the saint's work in mission is an affront to these "superpowers" and so must be snuffed out. But the saint accepts this willingly in the Christoform mode of obedience.[77] We could go as far as to propose the following claim, based on what has been argued earlier: if difficulty in individual prayer can be taken to be a positive indication of prayer's role in remaking the self outside itself for the sake of mission (cf. Section 5.2.1 *supra*), then worldly resistance to the action born of prayer is likewise a positive indication of prayer's role in the eschatological progress of history, in which the world itself is remade according to God's idea of it.

It is just this eschatological perspective that gives prayer its necessary "element of urgency" and in turn yields a properly Christian understanding of action.[78] The realized perspective is pivotal here. If in prayer, and especially in the parrhesiastic prayer that dares to draw on the heavenly reserves of the saints, the praying person enjoys real "insight" into the redeemed order of things—if in prayer the "walls separating heaven and earth" are truly "as glass"—then for that same praying person, who inevitably exists in and observes the world as it currently is, prevailing conditions come to be seen as intolerable and inadequate, as contrary to the will of God. Thus, an "attitude of revolt [*Auflehnung*]" can

---

74. Cf. *Prayer* (H), 128 and *LAC*, 94–5.

75. See *TuG*, 192–3.

76. *YCYYG*, 279.

77. Philip McCosker draws a useful distinction between what he calls "immolationist accounts of sacrifice, which involve the destruction of the 'victim' [as the *intended end* of the sacrifice], and oblationist accounts which emphasize the act of offering the *offerandum*, whether of self or something else" ("Sacrifice in Recent Roman Catholic Thought," in *Sacrifice and Modern Thought*, 132–46, here 133). In this sense, Balthasar's notion of sacrifice is oblationist, if also with the inbuilt understanding that the Christian oblation tragically evokes a certain hateful reaction. James Alison comes close to Balthasar's position in *Knowing Jesus* (London: SPCK, 1988), 49.

78. *Prayer* (H), 107.

often be an appropriate fruit of prayer.⁷⁹ It is not simply that contemplation mechanistically precedes action, but that both action and contemplation together—for the Christian—are motivated by love, and love is discovered in a uniquely immediate way in prayer.⁸⁰ In *Love Alone*, Balthasar describes prayer as a kind of harmonization with the divine love; elsewhere, he calls it "attunement."⁸¹ So attuned, the holy life will increasingly radiate this love in both action and contemplation.⁸² True love does not abide any artificial division between considering the beloved in the abstract and attending to them here and now. It is love, then, not some suicidal death drive, that leads Joan to the pyre and Christ to the Cross—it belongs to the fathomless depths of divine love, in turn, that God makes of Joan's pyre an "eternal beacon" which might illuminate the form of love alive in history.⁸³ Eschatological progress in history depends

---

79. *Prayer* (L), 182. Drawing on Barth, Ashley Cocksworth likewise concludes that "If prayer does not amount to public action in revolt against that which causes oppression, then it amounts to nothing" (Cocksworth, *Karl Barth on Prayer*, 166). Cocksworth acknowledges that this perspective can potentially become "too one-sided" (167); see the whole discussion 147–67.

80. *LAC*, 88. See also ET.1, 239 and *Prayer* (H), 104–5.

81. See *LAC*, 89; cf. GL.1, 91ff. See the remarks by Moser at *Love Itself is Understanding*, 250.

82. Cf. *Prayer* (H), 265.

83. *TuG*, 192; Brown, "Kneeling in the Streets," 805; see 804–6. Kilby worries that this "fold[s] the mystery of suffering into the mystery of God" and thereby threatens to obscure the fact that certain sufferings of others remain scandalously inaccessible to our own attempts at meaning (see Kilby, "Eschatology, Suffering, and the Limits of Theology" in *Game Over? Reconsidering Eschatology*, ed. Christophe Chalamet et al. [Berlin: De Gruyter, 2017], 279–91, here 291). Kilby asks whether or not the approach being proposed here implies an overambitious theodicy which lays claim to the sufferings of others as all simply, as it were, part of the plan (see 287–8). As usual, Kilby's concerns are pertinent, and in particular I share her view that theodicy is often practiced in a way that could be considered ethically dubious. As a way forward she suggests "restraint" both in the style and content of Christian eschatology, which, without abandoning the faith that on the last day all tears shall be wiped away (Rev. 21:4), nevertheless should not rush to "*apply* that belief to [each and every] situation" (290). In other words, Christian eschatology must retain a tragic sense of just that which it promises deliverance *from*. Although Kilby clearly has Balthasar in mind when calling for restraint (she names him at *op. cit.* 291), it is worth noting that Balthasar *does* at several places allow for just this kind of "unsynthesized" view of suffering. For one thing, there is the homily quoted earlier in which Balthasar acknowledges those "superpowers of darkness" in the face of which we seem to "lose all belief in the mission" (*YCYYG*, 279). These "superpowers of darkness" roughly correspond to Marilyn McCord Adams' notion of "horrendous evils" ("Horrendous Evils and the Goodness of God," in *The Problem of Evil*, eds. Marilyn McCord Adams and Robert Merrihew Adams [Oxford: Oxford University Press, 1990], 211), which Kilby appeals to at a key moment in her

upon the Christian's ability to tend to this fire, and it is here that prayer can come to be seen as the constant work that it is (cf. 1 Thess. 5:17).

Always it is God accomplishing the work. This is why the progress of salvation history is ultimately not reducible to "development," inasmuch as that word suggests incremental advances along some predetermined path to a given end.[84] "The world [on its own] will never transform itself into the kingdom of God through mere evolution (whether slow or fast)"—the "decision" of prayer is always needed.[85] To be perfectly clear, this does *not* mean that prayer should not aim at the transformation of "social structures"—indeed, Balthasar says, "we can say that *only* where this effect [i.e., the transformation of social structures] actually occurs are people really serious about Christianity."[86] The point is that such transformation must be seen in its proper theological context as the work of grace in history, nurtured by prayer and, therefore, a result of the cooperation of divine and human freedom. Such transformation is always liable to being undone, just as the disciples are liable to fall asleep despite Christ's call to stay awake. Christian action thus arises from the fact "that we have been commissioned to *act*, without reading into it any promise of success."[87] In other words, eschatology remains dramatic precisely in its relation to prayer, and it still makes sense to speak

---

essay. Furthermore, at TD.5, 210ff., Balthasar again considers the rage of the dragon at the end of time and tentatively describes "an eschatological 'tragedy' in the very midst of 'God's victory,'" the tragedy here being that precisely in light of the fullness of divine love the Satanic "No" will still ring out. This means that, in a certain manner of speaking, "a portion of God's plan for the world has failed, a portion of his creation has turned out to be meaningless" (212). Later, in TL.2, Balthasar again refuses to synthesize this final "No" into God's overall victory (which is nevertheless decisive): "The negativity of hatred and lying cannot be integrated in any way into the truth as one of its transitional 'moments.' The only attitude the truth can adopt toward it is unqualified rejection, that is, judgment" (322). At this point, the only hope, so to speak, is that the Satanic "No" is revealed to be literally groundless, to truly have no other basis than its hatred of the truth.

84. *TuG*, 193.

85. *YCYYG*, 294.

86. Ibid., The occasion of these striking remarks is a Christmas homily in which Balthasar explicitly considers political communism (291–4) and draws parallels to the way in which Christianity involves a "leveling downward" of all people (kings and shepherds alike) toward the pure poverty of the infant in the crib. When Christianity impugns its own credibility by neglecting to consider (or worse still, supporting), the structures which give rise to inequality, Balthasar admits, "communism must fill the gap with its [own] version of leveling" (293). The mistake comes in thinking that the "machinery of economics" operates in such a way as to abrogate the need for the "free decision on the part of individuals" (294). Cf. the similar remarks at *VBR*, 368–73, *EG*, 22, and *WiC?*, 45–6.

87. *TD.2*, 71; cf. *YCYYG*, 277 and *WiC?* 123.

of the "Final Judgment" as that Christ-saturated time toward which all prayer is building.[88]

6.4 Consolidation

"The transfigured paradisiacal world," Balthasar declares in one of his more ambitious aphorisms, "is none other than the one in which we presently live, only contemplated with different eyes."[89] How to gain this new sight—whence these "different eyes" that yield such a distinctive view of the world? Quite simply: prayer is the school of this new sight that casts the world in a new light. (The conclusion of the first chapter of the Letter to the Ephesians [e.g., Eph. 1:18] likewise makes the connection between prayer and this new sight explicit.) Prayer grants this view by entering completely into the perspective of the Son, who only sees the Father's Kingdom ahead of him. In prayer, especially the prayers of intercession in which love unifies a multitude of missions, one gains a "preview of things [...] to come."[90]

But prayer is more than mere anticipation which is content to catch glimpses of God's final action. God has already acted decisively in Christ, and in prayer Christ's love continues to be made present to history in ways that challenge everything that denies his spoken word of peace (Jn 14:27). Christian action depends upon a view of history as shaped and sanctified by prayer: *shaped* by prayer inasmuch as prayer grounds an eschatologically meaningful sense of the future and *sanctified* by prayer inasmuch as prayer describes the particular form of attention and responsibility that the individual owes to history as the realm in which our redemption is made effective. Action in this mode is urgent, indeed is transformative of the world and its structures, but is always shot through with the contemplative focus on the Son in whose love we are to abide with steadfast hope.

Healy describes eschatology as the "hidden heart of [Balthasar's] theological mission," and it is not unreasonable, based on the preceding considerations, to admit the plausibility of that claim.[91] Nor is that claim incompatible with my own in this work that prayer animates Balthasar's entire theological project. As an eschatological act par excellence, prayer locates us in God—and this location in God is understood not merely as a conceptual breakthrough (*theoria*), but as a new life (*praxis*) which makes demands of us, body and soul.[92]

---

88. In this sense, Balthasar's notion of prayer can go some ways toward addressing John Thiel's concern that contemporary Christianity has lost its sense for the "drama of salvation" (see Thiel, *Icons of Hope: The "Last Things" in Catholic Imagination* [Notre Dame: University of Notre Dame Press, 2013], 139).

89. See *GW*, 127.

90. *Prayer* (H), 148.

91. Healy, *The Eschatology of Hans Urs von Balthasar*, 17.

92. Again, *CM*, 38.

Put differently we could say that prayer reaches its highest degree of reality in its eschatological dimensions, for it is here, finally, that God proves what God is doing in prayer. Earlier (cf. Section 3.2 *supra*), I called prayer a form of indwelling in which the Spirit works to locate us at the very center of divine life, to place us at the "bosom of the Father" (Jn 1:18). We tend to resist this relocation since our sin produces feelings of alienation in us, so that we wrongly believe that we are unwanted or unwelcome (cf. Section 5.2.1 *supra*). Prayer reconciles us, however, to the fact that God not only finds us worthy of love, but that God wants more than anything to enter into a fruitful, cooperative relationship with us (cf. Sections 4.1.2 and 5.3.1 *supra*). This fruitful dialogue, this interplay of finite and infinite freedom, is essentially what prayer is. For us, as for Christ in mission, prayer becomes a mode of occupying that distance that draws us closer to the Father (cf. Sections 4.2.2 and 6.2.1 *supra*). To this extent, it is a grace that counteracts the effects of sin. In traversing this distance, we will not be able to neglect the missions that God bestows on each of us, missions which are oriented to the Kingdom and which in fact help to bring it about (cf. Section 6.3 *supra*). Thus, Christian prayer is nothing less than the existential mode of witness to and (therefore) work in and on behalf of the world. This mode of witness is revealed to be, in the end, not a creaturely innovation nor a pale imitation of divine love, but the creature's real participation in the Trinitarian life, which seeks ever-new ways of proving that "love alone is credible."

Chapter 7

PRAYER'S POWER

CRITICAL DIMENSIONS

I have covered a good deal of ground in the previous chapters. We have, by now, a fairly comprehensive answer to the question I posed at the outset of this book: What, for Balthasar, does prayer do? In short: prayer grants us a share in the Trinitarian life of love and trust, *kenosis* and *pleroma*, word and response. It is the realm of intimacy in which the Christian stands face to face with God, not with "downcast eyes and obsequious gestures" but as one invited into the dialogue.[1] Prayer precedes the praying person—since its source lies in, and its form derives from, the eternal dialogue of love which is the Trinity—and it leads the praying person on toward their future—indeed, toward the future of the whole world which groans for the eschatological *amen*. Ultimately what prayer *does* is nothing less than form the person who prays in the image of God who prays in and for the world, at the heart of the world. By forming persons thus, prayer serves to sanctify the world precisely through the transformative missions of these persons, whether these missions are great or small, public or anonymous.

In the course of the preceding considerations, I have made reference to the various social aspects of prayer (cf. Sections 1.2.3; 2.1.2; 3.3.2; and 5.2.2 *supra*, e.g.) These aspects, in turn, point us back to a claim I made in Chapter 2 that Balthasar's notion of prayer emerged in part as an attempt to offer an adequate model of engaged sanctity in response to the challenges of the modern era. I mean by this that prayer does more than just bear the not inconsiderable weight within Balthasar's system that I have shown it to do. It also serves a more specific and recognizably critical function as a form of witness in and to the world. This point was discussed in Chapter 2 with regard to the saint (i.e., the praying person par excellence) as a witness in the world, especially when that witness takes the form of an anonymous daily life of love and prayer like Gabrielle Pietzcker's (Section 2.1.1 *supra*). In the previous chapter, I further discussed how such a witness, when it meets a specific historical circumstance of injustice and violence, can result in the more dramatic example of a Joan of Arc (Section 6.3 *supra*). It seems advisable now, however, to expand upon this latter form of witness as a profound act of

---

1. Again, *Prayer* (H), 46.

freedom and liberation, in order to further elucidate just how radical Balthasar believes the act of prayer can be in the midst of a world that persists in saying "No" to God. Expanding upon this topic seems advisable, in part, lest the remarks from the previous chapter give the impression of one-sidedly equating prayer with protest. How does the particular form of witness grounded in prayer issue in a context that seems so opposed to it? What are the critical functions of prayer in such a context? This discussion will also provide an opportunity to treat again the important notion of *parrhesia* and its relation to prayer in ways that I could not go into in Chapter 5.

In doing so, as we will see, the "anonymous" witness is by no means eclipsed by the more visible sort—Gabrielle Pietzcker and Joan of Arc work toward the same goal. But it was Pietzcker herself who acknowledged, in a 1925 lecture, that the modern world requires visible, vivid, and engaged forms of sanctity: "Today," she said, "salvation is no more to come from those holy souls who remain *hidden* behind the cloister walls; the current moment [rather] calls for men and women who stay *out beyond the walls* and who can do so in the face of all the various dangers."[2] The eschatological dimensions of prayer discussed in the previous chapter are of decisive importance here: it is only in light of the realized perspective, according to which prayer names the realm in which nature and supernature meet, that the capacity for prayer to become critical really emerges. It also requires an eschatological faith, which appears as confidence, to see continuity between this world and the world to come (see Section 6.2 *supra*).[3] If, as I claimed at the end of the previous chapter, it is from the eschatological perspective that we see most clearly "what God is doing in prayer," then we are now left to consider some of the concrete effects of prayer in the world.[4]

---

2. Quoted by Thomas Krenski, *Hans Urs von Balthasars Literaturtheologie* (Hamburg: Kovač, 2007), 156; my translation. As King notes ("Theology under Another Form" 105), Pietzcker's influence upon her son can be rather clearly seen in lines like these (cf. *Razing the Bastions*, e.g.).

3. A similar point is made by Georges Wierusz Kowalski in regards to prayers of healing in "Prier pour Guérir," in *Revue de l'Institut Catholique du Paris* 40 (1991), 213–24, here 215: "L'audace de demander à Dieu la guérison pour quelqu'un repose sur l'assurance que l'intégrité corporelle retrouvée ne sera pas seulement un répit avant la mort, et encore moins l'illusion de la santé offerte à ceux qui seront finalement jetés dans la géhenne."

4. To clarify further: my claim at this point is not that *every* prayer necessarily issues in what I am calling in this chapter parrhesiastic protest against the powers of the world. There are those who pray whose mission does not lead them into explicit conflict with the "superpowers of darkness" mentioned in the last chapter. The primary point of the current chapter is to look more closely at *one of* the "concrete effects of prayer in the world," which is this visible parrhesiastic witness against injustice. However, it is necessary to stress at the same time that this explicit parrhesiastic witness is not categorically different than the essential stance of any genuine prayer, which has the boldness to identify oneself with God's "Yes" to the world (and to therefore align oneself *against* anything that insists on saying

I will proceed in this chapter by considering the picture of prayer as "encounter" between God and the world such as it is presented to be especially in Balthasar's 1953 book *Tragedy Under Grace*. In a way, this discussion serves to ratify the claims made in the previous chapter about the eschatological effects of prayer in that it shows what eschatologically significant prayer can look like. It also serves as a kind of capstone to the argument up to now by tying together several various points from the preceding chapters, while at the same time indicating prayer's centrality to the contemporary Christian "task" (which was an objective I declared at the outset of this book, cf. Section 2.3 *supra*). It is also my view that this aspect of prayer, according to Balthasar, is one of the most consistently neglected among his commentators.

The person who lives their life as prayer "out beyond the walls" of the cloister will inevitably be brought into contact (or even conflict) with worldly powers; prayer's relation to power is thus implicated. Seen from this perspective, prayer will be understood to have certain prophetic dimensions, some of which have already been indicated at various points above. But since genuine Christian prayer is always Christoform, since it is always participatory in the Son's particular mode of witnessing to the Father's love, this prophetic dimension will involve its own "Christological transpositions," which prevent us from merely opposing prayer or the praying person on the one hand to power on the other.[5] In particular, these Christological transposition apply to the notion of *parrhesia* such that that term is able to be understood in ways that go beyond what Foucault (as the foremost modern exponent of that term) could conceive of. In other words, even when it is fulfilling its critical functions vis-à-vis the powers of this world, prayer performs the fundamental task of Christian metaphysics in that it illuminates the form of love from within the very midst of history.

7.1 Prayer and Power

I have shown the centrality of mission-consciousness to Balthasar's anthropological thinking, and, therefore, to his conception of prayer. Missions are, by their nature, historically situated, and, accordingly, Balthasar's notion of prayer is fundamentally one in which the praying person "must make historical decisions"—and these are not as incidental or ancillary features to their prayer but as a central aspect of the prayer itself.[6] Prayer implicates the person's freedom as one who not only hears

---

"No" as I argued in Section 6.3 *supra*). That the essential "Yes" of prayer lies in continuity with the "No" to injustice is already indicated in the prototypical Marian prayer, in which the lowly handmaid denounces the proud and the powerful (cf. Lk. 1.46-55). Furthermore, Balthasar's view appears to be that these visible parrhesiastes are especially called for in the modern era, at a time when credible images of love alive in history appear so difficult to see.

5. Again, TD.5, 122.
6. *TuG*, 194.

but *responds to* God's word (cf. Section 5.3 *supra*). This Balthasar refers to as the praying person's unique *gravitas* (or their ability to "make themselves known") in prayer.[7] This *gravitas* not only expresses itself vis-à-vis the powers of the world, but is itself a kind of power exercised by the praying person. Earlier (Section 5.4) I described this power to hear and respond in terms of the Ignatian *elección*, choosing God's choice. Of course, on the broadest level, God's choice is for the world, in all its integrity. Thus why any understanding of prayer as an activity which lies somehow beyond the remit of worldly affairs constitutes a "fatal [. . .] apostasy from the real Christian task."[8]

7.1.1 The Example of the Prophets

Prayer's situatedness in history, and its relation to power, becomes apparent when one considers the example of prophetic prayers or the prophetic tradition more broadly: prayers for deliverance (2 Kgs 19:19 or Mic. 7:7, e.g.); prayers against unjust persecution (Hag. 2:22, e.g.); prayers calling for the reform of institutions, whether secular or ecclesial (Joel 113 or 2 Chron. 15:2-7, e.g.)—in all these instances, the prophet's prayers lead the prophet into the world.[9] The prophet maintains the unity of individual "hearing" and public "proclamation," since he knows that "hearing the word never takes place simply for the personal satisfaction of hearing it; it is always directed to a *common* obedience."[10] In prophetic witness, therefore, we see the concrete instances of the principle referred to earlier regarding the necessity of silence in prayer leading on naturally to the fullness of the word received as mission (see Section 5.3.2 *supra*): The prophets "are always men [*sic*] who have themselves heard the word individually, whose ability to hear has been tested in the school of solitude," and who are thus able to be trusted to act as the word's "representative" to the nation (cf. the commission to Ezekiel at Ezek. 3:24f.).[11] In both cases—in hearing and speaking—the prophet is only effective to the extent that he is transparent to the divine word; thus, a given prophet's personality will have less bearing upon the fulfillment of his mission than will the clarity of his mission-consciousness. Balthasar quotes from von Rad, who is

> so bold as to say that the prophet in the state in which he receives the revelation himself "became detached from his own personal likes and dislikes and was

---

7. GL.7, 241–2.
8. *TuG*, 107.
9. Abraham Heschel begins his classic study of the prophets by noting just how historically specific and even trivial their missions can seem to be, concerned as they are with the "daily occurrences" of society: "Instead of showing us a way through the elegant mansions of the mind, the prophets take us to the slums" (see Heschel, *The Prophets* [New York: Harper, 1962], 3–4).
10. *Prayer* (H), 86.
11. Ibid.

drawn into the emotions of the deity himself. It was not only the *knowledge* of God's designs in history that was communicated to him, but also the *feelings* in God's heart, wrath, love, sorrow, revulsion, and even doubt as to what to do or how to do it [Hos. 6:4; 11:8; Isa. 6:8]."[12]

Von Rad perhaps overstates the point here, but it is clear, at least, that for Balthasar the prophetic office involves becoming the "personified word of God for the people."[13] The prophet is in this way an exemplary praying person, one who has let the "centrifugal" momentum of prayer lead them out into a new existence in mission.[14]

As the example of the prophets clearly indicates, however, prayer of this sort tends to speak *against* something—whether persecution, the infidelity of Israel, or the primordial forces of chaos. Most often, this sense of opposition comes from within the very nation that the prophet arises out of and seeks to address (i.e., the prophet's own people). The prophet accepts this danger—indeed, is often explicitly warned of it (Ezek. 3:7)—but sets himself to mission nonetheless. As I argued earlier, availability is necessarily a maximal position (cf. Section 5.4 *supra*) and the prophet of all people cannot put conditions on the nature of the message he is to proclaim, precisely because it is not *his* message but God's. As I also argued earlier, worldly resistance to the action born of prayer can be a positive indication of prayer's role in the eschatological progress of history—thus the prophet's being scorned by his own people indicates that there *is* a people which God seeks to address and, in addressing, reform and reclaim as God's own. The prophet feels with a particular acuity the consequences of the "fundamental theodramatic law of world history" which I have alluded to several times already (Sections 4.1.1; 6.1; and 6.3 *supra*). Thus, Balthasar observes, "the period of the great [biblical]

---

12. GL.6, 218–19 (italics mine); quoting from von Rad, *Old Testament Theology*, Vol. II. This can also explain a certain degree of nescience in the prophetic mode of knowing, since a given prophet only represents a given aspect of God's word to the people. Thomas approaches a similar insight at *ST* II-II, q.171, a.4 when he concludes that the prophet need not know with certainty "all that can be known prophetically," but only those matters which bear directly on the message he has been given to proclaim.

13. GL.6, 249. Balthasar should not be understood here as subject to Heschel's critique of dogmatic theology, which, Heschel says, "has disregarded the prophet's part in the prophetic act" (Heschel, *The Prophets*, xiii). Although Balthasar clearly places the emphasis on the objectivity of mission-consciousness over against the obstacles to this which arise from the particulars of personality, he by no means neglects the prophet's "response" and unique "human situation" as necessary aspects to the fulfillment of mission. As Heschel puts it, "the prophet [. . .] speaks from the perspective of God as perceived from the perspective of his own situation" (xiv)—such is the same process of what I have referred to here as "hearing" and "proclaiming."

14. On the distinction between "centrifugal" and "centripetal" momentum in prayer, see, again, *Prayer* (H), 54 and 5.1 *supra*.

prophecy [. . .] is coextensive with the period of the kings" and during this period "God enters into a hitherto unheard-of kind of dialogue with the chosen people."[15] Not only does the invocation of a "dialogue" relationship here indicate the essentially prayerful nature of the relationship between God and Israel, but, more to the current point, prayer's critical function is said to be "coextensive" with the growth within history of the structures of worldly power. God shows God's commitment to continually expanding the scope of salvation history by eventually transcending the local jurisdictions of the kingdom period in the universal kingship of Christ (who recapitulates the roles of both king and prophet within himself for *all* peoples; accordingly, Christ knows to expect resistance from within his own people [cf. Lk. 4:24; Mt. 13:57; Mk 6:4; Jn 4:44]).

7.1.2 "The Encounter"

What the preceding considerations indicate is that the challenge of harmonizing "grace and power" cannot be resolved by simply "giving the precedence in principle to grace" and, in cases where the two come into tension, "demand[ing] an exclusive choice."[16] To do so would be to "neutralize" the central drama of world history and to give in to the sort of abstraction characteristic of the Scholasticism that Balthasar saw himself to be revising.[17] The prophet may well be a "voice in the wilderness," but he is sent precisely in order to find a hearing—to "prepare the way for the Lord" (Isa. 40:3; cf. Jn 1:23). In addition, neutralizing the world-historical drama would also present prayer as something essentially individualistic, the *monos pros monon*, which Balthasar considered characteristic of Greek and Greek-influenced notions of contemplation but incompatible with a genuinely Christian, biblical understanding of the same.[18] Rather, Balthasar emphasizes the way in which prayer makes claims upon the world, just as it makes claims upon the praying person. God does not will that prayer flourish at the world's expense (*ora contra mundi*, so to speak), but rather that it contributes to the conversion of the world by offering a credible witness of the sort of love that welcomes back the prodigal son with open arms (Lk. 15:27). Balthasar's opposition to a so-called two-tiered or extrinsicist ontology (supernature over against nature etc.) is well known.[19] Here the integrity

---

15. GL.6, 217 (my italics). Martti Nissinen takes a long view of the "coextensive" relationship between prophets and kings, tracing the relationship back to the ancient Mesopotamian empire and considering how the biblical notion of prophecy challenged while incorporating received notions of kingship (see the chapter "Prophets and Kings," in *Ancient Prophecy: Near Eastern, Biblical, and Greek Perspectives* [Oxford: Oxford University Pres, 2017], 257–96).

16. *TuG*, 107.

17. Ibid., 108.

18. *Prayer* (H), 87; cf. *2SS*, 462.

19. See, for example, *TKB*, 298. Balthasar was decisively influenced in this regard by his early encounters with Przywara and de Lubac. Among the numerous treatments

of Balthasar's perspective is seen to bear upon his concept of prayer inasmuch as he is not willing to oppose "the world of prayer" to "the world in itself."[20] To insist on the presence of some "contradiction" between these two realms would leave the Christian with no choice but to "flee into an unworldly holiness" that eschews any responsibility for the eschatological progress of history; and as I argued in the previous chapter, Balthasar's understanding of prayer as rooted in the realities of history stands firmly opposed to any such ahistorical approach.[21]

But if Balthasar wants to avoid asserting a necessary "contradiction" between grace and power, he nevertheless recognizes what he refers to as a *"refraction that exists between the spiritual and the worldly realms."*[22] This "refraction" is a consequence of sin (and indeed, it comports with the picture of sin as involving the mistaken belief that God and the world stand in competition with one another that I first presented in Section 5.2.1 *supra*). Thus, prayer's critical function lies not in rejecting but in reorienting worldly notions of power. This "encounter" between

---

of the theme, see the balanced discussion by Oakes in "Balthasar and *Ressourcement*: An Ambiguous Relationship," in *Ressourcement: A Movement for Renewal in Twentieth-Century Catholic Theology*, eds. Gabriel Flynn and Paul Murray (Oxford: Oxford University Press, 2012), 278–88, especially 284–8. Oakes highlights that although "Balthasar certainly voices his assent" to de Lubac's basic argument in *Surnaturel* (especially in the short book on de Lubac), he (i.e., Balthasar) nevertheless expresses some reservations (in the earlier Barth book, for instance) that the whole nature/grace debate, including de Lubac's contributions, risks giving the impression of nature as something less dynamic than it is. Balthasar's ambivalence here can be attributed in part to the fact, "insufficiently noted by most Balthasar scholars," that Balthasar never develops an extended, explicit doctrine of grace and nature (Oakes, "Balthasar and *Ressourcement*," 285, n.b. n.16), for fear that such a doctrine might obscure the event character of grace which is constantly operative in the world. Ultimately, for Balthasar, "No one [. . .] may construct a system rationalizing the relationship between nature and grace" (*GW*, 85).

20. Recall Balthasar's claim that, "There is in principle no need for any special way or effort in order to rise from nature to supernature" in prayer (*Prayer* [H], 45; cited in Section 5.2.1 *supra*).

21. *TuG*, 108. Balthasar's approach resonates with Daniélou's in this regard; see *Prayer as a Political Problem* (London: Burns & Oates, 1967). Daniélou argued that although it may be at times necessary to insist on a certain degree of "separation" between "Christianity and civilization" for practical purposes (in order to guarantee free religious expression, for instance), this separation must not be "transpose[d] [. . .] to the theoretical level" (21). In other words, "it is *unreal and dangerous* [. . .] to consider that the Church and the civil society ought to move in two separate worlds" (ibid.). Rather than betraying any integralist sympathies, Daniélou's concern here is to maintain the church as a church of the poor, one in which prayer is not "a privilege for a chosen group of spiritually-minded people" but a living, social reality (23). Notice this approach implies that "civilization is a conditioning factor" in prayer (25).

22. *TuG*, 127.

grace and power is clearly at stake in the confrontations that sometimes arise between the saint and the king, which Balthasar considers through the works of the poet Reinhold Schneider, for whom this was also a running theme. Las Casas confronting Charles V, Anselm of Canterbury confronting William II, Thomas More confronting Henry VIII, Teresa of Avila confronting Philip II, Joan of Arc confronting the English crown and the church itself—all these episodes and others were Schneider's subjects in various works, and in his book on Schneider Balthasar has the opportunity to reflect on them as concrete instances of the theodramatic theory he expounds at greater length in the systematics.[23] I already mentioned the case of Joan earlier in the context of a discussion of the sort of action born of prayer (Section 6.3 *supra*). Notably, Balthasar also adds to Schneider's list of examples, mentioning Maximilian Kolbe, Madeleine Delbrêl, and Alfred Delp in particular.[24] To be clear, Balthasar is interested in these individual episodes as synecdoches, which indicate the broader question of how grace and mission interact with history and power—the examples of Joan and Las Casas and the rest are particularly "dramatic" instances in which the question becomes "acute," but they should not for that reason be understood to rely upon dynamics of faith which are fundamentally different than those under which the "ordinary" Christian operates and which I have already discussed above with reference to the notion of *parrhesia* in prayer (Section 5.3.1 *supra*).[25] That being said, some saints—especially those marked by "representative" sanctity—are called upon to act in decisive and public ways, ways which might reform and inspire the world and church alike. It is not an exaggeration to say that Balthasar sees in such confrontations the potential to advance the eschatological progress of history. Prayer is central to this type of witness (in ways which I will discuss further in the following text), suggesting prayer's capacity to serve a critical function in the world. Balthasar is thus able to quote approvingly from Schneider at one key point that, "It is the one who prays who *accomplishes history*."[26]

How is prayer involved in this type of witness, such that we can be sure we are not just speaking of mere protest? At this point it is helpful to revisit the concept of *parrhesia*, which, as I argued earlier (Section 5.3.1), lies at the heart of Christian prayer. By affecting a theological transposition of the notion of *parrhesia*, Balthasar indicates new and exciting possibilities for an integrated form of witness in the modern era.

23. Balthasar's account of the saint and the king in *Tragedy Under Grace* corresponds especially to the treatment of "The Situation of the Witness" in *Theo-Drama* Vol. 3 (452–6).

24. TD.3, 453. That Balthasar's own examples are all individuals (and in Delbrêl's case, a laywoman) who resisted twentieth-century totalitarianism indicates the kind of engaged sanctity "beyond the cloister walls" that he associated with prayer and the contemporary Christian "task."

25. This also calls to mind the point first set forth in Chapter 2 that the saint's life represents an instance of living dogma, from which general theological truths can be drawn.

26. *TuG*, 111 (italics mine).

7.2 Parrhesia *Revisited*

It will be helpful to start by considering in more detail Michel Foucault's influential account of *parrhesia*, which I mentioned in the earlier discussion but did not treat at any length. Foucault's account not only helps us to see more clearly how *parrhesia* can function as a critical resource, but equally how a purely political or even ethical form of *parrhesia* needs to be complemented by certain theological arguments. My intention in this section is not necessarily to resolve any of the various exegetical and philosophical debates surrounding Foucault's understanding of the term; rather, I want to bring his reflections to bear on the theological account I have been developing up to now in order to show how prayer's critical dimensions might specifically apply to a social context.

7.2.1 *Foucault's Account*

The lectures[27] in which Foucault developed his account of *parrhesia* were delivered barely a year before his untimely death, and so his excavation of the concept should be located within a larger turn in his late thought toward a program of "self-care" (*epimeleia heautou*), understood as an ethics of life.[28] Furthermore, as Gutting notes, the timing of the lectures (and, significantly, the fact that the extant texts are extrapolated from transcriptions and listeners' notes) would recommend against considering this Foucault's settled treatment of the question or assuming we "know [. . .] how Foucault would have transformed this raw material had he ever decided to publish it [himself]."[29] Foucauldian *parrhesia*, then, is still to a large extent a speculative proposition—a fact not often enough noted in the relevant commentaries.

Nevertheless, in the relevant work by Foucault, and in the subsequent secondary literature, political *parrhesia* has been conceived of primarily as a form of "speaking

---

27. There are two editions of these lectures (which were originally delivered in English): *Fearless Speech*, ed. Pearson (Los Angeles: Semiotext(e), 2001) and the 2019 edition, *Discourse and Truth and Parrhesia* (*op. cit.*). Of the two, the more recent is the superior version, as the Pearson edition leaves out a certain amount of important material and is rendered less than perfectly. The 2019 edition also includes extensive transcripts of the question and answer sessions that followed Foucault's lectures, which are often useful. Finally, the 2019 edition includes a preparatory lecture Foucault gave a year before the Berkeley course at the University of Grenoble (*Discourse and Truth*, 1–38).

28. For discussion of Foucault's account of "self-care" or "care of the self," see Pierre Hadot, *Philosophy as a Way of Life: Spiritual Exercises from Socrates to Foucault* (Oxford: Blackwell, 1995); see also the briefer discussion by Julian Randall and Iain Munro, "Foucault's Care of the Self: A Case Study from Mental Health Work," *Organization Studies* 39, no. 11 (2010): 1485–504, 1495–8.

29. Gary Gutting, *Foucault: A Very Short Introduction* (Oxford: Oxford University Press, 2005), 109.

truth to power."[30] It was the parrhesiastes who spoke up when others could not or would not—the parrhesiastes who dared to challenge the king or the crowd by counseling against an ill-conceived course of action or by denouncing an unjust decision.[31] The parrhesiastes thus plays a special role within the *polis* and is in a certain sense responsible for its overall health. Notice that this implies that proper *parrhesia* must come "from 'below' and [be] oriented towards those 'above'"—the teacher or the king cannot exercise *parrhesia* since they control the power in a given relationship (but the would-be parrhesiastes can exercise *parrhesia* vis-à-vis these sources of authority).[32] Of decisive importance for the Greek sources that Foucault is drawing on is the question of truth. The parrhesiastes "takes a risk" in order to tell the truth as he or she sees it, even at the risk of inviting death, exile, or reprimand.[33] Indeed, parrhesiastic authority therefore derives from the statement in question's relation to the truth—a would-be parrhesiastes could speak boldly, publicly, and plainly but, if he or she happens to be wrong about whatever it is they are talking about, then they are nothing more than a chatterer, a tongue-wagger, or, worse, a deceiver (this is the major theme of *Ion*, which Foucault calls "*the parrhesiastic play*" and whose plot revolves around a case of mistaken identity).[34] So, "Not only is the parrhesiast [*sic*] sincere, not only does he state his opinion frankly, but his opinion is also the truth. He says what he knows to be true [. . .] There is [. . .] an exact coincidence between belief and truth."[35]

Now, of course, for Foucault, "truth" is not determined by reference to some external standard but as a function of power and the individual's relation to it. As he says at the conclusion of the *parrhesia* lectures, "My intention was not to deal with the problem of truth [in itself], but with the problem of the truth-teller, or of the activity of truth-telling."[36] He even describes a so-called game[37] or "contract/

---

30. See, for example, David Kim, "The Cosmopolitics of Parrhesia: Foucault and Truth-Telling as Human Right," in *Imagining Human Rights*, eds. Susanne Kaul and David Kim (Berlin: De Gruyter, 2015), 83–100; Andreas Folkers, "Daring the Truth: Foucault, Parrhesia, and the Genealogy of Critique," *Theology, Culture & Society* 33:1 (2016): 3–28; or José Luis Moreno Pestaña, "Isegoría y parrhesia: Foucault lector de Ión," *Isegoría: Revista de Filosofía Moral y Política* 49 (2013): 509–32.

31. As Foucault explains, this more normative sense of *parrhesia*—especially when it is seen as something admirable—is to be contrasted with the merely procedural sense of the term, which refers simply to the right of the citizen to speak ("free speech"). As ancient Greek political institutions came under increasing strain, *parrhesia* came to be seen as a dangerous feature of democracy that enabled "chatterers" to mislead and confuse public sentiment.

32. Foucault, *Discourse and Truth*, 44.

33. Ibid., 43.

34. See the discussion at ibid., 69–99.

35. Ibid., 44.

36. Ibid., 222.

37. Ibid., 43, 125, 185, and *passim*.

pact"[38] in which the king or sovereign explicitly grants license to the truth-teller to speak their mind under the promise not to punish them for what they say—provided what they say is indeed the truth (and, to complicate things further, provided the king receives it as such). Truth is contractually sought by the one with power, and the truth-teller must abide the terms of the contract, even if their goal is to subvert the power dynamic which makes their truth-telling possible in the first place. Therefore, even when seeking to critique, the parrhesiastes is always "historically dependent on and enmeshed in [the] autocracy" he or she seeks to correct.[39] As Raymie McKerrow has argued, Foucauldian *parrhesia* thus terminates in "never-ending skepticism [and] permanent criticism"—and, crucially, criticism of oneself as much as of the authority in relation to which one stands.[40] It was precisely this last aspect of ongoing self-criticism—what Foucault calls at one point "self-examination"—that made *parrhesia* such an essential aspect of ethical "self-care" that so defined Foucault's late period: truth-telling on this account requires that one be constantly willing to reconsider one's relation to truth and, equally, to constantly recommit oneself to speaking that truth.[41] The Delphic injunction *gnothi seauton* is therefore not understood as a call for pure introspection but requires that one examine the relationships, practices, and techniques of self-care, according to which one relates to oneself—and this one cannot do without *parrhesia*.[42]

Foucault thus presents the performance of *parrhesia* as a kind of office or discipline carried out not only for the sake of the political community (and this especially in times of crisis) but also and primarily for the parrhesiastes, who commits himself to a lifelong process of "self-care."

7.2.2 Theological Transposition

There are certain features of Foucault's account that resonate, however analogously, with the theological account of prayer that I have been developing throughout

---

38. Ibid., 74, 190, and *passim*.

39. Lida Maxwell, "The Politics and Gender of Truth-Telling in Foucault's Lectures on Parrhesia," *Contemporary Political Theory* 27 (2018): 1–21, here 6.

40. McKerrow's still-influential account is given at "Critical Rhetoric: Theory and Praxis," in *Communications Monographs* 56, no. 2 (1989): 91–111, see esp. 96–7. In the Berkeley lecture manuscript, Foucault refers to the "permanent reproblematization" that critical *parrhesia* requires (cf. *Discourse and Truth*, 226–35, third footnote). See also Foucault, "Is It Really Important to Think? An Interview," *Philosophical and Social Criticism* 9 (1989): 29–40.

41. See the discussion at *Discourse and Truth*, 211ff.

42. Ibid., 220. Parrhesia is a means of achieving harmony between *bios* and *logos*—between life itself and one's discourse concerning or about life; see the discussion by Maria Tamboukou, "Truth Telling in Foucault and Arendt: Parrhesia, the Pariah, and Academics in Dark Times," *Journal of Education Policy* 27, no. 6 (2012): 849–65, here 855.

the preceding chapters. Broadly, Foucault's emphasis on *parrhesia* as the ongoing process of reflection upon one's life as it stands in relation to the truth can be seen as a form of contemplation in which one reflects upon (discerns) one's mission and continually recommits oneself to it. More specifically, Foucault recognized the distinctive ways in which Christianity "impose[s] obligations of truth," in particular the obligation to *confess* both to propositional truths (in the form of dogmas, etc.) and existential truths (in the form of the holy life, etc.); thus, in this respect my argument about confession preceding *parrhesia* (cf. Sections 5.2.2 and 5.2.3 *supra*) resonates with this account, and Foucault can be said to agree with Balthasar—to some extent—that *parrhesia* is a necessary feature of the Christian life.[43] Developing these allusive resonances is a task that lies beyond the scope of this current chapter, however. More to the point, the Foucauldian notion of political *parrhesia* (i.e., parrhesiastes, vis-à-vis king) bears direct comparison to what Balthasar describes in the Schneider book as the "encounter" of grace and power (i.e., saint, vis-à-vis king); it is this comparison that I am interested in pursuing here.

It is in what we might call this moment of parrhesiastic witness common to both Foucault and Balthasar that certain essential differences in their accounts emerge, and thus it is to this moment that I want to devote some attention in order to suggest the ways in which these differences reveal the arguably *more* profound sort of witness that the theoparrhesiastes is ultimately capable of making. I will highlight three such differences.

First, the question of individual identity and the parrhesiastic task. For Foucault, the parrhesiastes is always, in the end, a solitary figure: the dissenter, the wise man, the martyr for truth—in any event the *parrhesiastes* stands apart from crowd as the one who dares to speak up. Foucault does discuss the role of schools and other forms of community life which were especially important to Epicurean and Stoic notions of *parrhesia*, but even in these cases the point of community life appears to have been to train the would-be parrhesiastes in the technical practices that were believed to instill and maintain *parrhesia*; ultimately, the parrhesiastes was expected to go out on his own and practice this skill in political life.[44] Theological *parrhesia*, on the other hand, could never accept this functional individualism since it begins from the proposition that *parrhesia* is a grace bestowed by God in prayer and mediated through mission in the church. Though a given saint may be in a position to "stand eye to eye" with the king, the saint never does so as a heroic individual but rather as one who bears witness to the faith of—and is therefore responsible to—a specific historical community which is the church.[45]

---

43. Foucault, *Discourse and Truth*, 4: "The obligation to say everything is quite unique in the Christian spirituality." Foucault is referring specifically to the practice of auricular confession to a spiritual director. See also *idem*, "Sexuality and Solitude," *London Review of Books* (May–June 1981).

44. Cf. Foucault, *Discourse and Truth*, 159–62.

45. *TuG*, 194.

Balthasar indicates this when, quoting from Schneider, he writes that whenever a saint has been called into an "encounter," there has stood behind the saint "an army of praying people who supported him."[46] In the decisive moment of encounter, the saint expresses "the innermost essence of what we mean by 'Church'"—indeed, in that moment the saint "lives [. . .] the destiny of the Church."[47] We have here the inverse corollary of the point which was made at the outset (Section 2.3 *supra*) that there is no private mystical insight in the church: Just as the saint's life contains theological content which can be generalized for the church as a whole, so too must their actions in furtherance of mission draw on the stockpile of faith that exists among the People of God. In both cases, prayer is seen to be the substance of ecclesial solidarity (cf. Section 4.3.1 *supra*).

A second point relates to the temporal aspects involved in the two types of *parrhesia*. Political *parrhesia* is a form of immanent critique—it exposes where power lies in relation to the speaker and thus raises critical questions about how that power is being distributed and exercised. Socratic *parrhesia* especially involves this first-person disclosure of "what you *are*—not your relation to the future or to a chain of events [as in the sort of self-knowledge disclosed by the oracle] but your [*current*] relation to truth."[48] Futurity on this account is arguably neglected, or even denied, if for no other reason than that the parrhesiastes always remains subject to the existing power structure—or, rather, to *some* power structure which will always stand over against him as the truth-teller.[49] On the other hand, theological *parrhesia* bears a necessary connection to the future. Recall

---

46. Ibid., 196.
47. TD.3, 453, *TuG*, 196.
48. Foucault, *Discourse and Truth*, 152.
49. Though he does not discuss Foucault or *parrhesia*, Lee Edelman's more recent attempt to deconstruct the very category of "the future" is worth mentioning here as an example of a form of critique that avoids the problem that Foucault seems to fall into. Edelman sets as his target the idea of "the Child," that is, the icon par excellence of (heterosexual) futurity, which, he argues, is used as the notional justification for the present order (the fact that social policies are so often justified with reference to "the children" or "future generations" seems to bear this out). Such appeals not only produce as their antithesis a category of undesirable persons who necessarily stand opposed to the future (i.e., the sterile homosexual, who cannot reproduce) but they also establish the conditions for an "endless" deferral of the coming future, a deferral which eventually ossifies into an ideology of the present. Such an order can thus be undermined precisely by an embodied critical response (Edelman's "queer death drive") that deliberately eschews the reproductive future; see Edelman, *No Future: Queer Theory and the Death Drive* (London: Duke University Press, 2004), especially the first chapter. One need not accept all aspects of Edelman's program in order to see the potential purchase it gains on social structures that claim to speak for the future. In particular, Foucault's parrhesiastic puzzle—how to speak truth to power when truth remains enmeshed in the operations of power?—is at least partially overcome by Edelman's refusal to play the game. The queer nihilist does not consider parrhesiastic

the aforementioned arguments about Christian prayer participating proleptically in the eschatological future (cf. Section 6.2.1 *supra*). As a function of mission born of prayer, the "encounter" is likewise future-oriented as an instance in which "the hour of God coalesces with the hour of the world."[50] It is in these moments (though not *only* in these moments) when (salvation) history has the opportunity to advance. Of course, for progress to come from these encounters, the king and the saint must agree—grace and power must harmonize. During these moments, therefore, "the world holds its breath."[51] Sometimes these encounters bear fruit. Las Casas eventually succeeds in convincing the emperor what justice requires regarding the treatment of the native Americans in Spanish colonies, for example. As often as not, however, the "refractions" between grace and power prevent any such harmonization—"the king turns aside" and the theoparrhesiastes is left to pay the price: "Becket stands as conscience before his king, and his brains are spattered over the tiles of the cathedral floor."[52] But—and here is where theological *parrhesia* shows its genuine basis in the future—it is precisely in these moments that the theoparrehsiastes is vindicated, for he has shown by his sacrifice that his mission extends beyond his own life. The fact that so many ostensibly "failed" encounters—Becket, Joan of Arc, Thomas More, Maximilian Kolbe, Edmund Campion, and so on—continue to live on in the memory of the faithful and the prayers of the church shows that their work in those decisive moments is still in some sense ongoing. Breuggeman's description of the prophets as "emancipated imaginers of alternative" applies just as well to these saints, inasmuch as they are able to conceive of something different than the current constellation of ever-shifting power(s).[53] The king cannot ultimately rob the saint of their future, even by inflicting death, for the simple reason that the saint does not disclose his or her *own* present truth in the encounter (a truth which would, in any case, live or die with the given speaker) but rather expresses his or her faith in the Kingdom to come—and by expressing it, helps to bring it about.

This leads directly on to the third decisive difference between political *parrhesia* and theological *parrhesia*, which has to do with the way in which the latter robs death of its "sting" (cf. 1 Cor. 15:55). For the political parrhesiastes, the parrhesiastic "game" can only go on so long as one is alive to take part—death (or, alternatively, exile) forecloses the possibility of exercising *parrhesia*. This finality is premised, ultimately, on the assumed "contradiction" between grace and power that Balthasar explicitly rejects. "In *parrhesia*," for Foucault, "the danger comes always from the

credibility something to be sought after, but rather lets their life—in all its "fatal [. . .] *juissance*" (*No Future*, 39)—offer its own testimony against the current order.

50. *TuG*, 194.
51. Ibid.
52. Ibid., 195.
53. Walter Breuggeman, *From Judgment to Hope: A Study on the Prophets* (London: Westminster John Knox, 2019), vii and *passim*.

fact that the said truth you say is able to hurt or anger the interlocutor."[54] This is the aforementioned "risk" of the parrhesiastic game, which assumes a zero-sum mentality. When Diogenes, the most famous of the Cynic parrhesiastes, engages in a dialogue with Alexander, he tries to "hurt [Alexander's] pride" in order to "[force Alexander] to recognize that he is not what he claims to be [i.e., brave, wise, etc.]."[55] The logic of the parrhesiastic game is fundamentally competitive and, in the terms of our earlier discussion, subject to the logic of sin. Theological *parrhesia*, on the other hand, as a prefiguration of the eschatological mode of relation, assumes no such competitive logic. The saint speaks not in order to threaten or to embarrass the king, but as a "summons" to his (i.e., the *king's*) own personal mission, which includes ruling justly, building peace, and so on. The saint sees clearly that they are both called to work toward the same goal (i.e., advancing the Kingdom), and, for this reason, seeks to reach out beyond the boundaries which have been established by the terms of the parrhesiastic game:

> Seen from the king's viewpoint, the encounter is an occasion for drawing boundaries and for conflict, but seen from the saint's viewpoint, it is an occasion for loosening the boundaries that maintain themselves and for the promise of unity [. . .] It is [therefore] not important that the saint perhaps falls when he bears witness at [the] boundaries, compared to the outcome—namely, that the boundary has for one moment become visible in its nonexistence.[56]

It is only on this account that death can be understood not to undo the performance of *parrhesia*. What theological *parrhesia* seeks to declare, finally, is the unity of *love*, in which "there is no enmity, no opposition, no division."[57]

All of these "transpositions" from political to theological *parrhesia* depend upon and are wholly grounded in Christ: "It is impossible to speak of the saint—of

---

54. Foucault, *Discourse and Truth*, 43. It was for this reason that a person who speaks up in such a way as to potentially incriminate *themself* (by testifying in a trial, say) is *not* exercising *parrhesia*.

55. Ibid., 176. It is true that this antagonistic form of *parrhesia* was particularly strong in Cynic-Stoic formulations. Socratic *parrhesia* is arguably less aggressive than the sort which was practiced by Diogenes, since it aimed primarily at the reform of the interlocutor. In either case, however, the parrhesiastes must expose the interlocutor in some way, must shame him or embarrass him. At the very least, there is no basis for *friendship* in philosophical *parrhesia*. Foucault clarifies: "A good parrhesiast does not hate you, but a good parrhesiast does not love you either. The good parrhesiast is someone with whom you have previously no particular relation, someone who is neutral" (Ibid., 189). It is just this neutrality that the theo-parrhesiastes (paradigmatically Christ) cannot abide (cf. Mt. 12:30, etc.)

56. *TuG*, 199; recall here Balthasar's claim that insisting on boundaries is the typical action of sinful humanity (cf. *YCYYG*, 266, e.g., and discussions in Sections 3.3.2 and 6.2.2 *supra*).

57. *TuG*, 199.

his office as witness in the Church and in history, of his [. . .] crossing over the boundary between the Church and the world through his committed action and [even] through his death—without continuously recalling the origin of all holiness, [. . .] namely, Jesus Christ."[58] In the first instance, Christ is theoparrhesiastes par excellence. He can speak the truth because he *is* the truth, and yet in his encounter with Pilate he does not seek to hurt him or expose Pilate's ignorance but rather invites him to see the truth which stands before him—"You have said that I am" (Jn 18:37). When "the encounter takes a tragic course, in a turning aside" and an abdication of responsibility by the worldly interlocutor, death is not the end.[59] Indeed, it is precisely by "voluntarily accept[ing] death into himself" that Christ crosses the final, seemingly insurmountable boundary, the boundary which had heretofore kept grace and power apart.[60] He does so, when the time comes, with a simple prayer of trust: "Into your hands I commit my Spirit" (Lk. 23:46). In doing so "he has proved that the undermost powerlessness is a function of the uppermost power."[61] Christ goes to the Cross, furthermore, not in the manner of a "conflict of one party against another" (he "does not fight directly" with the prince of this world) but as an uncompetitive parrhesiastic expression of the love that he is (1 Jn 4:8). Balthasar writes, "When Christ dies in the night and [crosses over into] hell, in[to] the realm far from God, this crossing of the boundary from the *civitas Dei* to the *civitas diaboli et mundi* is nothing other than the ecstasy of the love that remains itself, and remains at home with itself, as it crosses over."[62]

It was this same crossing over in love that motivated God's involvement in history in the first place. It is this crossing over in love that defines the Trinitarian life in itself. And it is this crossing over in love that the praying person is trained in through prayer. We have seen throughout this book the various and interconnected ways in which prayer describes a certain sort of relationship: one in which otherness is situated within love—a relationship in which I am not less myself for having found my home in Another. It is this unity in love that Christ expresses in his parrhesiastic prayer from the Cross. And it belongs to the uniquely Christian form of *parrhesia* to claim a share in this unity—to be able to say *amen*.[63] In this way, the Christian fulfills the decisive "task" of keeping alive a light in the darkness

---

58. Ibid.
59. Ibid., 195.
60. Ibid., 199–200.
61. Ibid.
62. Ibid., 204, 200; cf. *Prayer* (H), 112.
63. D. B. Hart captures this sentiment well when he writes that, "God's speech in creation does not, then, invite a speculative *nisus* toward silence—the silence of pure knowledge or of absolute saying—but doxology, an overabundance of words, hymnody, *prayer*" (David Bentley Hart, *The Beauty of the Infinite: The Aesthetics of Christian Truth* [Grand Rapids: Eerdmans, 2004], 298).

by witnessing to the eternal event of love which we participate in as prayer. "All of this is no abstruse metaphysics but the pure deed of God's miracle."[64]

7.3 Consolidation

I do not wish for my intentions in this chapter to be misunderstood. By focusing on the comparison with Foucault as much as I have, I make no claim to definitively resolving any of the fundamental inconsistencies that undoubtedly exist between his and Balthasar's accounts of *parrhesia*. My intention has been to show, rather, that Foucault's account brings certain distinctive features of *parrhesia* to the fore, features which are radically reconfigured in Balthasar's treatment. That Balthasar's reflections on *parrhesia* arrive some three decades before Foucault's Berkeley lectures suggests not only how creative and prescient a thinker Balthasar really was but also indicates the extent to which he considered prayer a holistic reality with actual historical consequences. (That Balthasar devotes no specific single work to *parrhesia*, however, has meant that I have mainly had to draw on the preceding chapters of this study as well as the one text that bears the closest resemblance to Foucault's analysis.)

Prayer's critical dimensions, then, lie, as I said, not in rejecting but in reorienting worldly notions of power. In the person of prayer's unique moment of witness, the world has a view to a vignette that discloses the whole history of grace writ large. No "encounter" of saint and king, however, can ultimately disclose more of the love of God than that most decisive encounter of Christ with the world—an encounter in which Christ sees all that is set against him as the bearer of God's love and carries out his mission nonetheless. It would be entirely contrary to the nature of divine love to remain closed in on itself, to refuse to enter into a "game" in which it was sure to be repeatedly spurned. It is altogether more fitting (yet for that reason no less miraculous) for that same love to "cross over" and prove itself, and to do so in a way that heals rather than embarrasses, that converts rather than condemns, and that, therefore, lives on when all else fades away. For those who embrace this same love, who commit themselves to it with their lives and in their prayers, they will likewise have no thought of remaining closed in on themselves, of holding back, of staying safe behind the "cloister walls." Rather they will find themselves out in the world, facing all the various dangers entailed therein but confident of the love that knows no limits: "Even though I walk through the valley of the shadow of death, I will fear no evil, for You are with me" (Ps. 23:4). What more radical challenge could be imagined to the world's sinful insistence on drawing boundaries, on setting things against one another, on fearing the power of death?[65]

---

64. *TuG*, 200.

65. Stephen Waldron develops this line of thought in explicitly political terms in the essay I first cited in Chapter 1 (again: "Hans Urs von Balthasar's Theological Critique of Nationalism," *Political Theology* 15, no. 5 [2014]: 406–20). Waldron shows that Balthasar's

164   *Balthasar and Prayer*

These critical dimensions of prayer by no means exhaust its mysterious depths. Sometimes prayer can do nothing more in the face of the world's power but cry "Stop!" (Amos 7:5). But we fail to grasp what Balthasar took to be the full importance of prayer—indeed, the *grace* of prayer—if we neglect its transformative parrhesiastic character. It is, to my view, one of the most distinctive features of his overall account, and the one that arguably holds the most promise for sustaining an engaged form of missionary love in the world today.

belief that the earthly and heavenly realms stand in no essential contradiction to one another leads ultimately to a "rejection of nationalistic ideology," inasmuch as any such ideology always depends on preserving "the nation" as a special vehicle of grace, set apart in some way. See especially the relevant remarks at TD.3, 422, where Balthasar plainly states his view that, "No national messianism has any theological significance." A Christian nation could only make such a claim precisely by *forgetting* Christianity's actual "prehistory" in Israel and replacing it with some abstract fiction—the German *Volk*, for instance ("Hitler's 'German Christians' [n.b. *Balthasar's* scare quotes] should be a constant warning for us here" [TL.3, 264]).

CONCLUDING REMARKS

What, in the end, has this book revealed about the theology of Hans Urs von Balthasar? I presume at this point that the arguments of the preceding chapters will stand or fall on their own merits, and I will refrain from simply re-narrating each of the various dimensions of prayer as I have presented them earlier. I will however summarize in broad terms the picture of prayer that has emerged from these investigations, clarify the contributions this work has made, and comment on how this account of prayer relates to our reading of Balthasar as a theologian. I will also draw out of these considerations those which I take to be the essential provocations of Balthasar's theology—provocations to do with how we understand the very nature and purpose of theology itself. These are provocations that, I believe, still deserve a hearing today. In the course of these remarks I will also note some lacunae and indicate possible trajectories for future research.

First, a summary of prayer according to Balthasar. Prayer is understood to be not an ascending act of the creature before God, but a grace that comes from the very heart of God. There is thus something (and the vague noun "something" is unavoidable here given the nature of all analogical language about God) about prayer that is revelatory of the mode of God's loving and, therefore, of God's very essence. Essentially what is implicated is the loving interaction of freedoms through which, as in a dialogue, word and response give rise to new significations of meaning. In prayer, the creature is formed in and conformed to this Trinitarian reality, which I have characterized repeatedly as a rhythmic interplay animated by love: disclosure and fidelity, revelation and covenant, word and response. It is this kind of relationship that God invites his people into—and which they, in turn, repeatedly dishonor by turning aside from in distraction (and so sin is in a sense essentially distraction). This underlines the extent to which prayer is understood by Balthasar to be a relational reality—not the *monos pro monon* of one alone with oneself but the decisive encounter with the living God who wants to know us as unique persons resolved to historical missions that build up the Kingdom.

The creaturely participation in this dialogue-relationship is founded on Christ, who expresses the "language of God" in human form.[1] It is thus precisely as a form of revelation that prayer lies at the heart of the person and mission of the Son who comes into the world in order to heal that which has been damaged by sin. Christ is a person of prayer not as a concession to his human nature but as an expression

---

1. Again, *MiH*, 275ff.

of his divine one. It is a significant feature of Balthasar's account that the unity of mission and identity in Christ secures prayer's basis in the eternal Trinitarian life. Christ brings the heavenly prayer to earth and opens it to the faithful through the Spirit, who then can be said to take guardianship of all prayer which is addressed to God. The Spirit's role here is entirely consonant with the Son's. As the one who testifies to the love between Father and Son *ad intra*, the Spirit is the one who leads the Son to the Father *ad extra*. Consequently, the creaturely share in Sonship will likewise be marked by this same Spirit-led movement toward the Father in prayer. We can thus say, following Balthasar, that it is the Son who makes creaturely prayer possible while the Spirit makes prayer effective. By extension, the church is seen to be established by and in ongoing dialogue with Christ's prayers for the salvation of the world (thus one concrete way in which the Spirit, as the "vehicle and interpreter" of Christ's prayers, can be said to have special guardianship of the church).[2] Inasmuch as the sacraments have been instituted as Christoform expressions of the "pure mutual relationship of God and man," they stand within the same theodramatic space opened up by Christ's prayers. Prayer thus describes the ontological situation of the creature who participates in the Son's eternal eucharistic stance, vis-à-vis the Father.[3] Creaturely and ecclesial prayer is seen here to be a form of mediated participation in the Trinitarian life.

Because to know God is to know God as love, to the extent that a creature enters into the rhythms of prayer (again: disclosure and fidelity, word and response), such a creature learns to see itself as one who is loved by God—as one whose voice is being invited into the eternal dialogue of love that prayer is. This shift of perception is itself a grace which overcomes the effects of sin, the primary one being the mistaken belief that we are not sought after by God, that we are unworthy of love. Once we see that we are located in the context of this dialogue-relationship, however, more and more possibilities for mission, understood as service in love, begin to emerge. That is, love learns to recognize love; indeed, love begets love.[4] As it was for the Son in mission, so too for the creature over the course of its life is prayer understood to be the substance of engaged obedience: prayer becomes the realm in which one demonstrates that theirs is a living faith, one which has made the "decision not to escape" which lies at the heart of the relationship.[5] For the same reason, prayer is understood to be the substance of ecclesial solidarity since it is as a community born of prayer, united by prayer, and engaged in the work of prayer that the church can be said to be a site of the Son's ongoing presence to history. Finally, to the extent that this community of prayer really does give rise to action in history, the effect of this will be to bring the world progressively more in line with God's intention for it as a place where death reigns no more, where every tear is wiped away, and where God is invited to dwell among God's people

---

2. Again, *Prayer* (H), 74.
3. Again, ET.2, 366.
4. Again, cf. *LAC*, 75.
5. Again, the phrase is Rowan Williams' from *On Christian Theology*, 122.

(cf. Rev. 21:1-8). In pursuit of such a world, men and women of prayer are called upon to live with a certain boldness—the boldness of faith which identifies itself in God's "Yes" to the world and, crucially, is bold enough to say "Yes" in return. Occasionally, depending on the exigencies of mission and circumstance, this boldness may lead a given individual into conflict with the powers of this world; in other cases, the same boldness is manifested by the "anonymous" witness of the one who persists in their everyday faith.

Such is the scope and status of prayer in Balthasar's theology. It is, as I claimed at the outset, central to his entire theological vision. Balthasar's account of prayer makes several critical contributions. First and most significantly, by locating genuine prayer entirely within the rhythms of Trinitarian love out of which all life flows, Balthasar distinguishes prayer from other forms of religious or devotional practice and secures its place as a central activity of Christian existence. He thus indicates the plausibility of the biblical injunction to "pray without ceasing" (cf. 1 Thess. 1:2; 2:13; 2 Thess. 1:11; 2:13; 5:17; Rom. 1:10; 1 Cor. 1:4; Eph. 5:20; Phil. 1:4; Col. 1:3; Phlm. 1:4; cf. Lk. 18:1) by showing prayer to be a mode of existence which can accurately be said to characterize a life of faith itself.[6] Second and relatedly, if prayer is the basis of Christian identity, then by that same token prayer is the basis of Christian mission (given the inseparability of identity and mission in the person of Christ), and so contemplation is seen here to bear a natural connection to action. This is really only the consequence of the previous point. If prayer is an entire mode of existence, then it will perforce include both action and contemplation, setting the two in mutual reciprocal relationship to one another rather than ranking them in terms of "higher" or "lower" activities as an older tradition of Christian Platonism was wont to do.[7] This in turn suggests a third strength of Balthasar's account, which is that it goes some substantial distance toward overcoming the largely sentimental hagiography of previous centuries, according to which sanctity was always in danger of being understood to be "self-sufficient."[8] Indeed, on this (semi-Pelagian) account the saint could seem less like a model of faith than a kind of ecclesial superhero. Against this sentimental view, Balthasar stresses repeatedly that sanctity is only "purposeful" to the extent that it illuminates the form of divine love in history—on this account, a given saint is to be remembered less for his or her subjective idiosyncrasies than for the objective "Yes" to God as evidenced by his or her life and mission.[9] Accordingly, sanctity can be seen to be not the remit of a chosen few but an option open to every person who bothers to turn to God in prayer. As a consequence of this point, prayer can then be said to provide a concrete basis for ecclesial solidarity inasmuch as it covers and includes a multitude of subjective personalities, states of mind,

---

6. Cf. *EG*, 54.
7. Refer again to the discussion in Section 6.3 *supra* and Balthasar's essay on this question at ET.1, 227–40.
8. Again, cf. *CSL*, 82.
9. Ibid., Cf. *GW*, 125–6.

historical and cultural contexts, and so on. Finally, since prayer is for Balthasar a form of mediated participation in the Trinitarian life, it can be said to introduce real responsibility—what Balthasar will call verticality—to the praying person's life.[10] Practically, this means that prayer can be a source of newness in a given life and indeed the life of the church (from this vantage point we have no reason to deny that prayer which does not lead to a conversion of life remains prethematic).

In addition to clearly bringing forward these important aspects of Balthasar's account, this study has advanced and defended a number of specific theological claims. Among the most important of these are: (i) that the idea of Trinitarian prayer, rather than signaling some mystic flight of fancy, in fact entails a deeply revisionist yet biblically grounded metaphysical argument about all created reality being located in God; (ii) that the unity of mission and identity in Christ (which is itself one of Balthasar's most important contributions) rests upon an understanding of Christ as a praying person, that is to say, one whose unique mission-identity is best understood as and at prayer; (iii) that the encounter with God in prayer has the effect upon the creature of personalizing them, not abstracting them from themself or annihilating their unique identity but locating that identity in a specific theodramatic context; (iv) that such a person will be possessed of a certain *parrhesia* which dares to speak with a boldness born of the faith that it participates in the future it hopes to bring about; and (v) that this eschatological future is the terminus of all prayer, such that prayer is itself already a proleptic participation in this future. These arguments have emerged in the context of Balthasar's theology, but taken together and thus arrayed they constitute a constructive theology of prayer.

In addition to these constructive theological points, I have also sought to make certain methodological contributions to Balthasar Studies. Most importantly, I have provided one strategy for finding one's way around Balthasar by showing the extent to which his incredibly varied theological writings are so often motivated by the central issue of prayer. Notably, I have made sure to cite a wide variety of sources (not just the systematic works from the famous trilogy) in order to show that this prayer heuristic holds across what I have called the three "categories" of Balthasar's writings. Likewise, I have provided a way of understanding the wildly disparate judgments on Balthasar's work that one finds represented among the secondary literature, and have done this in part by taking care to notice how various authors treat what I take to be the decisive question of prayer—and the attendant questions of theological method which are thereby raised.

These latter points deserve to be expanded upon. To return to my initial claim that there are "three waves" of English-language readers of Balthasar, we might now ask how the approach of this book bears upon those waves. Earlier I criticized the first wave (cf. Section 1.2.1 *supra*) for tending to reify Balthasar's thought more than engaging it. If Balthasar's theology is to be understood as arising from prayer, and if prayer for Balthasar is to be understood as a dialogue that requires the

---

10. On "horizontal" versus "vertical" prayer, see again GL.1, 192 or *Prayer* (H), 195.

free exchange of word and response, then it is precisely the first wave's tendency toward reification and systematization that constitutes the primary limitation of their approach. This is not to deny that Balthasar's theology holds a certain definite shape (as indeed the first wave so often emphasizes by focusing attention on the theological aesthetics), but it is to say that Balthasar's most significant theological contributions are speculative and allusive—to take his theology as a self-contained system is to miss its significant promise as a spur to new thinking. Whether any given speculation of Balthasar's proves fruitful is a separate matter; my narrow methodological point at the moment is that it is just this speculative nature of Balthasar's theology (with which the first wave so often express frustration) which we should expect of an approach which is so deeply intertwined with the question and practice of prayer. Theology, like prayer, should strive "not to say and think the same thing day after day," and it is what I called earlier the more daring Balthasar that we have to engage if we are to engage him honestly.[11] The first wave are often correct to point to the concrete form of Christ at the heart of Balthasar's system, but they err when they suggest that this encounter with Christ is for Balthasar something other than the dynamic, contingent, ongoing dialogue that prayer is. Another way of putting this is to say that prayer's role in Balthasar's theology should generally serve to open up new avenues of thought rather than shut them down.

Likewise, I faulted the second wave (cf. Section 1.2.2 *supra*) with their own failure to engage Balthasar in favor of simply disqualifying him from the realm of acceptable theological discourse. This disqualification was unfortunate, I argued, not only since it largely cedes the interpretive ground to the first wave (who will no doubt go on writing about Balthasar) but also since it fails to recognize that the proper mode of reception for Balthasar's theology is the mode in which it was conceived—that is, as part of an ecclesial ensemble, not as the product of a solitary eccentric or even an academic theologian. The harsh reactions to Balthasar which tend to predominate among the second wave, when they are not attributable to selective readings of the texts in question, often arise out of a failure to take his theology as an invitation to further dialogue. In this way, the defect of the second wave mirrors that of the first, inasmuch as both decline to go significantly further than Balthasar did himself. Sometimes (as with Beattie, for instance) this amounts to outright hermeneutical violence. More often (as with Kilby or Pitstick, for instance), it suggests that the authors simply find Balthasar's particular theological voice unworkable. But one consequence of associating prayer so closely with theology is that an ever-wider range of theological voices will be welcomed into the conversation. Just as there is no one way to pray, there is, in a manner of speaking, no one way to do theology. Thus one reason for Balthasar's own recourse

---

11. Again, *Prayer* (L), 112. Reno's frustrations with Balthasar are especially telling in this regard, especially in his call for a return to "textbook theology," which is of course precisely one of the methods of doing theology that Balthasar most despised (see "The Paradox of Hans Urs von Balthasar," 189).

to a number of nontraditional theological sources (Thérèse of Lisieux, Adrienne von Speyr, Reinhold Schneider), which I suggest is one concrete consequence of his doing theology as prayer. To be clear, this is no case for quietism or relativism when evaluating Balthasar's legacy. There is ample room to engage and indeed to disagree with his theology. But what I am suggesting is that this be done in the manner of prayer, which is to say, with an uncompetitive *parrhesia* that does not seek to silence or sanction but to "reason together" (Isa. 1:18) about the work that God does for and with the world.

And finally, I commended the third wave (cf. Section 1.2.3 *supra*) for understanding Balthasar's particular rhythms of thought and thus being able to engage him more fruitfully than the other two approaches. A contention of this work has been that the structure of Balthasar's theology is itself prayerful, and so by illuminating that structure (i.e., the structure of prayer) as Balthasar understood it, I have also thereby given an indication of how best to extract the most fertile theological material from this particular theologian. In this sense, this study has contributed to the momentum of the third wave. Although the various writers of the third wave are not as politically or ideologically homogenous as the other two, they are united by their insistence on doing theology *with* Balthasar, rather than *against* him or *like* him. In order to carry out this dialogue, it is necessary to bring in new topics, to raise new questions, to "[say] the same thing in different ways"[12]—thus, the third wave has engaged in the creative combinations I mentioned in Section 1.2.3 (Balthasar and liberation theology, Balthasar and Kierkegaard, Balthasar and Levinas, Balthasar and the East, and so on, as well as my own combination of Balthasar and Foucault in Chapter 7). At the same time, this approach recognizes the importance of letting Balthasar speak in his own voice, of not forcing him into categories which were not his own, lest any potential dialogue turn into a monologue. In this twofold sense—of listening and speaking, word and silence—third-wave approaches maintain the prayerful structure of Balthasar's thought, whether or not they take prayer as their explicit subject.

I have just said that this study contributes to the momentum of the third wave and that it does this by throwing some light on the structure of Balthasar's overall thought. The efforts of the third wave would likewise be advanced by developing a number of the specific aspects of Balthasar's thought which this work has exposed but not had the necessary space to develop at length, several of which have been raised in extended footnotes (Balthasar's relation to queer theory, for instance, or the parallel with Stanislavsky's method acting or else Balthasar's rich apocalyptic imaginary, especially vis-à-vis the figure of Satan). One point in particular, however, could sustain a number of relevant further investigations, namely the *parrhesia* aspect of prayer, especially as it relates to postmodern versions of *parrhesia* from Foucault onward. In pursuit of such a project, one could undertake to give a general account of theological *parrhesia* drawing on Balthasar but also Scripture, the

---

12. Again, *CL*, 57.

Fathers, and other modern theologians who discussed the term (such as Rahner)[13] in order to show more convincingly the centrality of this concept to the Christian spiritual life. After a general theological sense of the term has been established, Balthasar's particular understanding of it can be evaluated for its relative novelty, and a more meaningful localized exchange with Foucault could then be carried out. In turn, certain unresolved aspects of the Foucauldian account might come more clearly into focus (for instance, perhaps the Foucauldian/philosophical notion of *parrhesia* does in fact provide a basis for hope beyond death in ways which could be compared more favorably with the theological definition, but does so only when seen against a horizon of the future; thus, the theological comparison might help to clarify an implicit secular eschatology). This would be one such creative combination characteristic of the third wave. The *parrhesia* aspect of prayer in Balthasar could also fruitfully contribute to the burgeoning area of scholarship which seeks to understand Balthasar's thought in relation to liberation theology (Brown, Walatka, etc.), as well as related but broader considerations about how spiritual discipline relates to political liberation (Coakley, Eggemeier, etc.).[14] For the one who has found their voice in prayer, there is in this the freedom to likewise speak boldly to the world; this kind of bold speech can thus be a liberating praxis with the power to raise consciousness and interrupt prevailing cycles of violence. Along similar lines, it seems to me that the particular notion of *parrhesia* that Balthasar was developing could also contribute to the current efforts of some like David Newheiser to promote a "negative political theology" which can simultaneously critique and affirm political power without slipping into either pessimism or complicity.[15] These and other lines of inquiry suggest just how rich

13. Cf. Rahner's essay on "Boldness," in *Theological Investigations*, vol. VII: *Further Theology of the Spiritual Life I* (London: Darton, Longman and Todd, 1971), 260–7.

14. Cf. Matthew Eggemeier, "A Mysticism of Open Eyes: Compassion for a Suffering World and the *Askesis* of Contemplative Prayer," *Spiritus* 12, no. 1 (2012): 43–62.

15. See the special issue of *Modern Theology* 36:1 (2020), especially the introduction by Newheiser ("Why the World Needs Negative Political Theology," 5–12). As Newheiser explains, although the idea of a "negative political theology" can be traced back at least to Jacob Taube's work on Paul in the 1980s, the contributors to the *Modern Theology* symposium (including Amy Hollywood, Karen Kilby, Denys Turner, and William Cavanaugh) seek to develop a critical political stance that authentically expresses an apophatic theology, one which "affirms particular projects that it subjects, at the same time, to critique" (12). *Parrhesia* is a useful concept here, inasmuch as the proper exercise of *parrhesia* requires this same effort to weigh critique against affirmation (what Foucault called playing the parrhesiastic game); and therefore *parrhesia* in prayer is especially important as a kind of pedagogical practice that prepares the would-be parrhesiastes to speak in this uniquely difficult way. In this sense, prayer can be what Rowan Williams calls the "liberative non-place from which resistance arises" (see "Response to Amy Hollywood," 53–5, here 54), if indeed it involves the same dynamics of personalization and implicates the same relation to power that I have argued it does. That *parrhesia* seems to fit within a program that takes as

the concept is and what sort of constructive theological work might arise from these findings in the future.

If we can see now more clearly how the approach I have taken here recommends itself as a way of working within the Balthasarian *oeuvre*, there is still space to voice some reservations about choosing Balthasar as a dialogue partner. Even though I am convinced of its essential usefulness and its importance to his overall thought, I do not wish to merely endorse unreservedly every aspect of Balthasar's approach to the question of prayer. Several of my reservations have already been noted throughout this work: Balthasar's unfair characterizations of therapy, for instance, or the danger of his ranking two forms of sanctity, or the inherent danger of his speculative Trinitarian language. But even allowing for these concerns, one can still see how Balthasar's approach proceeds along the lines it does. More useful to notice at this point are what we might call the limits of the account itself. In other words, even if we grant the account of prayer that Balthasar wants to give, what more might we need to ask of him or, more likely, to seek from another source altogether? On this front there seems one especially prominent point to raise, which is that Balthasar's account of prayer's purpose and proper practice is clearly addressed primarily to Christians. While this is no inherent weakness (a Christian theologian can hardly be faulted for rendering a Christian account of prayer), it does perhaps create tensions at the edges of Balthasar's account. For instance, given that, for Balthasar, identity is tied to mission and mission is bestowed and confirmed in prayer, a non-Christian could reasonably ask whether or not they, as someone who does not pray in this way, is somehow less of a person in possession of a unique theodramatic identity than the Christian who prays. While this may seem like a critical point, and while it is not my intention to simply dismiss the charge as soon as I have raised it, there is also reason to suspect that it might be the result of a category error. As I noted earlier (cf. Section 5.1 *supra*), Balthasar explicitly declines in the first volume of the *Theo-Drama* to engage the general anthropological question—"What kind of creature is man?"—in favor of the more personal question—"Who am I?"—and, furthermore, puts this latter question in the distinctively theological register—"Who am I in relation to God?" (here the influence of Barth is apparent). Strictly speaking, mission-identity for Balthasar is not a general and necessary prerequisite to being human, but to being a Christian. This does not therefore imply that the Christian is some kind of superhuman, with an additional power (in this case, the power of prayer) above and beyond that which the non-Christian is capable of. It implies merely that the Christian is one possessed of a particular mission *qua* Christian, a point that seems a logical tautology when stated explicitly. And in any case, as I have shown at length earlier, this mission is presented by Balthasar not as an individual merit but a dynamic, ongoing grace mediated in and through the church and available in principle to every person, which challenges and changes the praying person even as they enter more fully into its mysterious depths. Prayer refers not to

---

its inspiration the discipline of *unsaying* that apophasis implies raises interesting questions both about *parrhesia* and about negative theology.

a higher order of being, but to the substance of the distinctively Christian existence spread out over a lifetime. Most important to notice, however, is that the Christian possessed of a mission works *on behalf of* the whole world—their unique mission-identity, therefore, does not serve to separate them from everyone else but to enable truly profound depths of solidarity with all those who work and hope for peace. I have stressed repeatedly throughout this study the various ways in which prayer is not seen by Balthasar as a privilege nor as a method of ascent away from the realities of the world, but a task of love which leads to service and to care for the other. While I believe these are relevant points that mitigate the danger of a tiered anthropology in Balthasar, and while I believe it is a mistake to read him as justifying any such hierarchy of praying Christians "above" non-Christians, it remains the case that his account, such as it is, may nevertheless give rise to this impression.[16] For this reason, its usefulness will be most apparent as a resource of Christian theology (though that is not to say comparative approaches can yield no fruit).

If this book has indeed succeeded in making any of these contributions, it has done so because it has insisted on reading Balthasar's theology not merely for what it has to say *about* prayer, but *as* a form of prayer itself. I do not make this claim lightly—I could even be said to do so reluctantly. To describe a given theologian's theology as a form of prayer often suggests to me some rhetorical sleight of hand. Usually the sentiment is piously intoned as a way to insulate said theologian from criticism or as a way for the would-be defender of said theologian to subtly indicate his or her own spiritual authority. As my way of proceeding has shown, however, to read a given theology as prayer need not for that reason place it beyond the scope of rigorous, critical discussion. Nor does it mean that such a theology loses a definite shape—indeed, I have shown that, for Balthasar, prayer has a specific shape and rhythm that a theology of prayer should to some extent replicate or, better yet, enact. I would like now to indicate some reasons why I think it is important that theology be done in this way.

The image of prayer that has emerged at this point is one of holistic engagement with God. Within the realm of prayer this engagement necessarily admits of a

---

16. Dermot Power, though clearly a sympathetic reader of Balthasar, notes the danger of reading Balthasar in an "elitist" way at *A Spiritual Theology of the Priesthood: The Mystery of Christ and the Mission of the Priest* (Edinburgh: T&T Clark, 1998), 141–2. According to Power, what is implicated here is the "scandal of particularity," which attends to any biblical theology of grace, such that "God in choosing some appears to be excluding others" (141 internal quotation marks omitted). Balthasar is clearly aware of this tension, even considering it to be a form of paradox (cf. *In Gottes Einsatz Leben*, 36–9). However, Power puts this tension in its proper theological context by highlighting that it is always "for the sake of and out of love for all" that God engages the particularity of a given person (or people, such as Israel; cf. *A Spiritual Theology of the Priesthood*, 142). That is, no mission is self-sufficient nor indeed self-serving. This relates to the concern that prayer can be misunderstood as a kind of Christian privilege since it suggests that the personal relationship between God and the praying person is simply not credible unless it manifests in a life of loving solidarity.

wide scope—various affects, petitions, states of mind, doubts, demands, words of thanksgiving and praise, questions, and the like, to say nothing of the "sighs too deep for words" (Rom. 8:26) which likewise express something of our sense of and desire for God. This wide scope of prayer is expressed with unique brilliance, for instance, in the Psalms. All of these various aspects of prayer take place, however, within a given structure or pattern of engagement between God and the praying person or people; this is the "dialogue-relationship" of prayer in all its various dimensions that I have sought to illuminate throughout this study. No matter how wide the horizon of prayer at any point becomes, the overall structure is already indicated in the simplest prayer, *amen*, which, as I argued earlier, is a reciprocal, dialogical affirmation that one locates oneself within the dynamic covenant relationship between God and God's people (cf. Section 3.3.2 *supra*). *Amen* expresses the confidence that one has been heard, if not that every word has been well chosen. Indeed, if one is being honest with oneself, one must acknowledge that the words one has chosen are likely to be inadequate in any number of ways given that the dialogue is with the infinite God who knows each praying person, their intentions and their desires, better even than they do themselves. No doubt pride is often at work here—we think we arrive at an insight in prayer when in fact we have been led to it, or we become convinced of the beauty of our own words such that they become the focus of our attention—but so too are distraction and lack of imagination obstacles to the kind of engagement with God that prayer exists in order to be. And yet, it is our very participation in the dialogue that forms us, that continually refines our language, that reveals the smallness of our preexisting categories, that continually leads us back to the source which is the self-gift of the Son who makes the dialogue possible for us in the first place. Seen from this perspective, the rules of the dialogue, so to speak, subtly shift: It is no longer a question of getting the "right words"—we cannot hope to outdo God's "omniloquence" in prayer.[17] But we can (and here ability implies obligation) find *our* voice in prayer, and can find a way to respond to the unique divine initiative that confronts us in our lives. We can and we must find a way to speak in the first person, to find a language that expresses something of what it is we actually believe since it is only such a language that has the potential to challenge us and, eventually, to convert our lives.

At first blush, this could seem like a trivial point, but it is in fact the constant and fundamental challenge of prayer. Many who experience difficulty in prayer stumble on precisely this point. The American writer Flannery O'Connor likened her experience of reading the traditional devotional literature to "wearing somebody else's finery," and Balthasar describes the same phenomenon on the first page of the prayer book by evoking the image of a hungry person watching someone else eat their fill.[18] One of the primary aims of Balthasar's account of prayer is to lead one

---

17. *Prayer* (H), 46.

18. Flannery O'Connor, Letter to Betty Hester from March 10, 1956 in *The Habit of Being* (New York: Farrar, Straus, and Giroux, 1978); Balthasar, *Prayer* (H), 7.

to overcome this deficit. Prayer's *parrhesia* is obviously implicated here, and this is one of my reasons for having highlighted it as much as I have. A key aspect of *parrhesia* is the willingness of the speaker to identify themselves with the content of their speech, and it is this self-identification—this *amen*—that lies at the heart of all genuine prayer. It is also this parrhesiastic *amen* that underlies the theological task, understood as one form of creaturely participation in the ongoing dialogue of conversion not only of the praying person but of the whole community that identifies itself in the covenant relationship.

Theology both participates in and is tasked with giving an account of this dialogue-relationship, and it is here that prayer and theology can be said to substantively overlap. Like prayer, indeed as prayer, theology draws from the same well of faith that dares to ask for what it needs in order to say what it must. Again, *parrhesia* is implicated. A theologian who merely adheres to given forms, who reinscribes existing patterns of meaning, shows thereby that he or she fails to understand the task and structure of theology. Such a theologian will have let the dialogue devolve into chatter, rather than finding their voice in order to "sing a new song" (Ps. 96:1). There is necessarily a certain boldness to good theology, then, even a sort of courage (recall that it was this boldness that most attracted the young Balthasar to theologians like Barth, Origen, and Maximus). Underlying this boldness, however, is the humility that the theologian must have before the dialogue itself—a dialogue which, after all, the theologian will never master but to which they are always accountable. The theologian, then, is pulled in two seemingly opposite directions: On the one hand, they must *listen*—to tradition, to scripture, to other theologians, but above all to the Word who confronts them with a particular mission—and on the other hand, they must *speak*—to their ecclesial community, to the academy, to the world at large, but above all to the God who addresses them as one possessed of a particular voice. This is a creative tension, one which can be detected in all great theological voices. Here again we have the dynamic interplay of word and silence, initiative and response, that lies at the heart of prayer; to locate this same interplay, this same rhythm, at the heart of theology is only to insist on the necessary integrity of a discourse which must be credible in order to be effective.

The value of this sort of theology becomes apparent when one considers the alternatives. Balthasar's concern, especially at the time of the famous "Theology and Sanctity" essay, was the divorce of theology from its ecclesial context, such that it had become just one more intellectual discipline among others (especially in the setting of the modern research university). When dogmatics cuts itself off from its source material in this way, when it neglects the "subjective aspect" of its objective teachings, it becomes abstract and sterile.[19] Theology's tendency to become sterile remains a pertinent concern today; indeed, in many places the trends which Balthasar was reacting to have only since accelerated. But it is in theology's capacity to prove not just sterile but oppressive that it must yet continue to heed Balthasar's more profound provocations. For Balthasar understood theology's unique capacity to impose silence

---

19. Again, see "Spirituality," in ET.1, 211.

(or what Rachel Muers called "muteness," which is a silence that "communicates nothing").[20] This imposed silence or muteness is to be carefully distinguished from what I called in Section 5.3.2 *supra* the "missionary silence" which is ready to say "Yes" and to make that "Yes" credible in the work of one's life. Muteness in this sense forecloses possibilities; it denies new significations. Theology can succeed in imposing this kind of muteness in a particularly profound way precisely because it dares to speak about and in a sense to God, and because, in turn, so many feel that that is a topic on which they have no right to speak (recall the dynamics of shame which operate on the person who undertakes to pray—Section 5.2.1 *supra*). A theology of this sort will react with hostility to disruption; it will stubbornly insist on repeating itself, and it will, given the opportunity, collaborate with violent structures for lack of a prophetic voice. A theology which operates so as to impose muteness can properly be called "mutilated" and closed off to the Spirit whose task it is to "sift, test, and refine" all speech addressed to God.[21] Such a theology obviously fails to either participate in or give an account of the dynamic dialogue-relationship between God and God's people.

I have emphasized repeatedly, however, that Balthasar indicates another way. At his best he is a theologian whose freedom of thought and breadth of vision create a space in which dialogue can take place. And he is this, when he is this, because his theology grows out of an engaged piety, a revolving, even restless concern to speak to God by speaking of God. No genuine Christian theologian can fear where this dialogue will lead, since its first word is the *amen* which is the Spirit's invitation to play midwife to a new birth of love. Conceived of as this open-ended participation in the dialogue of prayer, theology becomes simultaneously less predictable but more credible as a discourse of conversion, as the discourse of those who locate themselves within the living covenant relationship indicated by *amen*. Theology and prayer alike are both forms of speech addressed to God, and are both languages that attempt to describe the eschatological future while themselves participating in building up that future. They thus both bear the burden of keeping watch, of staying alert, of trying not to say the same thing every day, and of speaking in the first person. It is in these ways that theology can be its own form of mediated engagement with God. It is in these ways that the ever-further integration of prayer and theology can help to overcome some of the "damage" that has been done to the practice of prayer (to recall Winner's provocative term which I first raised in the Introduction *supra*) and even to prove to be a form of liberation. It would do this first by leading the individual to discover their voice, and then by requiring that they use it. It was because of his vision of theology as a form of this ongoing, future-oriented dialogue that Balthasar can be said to be a theologian of prayer par excellence. If, surveying the field, one was inclined to despair of so many contemporary theologians' apparent inability to speak with a

---

20. See Muers, "The Mute Cannot Keep Silent" 110 or *idem*, *Keeping God's Silence: Towards a Theological Ethics of Communication* (Oxford: Blackwell, 2004).

21. Hanvey, "Healing the Wound," 217.

boldness that manifests the hope that is in them (cf. 1 Pet. 3:15), then Balthasar's example still holds meaning for us today.

Finally, then, it is this keeping watch that lies at the heart of both prayer and of theology, and for the same reasons. The act of keeping watch, of holding attention, of keeping up the dialogue—this is no minor task, but the very essence of Christian hope. But it is just this hope that sustains us through the desert of history like manna from heaven. That prayer is this grace suggests God's profound respect for human freedom, since God wills to meet us in the personal dialogue-relationship of word and response. As such, it is precisely our freedom that is ratified in the context of this relationship, and it is our freedom which is shown to be our path toward God, rather than our primary obstacle. In this realm of freedom, this world of prayer, we will wander far and wide. These are the mysterious depths of prayer which echo the infinite depths of divine love. The Christian's bold faith is, simply put, that God does not leave us to wallow in these depths unaided, that in fact the Spirit of God carries us through these depths and helps to turn our inarticulate groans into something like a real conversation.

It is on this point that I would like to draw this book to a close, and to do so by giving the final word to Balthasar. In a compact aphorism, displaying both the depth of feeling and the psychological sensitivity for which he is not frequently enough recognized, Balthasar distills the essence of holiness as he sees it, which he defines as holding God's gaze. In this, all the essential aspects of the account I have presented are operative—decision, trust, surprise, action, and attention—even as they are put against the horizon of infinite love. Balthasar's words here seem at first to be deceptively simple, but, upon reflection, one is struck that what he describes is nothing less than the task of a lifetime, a task in which prayer plays the indispensable role:

> Holiness consists in enduring God's glance. It may appear mere passivity to withstand the look of an eye; but everyone knows how much exertion is required when this occurs in an essential encounter. Our glances mostly brush by each other indirectly, or they turn quickly away, or they give themselves not personally but only socially. So too do we constantly flee from God into a distance that is theoretical, rhetorical, sentimental, aesthetic, or, most frequently, pious. Or we flee from him to external works. And yet, the best thing would be to surrender one's naked heart to the fire of this all-penetrating glance. The heart would then itself have to catch fire, if it were not always artificially dispersing the rays that come to it as through a magnifying glass. Such enduring would be the opposite of a stoic's hardening his face: it would be yielding, declaring oneself beaten, capitulating, entrusting oneself, casting oneself into him. It would be childlike loving, since for children the glance of the father is not painful: with wide-open eyes they look into his. [Prayer thus conforms to] Augustine's formula on the essence of eternity: *videntem videre*—"to look at him who is looking at you."[22]

22. *GW*, 3–4.

APPENDIX

A Proposed Categorization of Balthasar's Major Works[1]

Category 1

Apocalypse of the German Soul
The Christian State of Life
Explorations in Theology, Vols. 1–5
"The Fathers, the Scholastics, and Ourselves"
Glory of the Lord, Vols. 1–7
Man in History
The Office of Peter and the Structure of the Church
Theo-Drama, Vols. 1–5
Theo-Logic, Vols. 1–3

Category 2

The Christian and Anxiety
"*Communio*—A Program"
Convergences
Dare We Hope That All Men Be Saved?
Engagement with God
Elucidations and *New Elucidations*
First Glance at Adrienne von Speyr
Love Alone is Credible
The Moment of Christian Witness
"On the Tasks of Catholic Philosophy in Our Time"
Razing the Bastions
A Theology of History
The Threefold Garland: The World's Salvation in Mary's Prayer
Truth Is Symphonic

---

1. For a discussion of the meaning and purpose of the categorization scheme, see Chapter 1 *infra*.

Category 3

Christian Meditation
The Grain of Wheat: Aphorisms
Heart of the World
Our Task
Test Everything and Hold Fast to What is Good
Who is a Christian?
You Crown the Year with Your Glory: Sermons

BIBLIOGRAPHY

Works By Hans Urs von Balthasar

Apokalypse der deutschen Seele: Studien zu einer Lehre von letzten Haltungen, Volumes 1–3. Salzburg: Pustet, 1937–9.

The Balthasar Reader. Edited by Medard Kehl and Werner Löser. Translated by Robert J. Daly and Fred Lawrence. New York: Crossroads, 1982.

"Catholicism and the Communion of the Saints." *Communio* 15 (1988): 163–8.

Christian Meditation. Translated by Mary Theresilde Skerry. San Francisco: Ignatius, 1989. [*Christlich meditieren*. Freiburg im Breisgau: Herder, 1984.]

The Christian and Anxiety. Translated by Dennis Martin and Michael Miller. San Francisco: Ignatius, 2000. [*Der Christ und die Angst*. Einsiedeln: Johannes, 1951.]

The Christian State of Life. Translated by Mary Francis McCarthy. San Francisco: Ignatius, 2002. [*Christlicher* Stand. Einsiedeln: Johannes, 1977.]

"Communio: A Program." *Communio: International Catholic Review* 33 (2006): 159–69.

Convergences: To the Source of Christian Mystery. Translated by E. A. Nelson. San Francisco, CA: Ignatius, 1983. [*Einfaltungen: Auf Wegen christlicher Einigung*. Munich: Kösel, 1969.]

Cosmic Liturgy: The Universe According to Maximus the Confessor. Translated by Brian Daley. San Francisco: Ignatius, 2003. [*Kosmische Liturgie: Das Weltbild Maximus' des Bekenners*. Einsiedeln: Johannes, 1961.]

Dare We Hope "That All May Be Saved"? With A Short Discourse on Hell. Translated by David Kipp and Lothar Krauth. San Francisco: Ignatius, 1988. [*Was dürfen wir hoffen?* Einsiedeln: Johannes, 1986; and *Kleiner Diskurs über die Hölle*. Ostfildern: Schwabenverlag, 1987.]

Does Jesus Know Us? Do We Know Him? Translated by Graham Harrison. San Francisco: Ignatius, 1983. [*Kennt uns Jesus? Kennen wir ihn?* Freiburg im Breisgau: Herder, 1980.]

Elucidations. Translated by John Riches. San Francisco: Ignatius, 1998. [*Klarstellungen: Zur Prüfung der Geister*. Freiburg im Breisgau: Herder, 1971.]

Engagement with God: The Drama of Christian Discipleship. Translated by John Halliburton. San Francisco: Ignatius, 2008. [*In Gottes Einsatz leben*. Einsiedeln: Johannes, 1971.]

Epilogue. Translated by Edward T. Oakes. San Francisco: Ignatius, 2004. [*Epilog*. Einsiedeln: Johannes, 1987.]

"Exerzitien und Theologie." *Orientierung: Katholische Blätter für weltanschauliche Information* 12 (1948): 229–32.

Explorations in Theology Volume 1: *The Word Made Flesh*. Translated by A.V. Littledale and Alexander Dru. San Francisco, CA: Ignatius, 1989. [*Skizzen zur Theologie* I: *Verbum Caro*. Einsiedeln: Johannes, 1960.]

Explorations in Theology Volume 2: *Spouse of the Word*. Translated by A.V. Littledale, Alexander Dru, John Saward, and Edward T. Oakes. San Francisco, CA: Ignatius, 1991. [*Skizzen zur Theologie* II: *Sponsa Verbi*. Einsiedeln: Johannes, 1961.]

Explorations in Theology Volume 3: *Creator Spirit*. Translated by Brian McNeil. San Francisco: Ignatius, 1993. [*Skizzen zur Theologie* III: *Spiritus Creator*. Einsiedeln: Johannes, 1976.]

Explorations in Theology Volume 4: *Spirit and Institution*. Translated by Edward T. Oakes. San Francisco: Ignatius, 1995. [*Skizzen zur Theologie* IV: *Pneuma und Institution*. Einsiedeln: Johannes, 1974.]

Explorations in Theology Volume 5: *Man Is Created*. Translated by Adrian Walker. San Francisco: Ignatius, 2014. [*Skizzen zur Theologie* V: *Homo Creatus Est*. Einsiedeln: Johannes, 1986.]

"The Fathers, the Scholastics, and Ourselves." Translated by Edward T. Oakes. *Communio: International Catholic Review* 24 (1997): 347–96.

First Glance at Adrienne von Speyr. Translated by Antje Lawry and Sergia Englund. San Francisco: Ignatius, 1981. [*Erster Blick auf Adrienne von Speyr*. Einsiedeln: Johannes, 1968.]

Fragen der Theologie Heute. Einsiedeln: Benziger, 1957.

The Glory of the Lord: A Theological Aesthetics, Volume 1: *Seeing the Form*. Edited by Joseph Fessio and John Riches. Translated by Erasmo Leiva-Merikakis. San Francisco, CA: Ignatius, 1982. [*Herrlichkeit: Eine theologische Ästhetik* I: *Schau der Gestalt*. Einsiedeln: Johannes, 1961.]

The Glory of the Lord: A Theological Aesthetics, Volume 2: *Studies in Theological Style: Clerical Styles*. Edited by John Riches. Translated by Andrew Louth, Francis McDonagh, and Brian McNeil. San Francisco: Ignatius, 1984. [*Herrlichkeit: Eine theologische Ästhetik* II: *Fächer der Stile: Klerikale Stile*. Einsiedeln: Johannes, 1962.]

The Glory of the Lord: A Theological Aesthetics, Volume 3: *Studies in Theological Style: Lay Styles*. Edited by John Riches. Translated by Andrew Louth, John Saward, Martin Simon, and Rowan Williams. San Francisco, CA: Ignatius, 1986. [*Herrlichkeit: Eine theologische Ästhetik* II: *Fächer der Stile: Laikale Stile*. Einsiedeln: Johannes, 1962.]

The Glory of the Lord: A Theological Aesthetics, Volume 4: *The Realm of Metaphysics in Antiquity*. Edited by John Riches. Translated by Brian McNeil, Andrew Louth, John Saward, Rowan Williams, and Oliver Davies. San Francisco, CA: Ignatius, 1989. [*Herrlichkeit: Eine theologische Ästhetik* III.1: *Im Raum der Metaphysik: Altertum*. Einsiedeln: Johannes, 1965.]

The Glory of the Lord: A Theological Aesthetics, Volume 5: *The Realm of Metaphysics in the Modern Age*. Edited by Brian McNeil and John Riches. Translated by Oliver Davies, Andrew Louth, Brian McNeil, John Saward, and Rowan Williams. San Francisco, CA: Ignatius, 1991. [*Herrlichkeit: Eine theologische Ästhetik* III.1: *Im Raum der Metaphysik: Neuzeit*. Einsiedeln: Johannes, 1965.]

The Glory of the Lord: A Theological Aesthetics, Volume 6: *Theology: The Old Covenant*. Edited by and John Riches. Translated by Brian McNeil and Erasmo Leiva-Merikakis. San Francisco, CA: Ignatius, 1991. [*Herrlichkeit: Eine theologische Ästhetik* III.2: *Theologie: Alter Bund*. Einsiedeln: Johannes, 1967.]

The Glory of the Lord: A Theological Aesthetics, Volume 7: *Theology: The New Covenant*. Edited by and John Riches. Translated by Brian McNeil. San Francisco, CA: Ignatius, 1989. [*Herrlichkeit: Eine theologische Ästhetik* III.2: *Theologie: Neuer Bund*. Einsiedeln: Johannes, 1969.]

"God Is His Own Exegete." Translated by Stephen Arndt. *Communio* 4 (1986): 280–7.

The God Question and Modern Man. Translated by Hilda Graef. New York: Seabury, 1967. [*Die Gottesfrage des heutigen Menschen*. Wien: Herold, 1956.]

"The Gospel as Norm and Test of All Spirituality of the Church." *Concilium* 1 (1965): 7–23.

The Grain of Wheat: Aphorisms. Translated by Erasmo Leiva-Merikakis. San Francisco, CA: Ignatius, 1995. [*Das Weizenkorn*. Einsiedeln: Johannes, 1953.]
Grundfragen der Mystik. Einsiedeln: Johannes, 1974.
Heart of the World. Translated by Erasmo Leiva-Merikakis. San Francisco, CA: Ignatius, 1979. [*Das Herz der Welt*. Zurich: Arche, 1945.]
In the Fullness of Faith: On the Centrality of the Distinctively Catholic. Translated by Graham Harrison. San Francisco: Ignatius Press, 1988. [*Katholisch: Aspekte des Mysteriums*. Einsiedeln: Johannes, 1975.]
"Kirche Zwischen Links und Rechts." *Civitas* 24 (1969): 440–6.
The Laity in the Life of the Counsels: The Church's Mission in the World. Translated by Brian McNeil and David C. Schindler. San Francisco, CA: Ignatius, 2003. [*Gottbereites Leben: Der Laie und der Rätestand. Nachfolge Christi in der heutigen Welt*. Einsiedeln: Johannes, 1993.]
Love Alone Is Credible. Translated by D. C. Schindler. San Francisco, CA: Ignatius, 2004. [*Glaubhaft ist nur Liebe*. Einsiedeln: Johannes, 1963.]
Man in History: A Theological Study. London: Sheed & Ward, 1968.
von Balthasar, Hans Urs and Joseph Ratzinger. *Mary: The Church at the Source*. Translated by Adrian Walker. San Francisco: Ignatius, 2005. [*Maria: Kirche im Ursprung*. Freiburg im Breisgau: Herder, 1980.]
Mary for Today. Translated by Robert Nowell. San Francisco, CA: Ignatius, 1988. [*Maria für heute*. Wien: Herder, 1987.]
"Die Metaphysik Erich Przywaras." *Schweizer Rundschau* 33 (1933): 489–99.
The Moment of Christian Witness. Translated by Richard Beckley. San Francisco, CA: Ignatius, 1994. [*Cordula oder der Ernstfall*. Einsiedeln: Johannes, 1966.]
My Work: In Retrospect. Translated by Brian McNeil, Kenneth Batinovich, John Saward and Kelly Hamilton. San Francisco, CA: Ignatius, 1993. [*Mein Werk: Durchblicke*. Einsiedeln: Johannes, 1990.]
Mysterium Paschale: The Mystery of Easter. Translated by Aidan Nichols. San Francisco, CA: Ignatius: 1990. [*Theologie der drei Tage*. Einsiedeln: Johannes, 1969.]
New Elucidations. Translated by Mary Theresilde Skerry. San Francisco, CA: Ignatius, 1986. [*Neue Klarastellungen*. Einsiedeln: Johannes, 1979.]
The Office of Peter and the Structure of the Church. Translated by André Emery. San Francisco, CA: Ignatius, 1986. [*Der antirömische Affekt: Wie rässt sich das Papsttum in der Gesamtkirche integrieren*. Freiburg im Breisgau: Herder, 1974.]
"On the Concept of Person." *Communio* 13 (1986): 18–26.
"On the Tasks of Catholic Philosophy in Our Time." Translated by Brian McNeil. *Communio* 20 (1993): 147–87. ["Von der Aufgaben der katholischen Philosophie in der Zeit." In *Annalen der Philosophischen Gesellschaft der Innerschweiz* 3:2/3 (1946/1947): 1–38.]
von Balthasar, Hans Urs, ed. *Origen: Spirit & Fire. A Thematic Anthology of His Writings*. Translated by Robert J. Daly. Washington, DC: Catholic University of America Press, 1984.
Our Task: A Report and a Plan. Translated by John Saward. San Francisco, CA: Ignatius, 1994. [*Unser Auftrag: Bericht und Entwurf*. Einsiedeln: Johannes, 1984.]
Prayer. Translated by Graham Harrison. San Francisco, CA: Ignatius, 1986. [*Das betrachtende Gebet*. Einsiedeln: Johannes, 1955.]
Prayer. Translated by A. V. Littledale. London: Geoffrey Chapman, 1961.
Presence and Thought: Essay on the Religious Philosophy of Gregory of Nyssa. Translated by Mark Sebanc. San Francisco, CA: Ignatius, 1995. [*Présence et pensée: essai sur la philosophie religieuses de Grégoire de Nysse*. Paris: Beauchesne, 1988.]

"Pourquoi Je Me Suis Fait Prêtre." In *Pourquoi je me suis fait prêtre. Témoignages recueillis*. Edited by Jorge Sans Vila. Tournai: Centre diocésain de documentation, 1961.

Razing the Bastions: On the Church in This Age. Translated by Brian McNeil. San Francisco, CA: Ignatius, 1993. [*Schleifung der Bastionen: Von der Kirche in dieser Zeit*. Einsiedeln: Johannes, 1952.]

"Realisticher Blick auf unsere Schweizer Situation." *Timor Domini* 7, no. 2 (1978).

"A Résumé of My Thought." Translated by Kelly Hamilton. *Communio: International Catholic Review* 15 (1988).

"Das Scholienwerk des Johannes von Scythopolis." *Scholastik* 15 (1940): 16–38.

A Short Primer for Unsettled Laymen. Translated by Michael Waldstein. San Francisco, CA: Ignatius, 1985. [*Kleine Fibel für verunsicherte Laien*. Einsiedeln: Johannes, 1980.]

Test Everything: Hold Fast to What Is Good: An Interview with Hans Urs von Balthasar by Angelo Scola. Edited by Angelo Scola. Translated by Maria Shrady. San Francisco, CA: Ignatius, 1989.

Theo-Drama: Theological Dramatic Theory Volume 1: *Prolegomena*. Translated by Graham Harrison. San Francisco: Ignatius, 1988. [*Theodramatik I: Prolegomena*. Einsiedeln: Johannes, 1983.]

Theo-Drama: Theological Dramatic Theory Volume 2: *Dramatis Personae: Man in God*. Translated by Graham Harrison. San Francisco, CA: Ignatius, 1990. [*Theodramatik II: Die Personen des Spiels: Der Mensch in Gott*. Einsiedeln: Johannes, 1976.]

Theo-Drama: Theological Dramatic Theory Volume 3: *Dramatis Personae: Persons in Christ*. Translated by Graham Harrison. San Francisco, CA: Ignatius, 1992. [*Theodramatik II: Die Personen des Spiels: Die Personen in Christus*. Einsiedeln: Johannes, 1978.]

Theo-Drama: Theological Dramatic Theory Volume 4: *The Action*. Translated by Graham Harrison. San Francisco, CA: Ignatius, 1994. [*Theodramatik III: Die Handlung*. Einsiedeln: Johannes, 1980.]

Theo-Drama: Theological Dramatic Theory Volume 5: *The Last Act*. Translated by Graham Harrison. San Francisco, CA: Ignatius, 1998. [*Theodramatik IV: Das Endspiel*. Einsiedeln: Johannes, 1983.]

Theo-Logic: Theological Logical Theory, Volume 1: *The Truth of the World*. Translated by Adrian J. Walker. San Francisco, CA: Ignatius, 2000 [*Theologik I: Wahrheit der Welt*. Einsiedeln: Johannes, 1985.]

Theo-Logic: Theological Logical Theory, Volume 2: *Truth of God*. Translated by Adrian J. Walker. San Francisco, CA: Ignatius, 2004. [*Theologik II: Wahrheit Gottes*. Einsiedeln: Johannes, 1985.]

Theo-Logic: Theological Logical Theory, Volume 3: *The Spirit of Truth*. Translated by Graham Harrison. San Francisco, CA: Ignatius, 2005. [*Theologik III: Der Geist der Wahrheit*. Einsiedeln: Johannes, 1987.]

A Theological Anthropology. New York: Sheed and Ward, 1967. [*Das Ganze im Fragment: Aspekte der Geschichtstheologie*. New York: Benziger, 1963.]

The Theology of Henri de Lubac. Translated by Joseph Fessio, Michael Waldstein, and Susan Clements. San Francisco, CA: Ignatius, 1991. [*Henri de Lubac: Sein organisches Lebenswerk*. Einsiedeln: Johannes, 1976.]

A Theology of History. San Francisco, CA: Ignatius, 1963. [*Theologie der Geschichte*. Einsiedeln: Johannes, 1950.]

The Theology of Karl Barth: Exposition and Interpretation. Translated by Edward T. Oakes. San Francisco, CA: Ignatius, 1992. [*Karl Barth: Darstellung und Deutung seiner Tehologie*. Einsiedeln: Johannes, 1976.]

The Threefold Garland: The World's Salvation in Mary's Prayer. Translated by Erasmo Leiva-Merikakis. San Francisco, CA: Ignatius, 1982. [*Der dreifache Kranz: Das Heil der Welt im Mariengebet.* Einsiedeln: Johannes, 1977.]

Tragedy Under Grace: Reinhold Schneider on the Experience of the West. Translated by Brian McNeil. San Francisco, CA: Ignatius Press, 1991.

Truth Is Symphonic: Aspects of Christian Personalism. Translated by Graham Harrison. San Francisco: Ignatius, 1987. [*De Wahrheit ist symphonisch: Aspekte des christlichen Pluralismus.* Einsiedeln: Johannes, 1972.]

Two Sisters in the Spirit: Therese of Lisieux and Elizabeth of the Trinity. Translated by Donald Nichols, Anne Elizabeth Englund, and Dennis Martin. San Francisco, CA: Ignatius, 1992. [*Schwestern im Geist: Therese von Lisieux und Elsabeth von Dijon.* Einsiedeln: Johannes, 1970.]

Unless You Become Like this Child. Translated by Erasmo Leiva-Merikakis. San Francisco, CA: Ignatius, 1991. [*Wenn ihr nicht werdet wie dieses Kind.* Ostfildern: Schwabenverlag, 1988.]

Verkaufe Alles und Folge Mir Nach. Einsiedeln: Johannes, 2015.

Balthasar, von Hans Urs with Joseph Ratzinger. "Warum ich noch ein Christ bin." In *Christ-Sein Heute: Zwei Plädoyers*, 7–72. Einsiedeln: Johannes, 2013.

Who is a Christian? Translated by John Cumming. London: Burns and Oates, 1968. [*Wer ist ein Christ?* Einsiedeln: Benziger, 1965.]

You Crown the Year with Your Goodness: Sermons through the Liturgical Year. Translated by Graham Harrison. San Francisco: Ignatius, 1989. [*"Du krönst das Jahr mit deiner Huld:" Radiopredigten.* Einsiedeln, Johannes, 1982.]

"Zur Überwindung der kirchlichen Flaute." *Vaterland* 150 (1978): 3.

Works by Other Authors

Adams, Marilyn McCord. "Horrendous Evils and the Goodness of God." In *The Problem of Evil*, edited by Marilyn McCord Adams and Robert Adams, 209–21. Oxford: Oxford University Press, 1990.

Adorno, Theodor. *Minima Moralia: Reflections from Damaged Life.* Translated by E. F. Jephcott. London: New Left Books, 1974.

Agamben, Giorgio. *Nudities.* Translated by David Kishik and Stefan Pedatella. Stanford: Stanford University Press, 2011.

Albus, Michael and Hans Urs von Balthasar. "Spirit and Fire: An Interview with Hans Urs von Balthasar." *Communio* 32, no. 3 (2005): 573–93.

Alison, James. *Knowing Jesus.* London: SPCK, 1988.

Alison, James. *On Being Liked.* New York: Herder and Herder, 2003.

Alison, James. "Prayer: A Case Study in Mimetic Anthropology." Self-published at http://www.jamesalison.co.uk/texts/eng54.html.

Althaus-Reid, Marcell. *Indecent Theology: Theological Perversions in Sex, Gender and Politics.* New York: Routledge, 2000.

Andrews, James. "'That the World May Know:' A Christological Ecclesiology of Prayer." *Modern Theology* 30, no. 4 (2014): 481–99.

Andrews, Michael. "How (Not) to Find God in All Things." In *The Phenomenology of Prayer*, edited by Bruce Ellis Benson and Norman Wirzba, 195–208. New York: Fordham University Press, 2005.

Arblaster, John and Rob Faesen, eds. *Mystical Doctrines of Deification: Case Studies in the Christian Tradition*. London: Routledge, 2018.

Arblaster, Wesley James. "A Semblance of Things Unseen: Damaged Experience and Aesthetic Recovery in Theodor Adorno and Hans Urs von Balthasar." Unpublished doctoral dissertation. University of Dayton, 2017.

Ashley, Matthew. "The Turn to Spirituality? The Relationship between Theology and Spirituality." In *Minding the Spirit: The Study of Christian Spirituality*, edited by Elizabeth Dreyer and Mar Burrows, 159–70. Baltimore: Johns Hopkins University Press, 2005.

Babini, Ellero. "Jesus Christ, Form and Norm of Man According to Hans Urs von Balthasar." *Communio: International Catholic Review* 16, no. 3 (1989): 446–57.

Barbarin, Philippe. *Théologie et Sainteté: Introduction à Hans-Urs von Balthasar*. Paris: Parole et Silence, 1999.

Barry, Richard. "Retrieving the Goat for Azazel: Balthasar's Biblical Soteriology." *Nova et Vetera*. 15, no. 1 (2017): 13–35.

Barth, Karl. Church Dogmatics I/1: *The Doctrine of the Word of God*. Edited by G. W. Bromiley and T. F. Torrance and translated by G.W. Bromiley. Edinburgh: T&T Clark, 1936, 1975, 2004.

Barth, Karl. Church Dogmatics III/3: *The Doctrine of Creation*. Edited by G. W. Bromiley and T. F. Torrance. Edinburgh: T&T Clark, 1960, 2010.

Barth, Karl. Church Dogmatics III/4: *The Doctrine of Reconciliation*. Edited by G. W. Bromiley and T.F. Torrance and translated by G. W. Bromiley. Edinburgh: T&T Clark, 1967, 2004.

Barth, Karl. *Prayer: 50th Anniversary Edition*. Translated by Sarah F. Terrien. Louisville, Kentucky: Westminster John Knox, 2002. [*La Prière*. Neuchâtel: Delachaux and Nestlé, 1949.]

Barron, Robert. *Exploring Catholic Theology: Essays on God, Liturgy, and Evangelization*. Grand Rapids, MI: Baker, 2015.

Barron, Robert. *The Priority of Christ: Toward a Postliberal Catholicism*. Grand Rapids, MI: Baker, 2007.

Bauer, Carlene. "God's Grandeur: The Prayer Journal of Flannery O'Connor." *The Virginia Quarterly Review* 90, no. 1 (2014): 218–21.

Bauman, Zygmunt. *Liquid Modernity*. Oxford: Blackwell, 2000.

Beattie, Tina. "A Man and Three Women: Hans, Adrienne, Mary and Luce." *New Blackfriars* 79, no. 927 (2004): 548–56.

Beattie, Tina. *New Catholic Feminism: Theology and Theory*. London: Routledge, 2005.

Beattie, Tina. "Sex, Death, and Melodrama: A Feminist Critique of Hans Urs von Balthasar." *The Way* 44, no. 4 (2005): 160–76.

Beattie, Tina. *Theology after Postmodernity: Divining the Void—A Lacanian Reading of Thomas Aquinas*. Oxford: Oxford University Press, 2013.

Beckman, Patricia. "Swimming in the Trinity: Mechthild of Magdeburg's Dynamic Play." *Spiritus: A Journal of Christian Spirituality* 4, no. 1 (2004): 60–77.

Bede. *Ecclesiastical History of the English People*. Translated by Leo Sherley-Price. London: Penguin, 1990 (revised edition).

Beiler, Martin. "Meta-Anthropology and Christology: On the Philosophy of Hans Urs von Balthasar." *Communio* 20 (1993): 446–57.

Benedict XVI, Pope. Encyclical Letter, *Deus Caritas Est*. December 25, 2005.

Bergem, Ragnar. "On the Persistence of the Genealogical in Contemporary Theology." *Modern Theology* 33, no. 3 (2017): 434–52.

Berger, David. "Woher kommen die Thesen Hans Urs von Balthasars zur Hölle? Oder: hatte 'Theologisches' doch recht?" *Theologisches Katholische Monatsschrift* 31 (2001): 267–8.
Bergson, Henri. *The Two Sources of Morality and Religion*. Notre Dame, IN: University of Notre Dame Press, 1977.
Bernstein, J. M. *Classic and Romantic German Aesthetics*. Cambridge: Cambridge University Press, 2003.
Best, Steven and Douglas Kellner. *The Postmodern Turn*. London: Guilford, 1997.
Bhattacharji, Santha and Dominic Mattos and Rowan Williams, eds. *Prayer and Thought in Monastic Tradition: Essays in Honour of Benedicta Ward SLG*. London: Bloomsbury, 2015.
Blankenhorn, Bernhard-Thomas. "The Good as Self-Diffusive in Thomas Aquinas." *Angelicum* 79, no. 4 (2002): 803–37.
Blankenship, Jane and Janette Kenner Muir. "On Imaging the Future: The Secular Search for 'Piety.'" *Communication Quarterly* 35no. 1 (1987): 1–12.
Block, Ed. *Glory, Grace, and Culture: The Work of Hans Urs von Balthasar*. Mahwah, NJ: Paulist, 2005.
Block, Ed. "Hans Urs von Balthasar's *Theodrama*: A Contribution to Dramatic Criticism." In *Renascene* 48, no. 2 (1996): 153–72.
Bloom, Anthony. *The Essence of Prayer*. London: Darton, Longman and Todd, 1986.
Blowers, Paul. *Maximus the Confessor: Jesus Christ and the Transfiguration of the World*. Oxford: Oxford University Press, 2016.
Boersma, Hans. *Nouvelle Théologie and Sacramental Ontology: A Return to Mystery*. Oxford: Oxford University Press, 2009.
Boff, Leonardo. *Trinity and Society*. Maryknoll: Orbis, 1988.
Borghesi, Massimo. *Jorge Mario Bergoglio: Una Biografia Intellettuale*. Milan: Jaca Book, 2017.
Bouillard, Henri. *Blondel and Christianity*. Washington, DC: Corpus, 1969.
Bourgeois, Jason Paul. *The Aesthetic Hermeneutics of Hans-Georg Gadamer and Hans Urs von Balthasar*. Oxford: Peter Lang, 2007.
Bremond, Henri. *A Literary History of Religious Thought in France from the Wars of Religion down to Our Own Times* Vol. 2: *The Coming of Mysticism (1590–1620)*. Translated by K. L. Montgomery. London: SPCK, 1930.
Breuggeman, Walter. *From Judgment to Hope: A Study on the Prophets*. London: Westminster John Knox, 2019.
Brotherton, Joshua R. "Damnation and the Trinity in Ratzinger and Balthasar." *Logos: A Journal of Catholic Thought and Culture* 18, no 3 (2015): 123–50.
Brower, Jay. "Critical Rhetoric's Truth-Telling Function." in *Atlantic Journal of Communication* 24, no. 5 (2016): 251–63.
Brown, Derek. "Kneeling in the Streets: Recontextualizing Balthasar." *New Blackfriars* 99 (2018): 788–806.
Bruaire, Claude. *L'Être et l'esprit*. Paris: Presses Universitaires de France, 1963.
Brümmer, Vincent. *What are We Doing When We Pray?* London: SCM, 1984.
Buckley, James. "Balthasar's Use of the Theology of Aquinas." *The Thomist* 59, no. 4 (1995): 517–49.
Buckley, Michael. "Seventeenth-Century French Spirituality: Three Figures." In *Christian Spirituality: Post-Reformation and Modern*, edited by Louis Dupré and Don E. Saliers, 30–62. New York: Crossroads, 1991.
Bunge, Gabriel. *Earthen Vessels: The Practice of Personal Prayer according to the Patristic Fathers*. Translated by Michael J. Miller. San Francisco: Ignatius, 2002.

Burnett, Joel. *Where Is God? Divine Absence in the Hebrew Bible*. Minneapolis, MN: Fortress Press, 2010.
Burrus, Virginia. *Saving Shame: Martyrs, Saints, and Other Abject Subjects*. Pennsylvania: University of Pennsylvania Press, 2018.
Busch, E. and J. Fangmeier and M. Geiger, eds. *Parrhesia: Fröhlich Zuversicht: Karl Barth zum 80 Geburstag am 10 Mai 1966*. Zürich: EVZ, 1966.
Bychkov, Oleg. *Aesthetic Revelation: Reading Ancient and Medieval Texts after Hans Urs von Balthasar*. Washington, DC: Catholic University of America Press, 2010.
Bychkov, Oleg and James Fodor. *Theological Aesthetics after von Balthasar*. Burlington, VT: Ashgate, 2008.
Caldecott, Stratford. "Theological Dimensions of Human Liberation." In *Communio* 22 (1995): 225–41.
Callahan, Ann. "The Concept of Person in the Theology of Hans Urs von Balthasar." Unpublished doctoral dissertation. Fordham University, 1993.
Campodonico, Angelo. "Hans Urs von Balthasar's Interpretation of the Philosophy of Thomas Aquinas." *Nova et Vetera* 8:1 (2010).
The Catechism of the Catholic Church. London: Burns and Oates, 1999 (revised edition).
Capole, Cornelia and Claudia Müller. *Hans Urs von Balthasar: Bibliography 1925–2005*. Einsiedeln: Johannes, 2005.
Caputo, John. *The Mystical Element in Heidegger's Thought*. New York: Fordham University Press, 1986.
Caputo, John. *The Prayers and Tears of Jacques Derrida: Religion without Religion*. Indianapolis: Indiana University Press, 1997.
Carlson, Thomas. "Postmetaphysical Theology." In *Cambridge Companion to Postmodern Theology*, edited by Kevin Vanhoozer. Cambridge: Cambridge University Press, 2006.
Carpenter, Anne M. *Theo-Poetics: Hans Urs von Balthasar and the Risk and Art of Being*. Minneapolis, MN: Fortress, 2014
Casarella, Peter. "Experience as a Theological Category: Hans Urs von Balthasar on the Christian Encounter with God's Image." *Communio* 20, no. 1 (1993).
Casarella, Peter. "The Expression and Form of the Word: Trinitarian Hermeneutics and the Sacramentality of Language in Hans Urs von Balthasar's Theology." *Renascence* 48, no. 2 (1996): 111–35.
Casarella, Peter and George Schner, eds. *Christian Spirituality and the Culture of Modernity: The Thought of Louis Dupré*. Grand Rapids, MI: Eerdmans, 1998.
Castro, Manuel Cabda. *Sein und Gott bei Gustav Siewerth*. Düsseldorf: Patmos, 1971.
Cavanaugh, William. *Theopolitical Imagination: Discovering the Liturgy as a Political Act in an Age of Global Consumerism*. London: T&T Clark, 2002.
Chappel, James. *Catholic Modern: The Challenge of Totalitarianism and the Remaking of the Church*. Cambridge, MA: Harvard University Press, 2018.
Chau, Carolyn. *Solidarity with the World: Charles Taylor and Hans Urs von Balthasar on Faith, Modernity, and Catholic Mission*. Eugene, OR: Cascade, 2016.
Chennattu, Rekha. *Johannine Discipleship as a Covenant Relationship*. Peabody, MA: Hendrickson, 2006.
Chia, Roland. "Theological Aesthetics or Aesthetic Theology? Some Reflections on the Theology of Hans Urs von Balthasar." *Scottish Journal of Theology* 49, no. 1 (1996): 75–95.
Chenu, Marie-Dominique. *Une École de Théologie: La Saulchoir*. Etiolles: Le Saulchoir, 1937.
Cihak, John. *Balthasar and Anxiety*. Edinburgh: T&T Clark, 2009.

Ciraulo, Jonathan. "Divinization as Christification in Erich Przywara and John Zizioulas." *Modern Theology* 32, no. 4 (2016): 479–503.
Clarke, William Norris. "Person, Being, and St. Thomas." *Communio* 19 (1992): 601–18.
Coakley, Sarah. "Deepening Practices: Perspectives from Ascetical and Mystical Theology." *Practicing Theology: Beliefs and Practices in Christian Life*, edited by Miroslav Volf and Dorothy Bass, 78–93. Grand Rapids, MI: Eerdmans, 2002.
Coakley, Sarah. *God, Sexuality, and the Self*. Cambridge: Cambridge University Press, 2013.
Coakley, Sarah. *The New Asceticism: Sexuality, Gender and the Quest for God*. London: Bloomsbury, 2015.
Coakley, Sarah. "'Persons' in the 'Social' Doctrine of the Trinity: A Critique of Current Analytic Discussion." In *The Trinity: An Interdisciplinary Symposium on the Trinity*, edited by Stephen T. Davis, Daniel Kendall, and Gerald O'Collins, 123–44. Oxford: Oxford University Press, 2002.
Coakley, Sarah. *Powers and Submissions*. Oxford: Blackwell, 2008.
Cocksworth, Ashley. *Karl Barth on Prayer*. London: Bloomsbury, 2015.
Cocksworth, Ashley. *Prayer: A Guide for the Perplexed*. London: Bloomsbury, 2018.
Colombo, J. A. *An Essay on Theology and History: Studies in Pannenberg, Metz, and the Frankfurt School*. Atlanta: Scholar's Press, 1990.
Congar, Yves. *I Believe in the Holy Spirit* (combined edition). Translated by David Smith. New York: Crossroad, 2000.
Corrigan, Kevn. "'Solitary' Mysticism in Plotinus, Proclus, Gregory of Nyssa, and Pseudo-Dionysius." *The Journal of Religion* 76, no. 1 (1996): 28–42.
Cortez, Marc. *Theological Anthropology: A Guide for the Perplexed*. London: Continuum, 2010.
Coyle, Justin Shaun. "The Very Idea of Subtler Language: The Poetics of Gerard Manley Hopkins in Charles Taylor and Hans Urs von Balthasar." *Heythrop Journal* 57 (2016): 820–33.
Crammer, Corinne. "One Sex or Two? Balthasar's Theology of the Sexes." In *Cambridge Companion to Hans Urs von Balthasar*, edited by Edward T. Oakes and David Moss, 93–112. Cambridge: Cambridge University Press, 2004.
Crosholz, Emily. "Descartes and the Individuation of Physical Objects." In *Individuation and Identity in Early Modern Philosophy: Descartes to Kant*, edited by Kenneth F. Barber and Jorge J. E. Garcia. Albany: State University of New York Press, 1994.
Crowe, Benjamin. "Heidegger and the Prospect of a Phenomenology of Prayer." In *The Phenomenology of Prayer*, edited by Bruce Ellis Benson and Norman Wirzba, 119–132. New York: Fordham University Press, 2005.
Cunningham, David. *These Three are One: The Practice of Trinitarian Theology*. Oxford: Blackwell, 1998.
Cusk, Rachel. *A Life's Work: On Becoming a Mother* (second edition). London: Faber & Faber, 2008.
Dadosky, John. "The Proof of Beauty: From Aesthetic Experience to the Beauty of God." In *Analecta Hermeneutica* 2 (2010): 1–15.
Daigler, Matthew. "Heidegger and von Balthasar: A Lover's Quarrel over Beauty and Divinity." In *American Catholic Philosophical Quarterly*. 69, no. 2 (1995): 375–94.
Daley, Brian. "Balthasar's Reading of the Church Fathers." In *Cambridge Companion to Hans Urs von Balthasar*, edited by Edward T. Oakes and David Moss, 187–206. Cambridge: Cambridge University Press, 2004.
Dallmayr, Fred. "Ontology of Freedom: Heidegger and Political Philosophy." In *Political Theory* 12, no. 2 (1984): 204–34.

Dalzell, Thomas. *The Dramatic Encounter of Divine and Human Freedom in the Theology of Hans Urs von Balthasar*. Oxford: Peter Lang, 1997.
Dalzell, Thomas. "The Enrichment of God in Balthasar's Trinitarian Eschatology." *Irish Theological Quarterly* 66, no. 1 (2001): 3–18.
Dalzell, Thomas. "Lack of Social Drama in Balthasar's Theological Dramatics." *Theological Studies* 60, no. 3 (1999): 457–75.
Daniélou, Jean. *Prayer as a Political Problem*. London: Burns & Oates, 1967.
Daniélou, Jean. *Prayer the Mission of the Church*. Edinburgh: T&T Clark, 1996.
Daniélou, Jean. "Les Orientations Présentes de la Pensée Religieuse." *Études* 249, no. 4 (1946): 5–21.
Danta, Chris. "The Poetics of Distance: Kierkegaard's Abraham." *Literature and Theology* 21, no. 2 (2007): 160–77.
Davies, Oliver. "The Theological Aesthetics." *Cambridge Companion to Hans Urs von Balthasar*, edited by Edward T. Oakes Oakes and David Moss, 131–42. Cambridge: Cambridge University Press, 2004.
Davies, Oliver. "Von Balthasar and the Problem of Being." In *New Blackfriars* 79, no. 923 (1998): 11–17.
Davis, Stephen and Daniel Kendall and Gerald O'Collins, eds. *The Trinity: An Interdisciplinary Symposium on the Trinity*. Oxford: Oxford University Press, 2002.
Davison, Scott. *Petitionary Prayer: A Philosophical Investigation*. Oxford: Oxford University Press, 2017.
D'Costa, Gavin. *Sexing the Trinity: Gender, Culture and the Divine*. London: SCM, 2000.
Delio, Ilia. "From Aquinas to Teilhard: Divine Action and the Metaphysics of Love." *Heythrop Journal* 59, no. 3 (2016): 468–83.
Delio, Ilia. "From Metaphysics to Kataphysics: Bonaventure's 'Good' Creation." *Scottish Journal of Theology* 64, no. 2 (2011): 161–79.
De Lubac, Henri. *Affrontements Mystiques*. Paris: Témoignage Chrétien, 1950.
De Lubac, Henri. *Catholicism: Christ and the Common Destiny of Man*. Translated by Lancelot Sheppard. London: Burns & Oates, 1962.
De Lubac, Henri. *The Discovery of God*. Translated by Alexander Dru. Edinburgh: T&T Clark, 1986.
De Lubac, Henri. *The Mystery of the Supernatural*. Translated by Rosemary Sheed. New York: Crossroad, 1998.
De Lubac, Henri. *Paradoxes of Faith*. San Francisco, CA: Ignatius, 2000.
De Lubac, Henri. *Surnaturel: Études Historiques*. Paris: Aubier, 1946.
De Lubac, Henri. *Theology in History*. San Francisco, CA: Ignatius, 1996.
De Lubac, Henri. "Un témoin du Christ dans l'Église: Hans Urs von Balthasar." In *Paradoxe et mystère de L'Église*. Paris: Aubier-Montaigne, 1967.
De Maeseneer, Yves. "Angels as Mirrors of the Human: The Anthropologies of Rilke and Bonaventure through the Lenses of Hans Urs von Balthasar." *Theologica*. 6, no. 1 (2016): 105–17.
De Margerie, Bertrand. "Note on Balthasar's Trinitarian Theology." *The Thomist* 64 (2000): 127–30.
Dimech, Pauline. *The Authority of the Saints: Drawing on the Theology of Hans Urs von Balthasar*. Eugene, OR: Wipf and Stock, 2017.
Doak, Mary. "Sex, Race, and Culture: Constructing Theological Anthropology for the Twenty-First Century." *Theological Studies* 80, no. 3 (2019): 508–29.
Dol, Jean-Noël. "L'inversion trinitaire chez Hans Urs von Balthasar." *Revue Thomiste* 100, no. 2 (2000): 201–38.

Donovan, Mary Ann. "The Vocation of the Theologian." *Theological Studies* 65 (2004): 3–22.
Doucet, Marcel. "Est-ce que le monothélisme a fait autant d'illustrés victimes? Réflexions sur un ouvrage de F.-M. Léthel." *Science et esprit* 35 (1983): 53–83.
Douglass, Scot. *Theology of the Gap: Cappadocian Language Theory and the Trinitarian Controversy*. Oxford: Peter Lang, 2005.
Drever, Matthew. "Prayer, Self-Examination and Christian Catechesis in Augustine and Luther." *Dialog* 55, no. 2 (2016): 147–57.
Dreyer, Elizabeth A. and Mark S. Burrows, eds. *Minding the Spirit: The Study of Christian Spirituality*. Baltimore, MD: Johns Hopkins University Press, 2004.
Dryberg, Torbon. *Foucault on the Politics of Parrhesia*. New York: Palgrave Macmillan, 2014.
Dubois, Elfiieda. "Fénelon and Quietism." In *The Study of Spirituality*, edited by Cheslyn Jones, Geoffrey Wainwright and Edward Yarnold, SJ, 408–15. London: SPCK, 1986.
Dünzl, Franz. *A Brief History of the Doctrine of the Trinity in the Early Church*. Translated by John Bowden. New York: T&T Clark, 2007.
Dupré, Louis. *The Enlightenment and the Intellectual Foundations of Modern Culture*. New Haven, CT: Yale University Press, 2004.
Dupré, Louis. "The Theological Aesthetics." In *The Cambridge Companion to Hans Urs von Balthasar*, edited by Edward T. Oakes and David Moss, 131–42. Cambridge: Cambridge University Press, 2004.
Dupré, Louis. *The Other Dimension: A Search for the Meaning of Religious Attitudes*. Garden City, NY: Doubleday, 1972.
Eggemeier, Matthew. "A Mysticism of Open Eyes: Compassion for a Suffering World and the *Askesis* of Contemplative Prayer." *Spiritus* 12, no. 1 (2012): 43–62.
Eikelboom, Lexi. "Erich Przywara and Giorgio Agamben: Rhythm as a Space for Dialogue between Catholic Metaphysics and Postmodernism." *Heythrop Journal* 57, no. 4 (2016): 1–12.
Eikelboom, Lexi. *Rhythm: A Theological Category*. Oxford: Oxford University Press, 2018.
Edelman, Lee. *No Future: Queer Theory and the Death Drive*. London: Duke University Press, 2004.
Elio, Guerriero. *Hans Urs von Balthasar: Eine Monographie*. Freiburg: Johannes, 1993.
Elio, Guerriero. *Il Dramma di Dio: Letteratura e Teologia in Hans Urs von Balthasar*. Milan: Jaca, 1993.
Endean, Philip. "Von Balthasar, Rahner, and the Commissar." *New Blackfriars* 79, no. 923 (1998): 33–8.
Escobar, Pedro. "Hans Urs von Balthasar: Christologian." *Communio* 2, no. 3 (1975): 300–16.
Espezel, Alberto. "La Cristología dramática de Balthasar." *Teología y Vida* 50 (2009): 305–18.
Euripides. *The Bacchae and Other Plays*. Translated by Philip Vellacott. London: Penguin, 1973 (revised edition).
Evagrius Ponticus. "On Prayer." In *Evagarius Ponticus*, edited by A. M. Cassidy. London: Routledge, 2006.
Evans, C. Stephen, ed. *Exploring Kenotic Christology: The Self-Emptying God*. Oxford: Oxford University Press, 2006.
Farris, Joshua and Charles Taliaferro, eds. *The Ashgate Research Companion to Theological Anthropology*. London: Routledge, 2015.

Feneuil, Anthony. "Becoming God or Becoming Yourself: Vladimir Lossky on Deification and Personal Identity." In *Theosis/Deification: Christian Doctrines of Divinization East and West*, edited by John Arblaster and Rob Faesen, 49–64. Leuven: Peeters, 2018.

Fiddes, Paul. "Sacrifice, Atonement, and Renewal." In *Sacrifice and Modern Thought*, edited by Julia Meszaros and Johannes Zachuber, 48–65. Oxford: Oxford University Press, 2013.

Fields, Stephen. "Balthasar and Rahner on the Spiritual Senses." *Theological Studies* 57 (1996): 224–41.

Finn, Geraldine. "The Politics of Spirituality: The Spirituality of Politics." In *Shadow of Spirit: Postmodernism and Religion*, edited by Berry and Wernick, 111–22. London: Routledge, 1992.

Fitzgerald, John, ed. *Friendship, Flattery, and Frankness of Speech: Studies on Friendship in the New Testament World*. Leiden: Brill, 1996.

Flannagan, Brian. "Reconciliation and the Church: A Response to Bruce Morrill." *Theological Studies* 75, no. 3 (2014): 624–34.

Flood, Gavin. *Religion and the Philosophy of Life*. Oxford: Oxford University Press, 2019.

Flood, Gavin. *The Truth Within: A History of Inwardness in Christianity, Hinduism, and Buddhism*. Oxford: Oxford University Press, 2013.

Folkers, Andreas. "Daring the Truth: Foucault, Parrhesia, and the Genealogy of Critique." *Theology, Culture and Society* 33, no. 1 (2016): 3–28.

Fot, Veronique. *Heidegger and the Poets: Poesis/Sophia/Techné*. London: Humanities, 1992.

Foucault, Michel. *Discourse and Truth and Parresia*. Edited by Henri-Paul Fruchaud and Daniele Lorenzini. London: University of Chicago Press, 2019.

Foucault, Michel. *Fearless Speech*. Translated by Joseph Pearson. Los Angeles, CA: Semiotext(e), 2001.

Foucault, Michel. *The Hermeneutics of the Subject*. Translated by Graham Burchell. New York: Palgrave Macmillan, 2005.

Foucault, Michel. "Is It Really Important to Think? An Interview." *Philosophical and Social Criticism* 9 (1989): 29–40.

Foucault, Michel. *Security, Territory, Population: Lectures at the Collège de Franc (1977–1978)*. Translated by Graham Burchell. New York: Picador, 2009

Foucault, Michel. "Sexuality and Solitude." *London Review of Books*. May–June 1981.

Frandsen, Henrik Vase. "Distance as Abundance: The Thought of Jean-Luc Marion." *Svensk Teologisk Kvartalskrift* 79 (2003): 177–86.

Frascati-Lochhead, Marta. *Kenosis and Feminist Theology: The Challenge of Gianni Vattimo*. Albany, NY: State University of New York Press, 1998.

Frohnen, Bruce and Jeremy Beer and Jeffrey Nelson, eds. *American Conservatism: An Encyclopedia*. Wilmington: ISI Books, 2006.

Furnal, Joshua. *Catholic Theology after Kierkegaard*. Oxford: Oxford University Press, 2015.

Gardner, Lucy. "Hans Urs von Balthasar: The Trinity and Prayer." In *A Transforming Vision: Knowing and Loving the Triune God*, edited by George Westhaver. London: SCM, 2018.

Gardner, Lucy and David Moss. "Difference: The Immaculate Concept? The Laws of Sexual Difference in the Theology of Hans Urs von Balthasar." *Modern Theology* 14, no. 3 (1998): 377–401.

Gardner, Lucy and David Moss and Ben Quash and Graham Ward. *Balthasar at the End of Modernity*. Edinburgh: T&T Clark, 1999.

Garrett, Lynn. "Ignatius Press' Papal Connection." In *Publishers Weekly* 252, no. 17 (2005): 7.
Garrigou-Lagrange, Ronald. *Christian Perfection and Contemplation, According to St Thomas Aquinas and St John of the Cross*. Translated by M. Timothea Doyle. St Louis, Missouri: Herder, 1937.
Gawronski, Raymond. *Word and Silence: Hans Urs von Balthasar and the Spiritual Encounter between East and West*. Kettering, OH: Angelico, 1995.
Geldhof, Joris. "*Cogitor Ergo Sum:*' On the Meaning and Relevance of Baader's Theological Critique of Descartes." *Modern Theology* 21, no. 2 (2005): 237–51.
Gensler, Harry and James Swindal, eds. *The Sheed and Ward Anthology of Catholic Philosophy*. London: Sheed and Ward, 2005.
Giles, Kevin. "Barth and Subordinationism." *Scottish Journal of Theology* 64, no. 3 (2011): 327–46.
Gillespie, Michael Allen and Lucas Perkins. "Political Anti-Theology." *Critical Review* 22, no. 1 (2010): 65–84.
Gschwandtner, Christina. "The Neighbor and the Infinite: Marion and Levinas on the Encounter between Self, Human Other, and God." *Continental Philosophy Review* 40 (2007): 231–49.
Godzieba, Anthony. "Ontotheology to Excess: Imagining God Without Being." In *Theological Studies* 56 (1995): 3–20.
Gonzalez, Michelle. "Hans Urs von Balthasar and Contemporary Feminist Theology." In *Theological Studies* 65 (2004): 566–95.
Gordon, Joseph K. "'The Incomprehensible Someone': Hans Urs von Balthasar on the Mission of the Holy Spirit for a Contemporary Theology of History." In *Theology in the Present Age: Essays in Honor of John D. Castelein*, edited by Christopher Ben Simpson and Steven D. Cone. Eugene, OR: Pickwick, 2013.
Goulding, Gill. "The Jesuit Imprint: Ignatian Insights into the Theology of Hans Urs von Balthasar." *Ultimate Reality and Meaning* 32, no. 1 (2009): 75–89.
Goulding, Gill. "Love Alone Is Credible." In *Apostolic Religious Life in America Today: A Response to the Crisis*, edited by Richard Gribble, 111–26. Washington, DC: Catholic University of America Press, 2001.
Gregory of Nyssa. *From Glory to Glory: Texts from Gregory of Nyssa's Mystical Writings*. Edited by Jean Daniélou. Yonkers, New York: St Vladimir's Seminary Press, 1997.
Griffiths, Paul. "Purgatory." In *Oxford Handbook of Eschatology*, edited by Jerry Walls, 430–4. Oxford: Oxford University Press, 2008.
Guardini, Romano. *The Art of Praying: The Principles and Methods of Christian Prayer*. Translated by Prince Leopold of Loewenstein-Wertheim. Manchester, NH: Sophia Institute, 1985 (revised edition).
Guardini, Romano. *The End of the Modern World: A Search for Orientation*. Translated by Joseph Theman and Herbert Burke. New York: Sheed and Ward, 1956.
Gutting, Gary. *Foucault: A Very Short Introduction*. Oxford: Oxford University Press, 2005.
Hadley, Christopher. "The All-Embracing Frame: Distance in the Trinitarian Theology of Hans Urs von Balthasar." Unpublished doctoral Dissertation. Marquette University, 2015.
Hadot, Pierre. *Philosophy as a Way of Life: Spiritual Exercises from Socrates to Foucault*. Oxford: Blackwell, 1995.
Hampson, Daphne, ed. *Swallowing a Fishbone? Feminist Theologians Debate Christianity*. London: SPCK, 1996
Han, Byung-Chul. *What is Power?* Cambridge: Polity, 2019.

Hanvey, James. "Continuing the Conversation." In *Radical Orthodoxy? A Catholic Enquiry*, edited by Laurence Paul Hemming, 149–71. Aldershot: Ashgate, 2000.

Hanvey, James. "Healing the Wound: Discourse of Redemption." In *Challenging Women's Orthodoxies in the Context of Faith*, edited by Susan Frank Parsons, 205–22. London: Routledge, 2000.

Hanvey, James. "Hegel, Rahner and Karl Barth: A Study in the Possibilities of a Trinitarian Theology." Unpublished doctoral dissertation. University of Oxford, 1990.

Hanvey, James. "In the Presence of Love: The Pneumatological Realization of the Economy: Yves Congar's *Le Mystère du Temple*." *International Journal of Systematic Theology* 7, no. 4 (2005): 383–98.

Hanvey, James. "Tradition as Subversion." *International Journal of Systematic Theology* 6:1 (2004): 50–87.

Hardon, John. "Karl Barth on Prayer." *Theological Studies* 14, no. 3 (1953): 443–51.

Harrison, Victoria. *The Apologetic Value of Human Holiness: Von Balthasar's Christocentric Philosophical Anthropology*. London: Kluwer, 2000.

Harrison, Victoria. "Homo Orans: Hans Urs von Balthasar's Christocentric Philosophical Anthropology." *Heythrop Journal* 40, no. 3 (1999): 280–300.

Harrison, Victoria. "Human Holiness as Religious *Apologia*." *International Journal for Philosophy of Religion* 46 (1999): 63–82.

Harrison, Victoria. "Personal Identity and Integration: Von Balthasar's Phenomenology of Human Holiness." *Heythrop Journal* 60 (1999): 424–37.

Hart, David Bentley. *The Beauty of the Infinite: The Aesthetics of Christian Truth*. Grand Rapids, Michigan: Eerdmans, 2004.

Healy, Nicholas and David L. Schindler. "For the Life of the World: Hans Urs von Balthasar on the Church as Eucharist." In *Cambridge Companion to Hans Urs von Balthasar*, edited by Edward T. Oakes and David Moss, 51–63. Cambridge: Cambridge University Press, 2004.

Healy, Nicholas. "Christ's Eucharist and the Nature of Love: The Contribution of Hans Urs von Balthasar." *The Saint Anselm Journal* 10, no. 2 (2015): 1–17.

Healy, Nicholas. "*Communio*: A Theological Journey." *Communio: International Catholic Review* 33 (2006): 117–30.

Healy, Nicholas. *The Eschatology of Hans Urs von Balthasar: Being as Communion*. Oxford: Oxford University Press, 2005.

Heaps, Jonathan and Neil Ormerod. "Statistically Ordered: Gender, Sexual Identity, and the Metaphysics of 'Normal.'" *Theological Studies* 80, no. 2 (2019): 346–69.

Heidegger, Martin. *Being and Time*. Translated by John Macquarrie and Edward Robinson. Oxford: Basil Blackwell, 1967.

Heidegger, Martin. *History and the Concept of Time: Prolegomena*. Translated by Theodore Kisiel. Indianapolis: Indiana University Press, 2009.

Heidegger, Martin. *Identity and Difference*. Translated by Joan Stambaugh. London: Harper & Row, 1969.

Heidegger, Martin. *An Introduction to Metaphysics*. Translated by Ralph Manheim. New Haven: Yale University Press, 1959.

Heiler, Friedrich. *Prayer: A Study in the History and Psychology of Religion*. Translated by Samuel McComb. Oxford: Oxford University Press, 1932.

Hegel, G. W. F. *Lectures on the Philosophy of Religion: The Lectures of 1827*. Edited by Peter C. Hodgson. Translated by R. F. Brown, Peter C. Hodgson, and J. M. Stewart. Oxford: Oxford University Press, 2006.

Hemming, Laurence Paul. "The Being of God: The Limits of Theological Thinking after Heidegger." *New Blackfriars* 85, no. 995 (2004): 17–32.
Hemming, Laurence Paul. *Heidegger's Atheism: The Refusal of a Theological Voice.* Notre Dame, Indiana: University of Notre Dame Press, 2002.
Hemming, Laurence Paul, ed. *Radical Orthodoxy? A Catholic Enquiry.* Aldershot: Ashgate, 2000.
Henrici, Peter. "Hans Urs von Balthasar: A Sketch of His Life." *Communio: International Catholic Review* 16 (1989): 306–50.
Henrici, Peter, ed. *Hans Urs von Balthasar: Ein grosser Churer Diözesan.* Freiburg: Academic Press Freiburg, 2006.
Henry, Michel. "The Critique of the Subject." *Topoi* 7, no. 2 (1988): 147–53.
Heschel, Abraham. *The Prophets.* New York: Harper, 1962.
Hill, William J. *The Three-Personed God: The Trinity as a Mystery of Salvation.* Washington, DC: The Catholic University of America Press, 1988.
Hitchcock, Nathan. *Karl Barth and the Resurrection of the Flesh: The Loss of the Body in Participatory Eschatology.* Eugene, Oregon: Wipf and Stock, 2013.
Hodgson, Peter C. *Hegel and Christian Theology: A Reading of the Lectures on the Philosophy of Religion.* Oxford: Oxford University Press, 2005.
Hoelzl, Michael and Graham Ward, eds. *Religion and Political Thought.* London: Bloomsbury, 2006.
Holmes, Urban. *Spirituality for Ministry.* San Francisco, CA: Harper & Row, 1982.
Hooks, Bell. "Theology as Liberatory Practice." *Yale Journal of Law and Feminism* 1 (1991): 1–12.
Hopko, Thomas. "God and Man in the Orthodox Church." In *God and Charity: Images of Eastern Orthodox Theology, Spirituality, and Practice*, edited by Thomas Hopko, 1–32. Brookline, MA: Holy Cross Orthodox Press, 1979.
Horosz, William. *Search Without Idols.* Leiden: Martinus Nijhoff, 1987.
Hösle, Vittorio. *A Short History of German Philosophy.* Translated by Steven Rendall. Oxford: Princeton University Press, 2017.
Howsare, Rodney and Larry Chapp, eds. *How Balthasar Changed My Mind: 15 Scholars Reflect on the Meaning of Balthasar for Their Own Work.* New York: Crossroad, 2008.
Howsare, Rodney. *Balthasar: A Guide for the Perplexed.* London: Bloomsbury, 2009.
Howsare, Rodney. *Hans Urs von Balthasar and Protestantism: The Ecumenical Implications of His Theological Style.* London: T&T Clark, 2005.
Huizinga, Johan. *Homo Ludens: A Study of the Play-element in Culture.* London: Routledge, 1949.
Hughes, Kevin. "Remember Bonaventure? (Onto)theology and Ecstasy." *Modern Theology* 19, no. 4 (2003): 529–45.
Hunt, Anne. *The Trinity and the Paschal Mystery: A Development in Recent Catholic Theology.* Collegeville, Minnesota: Liturgical Press, 1997.
Hvalvik, Reidar and Harl Olav Sandnes, eds. *Early Christian Prayer and Identity Formation.* Tübingen: Mohr Siebeck, 2014.
Ide, Pascal. *Être et Mystère: La Philosophie de Hans Urs von Balthasar.* Brussels: Culture et Vérité, 1995.
Ignatius of Loyola. *Personal Writings.* Translated by Joseph Munitiz and Philip Endean. London: Penguin: 2004.
Ignatius of Loyola. *Spiritual Exercises and Collected Works.* Edited by George Ganss. New York: Paulist, 1991.

International Theological Commission. "Theology Today: Perspectives, Principles and Criteria." 2011.
James, William. *The Varieties of Religious Experience: A Study in Human Nature*. New York: Collier-Macmillan, 1961.
Chrétien, Jean-Louis. "The Wounded Word: The Phenomenology of Prayer." In *Phenomenology and the "Theological Turn": The French Debate*, edited by Dominique Janicaud et al., 147–76. New York: Fordham University Press, 2000.
Jantzen, Grace. "Eros and the Abyss: Reading Medieval Mystics in Postmodernity." In *Literature & Theology* 17, no. 3 (2003): 244–64.
Jaspers, Karl. *Werke*, Vol. 1. Edited by Lambert Schneider. Munich: Kösel, 1962.
Jeanrond, Werner. *A Theology of Love*. London: T&T Clark, 2010.
Jensen, Matt. *Gravity of Sin: Augustine, Luther and Barth on Homo Incurvatus in Se*. London: T&T Clark, 2006.
Johnson, Elizabeth. *Friends of God and Prophets: A Feminist Theological Reading of the Communion of Saints*. London: Continuum, 1998.
Johnson, Elizabeth. *Truly Our Sister: A Theology of Mary in the Communion of Saints*. London: Continuum, 2006.
Johnson, Junius. *Christ and Analogy: The Christocentric Metaphysics of Hans Urs von Balthasar*. Minneapolis: Fortress, 2013.
Julian of Norwich. *Revelations of Divine Love*. Translated by Elizabeth Spearing. London: Penguin, 1998.
Jüngel, Eberhard. *God's Being Is in Becoming: The Trinitarian Being of God in the Theology of Karl Barth*. Translated by John Webster. Edinburgh: T&T Clark, 2006.
Jüngel, Eberhard. *Theological Essays*. Translated by John Webster. London: Bloomsbury T&T Clark, 2014.
Jones, Tasmin. "Dionysius in Hans Urs von Balthasar and Jean-Luc Marion." *Modern Theology* 24, no. 4 (2008): 743–54.
Kant, Immanuel. *Religion within the Boundaries of Mere Reason and Other Writings*. Translated by Allen Wood and George di Giovanni. Cambridge: Cambridge University Press, 1998.
Kapp, Volker and Helmuth Kiesel. *Theodramatik und Theatralität: Ein Dialog mit dem Theaterverständnis von Hans Urs von Balthasar*. Berlin: Duncker & Humblot, 2000.
Karavites, Peter. "*Gnome*'s Nuances: From Its Beginning to the End of the Fifth Century." *Classical Bulletin* 66 (1990): 9–34.
Kasper, Walter. *The God of Jesus Christ*. Translated by Matthew O'Connell. New York: Crossroads, 1992.
Kasper, Walter. *Jesus the Christ*. Translated by V. Green. Mahwah, New Jersey: Paulist, 1976.
Kasper, Walter. "Postmodern Dogmatics: Toward a Renewed Discussion of Foundations in North America." Translated by D. T. Asselin and Michael Waldstein. In *Communio: International Catholic Review* 17 (1990): 181–91.
Kasper, Walter. *Theology and Church*. London: SCM, 2012.
Kasper, Walter and Karl Lehmann. *Hans Urs von Balthasar: Gestalt und Werk*. Cologne: Communio, 1989.
Katz, Steven T., ed. *Mysticism and Philosophical Analysis*. London: Sheldon, 1978.
Keating, James. "Prayer and Ethics in the Thought of Hans Urs von Balthasar." *Irish Theological Quarterly* 62, no. 1 (1996): 29–37.
Kehl, Medard. "Hans Urs von Balthasar: Ein Porträt." In *In der Fülle des Glaubens: Hans Urs von Balthasar-Lesebuch*, edited by Löser, 13–60. Freiburg im Breisgau: Herder, 1980.

Kellner, Douglas. *Critical Theory, Marxism and Modernity*. Baltimore, MD: Johns Hopkins University Press, 1989.
Kelly, Anthony. *Upward: Faith, Church, and the Ascension of Christ*. Collegeville, MN: Liturgical Press, 2010.
Kennedy, Philip. *Twentieth-Century Theologians: A New Introduction to Modern Christian Thought*. New York: I.B. Taurus, 2010
Kerr, Fergus. "Adrienne von Speyr and Hans Urs von Balthasar." *New Blackfriars* 79, no. 923 (1988): 26-32.
Kerr, Fergus. *Twentieth-Century Catholic Theologians*. Oxford: Oxford University Press, 2006.
Kierkegaard, Søren. *Upbuilding Discourses in Various Spirits*. Translated and edited by Howard Hong and Edna Hong. Princeton: Princeton University Press, 1993.
Kilby, Karen. *Balthasar: A (Very) Critical Introduction*. Grand Rapids, Michigan: Eerdmans, 2012.
Kilby, Karen. "Eschatology, Suffering, and the Limits of Theology." In *Game Over? Reconsidering Eschatology*, edited by Christophe Chalamet et al., 279-91. Berlin: De Gruyter, 2017.
Kilby, Karen. *Karl Rahner: Theology and Philosophy*. London: Routledge, 2004.
Kilby, Karen. "Perichoresis and Projection: Problems with Social Doctrines of the Trinity." *New Blackfriars* 81, no. 95: 432-45.
Kim, David. "The Cosmopolitics of Parrhesia: Foucault and Truth-Telling as Human Right." In *Imagining Human Rights*, edited by Kaul and Kim, 83-100. Berlin: De Gruyter, 2015.
King, Jonathan. "Theology under Another Form: Hans Urs von Balthasar's Formation and Writings as a Germanist." Unpublished doctoral dissertation: Saint Louis University, 2016.
Klaghofer-Treitler, Wolfgang. *Gotteswort im Menschenwort: Inhalt und Form von Theologie nach Hans Urs von Balthasar*. Innsbruck: Tyrolia, 1992.
Koerpel, Robert. "The Form and the Drama of the Church: Hans Urs von Balthasar on Mary, Peter, and the Eucharist." *Logos: A Journal of Catholic Thought and Culture* 11:1 (2008): 70-95.
Koronkai, Zoltan. "The Relationship Between Prayer and Vocation in the Theology of Hans Urs von Balthasar." PhD Dissertation. Toronto: Regis College, 2007. ProQuest Dissertations Publishing.
Kowalski, Georges Wierusz. "Prier pour Guérir." *Revue de l'Institut Catholique du Paris* 40 (1991): 213-24.
Kovalishyn, Mariam Kamell. "The Prayer of Elijah in James 5: An Example of Intertextuality." *Journal of Biblical Literature* 137, no. 4 (2018): 1027-45.
Krenski, Thomas. *Hans Urs von Balthasar: Das Gottesdrama*. Mainz: Matthias-Grünewald, 1995.
Krenski, Thomas. *Hans Urs von Balthasars Literaturtheologie*. Hamburg: Kovač, 2007.
Kretzmann, Norman. "A General Problem of Creation: Why Would God Create Anything at All?" In *Being and Goodness: The Concept of the Good in Metaphysics and Philosophical Theology*, edited by Scott MacDonald, 208-28. Ithaca, NY: Cornell University Press, 1991.
Kristeva, Julia. *Melanie Klein*. Translated by Ross Guberman. New York: Columbia University Press, 2001.
Kristo, Jure. "The Interpretation of Religious Experience: What Do Mystics Intend When They Talk about Their Experiences?" *Journal of Religion* 62 (1982): 21-38.

Kuzma, Andrew. "Theo-Dramatic Ethics: A Balthasarian Approach to Moral Formation." Unpublished doctoral dissertation. Marquette University, 2016
Leclerq, Jean. *Love of Learning and the Desire for God: A Study of Monastic Culture*. Fordham, New York: Fordham University Press, 1983 (3rd revised edition).
LaCouter, Travis. "Competing Accounts of Progress: The Redemptive Purpose of Memory in J. B. Metz and Theodor Adorno." *Heythrop Journal* 59, no. 3 (2018): 544–60.
Lacugna, Catherine Mowry. *God for Us: The Trinity and Christian Life*. San Francisco, CA: Harper, 1973.
Ladd, George Eldon. *A Theology of the New Testament*. Grand Rapids, MI: Eerdmans, 1993.
Lane, Dermot. *Foundations for a Social Theology: Praxis, Process, and Salvation*. New York: Paulist, 1984.
Latour, Bruno. *We Have Never Been Modern*. Translated by Catherine Porter. Cambridge, MA: Harvard University Press, 1993.
Lauber, David. "Response to Alyssa Lyra Pitstick, *Light in Darkness*." In *Scottish Journal of Theology* 62, no. 2 (2009): 195–201.
Leahy, Breandán. *The Marian Principle in the Church According to Hans Urs von Balthasar*. Frankfurt am Main: Lang, 1996.
Leamy, Katy. *The Holy Trinity: Hans Urs von Balthasar and His Sources*. Eugene: Pickwick, 2015.
Leclercq, Jean. *Love of Learning and the Desire for God*. New York: Fordham University Press, 1983.
Leftow, Brian. "Anti Social Trinitarianism." In *The Trinity: An Interdisciplinary Symposium on the Trinity*, edited by Davis, Kendall and O'Collins, 203–50. Oxford: Oxford University Press, 2002.
Léthel, François-Marie. *Théologie de l'Agonie du Christ: La Libertè humaine du Fils de Dieu et son importance sotériologique mises en lumière par Saint Maxime le Confesseur*. Paris: Beauchesne, 1979.
Levering, Matthew and Nicholas Healy, eds. *Ressourcement after Vatican II: Essays in Honor of Joseph Fessio, S.J.* San Francisco: Ignatius, 2019
Levering, Matthew. *The Achievement of Hans Urs von Balthasar: An Introduction to His Theology*. Washington, DC: The Catholic University of America Press, 2019.
Levering, Matthew. "Balthasar on Christ's Consciousness on the Cross." *The Thomist* 65, no. 4 (2001): 567–81.
Levering, Matthew. *Engaging the Doctrine of the Holy Spirit: Love and Gift in the Trinity and the Church*. Grand Rapids, MI: Baker, 2016.
Levering, Matthew. *Scripture and Metaphysics: Aquinas and the Renewal of Trinitarian Theology*. Malden, MA: Blackwell, 2004.
Levertov, Denise. *Breathing the Water*. New York: New Directions, 1987.
Levertov, Denise. *A Door in the Hive*. New York: New Directions, 1989.
Levertov, Denise. *Oblique Prayers*. New York: New Directions, 1984.
Levinas, Emmanuel. *Totality and Infinity: Conversations with Philippe Nemo*. Translated by Alphonso Lingis. Pittsburgh: Duquesne University Press, 1969.
Levinas, Emmanuel. *Ethics and Infinity: Conversations with Philippe Nemo*. Translated by Richard A. Cohen. Pittsburgh: Duquesne University Press, 1985.
Levinas, Emmanuel. *Oneself as Another*. Translated by Kathleen Blamey. Chicago: University of Chicago Press, 1992.
Lilla, Mark. *The Shipwrecked Mind: On Political Reaction*. New York: New York Review of Books Press, 2016.

Linton, Marisa. *Choosing Terror: Virtue, Friendship and Authenticity in the French Revolution*. Oxford: Oxford University Press, 2013.
Lloyd, Vincent and David True. "What Political Theology Could Be." *Political Theology* 17, no. 6 (2016): 505–6.
Lochbrunner, Manfred. *Balthasariana: Studien und Untersuchungen*. Münster: Aschendorff, 2016.
Lochbrunner, Manfred. *Hans Urs von Balthasar und seine Literatenfreunde: neun Korrespondenzen*. Würzburg: Echter, 2007.
Lochbrunner, Manfred. *Hans Urs von Balthasar und seine Philosophenfreunde: fünf Doppelporträts*. Würzburg: Echter, 2005.
Lochbrunner, Manfred. *Hans Urs von Balthasar und seine Theologenkollegen: sechs Beziehungsgeschichten*. Würzburg: Echter, 2009.
Lonergan, Bernard. Collected Works, Volume 22: *Early Works on Theological Method*. Toronto: University of Toronto Press, 2010.
Lonergan, Bernard. *Collection: Papers by Bernard Lonergan*. Edited by F. E. Crowe. London: Darton, Longman and Todd, 1967.
Lonergan, Bernard. *Method in Theology*. New York: Herder & Herder, 1972.
Long, D. Stephen. *Saving Karl Barth: Hans Urs von Balthasar's Preoccupation*. Minneapolis: Fortress, 2014.
Long, D. Stephen. *Speaking of God: Theology, Language, and Truth*. Grand Rapids, MI: Eerdmans, 2009.
Longenecker, Richard. *Introducing Romans: Critical Issues in Paul's Most Famous Letter*. London: Eerdmans, 2011.
López, Antonio. "Eternal Happening: God as an Event of Love." *Communio* 32 (2005): 214–45.
Lösel, Steffen. *Kreuzwege: Ein Ökumenisches Gespräch mit Hans Urs von Balthasar*. Paderborn: Ferdinand Schöningh, 2001.
Lösel, Steffen. "Conciliar, Not Conciliatory: Hans Urs von Balthasar's Ecclesiological Synthesis of Vatican II." *Modern Theology* 24, no. 1 (2008): 23–49.
Lösel, Steffen. "Unapocalyptic Theology: History and Eschatology in Balthasar's *Theo-Drama*." *Modern Theology* 17, no. 2 (2001): 201–25.
Löser, Werner. *Im Geiste des Origenes: Hans Urs von Balthasar als Interpret die Theologie die Kirchenväter*. Frankfurt am Main: Knecht, 1976.
Löser, Werner. "The Ignatian *Exercises* in the Work of Hans Urs von Balthasar." In *Hans Urs von Balthasar: His Life and Work*, edited by David L. Schindler, 103–20. San Francisco: Ignatius, 1991.
Lossky, Vladimir. "Tradition and Traditions." In *In the Image and Likeness of God*, 141–68. Crestwood, New York: St Vladimir's Seminary Press.
Loughlin, Gerard, ed. *Queer Theology: Rethinking the Western Body*. Oxford: Blackwell, 2007.
Loughlin, Gerard. "Catholic Homophobia." *Theology* 121, no. 3 (2018): 188–96.
Loumagne, Megan. "Teresa of Avila on Theology and Shame." *New Blackfriars* 99, no. 1080 (2018): 388–402.
Louth, Andrew. "The Place of *Heart of the World* in the Theology of Hans Urs von Balthasar." In *The Analogy of Beauty: The Theology of Hans Urs von Balthasar*, edited by John Riches, 147–63. Edinburgh: T&T Clark, 1986.
Lubanda, François Kabeya. *La Descente aux Enfers chez Hans Urs von Balthasar pour Penser une Éthique de soins Palliatifs*. Zurich: Lit, 2019.
Macintosh, Douglas Clyde. "The Reaction against Metaphysics in Theology." University of Chicago doctoral dissertation, 1911.

Mackey, James. *Jesus the Man and the Myth*. New York: Paulist, 1979.
Macquarrie, John. *Paths in Spirituality*. New York: Harper & Row, 1972.
Manchester, Peter. *Temporality and Trinity*. New York: Fordham University Press, 2015.
Mahoney, John. *The Making of Moral Theology: A Study of the Roman Catholic Tradition*. Oxford: Clarendon, 1987.
Marchesi, Giovanni. *La Cristologia di Hans Urs von Balthasar: La Figura di Gesù Cristo, Espressione Visibile di Dio*. Rome: Università Gregoriana, 1977.
Mariani, Milena. "Non Più Servitori Muti di Dèi Muti: La *Parrhesia* in Hans Urs von Balthasar e Karl Rahner." *Politica e Religione* (2012/2013): 125–40.
Marías, Julián. *Metaphysical Anthropology: The Empirical Structure of Human Life*. University Park: Pennsylvania State University Press, 1971.
Marion, Jean-Luc. *The Erotic Phenomenon*. Translated by Stephen Lewis. Chicago: University of Chicago Press, 2007.
Marion, Jean-Luc. *God Without Being: Hors-Texte*. Translated by Thomas Carlson. Chicago: University of Chicago Press, 1991.
Marion, Jean-Luc. *The Idol and Distance*. Translated by Thomas Carlson. New York: Fordham University Press, 2001.
Marion, Jean-Luc. *In the Self's Place: The Approach of Saint Augustine*. Translated by Jeffrey Kosky. Stanford, CA: Stanford University Press, 2012.
Maritain, Jacques. *Distinguish to Unite, or the Degrees of Knowledge*. New York: Scribner, 1959.
Maréchal, Joseph. *Studies in the Psychology of the Mystics*. London: Burns Oates & Washbourne, 1927.
Marshall, Bruce. *Christology in Conflict: Identity of a Saviour in Rahner and Barth*. Oxford: Blackwell, 1987.
Martin, Jennifer Newsome. *Hans Urs von Balthasar and the Critical Appropriation of Russian Religious Thought*. Notre Dame, IN: University of Notre Dame Press, 2015.
Martos, Joseph. *Deconstructing Sacramental Theology and Reconstructing Catholic Ritual*. Eugene, Oregon: Wipf & Stock, 2015.
Matarazzo, James. *The Judgment of Love: An Investigation of Salvific Judgment in Christian Eschatology*. Eugene, OR: Pickwick, 2018.
Maximus the Confessor. *On the Cosmic Mystery of Jesus Christ: Selected Writings from St. Maximus the Confessor*. Translated by Paul Blowers and Robert Louis Wilken. Crestwood, New York: St. Vladimir's Seminary Press, 2003.
Maxwell, Lida. "The Politics and Gender of Truth-Telling in Foucault's Lectures on Parrhesia." *Contemporary Political Theory* 27 (2018): 1–21.
McCabe, Herbert. *God Matters*. London: Mowbray, 1987.
McCosker, Philip. "Sacrifice in Recent Roman Catholic Thought." In *Sacrifice and Modern Thought*, edited by Julia Meszaros and Johannes Zachuber, 132–46. Oxford: Oxford University Press, 2013.
McDonnell, Killian. "The Determinative Doctrine of the Holy Spirit." *Theology Today* 39, no. 2 (1982): 142–61.
McDonough, Richard. *Martin Heidegger's Being and Time*. Bern: Peter Lang, 2006.
McDowell, John. "'Openness to the World': Karl Barth's Evangelical Theology of Christ as the Pray-er." *Modern Theology* 25, no. 2 (2009): 253–83.
McDowell, John. "Prayer, Particularity and the Subject of Divine Personhood: Who are Brümmer and Barth Invoking When They Pray?" In *Trinitarian Theology After Barth*, edited by Myk Habets and Phillip Tolliday, 255–83. Eugene, Oregon: Pickwick, 2011.

McInroy, Mark. *Balthasar on the Spiritual Senses: Perceiving Splendour*. Oxford: Oxford University Press, 2014.
McIntosh, Mark A. *Christology from within: Spirituality and the Incarnation in Hans Urs von Balthasar*. South Bend, IN: University of Notre Dame Press, 1996.
McIntosh, Mark A. "Christology." In *Cambridge Companion to Hans Urs von Balthasar*, edited by Edward T. Oakes and David Moss, 24–36. Cambridge: Cambridge University Press, 2004.
McIntosh, Mark A. *Discernment and Truth: The Spirituality and Theology of Knowledge*. New York: Herder, 2004.
McIntosh, Mark A. "A Hagio-Theological Doctrine of God: Hans Urs von Balthasar on Three Carmelites." In *Irish Theological Quarterly* 59, no. 2 (1993): 128–42.
McIntosh, Mark A. "Hans Urs von Balthasar (1905–1988)." In *The Student's Companion to the Theologians*, edited by Ian Markham, 355–66. Oxford: Blackwell, 2013.
McIntosh, Mark A. *Mystical Theology: The Integrity of Spirituality and Theology*. Oxford: Blackwell, 1998.
McKerrow, Raymie. "Critical Rhetoric: Theory and Praxis." *Communications Monographs* 56, no. 2 (1989): 91–111.
McGill, Alan. "What Does Pope Francis Mean by His References to the Devil as a Being? An Intratextual, Cultural-Linguistic Perspective." *Heythrop Journal* 60 (2019): 769–82.
McGinn, Bernard. *The Calabrian Abbot: Joachim of Fiore in the History of Western Thought*. New York: Macmillan, 1985.
McGinn, Bernard. *Essential Writings of Christian Mysticism*. New York: Random House, 2006.
McGinn, Bernard. "The Letter and the Spirit: Spirituality as an Academic Discipline." In *Minding the Spirit: The Study of Christian Spirituality*, edited by Elizabeth Dreyer and Mar Burrows, 25–41. Baltimore, MD: Johns Hopkins University Press, 2005.
McGinn, Bernard. *The Presence of God: A History of Western Christian Mysticism*, Vol. 1: *The Foundations of Mysticism: Origins to the Fifth Century: The Presence of God*. New York: Crossroad, 1991.
McGinn, Bernard. *The Presence of God: A History of Western Christian Mysticism*, Vol. 3: *The Flowering of Mysticism: Men and Women in the New Mysticism, 1200–1350*. New York: Crossroad, 1998.
McGinn, Bernard. *The Presence of God: A History of Western Christian Mysticism*, Vol. 5: *The Varieties of Vernacular Mysticism, 1350–1550*. New York: Crossroad, 2012.
McGregor, Bede and Thomas Norris, eds. *The Beauty of Christ: An Introduction to the Theology of Hans Urs von Balthasar*. Edinburgh: T&T Clark, 1994.
McPartlan, Paul. "Who is the Church? Zizioulas and von Balthasar on the Church's Identity." *Ecclesiology* 4 (2008): 271–88.
Mechthild of Magdeburg. *Mechthild of Magdeburg: Selections from The Flowing Light of the Godhead*. Translated by Elizabeth Anderson. Cambridge: D.S. Brewer, 2003.
Meis, Anneliese. "El Ser, Plenitud Atravesada por la Nada, según Hans Urs von Balthasar." *Teología y Vida* 50 (2009): 387–419.
Merrigan, Terrence. "Conscience and Selfhood: Thomas More, John Henry Newman, and the Crisis of the Postmodern Subject." *Theological Studies* 73 (2012): 841–69.
Messmore, Ryan. "Rethinking the Appeal to Perichoresis in Contemporary Trinitarian Political Theology." Unpublished Doctoral Dissertation. University of Oxford, 2011.
Metz, Johann Baptist. *Faith in History and Society*. Translated by David Smith. London: Burns & Oates, 1980.

Metz, Johann Baptist. *Followers of Christ: Perspectives on the Religious Life*. Translated by Thomas Linton. London: Burns and Oates, 1978.

Metz, Johann Baptist. *A Passion for God: The Mystical-Political Dimension of Christianity*. Translated by J. Matthew Ashley. New York: Paulist, 1998.

Meuffels, Hans Otmar. *Einbergung des Menschen in das Mysterium der Dreieinigen Liebe: Eine Trinitarische Anthropologie nach Hans Urs von Balthasar*. Würzburg: Echter, 1991.

Michaels, J. Ramsey. *The Gospel of John*. Grand Rapids, MI: Eerdmans, 1971.

Milbank, John. *Theology and Social Theory*. Oxford: Blackwell, 1990.

Moltmann, Jürgen. *Spirit of Life: A Universal Affirmation*. Translated by Margaret Kohl. Minneapolis: Fortress, 1992.

Moltmann, Jürgen. *A Theology of Hope: On the Ground and Implications of a Christian Eschatology*. Translated from James Leitch. Minneapolis, MN: Fortress, 1993.

Moltmann, Jürgen. *The Trinity and the Kingdom: The Doctrine of God*. London: SCM Press, 1981.

Mongrain, Kevin. *The Systematic Thought of Hans Urs von Balthasar: An Irenaean Retrieval*. New York: Crossroad, 2002.

Mongrain, Kevin. "Von Balthasar's Way from Doxology to Theology." *Theology Today* 64 (2007): 58–70.

Moons, Jos. "The Difficulty of Prayer." *International Journal for Philosophy and Theology* 68, no. 2 (2017): 162–84.

Mongrain, Kevin. "*Lumen Gentium*'s Pneumatological Renewal: A 'Work in Progress.'" *Ecclesiology* 12 (2016): 147–64.

Moore, A.W. *The Evolution of Modern Metaphysics: Making Sense of Things*. Cambridge: Cambridge University Press, 2011.

Morrison, Glenn. *A Theology of Alterity: Levinas, von Balthasar, and Trinitarian Praxis*. Pittsburgh, PA: Duquesne University Press, 2013.

Moser, Matthew. *Love Itself is Understanding: Hans Urs von Balthasar's Theology of the Saints*. Minneapolis, MN: Fortress, 2016.

Muers, Rachel. *Keeping God's Silence: Towards a Theological Ethics of Communication*. Oxford: Blackwell, 2004.

Muers, Rachel. "The Mute Cannot Keep Silent: Barth, von Balthasar, and Irigaray, on the Construction of Women's Silence." In *Challenging Women's Orthodoxies in the Context of Faith*, edited by Susan Frank Parsons, 109–120. London: Routledge, 2000.

Murphy, Francesca. *God Is Not a Story: Realism Revisited*. Oxford: Oxford University Press, 2007.

Murphy, Francesca. "Immaculate Mary: The Ecclesial Mariology of Hans Urs von Balthasar." In *Mary: The Complete Resource*, edited by Sarah Jane Boss, 300–13. London: Continuum, 2007.

Murphy, Francesca. "The Trinity and Prayer." In *The Oxford Handbook of the Trinity*, edited by Gilles Emery and Matthew Levering, 505–17. Oxford: Oxford University Press, 2011.

Murphy, Francesca. "The Sound of the *Analogia Entis*, Part II." *New Blackfriars* 74, no. 877 (1993): 557–65.

Murphy, Michael. *A Theology of Criticism: Balthasar: Postmodernism, and the Catholic Imagination*. Oxford: Oxford University Press, 2008.

Neiman, Susan. *Evil in Modern Thought: An Alternative History of Philosophy*. Princeton: Princeton University Press, 2002.

Nelstrop, Louise with Kevin Magill and Bradley Onishi. *Christian Mysticism: An Introduction to Contemporary Theoretical Approaches*. Burlington, Vermont: Ashgate, 2009.

Newey, Edmund. *Children of God: The Child as a Source of Theological Anthropology*. Surrey: Ashgate, 2012.
Newheiser, David. "Why the World Needs Negative Political Theology." *Modern Theology* 36, no. 1 (2020): 5–12.
Nicholas of Cusa. *On God as Not-Other*. Translated by Jasper Hopkins. Minneapolis, MN: Arthur J. Banning Press, 1987.
Nichols, Aidan. "Adrienne von Speyr and the Mystery of Atonement." *New Blackfriars* 73, no. 856 (1992): 542–53.
Nichols, Aidan. *Divine Fruitfulness: A Guide to Balthasar's Theology Beyond the Trilogy*. Washington, DC: Catholic University of America Press, 2007.
Nichols, Aidan. *No Bloodless Myth: A Guide through Balthasar's Dramatics*. London: T&T Clark, 1999.
Nichols, Aidan. *Scattering the Seed: A Guide Through Balthasar's Early Writings on Philosophy and the Arts*. London: Bloomsbury, 2006.
Nichols, Aidan. "The Theo-Logic." *Cambridge Companion to Hans Urs von Balthasar*, edited by Oakes and Moss, 158–71. Cambridge: Cambridge University Press, 2004.
Nichols, Aidan. "Thomism and the Nouvelle Théologie." *The Thomist* 64:1 (2000): 1–19.
Nichols, Aidan. *The Word Has Been Abroad: A Guide Through Balthasar's Aesthetics*. Washington, DC: Catholic University of America Press, 1998.
Nichols, Robert. *The World of Freedom: Heidegger, Foucault, and the Politics of Historical Ontology*. Stanford, CA: Stanford University Press, 2014.
Nicholson, Graeme. "The Ontological Difference." *American Philosophical Quarterly* 33, no. 4 (1996): 357–74.
Nietzsche, Friedrich. *The Antichrist*. Translated by Thomas Common. Mineola, NY: Dover, 2004.
Nietzsche, Friedrich. *The Gay Science: With a Prelude in German Rhymes and an Appendix of Songs*. Edited by Bernard Williams and translated by Josefine Nauckhoff and Adrian Del Caro. Cambridge: Cambridge University Press, 2001.
Nissinen, Martti. *Ancient Prophecy: Near Eastern, Biblical, and Greek Perspectives*. Oxford: Oxford University Press, 2017.
O'Collins, Gerard. *Rethinking Fundamental Theology: Toward a New Fundamental Theology*. Oxford: Oxford University Press, 2011.
O'Collins, Gerard and Daniel Kendall. "The Faith of Jesus." *Theological Studies* 53 (1992): 403–23.
O'Connor, Flannery. *Mystery and Manners: Occasional Prose*. Edited by Sally Fitzgerald and Robert Fitzgerald. London: Faber & Faber, 2014.
O'Connor, Flannery. *A Prayer Journal*. New York: Farrar, Straus and Giroux, 2013.
O'Donnell, John. *Hans Urs von Balthasar*. London: Geoffrey Chapman, 1992.
O'Donnell, John. "In Him and Over Him: The Holy Spirit in the Life of Jesus." In *Gregorianum* 70, no. 1 (1989): 25–45.
O'Donnell, John. "Truth as Love: The Understanding of Truth according to Hans Urs von Balthasar." *Pacifica* 1 (1988): 189–211.
O'Hanlon, Gerard. *The Immutability of God in the Theology of Hans Urs von Balthasar*. Cambridge: Cambridge University Press, 1990.
O'Hanlon, Gerard. "The Jesuits and Modern Theology: Rahner, von Balthasar and Liberation Theology." *Irish Theological Quarterly* 58, no. 1 (1992): 25–45.
O'Hanlon, Gerard. "The Legacy of Hans Urs von Balthasar." *Doctrine and Life* 41 (1991): 401–10.

O'Hanlon, Gerard. "Theological Dramatics." *The Beauty of Christ: An Introduction to the Theology of Hans Urs von Balthasar*, edited by Bede McGregor and Thomas Norris, 92–111. Edinburgh: T&T Clark
O'Meara, Thomas F. *Erich Przywara, S.J.: His Theology and His World*. Notre Dame, Indiana: University of Notre Dame Press, 2002.
O'Regan, Cyril. *The Anatomy of Misremembering: Von Balthasar's Response to Philosophical Modernity*, Volume 1: *Hegel*. New York: Crossroad, 2014.
O'Regan, Cyril. "Balthasar and the Eclipse of Nietzsche." *Modern Theology* 35, no. 1 (2019): 103–21.
O'Regan, Cyril. "Balthasar: Between Tübingen and Postmodernity." *Modern Theology* 14, no. 3 (1998): 325–53.
O'Regan, Cyril. "Hans Urs von Balthasar and the Unwelcoming of Heidegger." In *Grandeur of Reason: Religion, Tradition, and Universalism*, edited by Conor Cunningham and Peter Candler, 264–98. London: SCM, 2010.
O'Regan, Cyril. "Martin Heidegger and Christian Wisdom." In *Christian Wisdom Meets Modernity*, edited by Kenneth Oakes, 37–57. London: Bloomsbury, 2009.
O'Regan, Cyril. "Von Balthasar and Thick Retrieval: Post-Chalcedonian Symphonic Theology." *Gregorianium* 77, no. 2 (1996): 227–60.
O'Reilly, Kevin. "'Father, If It Be Possible, Let This Cup Pass from Me': Christ's Prayer in Gethsamane According to St Thomas." *Nova et Vetera* 15, no. 2 (2017): 503–26.
O'Toole, Mark. "Freedom in the Anthropology of Hans Urs von Balthasar." MPhil Dissertation. Oxford: University of Oxford, 1992.
Oakes, Edward T. and David Moss, eds. *The Cambridge Companion to Hans Urs von Balthasar*. Cambridge: Cambridge University Press, 2004.
Oakes, Edward T. "Balthasar and *Ressourcement*: An Ambiguous Relationship." In *Ressourcement: A Movement for Renewal in Twentieth-Century Catholic Theology*, edited by Gabriel Flynn and Paul Murray, 278–88. Oxford: Oxford University Press, 2012.
Oakes, Edward T. "The Internal Logic of Holy Saturday in the Theology of Hans Urs von Balthasar." In *International Journal of Systematic Theology* 9, no. 2 (2007): 184–99.
Oakes, Edward T. *Pattern of Redemption: The Theology of Hans Urs von Balthasar*. New York: Continuum, 1994.
Oakes, Edward T. "What I Learned about Prayer from Hans Urs von Balthasar." *America Magazine*, August 2005.
Oakes, Kenneth, ed. *Christian Wisdom Meets Modernity*. London: Bloomsbury, 2009.
Olsen, Cyrus. "Act and Event in Rahner and von Balthasar: A Case Study in Catholic Systematics." *New Blackfriars* 89, no. 1019 (2008): 3–21.
Origen. *Selected Works*. Translated by Rowan Greer. New York: Paulist Press, 1979.
Osborn, Eric. *Tertullian: First Theologian of the West*. Cambridge: Cambridge University Press, 1997.
Oster, Stefan. "Thinking Love at the Heart of Things: The Metaphysics of Being as Love in the Work of Ferdinand Ulrich." *Communio* 37 (2010): 660–700.
Oullet, Marc. "The Foundations of Christian Ethics according to Hans Urs von Balthasar." In *Hans Urs von Balthasar: His Life and Work*, edited by D. L. Schindler, 419–34. San Francisco, CA: Ignatius, 1991
Oullet, Marc. "The Message of Balthasar's Theology to Modern Theology." *Communio* 23, no. 2 (1996): 270–99.
Pabst, Adrian. *Metaphysics: The Creation of Hierarchy*. Grand Rapids, MI: Eerdmans, 2012.

Pabst, Adrian. "The Politics of Paradox: Metaphysics beyond 'Political Ontology.'" *Telos* 161 (2012): 99–119.
Palakeel, Joseph. *The Use of Analogy in Theological Discourse*. Rome: Pontificia Università Gregoriana, 1995.
Pannenberg, Wolfhart. *What is Man? Contemporary Anthropology in Theological Perspective*. Minneapolis, Fortress, 1970.
Pattison, Stephen. *Shame: Theory, Therapy, Theology*. Cambridge: Cambridge University Press, 2000.
Papanikolaou, Aristotle. *The Mystical as Political: Democracy and Non-Radical Orthodoxy*. South Bend, IN: University of Notre Dame Press, 2012.
Papanikolaou, Aristotle. "Person, *Kenosis* and Abuse: Hans Urs von Balthasar and Feminist Theologies in Conversation." *Modern Theology* 19, no. 1 (2003): 41–65.
Pavlík, Jirí. "παρρησία in John Chrysostom's Homilies on the Gospel of Matthew." *Vigiliae Christianae* 73 (2019): 1–15.
Peelman, Achiel. *Hans Urs von Balthasar et la Théologie de l'histoire*. Bern: Lang, 1978.
Peelman, Achiel. "Hans Urs von Balthasar: Un Diagnostic Théo-logique de la Civilisation Occidentale." *Église et Théologie* 10 (1979): 257–74.
Peelman, Achiel. *Le Salut comme Drame Trinitaire: La Theodramatik de Hans Urs von Balthasar*. Paris: Médiaspaul, 2002.
Peels, Rik. "Replicability and Replication in the Humanities." *Research Integrity and Peer Review* 4, no. 2 (2019): 1–12.
Pestaña, José Luis Moreno. "Isegoría y parrhesia: Foucault lector de Ión." *Isegoría: Revista de Filosofia Moral y Politica* 49 (2013): 509–32.
Peterson, Paul Silas. "Anti-Modernism and Anti-Semitism in Hans Urs von Balthasar's *Apokalypse der deutschen Seele*." *Neue Zeitschrift für Systematische Theologie und Religionsphilosophie* 52, no. 3 (2010): 302–18.
Peterson, Paul Silas. *The Early Hans Urs von Balthasar: Historical Contexts and Intellectual Formation*. Boston: DeGruyter, 2015.
Pfau, Thomas. "On Attention." *Salmagundi* 194 (2017): 145–63.
Phan, Peter. "Roman Catholic Theology." In *The Oxford Handbook of Eschatology*, edited by Jerry Walls, 216–32. Oxford: Oxford University Press, 2008.
Philipon, M. M. *Sainte Thérèse de Lisieux: Une Voie Toute Nouvelle*. Paris: Desclée de Brouwer, 1946.
Philippe, Jacques. *Interior Freedom*. Translated by Helena Scott. New York: Scepter, 2007.
Picard, Max. *Die Welt des Schweigens*. Zurich: Rentsch, 1948.
Pinches, Charles. "Hauerwas and Political Theology: The Next Generation." *The Journal of Religious Ethics* 36, no. 3 (2008): 513–42.
Pitstick, Alyssa Lyra. "Development of Doctrine, or Denial? Balthasar's Holy Saturday and Newman's *Essay*." *International Journal of Systematic Theology* 11, no. 2 (2009): 129–45.
Pitstick, Alyssa Lyra. *Light in Darkness: Hans Urs von Balthasar and the Catholic Doctrine of Christ's Descent into Hell*. Grand Rapids, MI: Eerdmans, 2007.
Potter, Brett David. "Image and Kenosis: Assessing Jean-Luc Marion's Contribution to a Postmetaphysical Theological Aesthetics." *International Journal of Philosophy and Theology* 79, no. 1–2 (2018): 60–79.
Potworowski, Christophe. "The Attitude of the Child in the Theology of Hans Urs von Balthasar." In *Communio: International Catholic Review* 22, no. 1 (1995): 44–55.
Potworowski, Christophe. "Christian Experience in Hans Urs von Balthasar." *Communio* 20, no. 1 (1993): 107–17.

Power, Dermot. *A Spiritual Theology of the Priesthood: The Mystery of Christ and the Mission of the Priest*. Washington, DC: The Catholic University of America Press, 1998.
Prevot, Andrew. "Dialectic and Analogy in Balthasar's 'The Metaphysics of the Saints.'" *Pro Ecclesia* 26, no. 3 (2017): 261–77.
Prevot, Andrew. "The Gift of Prayer: Toward a Theological Reading of Jean-Luc Marion." *Horizons* 41 (2014): 250–74.
Prevot, Andrew. *Thinking Prayer: Theology and Spirituality amid the Crisis of Modernity*. Notre Dame, IN: University of Notre Dame Press, 2015.
Proceedings of the Catholic Theological Society of America. 51 (1996): 297–305.
Proceedings of the Catholic Theological Society of America. 61 (2006): 173–85.
Proceedings of the Catholic Theological Society of America. 68 (2013): 128–9.
Przywara, Erich. *Analogia Entis: Metaphysics: Original Structure and Universal Rhythm*. Translated by John Betz and David Bentley Hart. London: Eerdmans, 2014.
Przywara, Erich. *Deus Semper Major: Theologie der Exerzitien*. Munich: Herold, 1964.
Purcell, Michael. "Rahner amid Modernity and Post-Modernity." In *The Cambridge Companion to Karl Rahner*, edited by Marmion and Hines, 195–210. Cambridge: Cambridge University Press, 2005.
Quash, Ben. "Hans Urs von Balthasar." In *Modern Theologians: An Introduction to Christian Theology since 1918*, edited by David Ford, 106–23. Oxford: Blackwell, 2005.
Quash, Ben. "Ignatian Dramatics: First Glance at the Spirituality of Hans Urs von Balthasar." *The Way* 38:1 (1998): 77–86.
Rabinbach, Anson. *In the Shadow of Catastrophe: German Intellectuals between Apocalypse and Enlightenment*. Berkeley: University of California Press, 1997.
Rahner, Hugo. *Man at Play: Or, Do You Ever Practise Eutrapelia?* Translated by Brian Battershaw and Edward Quinn. London: Burns & Oates, 1965.
Rahner, Karl. *Encounters with Silence* (second edition). South Bend, IN: St Augustine's Press, 2001.
Rahner, Karl. *Foundations of Christian Faith: An Introduction to the Idea of Christianity*. Translated by William V. Dych. London: Darton Longman & Todd, 1978.
Rahner, Karl. "Hans Urs von Balthasar." *Civitas* 20 (1964–5): 601–4.
Rahner, Karl. *Hearers of the Word: Laying the Foundation for a Philosophy of Religion*. Translated by Joseph Donceel. New York: Continuum, 1994.
Rahner, Karl. *The Need and the Blessing of Prayer*. Translated by Bruce Gillette. Collegeville, MN: The Liturgical Press, 1997.
Rahner, Karl. *The Practice of Faith*. New York: Crossroad, 1983.
Rahner, Karl. *Theological Investigations*, Vol. 1: *God, Christ, Mary and Grace*. Translated by Cornelius Ernst. London: Darton, Longman, and Todd, 1961.
Rahner, Karl. *Theological Investigations*, Vol. 3: *The Theology of the Spiritual Life*. Translated by Karl H. Kruger and Boniface Kruger. New York: Crossroad, 1982.
Rahner, Karl. *Theological Investigations*, Vol. 7: *Further Theology of the Spiritual Life I*. Translated by David Bourke. London: Darton, Longman and Todd, 1971.
Rahner, Karl. *Theological Investigations*, Vol. 23: *Final Writings*. Translated by Joseph Donceel and Hugh Riley. London: Burns and Oates, 1992.
Rahner, Karl and Wilhelm Thüsing. *A New Christology*. London: Burns & Oates, 1980.
Rancour-Laferriere, Daniel. *Imagining Mary: A Psychoanalytic Perspective on Devotion to Mary*. London: Routledge, 2017.
Randall, Julian and Iain Munro. "Foucault's Care of the Self: A Case Study from Mental Health Work." *Organization Studies* 39, no. 11 (2010): 1485–504.

Ratzinger, Joseph. "Concerning the Notion of Person in Theology." *Communio* 17 (1990): 439–54.
Ratzinger, Joseph. *Eschatology: Death and Eternal Life* (second edition). Washington, DC: The Catholic University of America Press, 2006.
Ratzinger, Joseph. "Homily at the Funeral Liturgy of Hans Urs von Balthasar." In *Hans Urs von Balthasar: His Life and Work*, edited by D. L. Schindler, 291–5. San Francisco, CA: Ignatius, 1991.
Ratzinger, Joseph. *Milestones: Memoirs 1927–1977*. San Francisco, CA: Ignatius, 1998.
Richardson, Graeme. "Integrity and Realism: Assessing John Millbank's Theology." *New Blackfriars* 84, no. 988 (2003): 268–80.
Riches, John, ed. *The Analogy of Beauty: The Theology of Hans Urs von Balthasar*. Edinburgh: T&T Clark, 1986.
Rivera, Joseph. "The Call and the Gifted in Christological Perspective: A Consideration of Brian Robinette's Critique of Jean-Luc Marion." *Heythrop Journal* 51 (2010): 1053–60.
Redfern, Martin. *Hans Urs von Balthasar*. London: Sheed & Ward, 1972.
Reno, Russell. "The Paradox of Hans Urs von Balthasar." *How Balthasar Changed My Mind: 15 Scholars Reflect on the Meaning of Balthasar for their Own Work*, edited by Rodney Howsare and Larry Chapp, 172–90. New York: Crossroad, 2008.
Riga, Peter. "Toward a Theology of Protest." *The Thomist* 33:2 (1969): 229–50.
Robinette, Brian. "Contemplative Practice and the Therapy of Mimetic Desire." *Contagion: Journal of Violence, Mimesis, and Culture* 24 (2017): 73–100.
Robinette, Brian. "A Gift to Theology? Jean-Luc Marion's 'Saturated Phenomenon' in Christological Perspective." *Heythrop Journal* 48 (2007): 86–108.
Robinette, Brian. *Grammars of Resurrection: A Christian Theology of Presence and Absence*. New York: Crossroad, 2009.
Rosenberg, Randall. "Christ's Human Knowledge: A Conversation with Lonergan and Balthasar." *Theological Studies* 71 (2010): 817–45.
Ross, Maggie. *Silence: A User's Guide, Volume 2: Application*. London: Darton, Longman and Todd, 2017.
Roten, Johann. "Hans Urs von Balthasar's Anthropology in Light of His Marian Thinking." *Communio* 20, no. 2 (1993): 306–33.
Roten, Johann. "The Two Halves of the Moon: Marian Anthropological Dimensions in the Common Mission of Adrienne von Speyr and Hans Urs von Balthasar." In *Hans Urs von Balthasar: His Life and Work*, edited by D. L. Schindler, 65–86. San Francisco: Ignatius, 1991.
Rothkranz, Johannes. *Die Kardinalfehler des Hans Urs von Balthasar*. Durach: Anton Schmid, 1989.
Saarinen, Risto. "Love from Afar: Distance, Intimacy and the Theology of Love." *International Journal of Systematic Theology* 14, no. 2 (2012): 131–47.
Sabo, Theodore, Dan Lioy and Rikus Fick. "A Hesychasm before Hesychasm." *Journal of Early Christian History* 4, no. 1 (2014): 88–96.
Sachs, John Randall. "Spirit and Life: The Pneumatology and Christian Spirituality of Hans Urs von Balthasar." Unpublished Doctoral Dissertation. Tubingen: Eberhard Karls Universität zu Tübingen, 1984.
Sara, Juan. "Secular Institutes According to Hans Urs von Balthasar." *Communio* 29 (2002): 309–36.
Savage, Deborah. "The Nature of Woman in Relation to Man: Genesis 1 and 2 through the Lens of the Metaphysical Anthropology of Aquinas." *Logos: A Journal of Catholic Thought and Culture* 18, no. 1 (2015): 71–93.

Saward, John. "Mary and Peter in the Christological Constellation: Balthasar's Ecclesiology." In *The Analogy of Beauty: The Theology of Hans Urs von Balthasar*, edited by John Riches, 105–32. Edinburgh: T&T Clark, 1986.

Saward, John. *The Mysteries of March: Hans Urs von Balthasar on the Incarnation and Easter*. London: Collins, 1990.

Saward, John. "Towards an Apophatic Anthropology." *Irish Theological Quarterly* 41, no. 3 (1974): 222–34.

Saward, John. *The Sweet and Blessed Country*. Oxford: Oxford University Press, 2008.

Scerri, Hector, ed. *Living Theology: Studies on Karl Rahner, Yves Congar, Bernard Lonergan, Hans Urs von Balthasar*. Vatican City: Libreria Editrice Vaticana, 2007.

Sciglitano, Anthony. "Leaving Neo-Scholasticism Beyond: Aspirations and Anxieties." In *Josephinum Journal of Theology* 18, no. 1 (2011): 216–39.

Sciglitano, Anthony. *Marcion and Prometheus: Balthasar Against the Expulsion of Jewish Origins from Modern Religious Dialogue*. Freiburg im Breisgau: Herder, 2014.

Schindler, David C. "Metaphysics within the Limits of Phenomenology: Balthasar and Husserl on the Nature of the Philosophical Act." *Teología y Vida* 50 (2009): 243–58.

Schindler, David C. "A Very Critical Response to Karen Kilby: On Failing to See the Form." *Radical Orthodoxy: Theology, Philosophy, Politics* 3, no. 1 (2015): 68–87.

Schindler, David L., ed. *Hans Urs von Balthasar: His Life and Work*. San Francisco: Ignatius Pres, 1991.

Schindler, David L. *The Catholicity of Reason*. Grand Rapids, Michigan: Eerdmans, 2013.

Schindler, David L. "*Communio* Ecclesiology and Liberalism." *The Review of Politics* 60, no. 4 (1998): 775–86.

Schindler, David L. *Hans Urs von Balthasar and the Dramatic Structure of Truth: A Philosophical Investigation*. New York: Fordham University Press, 2004.

Schindler, David L. *Heart of the World, Center of the Church: Communio Ecclesiology, Liberalism, and Liberation*. Grand Rapids, MI: Eerdmans, 1996.

Schindler, David L. "Time in Eternity, Eternity in Time: On the Contemplative-Active Life." *Communio* 18 (1991): 53–68.

Schlesinger, Eugene. *Ite, Missa Est! A Missional Liturgical Ecclesiology*. Minneapolis: Fortress, 2017.

Schliesser, Benjamin. "'Exegetical Amnesia' and ΠΙΣΤΙΣ ΧΡΙΣΤΟΥ: The 'Faith *of* Christ' in Nineteenth-century Pauline Scholarship." *The Journal of Theological Studies* 66, no. 1 (2015): 61–89.

Schloesser, Stephen. *Jazz Age Catholicism: Mystic Modernisms in Postwar Paris: 1919–1933*. London: University of Toronto Press, 2005.

Schneiders, Sandra. "Spirituality in the Academy." *Theological Studies* 50, no. 4 (1989): 676–97.

Schrag, Calvin. *The Self after Postmodernity*. New Haven, CT: Yale University Press, 1997.

Schulz, Michael. "Beyond Being: Outline of the Catholic Heidegger School." *Studia Teologii Dogmatycznej* 3 (2017): 177–92.

Schumacher, Michele. "The Concept of Representation in the Theology of Hans Urs von Balthasar." *Theological Studies* 60 (1999): 53–71.

Schumacher, Michele. "Ecclesial Existence: Person and Community in the Trinitarian Anthropology of Adrienne von Speyr." *Modern Theology* 24, no. 3 (2008): 359–85.

Schumacher, Michele. *A Trinitarian Anthropology: Adrienne von Speyr and Hans Urs von Balthasar in Dialogue with Thomas Aquinas*. Washington, DC: Catholic University of America Press, 2014.

Schumacher, Michele, ed. *Women in Christ: Toward a New Feminism*. Grand Rapids, MI: Eerdmans, 2004.
Scola, Angelo. *Hans Urs von Balthasar: A Theological Style*. Grand Rapids, Michigan: Eerdmans, 1995.
Scola, Angelo. *The Nuptial Mystery*. Translated by Michelle Borras. Grand Rapids, MI: Eerdmans, 2005.
Segal, Julia. *Melanie Klein*. London: SAGE, 2004.
Sells, Michael. *Mystical Languages of Unsaying*. Chicago: University of Chicago Press, 1994.
Servais, Jacques, ed. *Hans Urs von Balthasar on the Ignatian Spiritual Exercises: An Anthology*. Translated by Thomas Jacobi and Jonas Wernet. San Francisco: Ignatius, 2019. [*Texte zum Ignatianischen Exerzitienbuch bei Hans Urs von Balthasar*. Einsiedeln: Johannes, 1993]
Servais, Jacques. "Balthasar as Interpreter of the Catholic Tradition." In *Love Alone is Credible: Hans Urs von Balthasar as Interpreter of the Catholic Tradition*, edited by David L. Schindler, 191–208. Grand Rapids, MI: Eerdmans, 2008.
Servais, Jacques. "The Community of St. John." *Communio* 19, no. 2 (1992): 208–19.
Servais, Jacques. "The Confession of the *Casta Meretrix*." *Communio* 40, no. 4 (2013): 642–62.
Servais, Jacques. "The Lay Vocation in the World According to Balthasar." *Communio* 23, no. 4 (1996): 656–76.
Servais, Jacques. *Théologie des Exercices Spirituels: Hans Urs von Balthasar interprète saint Ignace*. Paris: Culture et Vérité, 1996.
Shanley, Brian. "St. Thomas Aquinas, Onto-Theology, and Marion." *The Thomist* 60, no. 4 (1996): 617–25.
Shanks, Andrew. *God and Modernity: A New and Better Way to Do Theology*. London: Routledge, 2000.
Sheldrake, Philip. *Spirituality and History: Questions of Interpretation and Method*. New York: Crossroad, 1992.
Sheldrake, Philip. *Spirituality and Theology: Christian Living and the Doctrine of God*. London: Darton, Longman and Todd, 1998.
Sicari, Antonio. "Hans Urs von Balthasar: Theology and Holiness." In *Hans Urs von Balthasar: His Life and Work*, edited by D. L. Schindler, 121–32. San Francisco: Ignatius, 1991.
Siewerth, Gustav. *Metaphysik der Kindheit*. Eisiedeln: Johannesverlag, 1957.
Siewerth, Gustav. *Der Thomismus als Identitätssystem* (second edition). Frankfurt: Schulte-Bulmke, 1961.
Siewerth, Gustav. *Das Schicksal der Metaphysik von Thomas bis Heidegger*. Einsiedeln: Johannes, 1959.
Slater, Thomas. *A Manual of Moral Theology for English Speaking Countries*, Vol. 1 (fifth edition). London: Burns, Oates and Washbourne, 1925.
Smilansky, Saul. "A Moral Problem about Prayer." *Think* 36, no. 13 (2014): 105–13.
Sobrino, Jon. *Christology at the Crossroads*. Maryknoll, NY: Orbis, 1978.
Sohn, Hohyun. "Hans Urs von Balthasar and the East: Identity or Dialogue." *Heythrop Journal* 59, no. 3 (2018): 573–85.
Speyr, Adrienne von. *Confession: The Encounter with Christ in Penance*. Translated by A.V. Litteldale. Basel: Herder, 1964.
Speyr, Adrienne von. *The Cross: Word and Sacrament*. Translated by Graham Harrison. San Francisco, CA: Ignatius, 1983.

Speyr, Adrienne von. *The Book of All Saints*. San Francisco, CA: Ignatius, 2008.
Speyr, Adrienne von. *The World of Prayer*. Translated by Graham Harrison. San Francisco, CA: Ignatius Press, 1985.
Splett, Jörg. "Der Christ und seine Angst Erwogen mit Hans Urs von Balthasar." In *Gott für die Welt: Henri de Lubac, Gustav Siewerth und Hans Urs von Balthasar in ihren Grundanliegen*, edited by Reifenberg Peter and Anton van Hooff, 315–31. Mainz: Matthias-Grünwald 2001.
Stace, W. T. *Mysticism and Philosophy*. London: Macmillan, 1961.
Stanley, Timothy. "Before Analogy: Recovering Barth's Ontological Development." *New Blackfriars* 90, no. 1029 (2009): 577–601.
Steck, Christopher. *The Ethical Thought of Hans Urs von Balthasar*. New York: Crossroad, 2001.
Steinhauer, Hilda. *Maria als dramatische Person bei Hans Urs von Balthasar: Zum Mari, anischen Prinzip seines Denkens*. Innsbruck: Salzburger Theologische Studien, 2001.
Stratis, Justin. "Speculating about Divinity? God's Immanent Life and Actualistic Ontology." *International Journal of Systematic Theology* 12, no. 1 (2010): 20–32.
Stolz, Anselm. *Theologie der Mystik*. Regensburg: Pustet, 1936.
Sudbrack, Josef. "Prayer." *Sacramentum Mundi: An Encyclopedia of Theology*, Vol. 5. Edited by Karl Rahner. London: Burns & Oates, 1970.
Sullivan, Patricia. "Saints as the 'Living Gospel': Von Balthasar's Revealers of the Revealer, Rahner's Mediators of the Mediator." *Heythrop Journal* 55 (2014): 270–85.
Sutton, Matthew Lewis. "A Compelling Trinitarian Taxonomy: Hans Urs von Balthasar's Theology of the Trinitarian Inversion and Reversion." *International Journal of Systematic Theology* 14, no. 2 (2012): 161–76.
Sutton, Matthew Lewis. *Heaven Opens: The Trinitarian Mysticism of Adrienne von Speyr*. Minneapolis: Fortress, 2014.
Tamboukou, Maria. "Truth Telling in Foucault and Arendt: Parrhesia, the Pariah, and Academics in Dark Times." *Journal of Education Policy* 27, no. 6 (2012): 849–65.
Tanner, Kathryn. *Christ the Key*. Cambridge: Cambridge University Press, 2010.
Tanner, Kathryn. "Theological Reflection and Christian Practices." *Practicing Theology: Beliefs and Practices in Christian Life*, edited by Miroslav Volf and Dorothy Bass, 228–44. Grand Rapids, Michigan: Eerdmans, 2002.
Tellbe, Mikael. "Identity and Prayer." *Early Christian Prayer and Identity Formation*, edited by Reidar Hvalvik and Karl Olav Sandnes, 15–17. Tübingen: Mohr Siebeck, 2014.
Terrien, Samuel. *The Elusive Presence: Toward a New Biblical Theology*. Eugene, OR: Wipf and Stock, 2000.
Thacker, Justin. *Postmodernism and the Ethics of Theological Knowledge*. New York: Routledge, 2007.
Therborn, Göran. *The Ideology of Power and the Power of Ideology*. London: Verso, 1980.
Theobald, Christoph. "Le christianisme comme style. Entrer dans une manière d'habiter le monde." *Revue d'éthique et de théologie morale* 251 (2008): 235–48,
Thiel, John. *Icons of Hope: The "Last Things" in Catholic Imagination*. Notre Dame: University of Notre Dame Press, 2013.
Thompson, John. "Barth and Balthasar: An Ecumenical Dialogue." In *The Beauty of Christ: An Introduction to the Theology of Hans Urs von Balthasar*, edited by McGregor and Thomas, 171–92. Edinburgh: T&T Clark.
Thompson, Willam M., ed. *Bérulle and the French School: Selected Writings*. Translated by Lowell M. Glendon. New York: Paulist, 1989.

Todd, Richard. *The Sufi Doctrine of Man: The Metaphysical Anthropology of Sadr al-Dīn al-Qūnawī*. Leiden: Brill, 2014.
Tonstad, Linn Marie. "Everything Queer, Nothing Radical?" *Svensk Teologisk Kvartalskrift* 92 (2016): 118–29.
Tonstad, Linn Marie. *God and Difference: The Trinity, Sexuality, and the Transformation of Finitude*. New York: Routledge, 2015.
Tonstad, Linn Marie. "Sexual Difference and Trinitarian Death: Cross, Kenosis, and Hierarchy in the Theo-Drama." *Modern Theology* 26, no. 4 (2010): 603–31.
Tossou, K. J. *Streben nach Vollendung: Zur Pneumatologie im Werk Hans Urs von Balthasars*. Basel: Herder, 1983.
Tracy, David. "Trinitarian Speculation and the Forms of Divine Disclosure." In *The Trinity: An Interdisciplinary Symposium on the Trinity*, edited by Davis, Kendall and O'Collins, 273–92. Oxford: Oxford University Press, 2002.
Turek, Margaret. *Towards a Theology of God the Father: Hans Urs von Balthasar's Theodramatic Approach*. Oxford: Peter Lang, 2001.
Ulanov, Ann and Barry. "Prayer and Personality: Prayer as Primary Speech." In *The Study of Spirituality*, edited by Jones, Wainwright and Yarnold, 24–33. London: SPCK, 1986
Ulrich, Ferdinand. *Homo Abyssus: Das Wagnis der Seinsfrage*. Einsiedeln: Johannes, 1998.
van Erp, Stephan. *The Art of Theology: Hans Urs von Balthasar's Theological Aesthetics and the Foundations of Faith*. Leuven: Peeters, 2004.
van Oudtshoorn, Andre. "Prayer and Practical Theology." *International Journal of Practical Theology* 16, no. 2 (2013), 285–303.
Vanhoozer, Kevin. *Cambridge Companion to Postmodern Theology*. Cambridge: Cambridge University Press, 2003.
Vasko, Elisabeth. "The Difference Gender Makes: Nuptiality, Analogy, and the Limits of Appropriating Hans Urs von Balthasar's Theology in the Context of Sexual Violence." *Journal of Religion* 94, no. 4 (2014): 504–28.
Vermeulen, Timotheus and Robin van den Akker. "Notes on Metamodernism." *Journal of Aesthetics and Culture*. 2, no.1 (2010): 1–14.
Vogel, Jeffrey. "The Unselfing Activity of the Holy Spirit in the Theology of Hans Urs von Balthasar." *Logos* 10, no. 4 (2007).
Vogel, Jeffrey. "Suffering and the Search for Wholeness: Beauty and the Cross in Hans Urs von Balthasar and Contemporary Feminist Theologies." PhD Dissertation. Chicago, IL: Loyola University Chicago, 2009.
Verghese, Paul. "Monothelete Controversy: A Historical Survey." *Greek Orthodox Theological Review* 13, no. 2 (1968): 196–208.
Volf, Miroslav and Dorothy Bass, eds. *Practicing Theology: Beliefs and Practices in Christian Life*. Grand Rapids, MI: Eerdmans, 2002.
Volf, Miroslav. "'The Trinity is Our Social Program': The Doctrine of the Trinity and the Shape of Social Engagement." *Modern Theology* 14, no. 3 (1998): 403–23.
Walatka, Todd. *Von Balthasar and the Option for the Poor: Theodramatics in the Light of Liberation Theology*. Washington, DC: Catholic University of America Press, 2017.
Waldron, Stephen. "Hans Urs von Balthasar's Theological Critique of Nationalism." *Political Theology* 15, no. 5 (2014): 406–20.
Wallner, Karl. *Gott als Eschaton: Trinitarische Dramatik als Voraussetzung göttlicher Universalität bei Hans Urs von Balthasar*. Vienna: Heiligenkreuz Verlag, 1992.

Ward, Benedicta. "Miracles and History: A Reconsideration of the Miracle Stories Used by Bede." In *Essays in Commemoration of the Thirteenth Centenary of the Birth of the Venerable Bede*, edited by Gerald Bonner, 70–6. London: SPCK, 1976.
Ward, Graham, ed. *The Blackwell Companion to Postmodern Theology*. Oxford: Blackwell, 2001.
Ward, Graham. *How the Light Gets In: Ethical Life I*. Oxford: Oxford University Press, 2016.
Ward, Graham. *Christ and Culture*. Oxford: Blackwell, 2005.
Ward, Graham. *Cities of God*. London: Routledge: 2000.
Ward, Graham. *The Politics of Discipleship: Becoming Postmaterial Citizens*. Grand Rapids, Michigan: Baker, 2009.
Ward, Graham. "Transcorporeality: The Ontological Scandal." *Bulletin John Rylands Library* 80, no. 3 (1998): 235–52.
Ward, Graham. "The Voice of the Other." *New Blackfriars* 77, no. 909 (1996): 518–28.
Warren, Martin. "The Quakers as Parrhesiastes: Frank Speech and Plain Speaking as the Fruits of Silence." *Quaker History* 98, no. 2 (2009): 1–25.
Weil, Simone. *Gravity and Grace*. Translated by Emma Crawford and Mario von der Ruhr. New York: Routledge Press, 2002.
Weinandy, Thomas. "The Beatific Vision and the Incarnate Son." *The Thomist* 70 (2006): 605–15.
Westphal, Merold. *Overcoming Onto-Theology: Toward a Postmodern Christian Faith*. Fordham, New York: Fordham University Press, 2001.
Westphal, Merold. "Prayer as the Posture of the Decentered Self." *The Phenomenology of Prayer*, edited by Bruce Ellis Benson and Norman Wirzba, 13–31. New York: Fordham University Press, 2005.
White, Thomas Joseph. "Jesus' Cry on the Cross." *Nova et Vetera* 5, no. 3 (2007): 555–81.
White, Thomas Joseph. "The Voluntary Action of the Earthly Christ and the Necessity of the Beatific Vision." *The Thomist* 69 (2005): 497–534.
Williams, Rowan. "Balthasar and Rahner." In *The Analogy of Beauty: The Theology of Hans Urs von Balthasar*, edited by John Riches, 11–34. Edinburgh: T&T Clark, 1986.
Williams, Rowan. *Christ: The Heart of Creation*. London: Bloomsbury, 2018.
Williams, Rowan. *On Christian Theology*. Oxford: Blackwell, 2000.
Williams, Rowan. "Response to Amy Hollywood." *Modern Theology* 36:1 (2020): 53–55.
Williams, Rowan. "Theological Integrity." *New Blackfriars* 72, no. 847 (1991): 140–51.
Williams, Rowan. "Trinity and Revelation." *Modern Theology* 2, no. 3 (1986): 197–212.
Williams, Rowan. *Wrestling with Angels: Conversations in Modern Theology*. Edited by Mike Higton. London: SCM, 2007.
Wierciński, Andrzej, ed. *Between Friends: The Hans Urs von Balthasar and Gustav Siewerth Correspondence (1954–1963): A Bilingual Edition*. Konstanz: Verlag Gustav Siewerth Gesellschaft, 2007.
Wierciński, Andrzej. *Inspired Metaphysics? Gustav Siewerth's Hermeneutic Reading of the Ontotheological Tradition*. Toronto: The Hermeneutic Press, 2003.
Wigley, Stephen. *Karl Barth and Hans Urs von Balthasar: A Critical Engagement*. London: Bloomsbury, 2007.
Wilder, Amos. *Theopoetic: Theology and the Religious Imagination*. Philadelphia, PA: Fortress, 1976.
Winner, Lauren. *The Dangers of Christian Practice: On Wayward Gifts, Characteristic Damage, and Sin*. New Haven, CT: Yale University Press, 2018.
Wirzba, Norman. "The Work of Prayer." In *The Phenomenology of Prayer*, edited by Benson and Wirzba, 88–100. New York: Fordham University Press, 2005.

Woodward, Kenneth. *Making Saints: How the Catholic Church Determines Who Becomes a Saint, Who Doesn't, and Why*. New York: Touchstone, 1990.

Wyschogrod, Edith. *Saints and Postmodernism: Revisioning Moral Philosophy*. Chicago: University of Chicago Press, 1990.

Yannaras, Christos. *On the Absence and Unknowability of God: Heidegger and the Areopagite*. Translated by Haralambos Ventis and edited by Andrew Louth. London: T&T Clark International, 2005.

Yenson, Mark. *Existence as Prayer: The Consciousness of Christ in the Theology of Hans Urs von Balthasar*. New York: Peter Lang Publishing, 2014.

Yenson, Mark. "Making a Difference: Implications of Hans Urs von Balthasar's Neo-Chalcedonian Christology for Creation." In *To Discern Creation in a Scattering World*, edited by Frederiek Depoortere and Jacques Haers, 367–80. Leuven: Peeters, 2013.

Yoder, Timothy. "Hans Urs von Balthasar and Kenosis: The Pathway to Agency." PhD Dissertation. Chicago, IL: University of Chicago, 2013.

Zeitz, James V. "Pryzwara and von Balthasar on Analogy." *The Thomist: A Speculative Quarterly Review* 52, no. 3 (July 1988): 473–98.

Zimmerman, Michael. *Heidegger's Confrontation with Modernity: Technology, Politics, and Art*. Bloomington: Indiana University Press, 1990.

Zizioulas, John. *Communion and Otherness: Further Studies in Personhood and the Church*. London: T&T Clark, 2006.

INDEX

Adoptionism 84, 88
aletheia 66–9, 71, 89, 131
   and Christ 84, 97
   and *parrhesia* 119
amen 70–1, 86, 126, 162, 174–6
   eschatological *amen* 147
   Mary's *amen* (*see* Marian 'Yes')
   The Son's *amen* 81, 100
Annunciation 122, 138 n.53
Anselm of Canterbury 37, 154
apocalypse/apocalypticism 130–1
Augustine of Hippo 41, 113 n.29, 137, 177

Balthasar, Hans Urs von
   biography 12, 42–5
   categorization of works 8–10, 47, 104 n.120, 168
   difficulty in interpreting 7–11, 25
   engagement with Adrienne von Speyr 7, 21–2, 33, 46–7, 60, 94, 170
   engagement with Augustine 137
   engagement with Ferdinand Ulrich 75, 120 n.59
   engagement with Gustav Siewerth 75–7, 94
   engagement with Jean-Luc Marion 72–6
   engagement with Karl Barth 10, 43, 46–7, 59, 64
   engagement with Karl Rahner 27, 93, 105 n.125
   engagement with Martin Heidegger 30, 66–9, 74, 110–11
   engagement with Maximus the Confessor 8, 42, 82 n.11, 91–2, 117 n.46
   engagement with Thomas Aquinas 87, 93 n.63, 137
   feminist critics of 20–3, 90 n.50, 134 n.29
   on the integrity of theology and spirituality 1, 35–42, 175–7
   political theology and 32, 140–1, 171
   reception history 12–32
   sermons 9, 10, 138 n.53, 140
   supralapsarianism 117 n.46
   theodicy 143 n.83
   trilogy (*Herrlichkeit*, *Theodramatik*, and *Theologik*) 9, 12, 25, 45–6, 168
   views of Eastern spirituality 30–1, 118
   views of the laity 40 n.35, 103–4
Beattie, Tina 16, 20–3, 169
Benedict XVI (Joseph Ratzinger) 17, 20–1, 129, 138
bonum diffusivum sui 76
Bruaire, Claude 72, 75
Bulgakov, Sergei 31, 37

canonization. *See* saints
"centrifugal" prayer 110, 151
communion of saints 125, 136
confession 64, 71, 114–16, 122, 141, 158
covenant 69–70, 84–6

dialogism 108–9
"double portion" of grace 136–7
The Dragon. *See* Satan

Edelman, Lee 159 n.49
Elizabeth of the Trinity (Elizabeth Catez) 39, 63 n.34
emeth 66, 69–72, 89, 119, 131
   and Christ 84, 97
   the Eucharist 80–1, 98, 102. *See also* prayer, and sacrament

fides Christi 87–95, 102, 133

First Things (journal)   17–18
Foucault, Michel   119, 149, 155–61, 163, 170–1
"fundamental theodramatic law of world history"   83, 131, 142, 151

Gregory Nazianzus   90, 92

Hanvey, James   100, 134
Heart of the World (Balthasar)   9, 41, 48, 70, 113, 132
High Priestly Prayer (John 17)   59 n.13, 79, 90
Holy Spirit   5, 11, 23, 34, 39, 55, 75, 87, 125, 136, 146, 176, 177
  in the life of Christ   53, 80–1, 86, 95, 120, 135 (*see also* Trinitarian inversion)
  role in prayer   61–5, 102, 104, 166

Ignatian indifference   44, 97, 124
Ignatius of Loyola   10, 33 n.124, 71 n.86
Ignatius Press   16–17
the Immaculate Conception   100, 138 n.53
integralism   16, 53 n.21, 163
International Theological Commission   13, 42 n.41
Israel   85, 100, 151, 152, 164 n.65. See also covenant

Joan of Arc   44, 140–3, 148, 154
Johannesgemeinschaft (Community of St. John)   8 n.9, 9, 44, 54
John Paul II   16, 20–1, 38

kenosis   23, 29, 73, 77 n.116, 89, 92, 97, 102, 147
Kierkegaard, Søren   30, 139 n.57
Kilby, Karen   25–6, 28, 34 n.125, 38, 41, 50, 143 n.83
Kingdom of God   49, 127, 134, 139, 144–6, 160. See also prayer, eschatological dimensions of
"kneeling theology"   36–7, 44, 140–1
Kolbe, Maximilian   154, 160

Las Casas, Bartolome de   154, 160
Levertov, Denise   122

life   122–7, 132
listening   62, 98, 116–17, 170, 175
Lumen Gentium   55, 102, 141 n.72

manualism   43, 104 n.125, 130
Marian "Yes"   99, 122
martyrs/martyrdom   142, 154, 158
Marxism   129, 133 n.23
Moltmann, Jürgen   138–9
Moses   69, 85, 124
mysticism
  authority of the mystics   50, 111 n.23
  as dialogue   51–4
  legitimate *vs.* illegitimate   49–55
  and mission   53–5, 123–4
  mystical genitive (Deissmann)   94 (*see also fides Christi*)
  vacuum-plenum (Stace)   52

O'Connor, Flannery   174
ontological difference   71–7
ontology   59, 76, 79, 113, 152
ordo processionis   58, 66, 81
Origen of Alexandria   10, 42, 126 n.88, 175

parousia   49, 131
parrhesia
  Christological dimensions of   161–2
  death and   160–1
  ecclesial dimensions of   158–9
  Foucault's account of   155–7
  in prayer   117–19, 136, 171 n.15
Passion   25, 89, 135, 140
perichoresis   25, 79
Pietzcker, Gabrielle   38, 147–8
pistis Christou. See fides Christi
pleroma   89, 97, 102, 147
Pontius Pilate   115, 119, 162
prayer
  and action   45, 49, 90, 139–45
  anthropological dimensions of   107–28
    "horizontal" *vs.* "vertical" prayer   108, 115 n.43
  as apologia   48
  as attunement   143
  Christological dimensions of   79–97

confession and 64, 71, 114–16, 141, 158
critical dimensions of 147–64
death and 23, 94, 120, 143, 160–3
as dialogue 3, 49, 57–9, 64, 68, 81–3, 92, 109, 116–23, 131–2, 141, 152, 174–7
difficulty of 64, 112, 142, 174
ecclesiological dimensions of 98–105
as encounter 53, 62, 70–1, 99, 109, 116 n.44, 118, 152–4, 177
eschatological dimensions of 129–46, 148
and hope 44, 131, 133, 137–9, 177
as incorporation/divinization 4, 64, 71, 78
intercessory prayer 136–9
and liturgy 59, 62, 98–9, 116
methodological importance of 35–42, 168–70
and mission-consciousness 87–92, 123–7
as mystery 34, 47, 49, 78
naturalness of 112, 114, 118
ontology of 5, 59, 140, 166
as personalization 111, 115, 124–5
as petition 46, 59, 136
pneumatological dimensions of 61–5, 125
practical advice 120
as protest 149–54
and sacrament 102–4
and salvation history 83, 85 n.27, 133–45
and shame 111–14, 118, 122
and silence 52 n.97, 54, 114, 119–22, 128, 175–6
and sin 131–2, 174
Trinitarian dimensions of 4, 46, 57–61, 65–72
unceasing prayer 123, 167
as watching 131–4

Prayer (Balthasar) 45–9
the prophets 150–2, 160
Psalms 85, 174

Quietism. *See* prayer and silence

Rahner, Karl 14, 18 n.47, 60, 93, 171
"realized" eschatology 138, 142, 148
ressourcement 54, 91

saints 37–42, 50, 110 n.19. *See also* communion of saints
the Samaritan woman at the well (Jn 4:1–26) 70–1
Satan 91, 132 n.17, 144 n.83, 170
Schneider, Reinhold 44, 154, 159, 170
Scholasticism 16, 19, 42, 152
Second Vatican Council 13, 18, 30, 99, 102, 141 n.72
Speyr, Adrienne von 7, 9, 21–2, 25, 33, 66, 111, 115 n.40
Spiritual dryness 112. *See also* prayer and shame
The Spiritual Exercises 43–4, 71 n.86, 124

Temptation of Christ 90–2
The Theology of Karl Barth (Balthasar) 46, 64
therapy 115 n.43, 172
Thérèse of Lisieux (Marie Françoise-Thérèse Martin) 10, 64 n.45, 121, 136, 170
Thomas Aquinas 19, 76, 87, 122, 151 n.12
Trinitarian distance 72–7
Trinitarian inversion 62, 95–7
Trinitarian "surprise" (*Überraschung*) 67–8, 94, 109

violence 21, 43 n.48, 141–2, 160, 171

Ward, Graham 22, 45

www.ingramcontent.com/pod-product-compliance
Lightning Source LLC
Chambersburg PA
CBHW062221300426
44115CB00012BA/2163